THE COMPLETE GUIDE TO
THE HAZARDOUS WASTE
REGULATIONS

THE COMPLETE GUIDE TO THE HAZARDOUS WASTE REGULATIONS

A Comprehensive, Step-by-Step Guide to the Regulation of Hazardous Wastes Under RCRA, TSCA, HMTA, OSHA, and Superfund

SECOND EDITION

Travis P. Wagner

VAN NOSTRAND REINHOLD
New York

The author and publisher do not make any warranty or representation, expressed or implied, with respect to accuracy, completeness, or utility of the information contained in this document; nor does the author or publisher assume any liability with respect to the use of or reliance upon, or for damages resulting from the use of or reliance upon, any information, procedure, conclusion, or opinion contained in this document.

Copyright © 1991 by Travis P. Wagner

Library of Congress Catalog Card Number 90-12356
ISBN 0-442-00355-2

Manufactured in the United States of America

Published by Van Nostrand Reinhold
115 Fifth Avenue
New York, New York, 10003

Chapman and Hall
2–6 Boundary Row
London, SE1 8HN

Thomas Nelson Australia
102 Dodds Street
South Melbourne 3205
Victoria, Australia

Nelson Canada
1120 Birchmount Road
Scarborough, Ontario M1K 5G4, Canada

16 15 14 13 12 11 10 9 8 7 6 5 4 3

Library of Congress Cataloging-in-Publication Data

Wagner, Travis.
  The complete guide to the hazardous waste regulations : a
comprehensive, step-by-step guide to the regulation of hazardous
wastes under RCRA, TSCA, HMTA, OSHA, and Superfund / Travis P.
Wagner.
     p.   cm.
  Rev. ed. of: The complete handbook of hazardous waste regulation.
© 1988.
     ISBN 0-442-00355-2
     1. Hazardous wastes—Law and legislation—United States.
  I. Wagner, Travis. Complete handbook of hazardous waste regulation.
  II. Title.
KF3946.W34   1990
344.73′04622—dc20
[347.3044622]
                                                    90-12356
                                                         CIP

One of the greatest pleasures in life is to succeed where others said you would fail.

—Anonymous

Contents

Preface   xv

Acknowledgments   xvii

A Guide to Readers   xix

PART I—THE RESOURCE CONSERVATION AND RECOVERY ACT   1

Solid Waste Management   1

Hazardous Waste Management   2

CHAPTER 1   Key Definitions Under RCRA   7

CHAPTER 2   Hazardous Waste Identification   23

INTRODUCTION   23

SOLID WASTE   24

EXCLUDED WASTES   25

HAZARDOUS WASTE IDENTIFICATION   27

Listed Hazardous Wastes   28

Characteristics of Hazardous Wastes   33

Special Categories of Hazardous Waste   37

Special Exclusions   41

Hazardous Constituents   46

RECYCLING HAZARDOUS WASTES   47

Recycling Process   48

Requirements for Recycling   49

Burning and Blending of Waste Fuels   55

CHAPTER 3   Generators   61

INTRODUCTION   61
DEFINITION OF A GENERATOR   63
Requirements for All Generators   63
GENERATOR CATEGORIES   64
Counting Hazardous Waste   64
SMALL-QUANTITY GENERATORS (SQGs)   65
MEDIUM- AND LARGE-QUANTITY GENERATORS   66
Medium-Quantity Generators (MQGs)   71
Large-Quantity Generators (LQGs)   75

CHAPTER 4   Shipping and Transportation   80

TRANSPORTERS   80
General Requirements Under RCRA   80
General Requirements Under HMTA   83
SHIPPERS   84
Classification Procedure   85

CHAPTER 5   General Standards for Waste
Management Facilities   105

APPLICABILITY   105
EXCLUSIONS   106
GENERAL FACILITY STANDARDS   107
Notification and Record Keeping   107
General Waste Handling Requirements   110
Preparedness and Prevention   116
Contingency Plan and Emergency Procedures   117
Manifest System   119
GROUNDWATER MONITORING   120
Groundwater Monitoring at Interim Status Units   120
Groundwater Monitoring at Permitted Units   129
CLOSURE AND POST-CLOSURE   139
Closure Requirements   139
Post-Closure Requirements   154
FINANCIAL RESPONSIBILITY REQUIREMENTS   156
Financial Assurance   156
Liability Coverage   160

CHAPTER 6   Technical Standards for Waste
Management Units   161

INTRODUCTION   161
CONTAINER STORAGE UNITS   162
Container Management   162
Additional Requirements for Permitted Units   162

TANK SYSTEMS   163
  Special Requirements for Medium-Quantity Generators   164
  Accumulation Tanks for On-Site Generators   165
  Interim Status Tanks   165
  New Tank Systems   170
SURFACE IMPOUNDMENTS   171
  Interim Status Requirements   171
  Requirements for Permitted Surface Impoundments   173
WASTE PILES   174
  Interim Status Requirements   174
  Requirements for Permitted Waste Piles   175
LAND TREATMENT AREAS   175
  General Operating Requirements   175
LANDFILLS   177
INCINERATORS   178
  Interim Status Requirements   178
  Requirements for Permitted Incinerators   180
THERMAL TREATMENT UNITS   182
CHEMICAL, PHYSICAL, AND BIOLOGICAL
  TREATMENT UNITS   183
MISCELLANEOUS UNITS   183
  Introduction   183
  General Operating Requirements   184
UNDERGROUND INJECTION WELLS   184

CHAPTER 7   Permits and Interim Status   186

INTRODUCTION   186
INTERIM STATUS   187
  Operation During Interim Status   188
HAZARDOUS WASTE MANAGEMENT PERMITS   190
  Standards Applicable to All Permits   190
  Permit Application Process   192
  Permit Modifications   201
POST-CLOSURE PERMITS   208
RESEARCH, DEMONSTRATION, AND
  DEVELOPMENT PERMITS   209
EMERGENCY PERMITS   210

CHAPTER 8   Land Disposal Restrictions   211

OVERVIEW   211
  Applicability   212
  Treatment Standards   216
  Storage   220
PHASE I—SOLVENT AND DIOXIN CONTAINING
  WASTES   221
PHASE II—THE CALIFORNIA WASTES   223

CHAPTER 9   Corrective Action   227

OVERVIEW   227
PRIOR RELEASES   227
INTERIM STATUS CORRECTIVE ACTION ORDERS   230
BEYOND FACILITY BOUNDARIES   231
CORRECTIVE ACTION PROCESS   232
  RCRA Facility Assessment   233
  RCRA Facility Investigation   235
  Corrective Measures Study   236
  Remedy Selection   238
  Corrective Measures Implementation   238
  Public Participation   239

CHAPTER 10   Enforcement and State Authorization   240

RCRA'S ENFORCEMENT PROVISIONS   240
  Compliance Inspections   240
  Enforcement Options   242
  Administrative Actions   242
  Civil Actions   245
  Priority Classification Scheme   247
  EPA Action in Authorized States   249
STATE AUTHORIZATION   251
  Program Elements   252
  States with Different Programs   253
  Revising State Programs   254

PART II—SUPERFUND   257

  Relationship with Other Laws   259

CHAPTER 11   Key Definitions Under Superfund   261

CHAPTER 12   Reporting Requirements   273

SPILL REPORTING   273
  Superfund Reportable Quantities   274
  SARA Title III Reportable Quantities   278
  HMTA Reportable Quantities   279
  Clean Water Act Reporting Requirements   279
NOTIFICATION OF HAZARDOUS WASTE
  MANAGEMENT FACILITIES   280

CHAPTER 13   Response Actions Under Superfund   282

RESPONSE AUTHORITY   282
   National Contingency Plan   283
RESPONSE ACTIONS   284
   Removal Response Action   284
   Remedial Response Action   285
LIABILITY   285
   Defenses to Liability   287
   Miscellaneous Liability Provisions   289
FEDERAL FACILITIES   292

CHAPTER 14   Remedial Response   293

REMEDIAL RESPONSE ACTION PROCESS   293
   Determination of the Lead Agency   295
SITE DISCOVERY   296
PRELIMINARY ASSESSMENT   296
   Preliminary Assessment Goals   297
   Preliminary Assessment Petitions   298
SITE INSPECTION   298
HAZARD RANKING ANALYSIS   299
NATIONAL PRIORITIES LIST DETERMINATION   300
   Federal Facilities   301
   RCRA Facilities   301
REMEDIAL INVESTIGATION AND FEASIBILITY
   STUDY   302
   The RI/FS Process   302
   Remedial Investigation   306
   Feasibility Study   308
   Post RI/FS Action   312
   Cleanup Requirements   313
REMEDY SELECTION/RECORD OF DECISION   317
   Preferred Alternative Selection   317
   Public Comment   319
   Record of Decision   319
REMEDIAL DESIGN   320
REMEDIAL ACTION   320
PROJECT CLOSEOUT   321
   NPL Deletion   321
   Operation and Maintenance   322
   Final Project Closeout   322

CHAPTER 15   Miscellaneous Provisions Under Superfund   323

ENFORCEMENT   323
   Settlements   324

NATURAL RESOURCE DAMAGES   329
  Natural Resource Trustees   329
PUBLIC PARTICIPATION   330
  Citizen Suits   330
  Community Relations   331
WORKER SAFETY AND HEALTH PROGRAM   332
  Program Components   332

PART III—THE TOXIC SUBSTANCES CONTROL ACT   341

TSCA's RELATIONSHIP TO OTHER STATUTES   343

CHAPTER 16   Key PCB Definitions   347

CHAPTER 17   Use, Storage, and Disposal of PCBs 358

INTRODUCTION   358
WHAT PCBs ARE   359
PCBs IN ELECTRICAL EQUIPMENT   360
  Overview of the PCB Regulatory Program   361
  PCB Classifications   362
PROHIBITIONS   366
  Totally Enclosed Manner   366
AUTHORIZATIONS   367
  Transformers   367
  Capacitors   371
MARKING   372
INSPECTION   373
STORAGE   374
  Storage Area Requirements   374
DISPOSAL OF PCBs   377
  Disposal Facilities   377
  Disposal Requirements for PCB Items   377
TRACKING   380
  Record Keeping   385
TSCA ENFORCEMENT PROVISIONS   387
  Enforcement Overview   387
  Enforcement Provisions   388

CHAPTER 18   PCB Spill Cleanup Requirements   389

INTRODUCTION   389
  Compliance with the Policy   390
PCB SPILL REPORTING REQUIREMENTS   391
PCB SPILL CLEANUP REQUIREMENTS   392
  Small-Quantity Low-Concentration Spills   392

High-Concentration and Large Low-Concentration Spills   393
Post-Cleanup Sampling Requirements   395
Record-Keeping Requirements   396

APPENDIXES

Appendix A—RCRA Regulatory Compliance Checklist   397
Appendix B—TSCA Regulatory Compliance Checklist (PCB
    Compliance)   410
Appendix C—The RCRA-Listed Hazardous Wastes   415
Appendix D—The Hazardous Constituents (The Appendix
    VIII Constituents)   435
Appendix E—Groundwater Monitoring Constituents
    (The Appendix IX Constituents)   440
Appendix F—Classification of Permit Modifications   443
Appendix G—Information Sources   452
Appendix H—Acronyms   471
Index   477

Preface

Environmental regulation has fast become one of the most complicated and ambitious regulatory programs in our society. Because there are many regulations being promulgated and revised, it has become a nearly impossible task to stay current with them, let alone to understand the regulatory jargon. Thus, there is a need for a quality reference book that will cut through the regulatory language and present the material in a clear and concise manner.

My primary purpose in writing this book is to enable readers to understand the hazardous waste regulatory program of the United States Environmental Protection Agency (EPA). In my experiences, I have heard many wrong interpretations, as well as a basic misunderstanding of the regulations, which could be attributed to the many sources that explain the information in a piecemeal fashion. This book alleviates this problem by aggregating the information and presenting it in a straightforward manner. It is intended for industry, regulators, consultants, lawyers, and the public.

This book goes far beyond the typical inclusion of a copy of the various laws along with a brief summary. It is an in-depth, step-by-step guide to the regulations that contain compliance guidance, as well as EPA interpretations, which are not readily communicated. My experience as a technical information specialist on both the RCRA/Superfund and TSCA hotlines required research and answers to thousands of questions on this subject, and, combined with my field experience obtained as an environmental consultant, has enabled me to present this comprehensive collection of hazardous waste regulatory information. Responding to questions concerning regulations required the presentation of very technical information in general, understandable language to persons of varying backgrounds. I have written this book in that same manner.

To understand the program and the interrelationships among the statutes, it is important to review a brief history of the program.

Hazardous waste regulation is a relatively new initiative. The pollution scare and ecology movement in the 1960s brought about the first major attempts to rectify the adverse effects of environmental pollution. These first attempts were focused on the most visible media, air and surface water, with the passage of the Clean Air and Clean Water Acts. Because these new Acts prevented disposal of pollutants into the air or water, industry relied more heavily on land disposal of large amounts of wastes. Because inadequate and environmentally unsound practices for the disposal of hazardous wastes abounded, the nation became aware of a new pollution problem, hazardous and toxic substances contaminating groundwater and tainting drinking water wells. In response, Congress enacted the Resource Conservation and Recovery Act (RCRA) in 1976, which amended the Solid Waste Disposal Act of 1965, to control the generation, transportation, and management of hazardous wastes; and also in 1976, the Toxic Substances Control Act (TSCA) was enacted to regulate the use and management of toxic substances and specifically, polychlorinated biphenyls. In 1979, the Love Canal incident demonstrated the need for legislation to control and clean up past hazardous waste disposal sites that presented a dangerous threat to public health and the environment. To meet this need, Congress passed the Comprehensive Environmental Response, Compensation, and Liability Act (CERCLA, also called "Superfund") in 1980. In subsequent years, the EPA and Congress perceived shortcomings in both RCRA and CERCLA. Congress was able to implement sweeping changes to both statutes during their respective reauthorizations. The reauthorization of RCRA added the Hazardous and Solid Waste Amendments of 1984 (HSWA), which includes a mandate to stop relying on the traditional practice of land disposal. The reauthorization of CERCLA in 1986 added the Superfund Amendments and Reauthorization Act (SARA), which includes a mandate, as well as a substantially increased budget, to speed the cleanup of inactive waste management sites. This array of statutes, and their respective reauthorizations, constitutes the majority of the nation's hazardous waste regulatory program.

Acknowledgments

I would like to thank the following persons for their assistance and contributions in preparing this book:

Leigh Benson, LABAT-ANDERSON, Incorporated

Saskia Mooney, Resource Applications, Incorporated

Ingrid Rosencrantz, SAIC

Lance Traves, Clayton Environmental Services

Special thanks to Julie Steffen for the production of the tables, figures, and cover design; Suzanne Parent and Karen Burchard for editorial assistance; Kathie Gabriel for word processing, and Marat Perry for inspiration.

I would also like to express my gratitude to Alberta Gordon and Bob Esposito of Van Nostrand Reinhold for their assistance in this project.

A Guide to Readers

This book has been written and structured in the most straightforward manner possible, given the diversity of the audience and the nature of the subject. Some minor regulations, or regulations that affect a very small portion of the regulated community, have been purposely omitted. This book does not necessarily follow the regulations in the same order as the Code of Federal Regulations (CFR), because the CFR is not necessarily arranged in the most logical order for the purposes of easy understanding. However, *The Complete Guide to the Hazardous Waste Regulations* is structured to facilitate ease in understanding of the subject material. I recommend first reading the entire book through to obtain an understanding of how the various statutes and regulations are interrelated, and how they conflict. Afterward, review the book concurrently with the regulations to understand the intent of the regulations. Although this book is separated into three parts relating to the three major statutes (RCRA, CERCLA, and TSCA), other statutes are addressed throughout the various parts. As an aid, I have included regulatory compliance checklists and diagrams where appropriate.

It is important to note that, although the regulations are written in a clear-cut fashion, there are many factors that can affect their applicability or regulatory outcome. Close attention should be paid to the regulatory definitions of terms used throughout this book, as well as the regulations. Many people use the commonly implied meaning of a term instead of its regulatory meaning. Misunderstanding or ignorance of definitional usage accounts for a significant portion of noncompliance. Obviously, this book cannot provide individualized legal advice, and it is not intended to do so. However, it does provide the information needed to understand various regulatory situations and, thus, the necessary tools to make a prudent decision. I have tried to be as accurate and objective as possible and have not included material that judges the need, value, or practicality of the implementation of these regulations.

THE COMPLETE GUIDE TO THE HAZARDOUS WASTE REGULATIONS

PART 1

The Resource Conservation and Recovery Act

The Solid Waste Disposal Act (SWDA), enacted in 1965, was the first piece of federal legislation that addressed the Nation's waste management problem. The Act was amended significantly by the Resource Conservation and Recovery Act (RCRA) in 1976 and by the Hazardous and Solid Waste Amendments of 1984 (HSWA). These three acts collectively are referred to as RCRA (pronounced "wreckra").

The three major parts of RCRA are Subtitles C, D, and I. Subtitle C regulates hazardous waste, Subtitle D regulates solid waste (nonhazardous waste), and Subtitle I regulates underground storage tanks that hold petroleum products and hazardous substances (does not include wastes except for waste oil).

Solid Waste Management

Subtitle D of RCRA primarily regulates nonhazardous solid wastes and solid waste management facilities, such as nonhazardous industrial surface impoundments, construction/demolition debris landfills, municipal landfills, and "town dumps." It established a voluntary program through which participating states received federal financial and technical support to develop and implement solid waste management plans as well as operating standards for facilities. These standards, commonly called the Subtitle D criteria, set forth minimum operating requirements for environmentally acceptable facilities. These criteria are designed to:

1

- Protect groundwater, surface water, air, floodplains, and food crops.
- Prevent the transmission of disease.
- Ensure the safety of employees and nearby residents.

The solid waste management plan program essentially outlines steps that the state must take to ensure that the solid waste within its borders is managed in an environmentally sound manner and that resources are conserved and recovered whenever possible. A key component of Subtitle D is to identify inappropriately operated facilities, termed "open dumps," which are supposed to be closed or upgraded. The Environmental Protection Agency (EPA) periodically publishes a national inventory of open dumps.

EPA's role, with respect to state plans, is limited to setting the regulatory requirements that the state must follow in designing its plans, administering state grant programs, and approving state plans that comply with RCRA. In addition to state plans, RCRA requires EPA to prepare procurement guidelines, which allow federal agencies to procure recycled material in stipulated situations. These materials include recycled paper, kiln dust, oil, and rubber tires.

A significant number of sites contained in Superfund's National Priorities List (NPL) are solid waste landfills. (The NPL is a compilation of hazardous waste sites that pose a serious threat to human health and the environment.) As a result, HSWA has required EPA to scrutinize the current minimal Subtitle D criteria. EPA must revise the criteria for facilities that receive hazardous household waste and small-quantity generator (SQG) waste. At a minimum, the revisions must require groundwater monitoring, provide acceptable location standards for new facilities, outline adequate corrective action requirements, and establish some type of permit program.

Hazardous Waste Management

The Resource Conservation and Recovery Act (RCRA), enacted on October 21, 1976, regulates hazardous waste "from the cradle to the grave." The statute requires EPA to establish minimum acceptable requirements for all aspects of hazardous waste for generators and transporters as well as for treatment, storage, and disposal facilities.

The regulatory framework established under Subtitle C was designed to protect human health and the environment from the effects of improper management of hazardous waste. Determining what is a *hazardous waste* is therefore a key question because only those wastes that meet the definition of hazardous waste are subject to Subtitle C. Making this determination can be a very complex exercise. The universe of potential hazardous wastes is large and diverse, consisting of chemical products, generic waste streams, and specialized by-products. The terms "hazardous waste" and "toxic waste" are often used interchangeably; however, regarding the Subtitle C regulations, there is an important distinction between the two. Hazardous waste denotes a regulated waste; only certain waste streams are designated as hazardous. This designation is not based solely on toxicity; it also includes other physical characteristics that present an environmental or health threat, as well as the quantity generated, damage case history, and environmental fate. Toxic waste is a phrase used primarily by the media and the public. Although every waste stream is toxic to some degree, only some wastes are classified as hazardous specifically because of their toxicity. Toxic simply means that it has the ability to cause harm. Thus, those wastes that pose a serious threat when mismanaged must be differentiated.

Applicability of RCRA

RCRA was enacted in 1976, but it was not until May 19, 1980, that EPA finalized the first phase of the RCRA hazardous waste regulatory program. The May 19th rule did not become effective until November 19, 1980. By this date, hazardous waste management facilities had to either close or comply with RCRA. Except for a few provisions (e.g., corrective action) waste disposed of before November 19, 1980, is not subject to RCRA but is subject to Superfund. RCRA is written in the present tense and its regulatory scheme is prospective. Therefore, EPA believes that Congress intended the hazardous waste regulatory program under Subtitle C of RCRA to control primarily hazardous waste management activities that take place after the effective date of the Phase I regulations (November 19, 1980). Thus, the Subtitle C regulations did not by their terms apply to inactive (either closed or abandoned) disposal facilities. This statement can be found in the May 19, 1980, *Federal Register*, volume 45, page 33170 (cited as 45 *FR* 33170). However, hazardous waste placed in a surface impoundment, tank, or drum before November 19, 1980, and that remained in *storage* after that date, is subject to RCRA. This is considered active storage. Active storage, on or after November 19, 1980, is subject to RCRA requirements. This decision is based on *Environmental Defense Fund* v. *J. Lamphier*, 714 F.2nd (1983).

Regulatory Sections

The Subtitle C regulations are contained in Title 40 of the *Code of Federal Regulations*. (Regulatory compliance checklists for many of the Subtitle C requirements are contained in Appendix A of this book.) The codified regulations are organized into Parts. The codified regulatory Parts are as follows:

Part 260   Definitions, petitions for rulemaking changes, and delisting procedures
Part 261   Hazardous waste identification
Part 262   Generator standards
Part 263   Transporter standards
Part 264   Treatment, storage, and disposal facilities: final operating standards
Part 265   Treatment, storage and disposal facilities: interim status standards
Part 266   Hazardous waste fuel burned for energy recovery, used oil fuel, and process-specific regulatory standards
Part 268   Land disposal restrictions
Part 270   Permits and operation during interim status
Part 271   State programs

State Requirements

RCRA encourages states to develop and operate their own hazardous waste programs as an alternative to EPA management. Thus, the hazardous waste regulatory program described in this book may be run by EPA or a state agency. However, for a state to have jurisdiction over its hazardous waste program, it must receive EPA approval by showing that its program is at least as stringent as the EPA program; and in many approved states the program is identical. Chapter 10 explains the requirements for a state to obtain authorization.

Petitions

RCRA contains provisions (codified in Part 260) that allow any person to petition the EPA Administrator to modify or revoke any provision in Parts 260 through 265. The general informational requirements for a petition include:

- Petitioner's name and address.
- A statement of the petitioner's interest in the proposed action.

- A description of the proposed action, including (where appropriate) suggested regulatory language.
- A statement of the need and justification for the proposed action, including any supporting tests, studies, or other relevant information.

Specialized information is required for a petition, depending on the changes being sought. This information is contained in Subpart C of 40 CFR.

The EPA Administrator must make a tentative decision to grant or deny a petition and publish a notice of the tentative decision, in the form of either an advanced notice of proposed rulemaking (ANPR), a proposed rule, or a tentative determination to deny the petition in the *Federal Register* to allow public comment. An informal public hearing may be held if the Administrator decides that one is warranted or if one is requested.

After evaluating all public comments, the Administrator must make a final decision by publishing in the *Federal Register* a regulatory amendment or a denial of the petition.

Chapter 1

Key Definitions Under RCRA

This chapter contains key regulatory definitions of RCRA terms used throughout Part I. These definitions are listed in 40 CFR 260.10, 268.3, and 270.2.

Aboveground tank means a device meeting the definition of "tank" in Section 260.10 and that is situated in such a way that the entire surface area of the tank is completely above the plane of the adjacent surrounding surface and the entire surface area of the tank (including the tank bottom) is able to be visually inspected.

Active life of a facility means the period from the initial receipt of hazardous waste at the facility until the Regional Administrator receives certification of final closure.

Active portion means which portion of a facility where treatment, storage, or disposal operations are being or have been conducted after the effective date of Part 261 of this chapter and which is not a closed portion. (See also "closed portion" and "inactive portion.")

Ancillary equipment means any device including, but not limited to, such devices as piping, fittings, flanges, valves, and pumps that is used to distribute, meter, or control the flow of hazardous waste from its point of generation to a storage or treatment tank(s), between hazardous waste storage and treatment tanks to a point of disposal on-site, or to a point of shipment for disposal off-site.

Application means the EPA standard national forms for applying for a permit, including any additions, revisions or modifications to the forms; or forms approved by EPA for use in approved States, including any approved modifications or revisions. Application also includes the information required by the Director under §§270.14 through 270.29 (contents of Part B of the RCRA application).

Approved program or *approved state* means a State which has been approved or authorized by EPA under Part 271.

Aquifer means a geologic formation, group of formations, or part of a formation capable of yielding a significant amount of ground water to wells or springs.

Authorized representative means the person responsible for the overall operation of a facility or an operational unit (i.e., part of a facility), e.g., the plant manager, superintendent or person of equivalent responsibility.

Boiler means an enclosed device using controlled flame combustion and having the following characteristics:

(1)(i) The unit must have physical provisions for recovering and exporting thermal energy in the form of steam, heated fluids, or heated gases; and

(ii) The unit's combustion chamber and primary energy recovery section(s) must be of integral design. To be of integral design, the combustion chamber and the primary energy recovery section(s) (such as waterwalls and superheaters) must be physically formed into one manufactured or assembled unit. A unit in which the combustion chamber and the primary energy recovery section(s) are joined only by ducts or connections carrying flue gas is not integrally designed; however, secondary energy recovery equipment (such as economizers or air preheaters) need not be physically formed into the same unit as the combustion chamber and the primary energy recovery section. The following units are not precluded from being boilers solely because they are not of integral design: process heaters (units that transfer energy directly to a process stream) and fluidized bed combustion units; and

(iii) While in operation, the unit must maintain a thermal energy recovery efficiency of at least 60 percent, calculated in terms of the recovered energy compared with the thermal value of the fuel; and

(iv) The unit must export and utilize at least 75 percent of the recovered energy, calculated on an annual basis. In this calculation, no credit shall be given for recovered heat used internally in the same unit. (Examples of internal use are the preheating of fuel or combustion air, and the driving of induced or forced draft fans or feedwater pumps); or

(2) The unit is one which the Regional Administrator has determined, on a case-by-case basis, to be a boiler, after considering the standards in §260.32.

Certification means a statement of professional opinion based upon knowledge and belief.

Closed portion means that portion of a facility which an owner or operator has closed in accordance with the approved facility closure plan and all applicable closure requirements. (See also "active portion" and "inactive portion.")

Closure means the act of securing a hazardous waste management facility pursuant to the requirements of 40 CFR Part 264.

Component means either the tank or ancillary equipment of a tank system.

Confined aquifer means an aquifer bounded above and below by impermeable beds or by beds of distinctly lower permeability than that of the aquifer itself; an aquifer containing confined ground water.

Container means any portable device in which a material is stored, transported, treated, disposed of, or otherwise handled.

Contingency plan means a document setting out an organized, planned, and coordinated course of action to be followed in case of a fire, explosion, or release of hazardous waste or hazardous waste constituents which could threaten human health or the environment.

Corrosion expert means a person who, by reason of his knowledge of the physical sciences and the principles of engineering and mathematics, acquired by a professional education and related practical experience, is qualified to engage in the practice of corrosion control on buried or submerged metal piping systems and metal tanks. Such a person must be certified as being qualified by the National Association of Corrosion Engineers (NACE) or be a registered professional engineer who has certification or licensing that includes education and experience in corrosion control on buried or submerged metal piping systems and metal tanks.

Designated facility means a hazardous waste treatment, storage, or disposal facility which has received an EPA permit (or a facility with interim status) in accordance with the requirements of Parts 270 and 124 of this chapter [40 CFR], a permit from a State authorized in accordance with Part 271 of this chapter [40 CFR], or that is regulated under

§261.6(c)(2) or Subpart F of Part 266 of this chapter [40 CFR], and that has been designated on the manifest by the generator pursuant to §262.20.

Director means the Regional Administrator or the State Director, as the context requires, or an authorized representative. When there is no approved State program, and there is an EPA administered program, Director means the Regional Administrator. When there is an approved State program, Director normally means the State Director. In some circumstances, however, EPA retains the authority to take certain actions even when there is an approved State program. In such cases, the term Director means the Regional Administrator and not the State Director.

Discharge or *hazardous waste discharge* means the accidental or intentional spilling, leaking, pumping, pouring, emitting, emptying, or dumping of hazardous waste into or on any land or water.

Disposal means the discharge, deposit, injection, dumping, spilling, leaking, or placing of any hazardous waste into or on any land or water so that such hazardous waste or any constituent thereof may enter the environment or be emitted into the air or discharged into any waters, including ground water.

Disposal facility means a facility or part of a facility at which hazardous waste is intentionally placed into or on any land or water, and at which waste will remain after closure.

Draft permit means a document prepared under §124.6 indicating the Director's tentative decision to issue or deny, modify, revoke and reissue, terminate, or reissue a permit. A notice of intent to terminate a permit, and a notice of intent to deny a permit, as discussed in §124.5, are types of draft permits. A denial of a request for modification, revocation and reissuance, or termination, as discussed in §124.5 is not a "draft permit." A proposed permit is not a draft permit.

Elementary neutralization unit means a device which:

> (1) Is used for neutralizing wastes which are hazardous wastes only because they exhibit the corrosivity characteristic defined in §261.22 of this chapter [40 CFR], or are listed in Subpart D of Part 261 of this chapter [40 CFR] only for this reason; and

> (2) Meets the definition of tank, container, transport vehicle, or vessel in §260.10 of this chapter [40 CFR].

Emergency permit means a RCRA permit issued in accordance with §270.61.

EPA hazardous waste number means the number assigned by EPA to each hazardous waste listed in Part 261, Subpart D, of this chapter [40 CFR] and to each characteristic identified in Part 261, Subpart C, of this chapter [40 CFR].

EPA identification number means the number assigned by EPA to each generator, transporter, and treatment, storage, or disposal facility.

Equivalent method means any testing or analytical method approved by the Administrator under §§260.20 and 260.21.

Existing hazardous waste management (HWM) facility or *existing facility* means a facility which was in operation or for which construction commenced on or before November 19, 1980. A facility has commenced construction if:

(1) The owner or operator has obtained the Federal, State, and local approvals or permits necessary to begin physical construction; and either

(2)(i) A continuous on-site, physical construction program has begun; or

(ii) The owner or operator has entered into contractual obligations—which cannot be canceled or modified without substantial loss—for physical construction of the facility to be completed within a reasonable time.

Existing portion means that land surface area of an existing waste management unit, included in the original Part A permit application, on which wastes have been placed prior to the issuance of a permit.

Existing tank system or *existing component* means a tank system or component that is used for the storage or treatment of hazardous waste and that is in operation, or for which installation has commenced on or prior to July 14, 1986. Installation will be considered to have commenced if the owner or operator has obtained all Federal, State, and local approvals or permits necessary to begin physical construction of the site or installation of the tank system and if either (1) a continuous on-site physical construction or installation program has begun, or (2) the owner or operator has entered into contractual obligations—which cannot be canceled or modified without substantial loss—for physical construction of the site or installation of the tank system to be completed within a reasonable time.

Facility means all contiguous land, and structures, other appurtenances, and improvements on the land, used for treating, storing, or disposing of hazardous waste. A facility may consist of several treatment, storage, or disposal operational units (e.g., one or more landfills, surface impoundments, or combinations of them).

Final closure means the closure of all hazardous waste management units at the facility in accordance with all applicable closure requirements so that hazardous waste management activities under Parts 264 and 265 of this chapter [40 CFR] are no longer conducted at the facility unless subject to the provisions in §262.34.

Food-chain crops means tobacco, crops grown for human consumption, and crops grown for feed for animals whose products are consumed by humans.

Free liquids means liquids which readily separate from the solid portion of a waste under ambient temperature and pressure.

Freeboard means the vertical distance between the top of a tank or surface impoundment dike, and the surface of the waste contained therein.

Generator means any person, by site, whose act or process produces hazardous waste identified or listed in Part 261 of this chapter [40 CFR] or whose act first causes a hazardous waste to become subject to a regulation.

Ground water means water below the land surface in a zone of saturation.

Hazardous waste means a hazardous waste as defined in Section 261.3 of this chapter [40 CFR].

Hazardous waste constituent means a constituent that caused the Administrator to list the hazardous waste in Part 261, Subpart D, of this chapter [40 CFR], or a constituent listed in table 1 of Part 261.24 of this chapter [40 CFR].

Hazardous waste management unit is a contiguous area of land on or in which hazardous waste is placed, or the largest area in which there is significant likelihood of mixing hazardous waste constituents in the same area. Examples of hazardous waste management units include a surface impoundment, a waste pile, a land treatment area, a landfill cell, an incinerator, a tank and its associated piping and underlying containment system, and a container storage area. A container alone does not constitute a unit; the unit includes containers and the land or pad upon which they are placed.

In operation refers to a facility which is treating, storing, or disposing of hazardous waste.

Inactive portion means that portion of a facility which is not operated after the effective date of Part 261 of this chapter [40 CFR].

Incinerator means any enclosed device using controlled flame combustion that neither meets the criteria for classification as a boiler nor is listed as an industrial furnace.

Incompatible waste means a hazardous waste which is unsuitable for:

(1) Placement in a particular device or facility because it may cause corrosion or decay of containment materials (e.g., container inner liners or tank walls); or

(2) Commingling with another waste or material under uncontrolled conditions because the commingling might produce heat or pressure, fire or explosion, violent reaction, toxic dusts, mists, fumes, or gases, or flammable fumes or gases.

Individual generation site means the contiguous site at or on which one or more hazardous wastes are generated. An individual generation site, such as a large manufacturing plant, may have one or more sources of hazardous waste but is considered a single or individual generation site if the site or property is contiguous.

Industrial furnace means any of the following enclosed devices that are integral components of manufacturing processes and that use controlled flame devices to accomplish recovery of materials or energy:

(1) Cement kilns
(2) Lime kilns
(3) Aggregate kilns
(4) Phosphate kilns
(5) Coke ovens
(6) Blast furnaces
(7) Smelting, melting, and refining furnaces (including pyrometallurgical devices such as cupolas, reverberator furnaces, sintering machines, roasters, and foundry furnaces)
(8) Titanium dioxide chloride process oxidation reactors
(9) Methane reforming furnaces
(10) Pulping liquor recovery furnaces
(11) Combustion devices used in the recovery of sulfur values from spent sulfuric acid

(12) Such other devices as the Administrator may, after notice and comment, add to this list on the basis of one more of the following factors:

(i) The design and use of the device primarily to accomplish recovery of material products;

(ii) The use of the device to burn or reduce raw materials to make a material product;

(iii) The use of the device to burn or reduce secondary materials as effective substitutes for raw materials, in processes using raw materials as principal feedstocks;

(iv) The use of the device to burn or reduce secondary materials as ingredients in an industrial process to make a material product;

(v) The use of the device in common industrial practice to produce a material product; and

(vi) Other factors, as appropriate.

Inground tank means a device meeting the definition of tank in §260.10 whereby a portion of the tank wall is situated to any degree within the ground, thereby preventing visual inspection of that external surface area of the tank that is in the ground.

Injection well means a well into which fluids are injected. (See also "underground injection.")

Inner liner means a continuous layer of material placed inside a tank or container which protects the construction materials of the tank or container from the contained waste or reagents used to treat the waste.

Installation inspector means a person who, by reason of his knowledge of the physical sciences and the principles of engineering, acquired by a professional education and related practical experience, is qualified to supervise the installation of tank systems.

International shipment means the transportation of hazardous waste into or out of the jurisdiction of the United States.

Land disposal means placement in or on the land and includes, but is not limited to, placement in a landfill, surface impoundment, waste pile, injection well, land treatment facility, salt dome formation, salt bed formation, underground mine or cave, or placement in a concrete vault or bunker intended for disposal purposes.

Landfill means a disposal facility or part of a facility where hazardous waste is placed in or on land and which is not a pile, a land treatment facility, a surface impoundment, an injection well, a salt dome formation, a salt bed formation, an underground mine, or a cave.

Landfill cell means a discrete volume of a hazardous waste landfill which uses a liner to provide isolation of wastes from adjacent cells or wastes. Examples of landfill cells are trenches and pits.

Land treatment facility means a facility or part of a facility at which hazardous waste is applied onto or incorporated into the soil surface; such facilities are disposal facilities if the waste will remain after closure.

Leachate means any liquid, including any suspended components in the liquid, that has percolated through or drained from hazardous waste.

Leak-detection system means a system capable of detecting the failure of either the primary or secondary containment structure or the presence of a release of hazardous waste or accumulated liquid in the secondary containment structure. Such a system must employ operational controls (e.g., daily visual inspections for releases into the secondary containment system of aboveground tanks) or consist of an interstitial monitoring device designed to detect continuously and automatically the failure of the primary or secondary containment structure or the presence of a release of hazardous waste into the secondary containment structure.

Liner means a continuous layer of natural or man-made materials, beneath or on the sides of a surface impoundment, landfill, or landfill cell, which restricts the downward or lateral escape of hazardous waste, hazardous waste constituents, or leachate.

Major facility means any facility or activity classified as such by the Regional Administrator, or, in the case of approved State programs, the Regional Administrator in conjunction with the State Director.

Management or *hazardous waste management* means the systematic control of the collection, source separation, storage, transportation, processing, treatment, recovery, and disposal of hazardous waste.

Manifest means the shipping document EPA form 8700-22 and, if necessary, EPA form 8700-22A, originated and signed by the generator in accordance with the instructions included in the Appendix to Part 262.

Manifest document number means the U.S. EPA twelve-digit identification number assigned to the generator plus a unique five-digit document number assigned to the Manifest by the generator for recording and reporting purposes.

Mining overburden returned to the mine site means any material overlying an economic mineral deposit that is removed to gain access to that deposit and is then used for reclamation of a surface mine.

Miscellaneous unit means a hazardous waste management unit where hazardous waste is treated, stored, or disposed of and that is not a container, tank, surface impoundment, pile, landfill, incinerator, boiler, industrial furnace, underground injection well with appropriate technical standards under 40 CFR Part 146, or unit eligible for a research, development, and demonstration permit under §270.65.

Movement means that hazardous waste transported to a facility in an individual vehicle.

New hazardous waste management facility or *new facility* means a facility which began operation, or for which construction commenced, after October 21, 1976. (See also "Existing hazardous waste management facility.")

New tank system or *new tank component* means a tank system or component that will be used for the storage or treatment of hazardous waste and for which installation has commenced after July 14, 1986; except, however, for purposes of §§264.193(g)(2) and 265.193(g)(2), a new tank system is one for which construction commences after July 14, 1986. (See also "existing tank system.")

On Ground Tank means a device meeting the definition of "tank" in §260.10 and that is situated in such a way that the bottom of the tank is on the same level as the adjacent surrounding surface so that the external tank bottom cannot be visually inspected.

Off-Site means any site which is not on-site.

On-Site means the same or geographically contiguous property which may be divided by public or private right-of-way, provided the entrance and exit between the properties is at a crossroads intersection, and access is by crossing, as opposed to going along, the right-of-way. Noncontiguous properties owned by the same person but connected by a right-of-way which he controls and to which the public does not have access, is also considered on-site property.

Open burning means the combustion of any material without the following characteristics:

(1) Control of combustion air to maintain adequate temperature for efficient combustion,

(2) Containment of the combustion reaction in an enclosed device to provide sufficient residence time and mixing for complete combustion, and

(3) Control of emission of the gaseous combustion products (see also "incineration" and "thermal treatment").

Operator means the person responsible for the overall operation of a facility.

Owner means the person who owns a facility or part of a facility.

Partial closure means the closure of a hazardous waste management unit in accordance with the applicable closure requirements of Parts 264 or 265 of this chapter [40 CFR] at a facility that contains other active hazardous waste management units. For example, partial closure may include the closure of a tank (including its associated piping and underlying containment systems), landfill cell, surface impoundment, waste pile, or other hazardous waste management unit, while other parts of the same facility continue to operate.

Permit means an authorization, license, or equivalent control document issued by EPA or an approved State to implement the requirements of this part [270] and Parts 271 and 124. Permit includes permit by rule (§270.60), and emergency permit (§270.61). Permit does not include RCRA interim status (Subpart G of this part), or any permit which has not yet been the subject of final agency action, such as a draft permit or proposed permit.

Person means an individual, trust, firm, joint stock company, Federal Agency, corporation (including a government corporation), partnership, association, State, municipality, commission, political subdivision of a State, or any interstate body.

Personnel or *facility personnel* means all persons who work at, or oversee the operations of, a hazardous waste facility, and whose actions or failure to act may result in noncompliance with the requirements of Parts 264 or 265 of 40 CFR.

Pile means any non-containerized accumulation of solid, nonflowing hazardous waste that is used for treatment or storage.

Point source means any discernible, confined, and discrete conveyance, including, but not limited to any pipe, ditch, channel, tunnel, conduit, well, discrete fissure, container, rolling stock, concentrated animal feeding operation, or vessel or other floating craft, from which pollutants are or may be discharged. This term does not include return flows from irrigated agriculture.

Publicly owned treatment works or *POTW* means any device or system used in the treatment (including recycling and reclamation) of municipal sewage or industrial wastes of a liquid nature which is owned by a "State" or "municipality" (as defined by Section 502(4) of the CWA). This definition includes sewers, pipes, or other conveyances only if they convey wastewater to a POTW providing treatment.

Regional Administrator means the Regional Administrator for the EPA Region in which the facility is located, or his designee.

Representative sample means a sample of a universe or whole (e.g., waste pile, lagoon, ground water) which can be expected to exhibit the average properties of the universe or whole.

Run-off means any rainwater, leachate, or other liquid that drains over land from any part of a facility.

Run-on means any rainwater, leachate, or other liquid that drains over land onto any part of a facility.

Saturated zone or *zone of saturation* means that part of the earth's crust in which all voids are filled with water.

Schedule of compliance means a schedule of remedial measures included in a permit, including an enforceable sequence of interim requirements (for example, actions, operations, or milestone events) leading to compliance with the Act and regulations.

Site means the land or water area where any facility or activity is physically located or conducted, including adjacent land used in connection with the facility or activity.

Sludge means any solid, semi-solid, or liquid waste generated from a municipal, commercial, or industrial wastewater treatment plant, water supply treatment plant, or air pollution control facility exclusive of the treated effluent from a wastewater treatment plant.

Solid waste means a solid waste as defined in §261.2 of this chapter [40 CFR].

Solid waste management unit means any discernible waste management unit at a RCRA facility from which hazardous waste or constituents might migrate, irrespective of whether the unit was intended for the management of solid and/or hazardous waste.

The solid waste management unit definition includes:

(a) Containers, tanks, surface impoundments, container storage areas, waste piles, land treatment units, landfills, incinerators, underground injection wells, and other physical, chemical and biological units, including those units defined as regulated units under RCRA;

(b) Recycling units, wastewater treatment units, and other units which EPA has generally exempted from standards applicable to hazardous waste management units; and

(c) Areas associated with production processes at facilities which have become contaminated by routine, systemic, and deliberate discharges of waste or constituents.

State means any of the several States, the District of Columbia, the Commonwealth of Puerto Rico, the Virgin Islands, Guam, American Samoa, and the Commonwealth of the Northern Mariana Islands.

State Director means the chief administrative officer of any State agency operating an approved program, or the delegated representative of the State Director. If responsibility is divided among two or more State agencies, State Director means the chief administrative officer of the State agency authorized to perform the particular procedure or function to which reference is made.

Storage means the holding of hazardous waste for a temporary period, at the end of which the hazardous waste is treated, disposed, or stored elsewhere.

Sump means any pit or reservoir that meets the definition of tank and those troughs/trenches connected to it that serves to collect hazardous waste for transport to hazardous waste storage, treatment, or disposal facilities.

Surface impoundment or *impoundment* means a facility or part of a facility which is a natural topographic depression, man-made excavation, or diked area formed primarily of earthen materials (although it may be lined with man-made materials), which is designed to hold an accumulation of liquid wastes or wastes containing free liquids, and which is not an injection well. Examples of surface impoundments are holding, storage, settling, and aeration pits, ponds, and lagoons.

Tank means a stationary device, designed to contain an accumulation of hazardous waste, which is constructed primarily of non-earthen materials (e.g., wood, concrete, steel, plastic) which provide structural support.

Tank system means a hazardous waste storage or treatment tank and its associated ancillary equipment and containment system.

Thermal treatment means the treatment of hazardous waste in a device which uses elevated temperatures as the primary means to change the chemical, physical, or biological character or composition of the hazardous waste. Examples of thermal treatment processes are incineration, molten salt, pyrolysis, calcination, wet air oxidation, and microwave discharge. (See also "incinerator" and "open burning.")

Totally enclosed treatment facility means a facility for the treatment of hazardous waste which is directly connected to an industrial production process and which is constructed and operated in a manner which prevents the release of any hazardous waste or any constituent thereof into the environment during treatment. An example is a pipe in which waste acid is neutralized.

Transfer facility means any transportation related facility including loading docks, parking areas, storage areas, and other similar areas where shipments of hazardous waste are held during the normal course of transportation.

Transport vehicle means a motor vehicle or rail car used for the transportation of cargo by any mode. Each cargo-carrying body (trailer, railroad freight car, etc.) is a separate transport vehicle.

Transportation means the movement of hazardous waste by air, rail, highway, or water.

Transporter means a person engaged in the off-site transportation of hazardous waste by air, rail, highway, or water.

Treatment means any method, technique, or process, including neutralization, designed to change the physical, chemical, or biological character or composition of any hazardous waste so as to neutralize such waste, or so as to recover energy or material resources from the waste, or so as to render such waste non-hazardous or less hazardous; safer to transport, store, or dispose of; or amenable for recovery, amenable for storage, or reduced in volume.

Treatment zone means a soil area of the unsaturated zone of a land treatment unit within which hazardous constituents are degraded, transformed, or immobilized.

Underground injection means the subsurface emplacement of fluids through a bored, drilled, or driven well; or through a dug well, where the depth of the dug well is greater than the largest surface dimension. (See also "injection well.")

Underground tank means a device meeting the definition of "tank" in §260.10 whose entire surface area is totally below the surface of and covered by the ground.

Unfit-for use tank system means a tank system that has been determined through an integrity assessment or other inspection to be no longer capable of storing or treating hazardous waste without posing a threat of release of hazardous waste to the environment.

United States means the 50 States, the District of Columbia, the Commonwealth of Puerto Rico, the U.S. Virgin Islands, Guam, American Samoa, and the Commonwealth of the Northern Mariana Islands.

Unsaturated Zone or *Zone of Aeration* means the zone between the land surface and the water table.

Uppermost aquifer means the geologic formation nearest the natural ground surface that is an aquifer, as well as lower aquifers that are hydraulically interconnected with this aquifer within the facility's property boundary.

Vessel includes every description of watercraft, used or capable of being used as a means of transportation on the water.

Wastewater treatment unit means a device which:

(1) Is part of a wastewater treatment facility which is subject to regulation under either Section 402 or 307(b) of the Clean Water Act; and

(2) Receives and treats or stores an influent wastewater which is a hazardous waste as defined in §261.3 of this chapter [40 CFR], or generates and accumulates a wastewater treatment sludge which is a hazardous waste as defined in §261.3 of this chapter [40 CFR], or treats or stores a wastewater treatment sludge which is a hazardous waste as defined in §261.3 of this chapter [40 CFR]; and

(3) Meets the definition of tank in §260.10 of this chapter [40 CFR].

Water (Bulk Shipment) means the bulk transportation of hazardous waste which is loaded or carried on board a vessel without containers or labels.

Well means any shaft or pit dug or bored into the earth, generally of a cylindrical form, and often walled with bricks or tubing to prevent the earth from caving in.

Zone of engineering control means an area under the control of the owner/operator that, upon detection of a hazardous waste release, can be readily cleaned up prior to the release of hazardous waste or hazardous constituents to ground water or surface water.

Chapter 2

Hazardous Waste Identification

Because only those wastes that meet the definition of hazardous are subject to Subtitle C of RCRA, the identification process is crucial to determining a generator's applicability to RCRA.

INTRODUCTION

The determination of a waste as a RCRA hazardous waste is the most important, and by far the most complex, step in ascertaining one's responsibility under RCRA. Because only those wastes that meet the definition of *hazardous* are subject to Subtitle C of RCRA, careful attention should be paid to each step in the determination of a waste as hazardous. It is strongly recommended that one read the entire chapter before arriving at a determination for a waste.

The Identification Process

Although this book uses a step-by-step identification process, many factors can affect the classification of a waste throughout the process, and they may not necessarily appear in a logical order. This is mainly because of EPA's redefinition of solid waste and because certain hazardous wastes are subject to special considerations under various sections of RCRA. For the purposes of simplifying this procedure, a basic process is used as outlined in Figure 2-1.

The first step is to determine if the waste is classified as solid waste

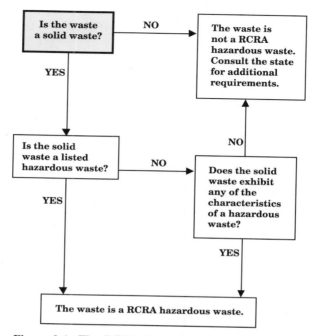

Figure 2-1. The RCRA Hazardous Waste Identification Process

under RCRA. The definition of solid waste is very broad and covers most waste-type items. Assuming that the waste meets the definition of solid waste, the next step is to determine if the waste is specifically excluded. That is, Congress and EPA have listed certain wastes that are specifically excluded from the definition of solid and hazardous waste. The next step is to determine if the waste is a listed hazardous waste; that is, is the waste or the process that generated the waste specifically listed in Subpart D of Part 261? Assuming that it is not, the next step is to determine if the waste exhibits any of the four characteristics of hazardous waste. If the waste exhibits a characteristic, it is hazardous; if not, the waste is not hazardous. Finally, if the hazardous waste is to be recycled, it is necessary to determine how it is hazardous, what type of material it is, and how it is to be recycled to determine how it is regulated. Each step and each criterion are explained in detail in the following sections.

SOLID WASTE

For a material to be classified as a hazardous waste it must first meet the definition of solid waste under 40 CFR 261.2. Hazardous waste is a subset of solid waste. Thus, if a material does not meet the definition of solid waste, it cannot be classified as a hazardous waste. The term solid waste does not refer to a material's physical state per se; it is a regulatory term only. Thus, industrial wastewater may be a solid waste.

A *solid waste* is any discarded material that is not excluded by 40 CFR 261.4(a) or that has been delisted. (Delisting is the process by which a generator has a listed hazardous waste reclassified as a nonhazardous waste through a petition.) However, delisted materials are still solid wastes unless they are granted a variance under 40 CFR 260.30 or 260.31. A *discarded material* is any material that is disposed, stored, or treated before its disposal; that is burned as a fuel, treated, recycled, abandoned, considered inherently wastelike (e.g., certain dioxin wastes); or that is stored or accumulated before recycling. There are some exceptions to the definition of solid waste regarding specific recycling activities [40 CFR 261.6(a)(2)].

EXCLUDED WASTES

The following wastes are not subject to Subtitle C requirements because they are either excluded from the statutory definition of solid waste (Section 3001 of RCRA) based on EPA's interpretation, not intended by Congress to be regulated under Subtitle C based on EPA's interpretation of RCRA's legislative history indicating congressional intent, or subject to regulation under other EPA statutes (see Table 2-1).

The following materials are excluded from the definition of solid waste:

1. Domestic sewage [40 CFR 261.4(a)(1)(i)].
2. Any mixture of domestic sewage and any other waste that passes through a sewer system to a publicly owned treatment works (POTW) [40 CFR 261.4(a)(1)(ii)].

   This means a person may legally dispose of hazardous waste into a POTW system under RCRA, except that storage or treatment prior to discharging into a POTW is not excluded from RCRA and is subject to applicable storage regulations. However, POTWs are subject to applicable pretreatment standards under the Clean Water Act (CWA). (POTWs have local jurisdiction. Thus, they can legally prohibit discharges that interfere with the operation of their system or that may cause them to violate their National Pollutant Discharge Elimination System [NPDES] permit.)
3. Industrial wastewater discharges that are point source discharges subject to Section 402 of the Clean Water Act (CWA) [40 CFR 261.4(a)(2)].

   This exclusion applies only to the actual point source discharge.

Table 2-1. Exclusions from Subtitle C of RCRA.

Excluded from solid waste definition	Excluded from hazardous waste definition
Domestic sewage	Household wastes
Mixtures of domestic sewage and wastes going to POTW	Agricultural wastes used as fertilizers
Industrial point source discharges under §402 CWA	Mining overburden returned to site
Irrigation return flows	Discarded wood treated with arsenic
Source, special nuclear, or byproduct material under AEA	Chromium wastes
In situ mining waste	Petroleum-contaminated media from tank cleanup
Reclaimed pulping liquors	*Specific ore processing wastes
Regenerated sulfuric acid	*Specific utility wastes
Secondary materials returned to the original process under certain conditions	* Oil and gas exploration, development, and production wastes
	*Cement kiln dust
*Special study wastes.	

— RCRA covered wastes by definition are "solid wastes"

It does not exclude industrial wastewaters while they are being collected, stored, or treated prior to discharge, nor does it exclude sludges that are generated by industrial wastewater treatment.

4. Irrigation return flows [40 CFR 261.4(a)(3)].
5. Materials defined as source, special nuclear, or by-product material by the Atomic Energy Act [40 CFR 261.4(a)(4)].
6. Materials generated as a result of in situ mining techniques that are *not* removed from the ground during extraction. If materials are removed, they are subject to regulation [40 CFR 261.4(a)(5)].
7. Pulping liquors used in the production of paper in the Kraft paper process [40 CFR 261.4(a)(6)].

8. Spent sulfuric acid used to produce virgin sulfuric acid [40 CFR 261.4(a)(7)].

9. Secondary materials that are reclaimed and returned to the original process or processes in which they were generated, provided that only tank storage is used, the material is not burned, the material is not used to produce a fuel, and the material is not accumulated for more than 12 months prior to reclamation [40 CFR 261.4(a)(8)].

The following materials, which are classified as solid wastes, are excluded from the definition of hazardous wastes:

1. All household wastes and resource recovery facilities that burn only household waste. (Hotel, motel, septic sewage, and campground waste are all considered household waste [40 CFR 261.4(b)(1)].)

2. Manure and crops returned to the soil as fertilizers [40 CFR 261.4(b)(2)].

3. Mining overburden returned to the mine site from mining operations [40 CFR 261.4(b)(3)].

4. Fly ash waste, bottom ash waste, slag waste, and flue gas emission control waste generated primarily from the combustion of coal or other fossil fuels (the "utility waste exemption") [40 CFR 261.4(b)(4)].

5. Drilling fluids, produced waters, and other wastes associated with the exploration, development, or production of crude oil, natural gas, or geothermal energy [40 CFR 261.4(b)(5)].

6. Wastes containing primarily trivalent chromium instead of hexavalent chromium and specified wastes from the tannery industry [40 CFR 261.4(b)(6)].

7. Specified solid wastes from the extraction and beneficiation of ores and minerals [40 CFR 261.4(b)(7)].

8. Cement kiln dust [40 CFR 261.4(b)(8)].

9. Discarded wood that fails only the toxicity characteristic test (a test to determine if a waste exhibits a hazardous characteristic) for arsenic as a result of being treated with arsenical compounds [40 CFR 261.4(b)(9)].

10. Petroleum-contaminated media and debris that fails only the toxicity characteristic *and* are subject to the corrective action requirements under 40 CFR 280, underground storage tanks [40 CFR 261.4(b)(10)].

HAZARDOUS WASTE IDENTIFICATION

In determining if a waste is hazardous (assuming that it is a solid waste and is not excluded), the protocol is first to determine if it is a RCRA-listed hazardous waste. If it is not listed, a generator then must determine if the waste exhibits any of the characteristics of hazardous waste: ignitability, corrosivity, reactivity, and/or toxicity. If a listed hazardous waste also exhibits a characteristic, only the listing code and not the characteristic code need be recorded. In addition, there are other hazardous wastes, such as waste mixtures, wastes derived from processing wastes, and wastes contained in nonwastes, that meet the definition of hazardous. Table 2-2 lists all of the categories of hazardous wastes.

The RCRA-listed hazardous wastes are listed in 40 CFR 261.30 through 261.33, as well as in Appendix C of this book. The characteristics of hazardous waste are contained in 40 CFR 261.20 through 261.24.

The EPA manual *Test Methods for Evaluating Solid Waste, Physical/Chemical Methods*, more commonly known as SW-846, provides information on sampling and analyzing procedures for complying with RCRA. However, the general use of SW-846 for testing purposes is not necessarily required. One must refer to the regulatory text to determine if a specific test method is required, and in some cases specific test methods from SW-846 are mandatory. The manual is available from the U.S. Government Printing Office. (See Appendix G for further information.)

Listed Hazardous Wastes

EPA has listed specific hazardous wastes based on the criteria set forth in 40 CFR 261.11. If a waste meets the listing definition, it is presumed to be hazardous regardless of its concentration. However, generators have the opportunity to demonstrate that a listed waste is not hazardous by petitioning to delist a waste at a particular generation site based on specified criteria. A more detailed discussion of delisting appears later in this chapter.

EPA has listed wastes according to their toxicity, reactivity, corrosivity, and ignitability. For hazardous wastes listed because they meet the criteria of toxicity, EPA's principal focus is on the identity and concentration of the waste's constituents and the nature of the toxicity presented by the constituents. If a waste contains significant concentrations of hazardous waste constituents, EPA is likely to list the waste as hazardous unless it is evident that the waste constituents are incapable of migrating in significant concentrations even if improperly managed, or that the waste constituents are not mobile or persistent should they migrate.

A detailed justification for listing each hazardous waste is contained in EPA's *Listing Background Documents*. The listing documents are

Table 2-2. Categories of hazardous waste.

RCRA Hazardous Wastes		
Listed hazardous wastes	Characteristic hazardous wastes	Other hazardous wastes
• Nonspecific sources (F codes) • Specific sources (K codes) • Commercial chemical products – Acutely hazardous (P codes) • Commercial chemical products – Nonacutely hazardous (U codes)	• Ignitable • Corrosive • Reactive • Toxic	• Mixtures (hazardous and nonhazardous) • Derived–from wastes (treatment residues) • Materials containing listed hazardous wastes

organized into the following sequence: (1) the EPA Administrator's basis for listing the waste or waste stream; (2) a brief description of the industries generating the listed waste stream; (3) a description of the manufacturing process or other activity that generates the waste; (3a) identification of waste composition, constituent concentrations, and annual quantity generated; (4) a summary of the adverse health effects of each of the waste constituents of concern; and (5) a summary of damage case histories involving the waste. The listing background documents, prepared for each listed waste, are located at EPA's RCRA regulatory dockets.

The listed hazardous wastes include material-specific and process-specific wastes. The listed wastes, contained in Appendix C of this book, are separated into the following categories:

- Wastes from nonspecific sources (F codes)
- Wastes from specific sources (K codes)
- Commercial chemical products (U and P codes)

Some of the listed wastes are classified as acutely hazardous waste, designated with an H. These wastes are subject to reduced weight limits regarding generator categories and more stringent requirements concerning the determination of empty containers, as discussed later in this chapter and in Chapter 3.

Wastes from Nonspecific Sources

The first category of listed hazardous wastes is generally material-specific wastes generated by a variety of processes. This category of wastes includes solvent wastes, electroplating wastes, metal heat treating wastes, and dioxin-containing wastes.

Solvent Wastes

Solvent wastes are designated as wastes F001 through F005 (see Appendix C). For a waste to be classified as a *solvent* waste, the purpose of the material must have been to mobilize or solubilize a constituent. Thus, if a material was used solely as a reactant or a feedstock, it is not classified as a solvent waste (OSWER Directive 9444.08).

The mere presence of any of the components listed in F001 through F005 in a waste does not necessarily render the waste a listed hazardous waste. A material will meet the listing criteria if it is a solvent with a sole active ingredient that is listed, and it also can meet the listing criteria if it is a solvent mixture. A *solvent mixture*—which is a commercial blend that has any of the listed components that fall under the heading of solvent waste except F003 wastes (i.e., F001, F002, F004, F005), alone or in any combination that equals 10 percent or more of the blend prior to use—will constitute a listed hazardous waste when the material is spent. (*Spent* refers to any material that has been used and as a result of contamination can no longer serve its intended purpose without processing.) It is important to note that if a mixture had 10 percent of solvent before use, and the resultant mixture contains less than 10 percent, it is still a hazardous waste. This is because the solvent mixture rule's 10 percent threshold is applicable before the solvent is used, not when it is spent.

Electroplating Wastes

The wastes F006, F007, F008, and F009 are the electroplating wastes. Previously, EPA's definition of electroplating included electroless plating, anodizing, chemical etching and milling, printed circuit board manufacturing, and chemical conversion coating (i.e., coloring, chromating, phosphating, and immersion plating). However, on December 2, 1986 (51 *FR* 43351), EPA redefined electroplating wastes. The new definition does not include electroless plating, chemical conversion coating, or printed circuit board manufacturing. However, these processes may fall under another listing category or exhibit a characteristic of hazardous waste. Further clarification of the individual processes are included in EPA's *Listing Background Documents*.

Metal Heat Treating Wastes

The wastes F010, F011, and F012 are the metal heat treating wastes. Metal heat treatment involves case hardening by carburizing, which adds carbon to the surface of steel. Liquid carburizing, which uses cyanides as the source of carbon, is accomplished by submerging the metal in a molten salt bath containing sodium cyanide. Sodium cyanide also is used in the case hardening of steel using either the liquid nitriding or carbonitriding processes. The associated wastes include quenching bath residues from oil baths, salt bath pot cleaning, and quenching wastewater treatment sludges all from metal heat treating operations only when cyanides (complex or free) are used in the process.

Dioxin Wastes

The wastes F020, F021, F022, F023, F026, F027, and F028 are termed the "dioxin wastes" and are classified as acutely hazardous. These wastes are hazardous whether dioxin is present or not, because dioxin itself is not considered a hazardous waste but may be a component of the above-listed wastes.

The F027 listing covers *unused* formulations containing tri-, tetra-, and pentachlorophenol (PCP). This has significant implications concerning the pesticide registration cancellation of pentachlorophenol under the Federal Insecticide, Fungicide, and Rodenticide Act (FIFRA) because persons may still have unused pentachlorophenol that cannot be sold or used. Currently, few facilities are permitted to store or dispose of the dioxin wastes, and storing these wastes on-site without a permit or interim status is a violation of RCRA.

Wastes from Specific Sources

The second category of listed hazardous wastes includes those generated from specific sources. These wastes, under the designation of K codes, are listed according to the specific industrial process that generates the waste rather than what is generated per se. For example, most hazardous wastes are listed by a chemical name, such as benzene, whereas the K-listed wastes are listed by the specific industrial process, such as *Untreated process wastewater from the production of toxaphene* (K098). The categories of hazardous waste, under the K-code designations, include: wood preservation, inorganic pigments, organic chemicals, inorganic chemicals, pesticides, explosives, petroleum refining, iron and steel, secondary lead, veterinary pharmaceuticals, ink formulation, and coking.

Commercial Chemical Products

The third category of listed hazardous wastes includes commercial chemical products, designated by either a U- or a P-code. All of the P-code wastes are considered acutely hazardous and are subject to further restrictions concerning empty containers and weight limits. For a waste to be categorized as a U or a P waste, it must be a commercial chemical product in an *unused* form. The definition of commercial chemical products includes technical grades, pure forms, off-specification products, or sole active ingredient products. Once a material is spent, it does not meet any of the U or P listings, but may meet one of the other listings or exhibit a characteristic. If a material contains more than one active ingredient that is a listed U- or P-code substance, it does not receive the U or P listing and can only be hazardous by another listing or if it exhibits a hazardous characteristic. For example, unused technical grade toluene that is to be discarded is identified as a listed hazardous waste, U220. However, if that same toluene were used as a solvent, the spent material would be considered a listed hazardous waste, F005.

A commercial chemical product is not considered a hazardous waste unless it is intended to be discarded or it is spilled, in which case the spill cleanup residue attains the appropriate U or P code listing. Thus, a material can be stored indefinitely without RCRA restraints if the intent is to use it or to have it recycled. These activities are not included in the definition of recycling for commercial chemical products: a U- or a P-code product is mixed with used oil or other material and applied to the land as a dust suppressant or for road treatment; products are otherwise applied to the land in lieu of their original intended use; they are contained in products that are applied to the land in lieu of their use; or they are used as a fuel [40 CFR 261.33].

Delisting

Delisting is a formal request by petition for a generator to reclassify a listed hazardous waste to a nonhazardous waste at the generation site. The requirements to be followed in submitting a delisting petition are set forth in 40 CFR 261.22.

A waste is listed by EPA if it contains 40 CFR Part 261, Appendix VIII, hazardous constituents, or if it exhibits a characteristic of hazardous waste (is ignitable, corrosive, reactive, or toxic). Part 261, Appendix VII, categorizes the listed wastes and, for each waste, lists the hazardous constituents for which the waste is listed. A petitioner must demonstrate that the Appendix VIII hazardous constituents for which the waste was listed are not present in the waste and that the waste does not exhibit any of the characteristics. A facility also must demonstrate that the waste will not be hazardous for other reasons. This includes other Appendix VIII hazardous constituents.

EPA has outlined additional information that a petitioner should include to satisfy the requirements for delisting (OSWER Directive 9433.07):

- A list of raw materials and a description and schematic diagram of manufacturing processes that may contribute waste, wastewater, or rinse water to the waste stream.
- An evaluation of representative samples for the characteristics of hazardous waste, including an analysis of the potential for sulfide and cyanide gas generation.
- The total oil and grease and total organic carbon (TOC) content of the waste.
- A statement indicating that samples analyzed and reported in the petition are considered representative of any potential variation.
- The average and maximum quantities of waste generated per month and per year.
- The quality assurance procedures followed during sampling and analysis.
- An explanation of why planned changes of equipment, feedstock materials, and manufacturing processes will not alter the chemical makeup of the waste stream.

Characteristics of Hazardous Waste

Section 3001 of RCRA required EPA to develop and promulgate criteria for identifying characteristics of hazardous waste that are separate from the listed wastes. Characteristics were selected that were measurable by standard available testing protocols. Thus, EPA established that ignitability, corrosivity, reactivity, and toxicity as the characteristics of hazardous waste. The responsibility for determining whether a waste exhibits a characteristic rests with the generator.

Ignitability

A waste is an ignitable waste, designated as D001, if it meets any of the following conditions:

1. It is a *liquid* that has a flash point of less than 140°F as determined by either a Pensky-Martens or a Setaflash closed-cup test.

   A liquid is that material, called the liquid phase, that is obtained from the waste in step 2 (Separation Procedure) of the Extraction Procedure Test, Method 1310. The liquid extract is the liquid and is subject to the ignitability analysis.

   There is an exclusion in 40 CFR 261.21(a)(1) from the ignitability characteristic for aqueous solutions that fail the flash point test and contain less than 24 percent alcohol. Originally, this exclusion was intended for alcoholic beverages such as wine (45 FR 33108, May 19, 1980). However, the regulatory language is ambiguous regarding the extent of this exclusion. OSWER Directive 9443.02 states that "while the Agency's intent was that this exemption apply to potable beverages only, because the term alcohol was used instead of ethanol, all aqueous wastes which are ignitable only because they contain alcohols (here using the term alcohol to mean any chemical containing the hydroxl [—OH] functional group) are excluded from regulation." The directive also defines the term "aqueous solution" by stating: "With respect to what constitutes an aqueous solution, such a solution is one in which water is the primary component. This means that water constitutes at least 50 percent by weight of the sample."

2. It is a *solid* that can spontaneously combust through friction, absorption, or loss of moisture. At this time, there is no standardized test for this determination.

3. It is an *ignitable [flammable] compressed gas* as defined by the Department of Transportation (DOT) in 49 CFR 173.300.

   An ignitable compressed gas must first meet the definition of a compressed gas, which is "any material or mixture having in the container an absolute pressure exceeding 40 psi at 70°F or, regardless of the pressure at 70°F, having an absolute pressure exceeding 104 psi at 130°F; or any liquid flammable mixture having a vapor pressure exceeding 40 psi absolute at 100°F." A material meeting the definition of a compressed gas is considered ignitable if it is either a mixture of 13 percent or less (by volume) with air forms a flammable mixture or the flammable range with air is wider than 12 percent regardless of the lower limit; the flame projects more than 18 inches beyond the ignition source with the valve opened fully, or the flame flashes back and burns at the valve with any degree of valve opening; or there is any significant propagation of flame away from the ignition source.

4. It is an *oxidizer* as defined by DOT in 49 CFR 173.151.

   An oxidizer is a substance that yields oxygen readily when involved in a fire, thereby accelerating and intensifying the combustion of organic material. There is no prescribed test for determining this classification. DOT does give examples of oxidizers such as chlorate, permanganate, inorganic peroxide, or nitrates.

Corrosivity

A waste is a corrosive waste, designated as D002, if it meets any of the following criteria:

1. It is *aqueous* and has a pH of 2 or less or 12.5 or more; or
2. It is a *liquid* and corrodes steel at a rate of 6.35 mm or more per year as determined by the National Association of Corrosion Engineers (NACE).

   Wastes in a solid phase, as determined by the Separation Procedure of the Extraction Procedure Test, Method 1310, are not considered corrosive wastes (45 FR 33108, May 19, 1980).

Reactivity

A waste is a reactive waste, designated as D003, if it has the capability to explode or undergo violent chemical change in a variety of situations. This characteristic is used to identify wastes that, because of their extreme instability and tendency to react violently or explode, pose a threat to human health and the environment at all stages of the waste handling process. The criteria for reactivity of a waste are:

1. Instability and readiness to undergo violent change.
2. Violent reactions when mixed with water.
3. Formation of potentially explosive mixtures when mixed with water.
4. Generation of toxic fumes in quantities sufficient to present a danger to human health or the environment when mixed with water.
5. Cyanide or sulfide-bearing material that generates toxic fumes when exposed to acidic conditions.
6. Ease of detonation or explosive reaction when exposed to pressure or heat.

7. Ease of detonation or explosive decomposition or reaction at standard temperature and pressure.
8. Defined as a forbidden explosive or a Class A or Class B explosive by DOT.

The reactivity characteristic, however, requires a determination based more on judgment than a standardized quantitative determination except for explosives (Class A or B) and toxic (sulfide and cyanide) gas generation. For sulfide and cyanide gas generation, using the prescribed test methods in SW-846, if free (not total) cyanide is generated at 250 mg/kg of waste or more, or free sulfide is generated at 500 mg/kg of waste, the material is considered a reactive hazardous waste.

Toxicity

EPA has determined that one of the most significant dangers posed by hazardous waste stems from the leaching of toxic constituents of land-disposed wastes into groundwater. Consequently, the Toxicity Characteristic (TC) is designed to identify wastes that are likely to leach hazardous constituents into groundwater under improper management conditions. (The TCLP replaced the Extraction Procedure Toxicity Test on March 29, 1990 (55 *FR* 11798).) EPA established a testing procedure that extracts constituents from a solid waste in a manner that simulates the leaching action that can occur in a landfill. EPA made the assumption that industrial waste would be co-disposed of with nonindustrial waste in an actively decomposing municipal landfill situated over an aquifer. It is important to note that, for the purposes of determining whether a waste is hazardous when using the toxicity test, it is irrelevant whether generators actually do co-dispose of their hazardous waste in a municipal landfill or in any type of landfill.

The extraction procedure of the TC is also known as the toxicity characteristic leaching procedure test (TCLP). This test requires the following basic steps:

- If the waste is liquid (i.e., contains less than 0.5% solids), after it is filtered the waste itself is considered the extract (simulated leachate).
- If the waste contains greater than 0.5% solid material, the solid phase is separated from the liquid phase, if any. If required, the particle size of the solid phase is reduced until it passes through a 9.5 mm sieve.
- For analysis other than for volatiles, the solid phase is then placed

in a rotary agitation device with an acidic solution and rotated at 30 rpm for 18 hours. The pH of the solution is approximately 5, unless the solid is more basic, in which case a solution with a pH of approximately 3 is used. After extraction (rotation), solids are filtered from the liquid extract and discarded.

- For volatiles analysis a solution of pH 5 is used, and a Zero Headspace Extraction Vessel (ZHE), which does not allow headspace to develop, is used for liquid/solid separation, agitation, and filtration.
- Liquid extracted from the solid/acid mixture is combined with any original liquid separated from the solid material is analyzed for the presence of the contaminants listed in Table 2-3.
- If *any* of the contaminants in the extract meets or exceeds any of the maximum levels listed in Table 2-3, the waste is classified as a TC hazardous waste.

Special Categories of Waste

The following sections outline the requirements for special categories of hazardous waste. These categories are found in different sections throughout the regulations but have been grouped here for easier reference. They include:

- Mixtures
- Wastes derived from the management of other wastes
- Wastes contained in nonwastes
- Medical wastes
- Low-level radioactive mixed wastes

Mixtures

A mixture of hazardous waste and a solid (nonhazardous) waste is considered a hazardous waste [40 CFR 261.3(a)(2)(iii)]. (There is no *de minimis* amount that qualifies for an exclusion from the mixture rule except for some *de minimis* mixtures in wastewater treatment systems meeting certain conditions.) However, if the mixture is hazardous solely because of a characteristic, and the resultant mixture no longer retains that characteristic, it is not considered a hazardous waste. An example is F003 (a listed waste), which is listed solely because of the ignitability characteristic. Hence, a mixture of F003 and a nonignitable, nonhazardous waste will become nonhazardous provided that the mixture no longer exhibits the ignitability characteristic (46 *FR* 56588, November 17, 1981).

Table 2-3. Toxicity characteristic levels.

EPA HW No.	Contaminant	Limit (mg/1)
D004	**Arsenic**	**5.000**
D005	**Barium**	**100.0**
D018	Benzene	0.5
D006	**Cadmium**	**1.0**
D019	Carbon Tetrachloride	0.5
D020	Chlordane	0.03
D021	Chlorobenzene	100.0
D022	Chloroform	6.0
D007	**Chromium**	**5.0**
D023	o-Cresol	200.0*
D024	m-Cresol	200.0*
D025	p-Cresol	200.0*
D026	Cresol	200.0*
D016	**2,4-D**	**10.0**
D027	1,4-Dichlorobenzene	7.5
D028	1,2-Dichloroethane	0.5
D029	1,1-Dichloroethylene	0.7
D030	2,4-Dinitrotoluene	0.13
D012	**Endrin**	**0.02**
D031	Heptachlor	0.008
D032	Hexachlorobenzene	0.13
D033	Hexachlorobutadiene	0.5
D034	Hexachloroethane	3.0
D008	**Lead**	**5.0**
D013	**Lindane**	**0.4**
D009	**Mercury**	**0.2**
D014	**Methoxychlor**	**10.0**
D035	Methyl Ethyl Ketone	200.0
D036	Nitrobenzene	2.0
D037	Pentachlorophenol	100.0
D038	Pyridine	5.0
D010	**Selenium**	**1.0**
D011	**Silver**	**5.0**
D039	Tetrachloroethylene	0.7
D015	**Toxaphene**	**0.5**
D040	Trichloroethylene	0.5
D041	2,4,5-Trichlorophenol	400.0
D042	2,4,6-Trichlorophenol	2.0
D017	**2,4,5,-TP Silvex**	**1.0**
D043	Vinyl Chloride	0.2

*If the concentrations for o-, m-, and p-cresol cannot be differentiated, the total cresol concentration is used.

The constituents in bold are the original EP toxicity constituents.

However, treating hazardous waste without a permit may be prohibited, as described in Chapters 3 and 7.

Wastewater treatment systems subject to either an NPDES permit or pretreatment standards have specific exclusions from the mixture rule for the effluent under 40 CFR 261.3(a)(2)(iv). These exclusions include wastewater mixed with specified spent solvents, *de minimis* losses, and laboratory wastes. All of these exclusions are subject to certain conditions.

Derived-From Rule

Any solid waste generated from the treatment, storage, or disposal of a hazardous waste, including any sludge (pollution control residue), spill residue, ash, leachate, or emission control dust, will remain a hazardous waste unless it is delisted, or, in the case of a characteristic waste, the waste no longer exhibits the characteristic [40 CFR 261.3(c)].

This rule can have serious implications during the on-site treatment of hazardous wastes during a corrective action; that is, persons who are treating hazardous wastes (e.g., mobile incineration, fixation, land treatment) will still have to contend with hazardous waste although the toxicity of the waste is greatly reduced. This situation can be illustrated by the following example: as a result of a spill, a site has 5000 yards of soil contaminated with 1000 parts per million (ppm) of tetrachloroethylene product (U210). A mobile thermal treatment device is brought on-site to treat the soil. After the treatment process, the resultant tetrachloroethylene level in the soil is less than 1 ppm. However, according to the derived-from rule, all of the remaining contaminated soil will still be classified as a hazardous waste unless the waste is delisted.

Contained-In Rule

The mixture rule requires that a hazardous waste be mixed with a *solid waste* for it to be regulated under the provisions of the mixture rule. However, there are some instances where a hazardous waste is mixed with a material that is not considered a solid waste. For example, if a surface impoundment leaks a listed hazardous waste into the groundwater, the resulting contaminated groundwater is not a hazardous waste, as the groundwater is not considered a solid waste at the time when the waste and groundwater mix because it is not *discarded*. However, the groundwater, once contaminated, contains a listed hazardous waste. The hazardous waste component itself will remain hazardous, and must be managed as hazardous waste although the groundwater itself, if it did not contain any of the hazardous waste, would not be considered hazardous. Hence, the groundwater contaminated with hazardous waste must be handled as if the groundwater itself were hazardous because the hazardous waste leachate is subject to regulation under Subtitle C of RCRA (OSWER Directive 9481.00-6).

Medical Wastes

With increasing concern over various public health issues and extensive press coverage of medical waste washing ashore, Congress decided in the late 1980s that action must be taken. However, the actual health threat and appropriate requirements for controlling the problem were not known; so Congress mandated a pilot program focusing on a limited number of states. Thus, Congress enacted the Medical Waste Tracking Act of 1988. This act required EPA to establish regulations for the identification, transportation, and management of medical wastes.

Because the act affected only a limited universe when this book was written, the requirements contained in 40 CFR Part 259 are not discussed in detail here. However, the definition of medical waste is presented below for classification purposes.

Pursuant to 40 CFR 259.10(a), the definition of medical waste is:

Medical waste means solid waste that is generated in the diagnosis, treatment (e.g., provision of medical services), or immunization of human beings or animals, in research pertaining thereto, or in the production or testing of biologicals. The term does not include any hazardous waste identified or listed under Part 261 of this chapter [40 CFR] or any household waste as defined in 40 CFR 261.4(b).

Low-Level Radioactive Mixed Wastes

A low-level radioactive waste (LLW) is radioactive material that (a) is not high-level radioactive waste, spent nuclear fuel, or by-product material as defined in Section 11(e)(2) of the Atomic Energy Act (AEA) (i.e., uranium or thorium mill tailings) and (b) is classified by the Nuclear Regulatory Commission (NRC) as a low-level radioactive material.

If a low-level radioactive waste contains a listed RCRA hazardous waste, or the LLW exhibits a characteristic of hazardous waste, the material is classified as a mixed low-level waste and thus must be managed and disposed of in compliance with EPA regulations, 40 CFR Parts

124 and 260 through 280, and with NRC regulations, 10 CFR Parts 20, 30, 40, 61, and 70. The management and disposal of mixed low-level radioactive wastes also must be in compliance with state requirements, in states that are EPA-authorized for the hazardous components of the waste, and with the NRC agreement state radiation control programs for the low-level radioactive portion of the waste (OSWER Directive 9440.00-1).

Special Exclusions

There are materials that have some degree of exclusion contingent upon compliance with specified criteria. These materials include:

- Product storage waste
- Samples (laboratory and treatability)
- Empty containers

Product Storage Waste

Any waste generated in a product or raw material storage tank, product transport vehicle or vessel, or manufacturing process unit is not subject to Subtitle C until it exits from that unit, or the waste remains in the unit 90 days after the unit ceases operation [40 CFR 261.4(c)]. This exclusion does not apply to surface impoundments.

Samples

There are two exclusions from Subtitle C of RCRA for samples. One exclusion, under 40 CFR 261.4(d), covers laboratory samples of waste that are used for the purposes of waste identification. The second exclusion, under 40 CFR 261.4(e), covers samples of hazardous waste being used in treatability studies.

Laboratory Samples

There is a conditional exclusion for laboratory samples under 40 CFR 261.4(d). For a sample to be excluded, it must be in the process of being analyzed for the sole purpose of hazardous waste identification, in which case the sample would be excluded from RCRA during its storage and transportation. However, there may be Department of Transportation

(DOT) requirements. Once the sample has been analyzed, it must be sent immediately back to the sample collector. If the laboratory keeps the sample or does not send it back to the original sample collector, the sample is no longer excluded and is subject to applicable regulations. If the sample is sent back to the collector, the collector becomes the generator. If the laboratory keeps the sample, it will be considered the generator.

Treatability Study Samples

Under 40 CFR 261.4(e), hazardous waste samples used in small-scale treatability studies are conditionally excluded from Subtitle C regulation. Generators of the waste samples and owners/operators of laboratories or treatment facilities conducting treatability studies will be excluded from the Subtitle C hazardous waste regulations, including the permitting requirements, provided that certain conditions are met.

A *treatability study* is a study in which a hazardous waste is subjected to a treatment process to determine:

- Whether the waste is amenable to the treatment process.
- What pretreatment (if any) is required.
- The optimal process conditions needed to achieve the desired treatment.
- The efficiency of a treatment process for a specific waste or wastes.
- The characteristics and volumes of residuals from a particular treatment process.

Also included in the definition of treatability study for the purpose of the 40 CFR 261.4(e) and (f) exemptions are liner compatibility, corrosion, and other material compatibility studies (e.g., leachate collection systems, geotextile materials, pumps, and personal protective equipment) and toxicological and health effects studies.

A *treatability study* is not a means to commercially treat or dispose of hazardous waste. In addition, this definition does not apply where the practice could result in a significant uncontrolled release of hazardous constituents to the environment. It would, then, not include open burning or any type of treatment involving placement of hazardous waste on the land, such as in-situ stabilization (53 *FR* 27293, July 19, 1988).

Under this section, waste samples are excluded from Subtitle C when:

- The sample is being collected and prepared for transportation by the generator or sample collector.
- The sample is being accumulated or stored by the generator or

sample collector prior to transportation to a laboratory or testing facility.

- The sample is being transported to the laboratory or testing facility for the purposes of conducting a treatability study.

These exclusions are applicable to samples of hazardous waste being collected and shipped for the purposes of conducting treatability studies, provided that:

- The generator sends, or the sample collector uses in the treatability study, no more than 1000 kg of any nonacute hazardous waste; 1 kg of acute hazardous waste; or 250 kg of soil, water, or debris contaminated with acute hazardous waste for each process being evaluated for each generated waste stream (i.e., not limited to the waste code, but to the waste stream).
- The sample is packaged so that it will not leak, spill, or vaporize from its packaging during shipment.

The transportation of the sample must comply with DOT or USPS shipping requirements. However, if DOT, USPS, or other shipping requirements do not apply, the following information must accompany the sample:

- The name, mailing address, and telephone number of the originator of the sample.
- The name, address, and telephone number of the facility that will perform the treatability study.
- The quantity of the sample.
- The date of shipment.
- A description of the sample, including its EPA hazardous waste number.

A facility or laboratory conducting treatability testing is excluded from Parts 124, 262 through 266, 268, and 270 provided that certain conditions are met. EPA has determined (53 *FR* 27297, July 19, 1988) that mobile treatment units (MTUs) conducting treatability studies may qualify for this exemption. However, each MTU or group of MTUs operating at the same location is subject to the treatment rate, storage, and time limitations and the notification, record keeping, and reporting requirements that are applicable to stationary laboratories or testing facilities conducting treatability studies. That is, a group of MTUs operating at one location will be treated as one MTU facility for purposes of 40 CFR 261.4(e) and (f). Furthermore, these requirements apply to each location where an MTU will conduct treatability studies.

The requirements for compliance with the exclusion are that the MTU must:

- Notify EPA at least 45 days before conducting any treatability studies.
- Obtain an EPA identification number.
- Test no more than 250 kg of hazardous waste per day.
- Maintain records that document compliance with the treatment rate limits, storage time, and quantity limits.
- Maintain on-site all treatability contracts and shipping papers for at least three years. The information must include:
  - The name, address, and EPA identification number of the generator or sample collector of each waste sample.
  - The date when the shipment was received.
  - The quantity of waste received and in storage.
  - The date when the treatment study was initiated and the amount of waste introduced to treatment each day.
  - The date when the treatability study was concluded.
  - The date when any unused sample or residues generated from the treatability study were returned to the generator or sample collector or sent off-site to a designated facility (including the designated facility's name and EPA identification number).
- Submit an annual report to EPA, by March 15, estimating the number of studies and the amount of waste expected to be used in treatability studies during the current year. The report covering the previous year must include information on:
  - The name, address, and EPA identification number of the facility conducting the treatability studies.
  - The types (by process) of treatability studies conducted.
  - The names and addresses of persons for whom studies have been conducted (including their EPA identification numbers).
  - The total quantity of waste in storage each day.
  - The quantity and types of waste subjected to treatability studies.
  - When each treatability study was conducted.
  - The final disposition of residues and unused samples from each treatability study.
- Notify EPA by letter when a facility is no longer planning to conduct treatability studies at the site.

Empty Containers

Any hazardous waste remaining in a container that is considered *empty* (as defined by the definitions listed below) is no longer a listed hazardous waste. However, EPA interprets 40 CFR 261.7 to read that the waste remaining in an empty container does not meet the definition of a listed waste but can be hazardous by a characteristic of hazardous waste when it exits the container (OSWER Directive 9441.25).

Nonacutely Hazardous Waste Containers

A nonacutely hazardous waste container is considered *empty* if it is thoroughly emptied using common industry practices and contains less than 1 inch of residue on the bottom, or less than 3 percent by weight for containers less than 110 gallons, or less than 0.3 percent by weight for containers greater than 110 gallons [40 CFR 261.7(b)(1)].

Acutely Hazardous Containers

A container or liner holding an acutely hazardous waste (P-code and certain F-code wastes) must be triple-rinsed with an appropriate solvent, rinsed using another method shown to be equivalent, or have the liner removed to be considered *empty* [40 CFR 261.7(b)(3)].

Paper Bags

A paper bag that contained an acutely hazardous waste (P-code and certain F-code wastes) is considered *empty* by repeatedly beating an inverted bag to ensure thorough emptiness (OSWER Directive 9441.15).

Compressed Gas Containers

A container holding a hazardous waste that is a compressed gas must be emptied until the pressure of the material inside the container is equal to atmospheric pressure. When the pressures are equal, the container is considered *empty* [40 CFR 261.7(b)(2)].

Tanks

There is no definition for an empty tank. Although the empty container definition is commonly applied, the tank owner should check with the state or appropriate EPA Regional Office for a conclusive determination.

Drum Reconditioner

A drum reconditioner who recycles empty hazardous waste containers and generates residue as a result of reconditioning the containers must analyze the residues for the characteristics of a hazardous waste. Although the containers were empty, a new waste (the residue) has been generated, and it must be tested for the characteristics (45 *FR* 78529, November 25, 1980).

Hazardous Constituents

Hazardous constituents are used for a number of provisions including monitoring and analysis, delisting, listing hazardous wastes, and corrective action. RCRA uses the following categories of constituents:

- Appendix VIII constituents
- Appendix VII constituents
- Appendix IX constituents

Appendix VIII Constituents

The Appendix VIII constituents, found in Appendix VIII of Part 261 (and Appendix D of this book), also are known as the *hazardous constituents*. The Appendix VIII list is composed of priority pollutants under the Clean Water Act, Department of Transportation's hazardous substances, EPA's Carcinogen Assessment Group (CAG) list, and substances with carcinogenicity potential or that have a low LD_{50} on the National Institute of Occupational Safety and Health (NIOSH) *Registry of Toxic Effects of Chemical Substances* (RTECS). These constituents are used as a basis for EPA to list a waste as hazardous, for delisting wastes, and as a trigger for corrective action.

If a generator tests a waste and finds Appendix VIII constituents, this finding does not render the waste hazardous; the generator must use other criteria for this determination. The Appendix VIII constituents are justification for EPA to list a hazardous waste. Only the EPA Administrator can designate a listed hazardous waste through a formal rulemaking procedure. The corrective action provision under Section 3004(u) of HSWA uses the Appendix VIII constituents as a trigger for corrective action at facilities. (See Chapter 9 for further information.)

Appendix VII Constituents

The Appendix VII constituents, found in Appendix VII of Part 261, also are known as the *hazardous waste constituents*. Appendix VII is basically a catalog of those hazardous constituents listed in Appendix VIII whose presence caused EPA to list the waste as hazardous. Grouped by waste stream, Appendix VII names the specific Appendix VIII constituent(s) that caused the waste to be listed. It is important to realize, however, that this list is not a complete list of constituents of concern. It contains only the hazardous constituents used to justify the listing.

Appendix IX Constituents

The Appendix IX constituents, found in Appendix IX of Part 264 (and Appendix E of this book), are substances specifically designed for monitoring groundwater at permitted facilities. Previously, the entire Appendix VIII list was required for monitoring purposes. However, a number of these Appendix VIII constituents were impossible to test for in water, unstable in water, or inappropriate for groundwater characterization. Thus, the Appendix IX list was developed to select constituents that are appropriate for characterizing the underlying groundwater. This list, used primarily for the RCRA groundwater requirements, was promulgated on July 9, 1987 (52 *FR* 25942).

RECYCLING HAZARDOUS WASTE

Under Subtitle C of RCRA, EPA has the authority to regulate hazardous wastes. Hazardous wastes, however, are defined in the statute as a subset of solid wastes. EPA does not subscribe to the view that only those materials that are thrown away are solid wastes. Many recycling practices are characterized by elements of discarding that afford jurisdiction under Subtitle C. Thus, it is necessary to define what a solid waste is to determine the extent of EPA's jurisdiction under Subtitle C.

EPA completely restructured and revised the definition of solid waste on January 4, 1985 (50 *FR* 614). (Although this redefinition of solid waste is still involved in litigation, the majority of the action remains intact.) Thus, determining if a material is a solid waste is a fairly straightforward exercise unless the material will be recycled. The redefinition of solid waste focused primarily on regulating recycling activities that EPA determined were potentially a threat to human health and the environment.

Initially, a person determining the status of a waste should ignore the fact that the waste will be recycled. Given this approach, one should then proceed with the following protocol:

- Is it a solid waste?
- Is it excluded from the definition of hazardous waste?
- Is it a listed hazardous waste?
- Is it a characteristic hazardous waste?

If the waste is to be recycled, the regulations do not expressly require the following protocol, but inherently force one to answer these questions:

- Would it be a solid waste if the recycling question were ignored?
- Is it excluded from the definition of hazardous waste?
- Would it be a listed hazardous waste?
- Would it be a characteristic hazardous waste?
- Is it a solid waste when recycled in the manner of recycling planned?

Notice the extra step at the end. This step is required because materials to be recycled are in fact classified as a solid waste depending on the type of hazardous waste (i.e., listed or characteristic). The reason why this is the final determination is that, to answer the question, one must know if the material *would* be a listed or characteristic waste. Admittedly, this procedure is somewhat cumbersome; however, by following a simple rule one can lessen or avoid this confusion:

> If you intend to recycle your waste, first determine if it would be a listed or characteristic hazardous waste; then classify it accordingly under the definition of solid waste depending on the recycling activity.

Recycling Process

The actual recycling process, except waste burned as fuel and use constituting disposal, is unregulated. For example, a generator can distill solvents on-site without the distillation unit being regulated (OSWER Directive 9441.24). However, generation, transportation, and storage prior to recycling are regulated unless the specific waste is not a solid waste. Thus, a facility that distills solvents from off-site sources must have interim status or a permit for the storage of the waste solvents. A generator may recycle and/or store wastes prior to recycling them without interim status or a permit, provided that the waste is generated on-site and the accumulation is done in accordance with 40 CFR 262.34 (i.e., accumulation is for less than 90 days).

In most cases the waste generated from the treatment and storage of hazardous waste remains a hazardous waste. However, there is an exclusion for products derived from hazardous waste. For example, if a person places spent solvent in a distillation unit, the material distilled will no longer be regulated if it is considered a product. Only the still bottoms remain regulated because they were derived from hazardous waste and are themselves waste [40 CFR 261.3(c)(2)(i)].

Exclusions

40 CFR 261.6(a)(3) excludes certain recyclable materials from regulation under Parts 262 through 266. These materials are:

- Used oil that is recycled in some way other than burning for energy recovery.
- Industrial ethyl alcohol.
- Scrap metal.
- Used batteries returned for regeneration (does not include reclamation).
- Fuels produced from the refining of oil-bearing wastes from normal processes at petroleum refineries.
- Oil reclaimed from hazardous waste generated as a result of normal petroleum refining operations.
- Coke and coal tar from the iron and steel industry that contains waste code K087.

In addition, 40 CFR 261.2(e) also excludes certain recyclable materials. These materials include:

- Materials used or reused as ingredients to make a product, provided that they are not reclaimed before use.
- Wastes used or reused as effective substitutes for commercial products without prior reclamation.
- Wastes returned to the original process from where they were first generated without first being reclaimed.

Requirements for Recycling

If the intent is to recycle a waste, what the waste is and how it is to be recycled must be known to determine how it is regulated under Subtitle C as shown in Table 2-4 and Figure 2-2. The regulatory requirements are separated into two categories: secondary materials and recycling activities.

Table 2-4. Classification of secondary materials when recycled.

Secondary material	*Recycling Activity			
	Use constituting disposal	Reclamation	Speculative accumulation	Burned as fuel
Spent materials, listed or exhibiting a characteristic	Yes	Yes	Yes	Yes
Sludges, listed	Yes	Yes	Yes	Yes
Sludges, exhibiting a characteristic	Yes	No	Yes	Yes
Byproducts, exhibiting a characteristic	Yes	No	Yes	Yes
Byproducts, listed	Yes	Yes	Yes	Yes
Commercial chemical products	Yes	No	No	Yes

*Yes means the material is a solid waste, no means the material is not a solid waste.

Secondary Materials

The definition of solid waste under 40 CFR 261.2 also distinguishes five types of secondary materials:

- Spent materials
- Sludges
- By-products
- Commercial chemical products
- Scrap metal

Spent Materials

Spent materials are materials that have been used and as a result of such use have become contaminated by physical or chemical impurities such that they can no longer serve the purpose for which they were produced without regeneration [40 CFR 261.1(c)(1)]. The following materials are considered spent after use: wastewater, solvents, catalysts, acids, pickle liquor, foundry sands, lead-acid batteries, and activated

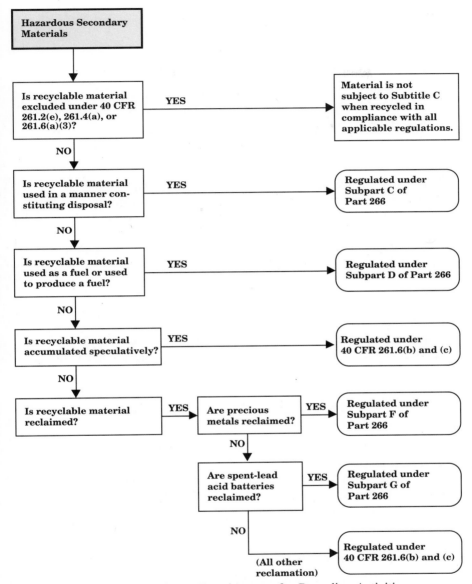

Figure 2-2. Regulatory Requirements for Recycling Activities

carbon. (Spent activated carbon also can be classified as a sludge if it was used as a pollution control device.)

Sludges

Sludges are residues from pollution control technology [40 CFR 260.10]. Examples include bag house dusts, flue dusts, wastewater treatment sludges, and filter cakes.

By-products

By-products include residual materials resulting from industrial, commercial, or agricultural operations that are not primary products, are not produced separately, are not fit for a desired end use without substantial further processing, and are not spent materials, sludges, commercial chemical products, or scrap metals [40 CFR 261.1(c)(3)]. Examples of by-products include mining slags, drosses, and distillation column bottoms.

Commercial Chemical Products

Commercial chemical products include commercial chemical products and intermediates, off-specification variants, spill residues, and container residues that are listed in 40 CFR 261.33 or that exhibit a hazardous waste characteristic.

Scrap Metal

Scrap metal is bits and pieces of metal parts that are generated by metal processing operations or result from consumer use (e.g., bars, turnings, rods, sheets, wire), or metal pieces that may be combined along with bolts or soldering (e.g., radiators, scrap automobiles, railroad boxcars), which when worn or superfluous can be recycled [40 CFR 261.1(c)(6)].

Recycling Activities

The definition of solid waste under 40 CFR 261.2 identifies four types of recycling activities for which recycled wastes may be subject to Subtitle C regulation:

- Speculative accumulation.
- Use constituting disposal.

- Reclamation.
- Burning wastes or waste-derived fuels for energy recovery (discussed below in a separate subsection).

Speculative Accumulation

Any hazardous secondary material not otherwise defined as a solid waste when recycled is considered a solid waste if it is accumulated before recycling, unless it can be shown that (1) the material is potentially recyclable and has a feasible means of being recycled, and (2) at least 75 percent of the accumulated material is recycled in one calendar year. The only exceptions to this rule are hazardous commercial chemical products (listed or characteristic) that are not considered wastes when stored prior to recycling. The 75 percent requirement may be calculated on the basis of either volume or weight and applies to waste accumulated during a calendar year beginning with the first day of January [40 CFR 261.1(c)(8)].

Use Constituting Disposal

A waste that is managed in such a way that it is considered use constituting disposal is a hazardous waste. *Use constituting disposal* is defined [40 CFR 261.2(c)] as either:

- Applying materials to the land or placing them on the land in a manner constituting disposal.
- Applying materials contained in a product to the land or placing them on the land in a manner constituting disposal.

Examples of such use include use as a fill, cover material, fertilizer, soil conditioner, or dust suppressor, or use in asphalt or building foundation materials.

As noted above, all hazardous secondary materials are considered solid wastes when applied to the land in these ways, except for listed commercial chemical products whose ordinary use involves application to the land. Therefore, hazardous waste generator, transporter, and storage requirements apply prior to use, and applicable land disposal requirements under Parts 264 and 265 apply to the activity itself.

Products that include listed hazardous wastes as ingredients are classified as solid wastes when placed directly on the land for beneficial use, unless and until the products are formally delisted. Products that include characteristic hazardous wastes as ingredients are classified as solid wastes only if the products themselves exhibit hazardous waste characteristics.

Reclamation

Reclamation is defined as the regeneration of waste materials or the recovery of material with value from wastes [40 CFR 261.4(c)(4)]. Reclamation includes such activities as dewatering, ion exchange, distillation, and smelting. However, simple collection, such as collection of solvent vapors, is not considered reclamation. Use of materials as feedstocks or ingredients, such as the use of a material as a reactant in the production of a new product, also is not considered reclamation.

Special Recycling Activities

Precious Metal Recovery

Hazardous wastes that contain precious metals are subject to reduced requirements when being recycled [40 CFR 266.70]. The *precious metals* include gold, silver, platinum, palladium, iridium, osmium, rhodium, and ruthenium. These reduced requirements are that:

- Generators and transporters must have an EPA identification number and must use a uniform manifest.
- Treatment, storage, and disposal facilities must have an EPA identification number, comply with manifest requirements, and keep records to demonstrate that 75 percent of all received wastes are being recycled per calendar year to satisfy the speculative accumulation provision.

The reclaimer is not required to comply with the technical standards of Parts 264 or 265 for precious metal recovery operations. A reclaimer can be considered a *designated facility* (see definition) if a Part A permit application is filed with an attached statement explaining that only precious metal reclamation will be conducted. However, the facility will not receive interim status for the precious metal recovery operations unless it is requested. The Part B permit application is not required for these operations.

Lead-Acid Batteries

Persons who generate, transport, or collect spent lead-acid batteries, and who do not also recover the lead from the batteries, are not subject to regulation under Parts 262 through 265 [40 CFR 266.80]. Reclaimers of lead from these batteries must notify EPA, and, if they store the batteries prior to reclamation, comply with the storage facility requirements of Parts 264 and 265 Subparts A through L, with the exception of waste characterization [40 CFR 264.14 and 265.23] and manifest-related requirements [40 CFR 264.71 and 72 and 40 CFR 265.71 and 72].

It is important to note that cracking batteries is considered reclamation, and thus is regulated. Generators should not drain the acid or otherwise crack a battery to recover the lead plates, or they will be considered recyclers subject to regulation.

Burning and Blending of Waste Fuels

Another form of recycling is the burning of hazardous waste and used oil as fuel for legitimate energy recovery regulated under 40 CFR Part 266. *Legitimate energy recovery* means a heating value of 5000 to 8000 Btu/lb in an industrial furnace or boiler (see definitions). There are two categories of waste fuel: hazardous waste fuel and used oil fuel. The burning of hazardous waste fuel in a unit other than an industrial furnace or boiler or the burning of fuel with a heating value less than 5000 to 8000 Btu/lb must comply with the incinerator standards under Parts 264 and 265 as well as the requirement to obtain a permit or interim status.

Hazardous Waste Fuel

The hazardous-waste-as-fuel activities were promulgated (50 *FR* 49164, November 29, 1985) to institute administrative controls for marketers and burners of hazardous waste fuels. The rule applies to the generation, transportation, and storage of all hazardous waste used as fuels or used to produce a fuel. The rule also prohibits the burning of hazardous waste fuels in nonindustrial boilers, unless the boiler complies with the incinerator standards under Parts 264 and 265.

Hazardous waste fuel is any hazardous waste (listed or that exhibits a hazardous waste characteristic) that is being burned for legitimate energy recovery. Any used oil that is mixed with any hazardous waste is considered a hazardous waste fuel when being burned.

Prohibitions

A person may market a hazardous waste fuel only to other marketers who have notified EPA of their hazardous waste fuel activities, have obtained an EPA identification number, and use burners that have an industrial furnace or boiler. This prohibition is in response to previous instances in which contaminated fuels were burned in furnaces contained in apartment buildings [40 CFR 266.31(a)].

The waste-as-fuel regulations require all marketers and burners to notify EPA of this activity, even if they have previously notified and received an EPA identification number for other activities.

No hazardous waste fuel may be burned in a cement kiln located within the incorporated boundaries of a city whose population is 500,000 or greater [40 CFR 266.31(c)].

Marketers

A *marketer* is any person who sends hazardous waste fuel directly to a burner; produces, processes, or blends hazardous waste fuel; or distributes hazardous waste fuel but does not produce, process, or blend the fuel. The term marketer has no association with monetary transactions. Thus, a person who distributes hazardous waste fuel for no monetary profit would still be considered a marketer [40 CFR 266.34].

According to 40 CFR 266.34, marketers of hazardous waste fuel must:

- Notify EPA of regulated waste-as-fuel activities.
- Comply with the appropriate accumulation requirements, that is, 90 days for on-site generators under 40 CFR 262.34, or a permit or interim status for nongenerators. (Storage requirements for generators and nongenerators are addressed in Chapters 3 and 5, respectively.)
- Use a manifest for all off-site shipments.
- Obtain a one-time certification from the burner or another marketer before initiating a shipment. This certification must state that the burner or marketer is in compliance with all applicable requirements of the waste-as-fuel regulations. A copy of this certification must be kept for at least three years.

Generators

Generators of hazardous waste fuel are subject to the same requirements as other hazardous waste generators under 40 CFR Part 262. However, if a generator were to send hazardous waste fuel directly to a burner, the generator would become a marketer and would also have to comply with the marketer requirements [40 CFR 266.32(b)].

Transporters

Transporters of hazardous waste fuel are subject to the Part 263 requirements for transporters as well as applicable Department of Transportation (DOT) requirements discussed in Chapter 4 [40 CFR 266.33].

Burners

According to 40 CFR 266.35, burners of hazardous waste fuel must:

- Notify EPA of the hazardous waste fuel burning.
- Retain a copy of each certification that was sent to a marketer for at least three years.
- Comply with the applicable storage requirements. This means either storing 90 days under 40 CFR 262.34 if the burner is burning only hazardous waste fuel generated on-site, or, if the burner is burning hazardous waste fuel generated off-site, filing a part A permit application as a storage facility to obtain interim status to store waste before burning.

Used Oil Fuel

The second part of the waste-as-fuel activities covers the burning of used oil for energy recovery. *Used oil* means oil that is refined from crude oil, is used, and, as a result of that use, is contaminated by physical or chemical means [40 CFR 266.40(b)]. Currently, used oil is not considered a hazardous waste unless it exhibits a hazardous waste characteristic *and* will be discarded. If, however, the intent is to dispose of used oil, the generator must determine if the oil is hazardous (by the characteristics) and determine the applicable requirements. The following regulations govern only the burning of used oil. Other used oil recycling (not including disposal) activities are not currently regulated.

Used oil mixed with any hazardous waste is subject to regulation under the hazardous-waste-as-fuel requirements discussed in the previous section [40 CFR 266.40(c)].

Any used oil that contains more than 1000 ppm of total halogens (fluorine, chlorine, bromine, iodine, and astatine) is assumed to have been mixed with a hazardous waste and would be regulated as a hazardous waste fuel under Part 266, Subpart D [40 CFR 266.40(c)]. However, provided that it can be demonstrated that mixing has not occurred (i.e., by labels or other documentation), the oil may be handled under the used oil rules. For example, commercial cutting oils may contain chlorinated substances as additives. Thus, used cutting oil containing

Table 2-5. Specification levels for used oil fuels.

Specification	Maximum level
Arsenic concentration	5 ppm
Cadmium concentration	2 ppm
Chromium concentration	10 ppm
Lead concentration	100 ppm
Total halogen concentration	4,000 ppm
Flash Point	100 °F (minimum)

chlorine at a concentration higher than 1000 ppm may not have been mixed with a hazardous waste.

Specification oil is any used oil that does not exceed any of the specification levels in Table 2-5. However, all used oil being burned for energy recovery, unless it is a hazardous waste fuel, is assumed to be off-specification oil unless demonstrated otherwise. This demonstration can be accomplished by a laboratory analysis.

It may be demonstrated that used oil with more than 1000 ppm of total halogens has not been mixed with hazardous wastes. If this is demonstrated, and the total halogen level is below 4000 ppm, it is considered specification oil. If the level is above 4000 ppm, it is considered off-specification oil. Otherwise, the oil must be treated as a hazardous waste fuel [40 CFR 266.40(c)]. This demonstration can be accomplished by a laboratory analysis. A total chlorine test may be used instead of a total halogen test to satisfy this requirement.

Off-specification oil is any used oil that exceeds any specification level identified in Table 2-5. However, off-specification oil may be blended to meet the specification without a permit or interim status. Blending is considered treatment prior to recycling and thus is not regulated [40 CFR 266.40(e)].

Requirements

The initial party to document a fuel as specification oil must retain all appropriate paperwork substantiating the claim for three years, except for burners who burn specification oil that they generate on-site [40 CFR 266.43(b)(6)].

Specification oil may be burned in any device, whereas off-specification oil may be burned only in boilers, furnaces, and used oil-fired space heaters (under certain constraints) [40 CFR 266.41(b)].

Off-specification oil may be marketed only to burners or other marketers who have notified EPA of their used oil management activities and have an EPA identification number. Generators of off-specification oil are subject to regulation only if they burn the oil on-site or market the oil directly to a burner. Transporters are not subject to these regulations unless they are also marketers [40 CFR 266.41(a)].

Marketers

Marketers of used oil fuel are those who generate and market fuel directly to a burner; receive used oil from other generators and produce, process, or blend the used oil fuel (including persons sending blended or processed used oil to brokers or other intermediaries); and distribute but do not process or blend used oil fuel [40 CFR 266.43(a)].

The marketer must notify EPA of used oil fuel activities with EPA form 8700-12. The notification is required even if the marketer has previously notified EPA of other hazardous waste activities [40 CFR 266.43(b)(3)].

A marketer must conduct and maintain records of analyses unless the marketer handles the oil as off-specification oil fuel [40 CFR 266.43(b)(ii)].

The marketer must obtain a one-time certification from the burner or marketer before initiating a shipment. The certification must state that the burner or marketer has notified EPA of its used oil fuel activities, and that, if the receiving facility is a burner, the facility will burn the off-specification oil only in an industrial furnace or boiler [40 CFR 266.43(b)(5)].

Invoice System

Because used oil fuel is not a hazardous waste (unless it exhibits a hazardous waste characteristic), an invoice system is required instead of a manifest [40 CFR 266.43(b)(4)]. A copy of each invoice received or sent must be retained for at least three years. When a marketer initiates a shipment of off-specification oil, an invoice containing the following information must be sent to the receiving facility:

- An invoice number.
- Marketer's EPA identification number.

- Receiving facility's EPA identification number.
- Names and addresses of both the receiving and the shipping facility.
- Quantity of off-specification oil fuel.
- The date(s) of shipment or delivery.
- The statement *This used oil is subject to EPA regulation under 40 CFR Part 266.*

Burners

A burner may burn off-specification oil only in an industrial furnace, a boiler, or a used-oil-fired space heater (provided that the used oil for the space heater is generated on-site or is from do-it-yourself oil changers only) [40 CFR 266.41(b)].

A burner of either specification or off-specification used oil fuel must notify EPA of its used oil fuel activities (except for using a used-oil-fired space heater). This notification must state the location and a general description of the used oil management activities [40 CFR 266.44(c)].

Before accepting an off-site shipment of off-specification oil, the burner must certify to the shipper that EPA has been notified of its used oil fuel activities and that burning will only be done in an industrial furnace or boiler [40 CFR 266.44(c)].

A burner must maintain a copy of each invoice it has received or any waste analysis conducted on the used oil for at least three years [40 CFR 266.44(e)].

Chapter 3

Generators

RCRA, the Hazardous Materials Transportation Act (HMTA), and Superfund all place the greatest accountability for the environmentally sound disposition of hazardous wastes on the generator. Therefore, it is essential that close attention be paid to the requirements to ensure compliance.

This chapter defines generator, describes the waste counting requirements, and outlines the requirements for each generator category.

INTRODUCTION

Compared to the other provisions of RCRA, the regulations for hazardous waste generators are short and easily comprehensible. Generators of hazardous waste must comply with the regulations set out in 40 CFR Part 262, the standards of which are designed to ensure, among other things, proper record keeping and reporting; the use of the Uniform Hazardous Waste Manifest system to track shipments of hazardous waste; the use of proper labels, markings, and containers; proper storage; and the delivery of the waste to a permitted treatment, storage, or disposal facility.

The key in determining the requirements for hazardous waste generators is to determine how much hazardous waste is generated at a facility *per* calendar month. The three categories of hazardous waste generators, based on the amount of waste generated, are:

- Small-quantity generators (less than 100 kg/mo)
- Medium-quantity generators (between 100 and 1000 kg/mo)
- Large-quantity generators (1000 kg/mo or greater)

Table 3-1. Requirements for generators of hazardous waste.

	Requirements		
	Small-quantity generators	Medium-quantity generators	Large-quantity generators
Quantity limits	<100 kg/mo **	100–1000 kg/mo	1000 kg/mo or greater
Management of waste	State-approved or RCRA-permitted	RCRA-permitted facility	RCRA-permitted facility
Manifest	Not required*	Required	Required
Exception report	Not required	Required after 60 days	Required after 45 days
Biennial report	Not required	Not required	Required
Personnel training	Not required	Basic training required	Full training required
Contingency plan	Not required	Basic plan required	Full plan required
EPA ID number	Not required*	Required	Required
On-site storage limits	May accumulate up to 999 kg	May accumulate up to 6000 kg for up to 180 days (or 270 days if will transport waste over 200 miles)	May accumulate any quantity up to 90 days
Storage requirements	None	Basic requirements with the technical standards under Part 265 for containers or tanks	Full compliance with technical standards under Part 265 for containers or tanks

*Although not legally required under RCRA, many transporters will not handle hazardous waste without these items.

** Or <1 kg/mo acutely hazardous waste

Each generator category has a unique set of requirements as shown in Table 3-1. As expected, the stringency of regulation increases with the amount of hazardous waste generated.

DEFINITION OF A GENERATOR

A *generator* is any person, by site, whose act or process produces hazardous waste or whose act first causes a hazardous waste to become subject to regulation [40 CFR 260.10].

There are instances in which two or more parties fit the definition of a generator. As an example, an owner of a raw material product storage tank hires a contractor to clean out the tank residue; the contractor generates the waste, but the tank owner owns the facility, tank, and residue. EPA would like for the parties to select a person to accept the duties of the generator, although in this example EPA would normally define the owner of the tank as the generator (45 *FR* 72026, October 30, 1980). However, EPA may apply the definition of generator to each of these parties because it is the *act or process* of each of these parties that produces the hazardous waste. EPA has stated (OSWER Directive 9451.01) that it will hold the persons who *generated* the waste jointly and severally liable even though the persons may not be the owners or operators of the facility. Thus, all persons who may fit the regulatory definition of a generator are potentially liable as the generator even though they may not have accepted the duties of the generator.

Requirements for All Generators

A generator of *any* amount of waste must determine if the waste is hazardous [40 CFR 261.11] by following the protocol as outlined in Figure 2-1. It first must be determined if the waste is a listed hazardous waste, and, if not, if it exhibits a hazardous waste characteristic by either testing it using approved methods or by applying knowledge of the characteristics of the waste in light of the materials and processes used [40 CFR 262.11(c)]. However, EPA does not recognize the defense of a good-faith mistake in identifying one's waste (45 *FR* 12727, February 26, 1980). If the waste is determined to be hazardous, the generator must refer to Parts 264, 265, and 268 to determine if the waste's management is restricted in any way. These management restrictions focus on land disposal restrictions [40 CFR 262.11(d)].

GENERATOR CATEGORIES

Prior to the Hazardous and Solid Waste Amendments of 1984 (HSWA), there were two categories of hazardous waste generators: those generating less than 1000 kg/mo and those generating 1000 kg/mo or more. HSWA reorganized the categories of hazardous waste generators into three tiers based on the generation of nonacutely hazardous waste per month: less than 100 kg, from 100 kg to 1000 kg, and 1000 kg or more. Although the categories were restructured, they have not been given standardized names. Various publications, as well as EPA itself, have created confusion among the regulated community by using differing terms that are nondescriptive. For the purposes of better understanding the generator requirements, this book uses the following terms: small-quantity generators (<100 kg/mo), medium-quantity generators (100–1000 kg/mo), and large-quantity generators (1000 kg/mo or more).

It is important to note that regardless of the regulatory status of a generator's hazardous waste under RCRA, Superfund does not exclude a generator's hazardous waste based on the amount or management of the waste. Thus it is in the generator's best interest to ensure that the hazardous waste is managed in the most secure manner possible. If a generator's hazardous waste is ever involved in a release, the generator is potentially liable for all or part of the cleanup costs. (See Chapter 14 for further discussion.)

Counting Hazardous Waste

To determine the appropriate generator category and the requirements that must be met, the quantity of hazardous wastes generated by a facility must be counted on a calendar-month basis. In general, a generator must tally the weight of all hazardous wastes generated in a calendar month. The total weight of *countable* hazardous wastes determines the appropriate generator category and applicable requirements as outlined in Table 3-1.

Hazardous wastes *must* be counted if they are:

- Generated and accumulated on-site for *any* period of time prior to their subsequent management.
- Placed directly into an on-site Subtitle C regulated treatment, storage, or disposal unit.
- Generated from a product storage tank or manufacturing process unit.

Hazardous wastes do *not* have to be counted if they are:

- Specifically excluded from regulation; these wastes include spent lead-acid batteries, used oil, and commercial chemical products sent off-site for reclamation.
- Nonacutely hazardous waste remaining in an *empty container.*
- Managed in an elementary neutralization unit, totally enclosed treatment unit, or wastewater treatment unit as these units are defined in 40 CFR 261.10.
- Discharged directly to a publicly owned treatment works (POTW) without being accumulated or treated prior to discharge.
- Produced from the on-site treatment of previously counted hazardous waste. For example, a facility generates 995 pounds of methyl ethyl ketone (MEK), then distills the spent MEK in the facility's on-site distillation unit. The distillation unit, after the distillation process, generates 15 pounds of waste MEK still bottoms. However, because the facility already counted the spent MEK before it was treated, the still bottoms do not have to be counted, as, technically, this is still the same waste.

Changing Generator Categories

Because a generator is subject to regulations that correspond to the amount of hazardous waste generated *per* calendar month, it is possible to change categories on a monthly basis. As an example, a generator normally produces less than 100 kg/mo; however, once a year, the generator conducts a facility-wide product storage and manufacturing process unit clean-out. This annual operation generates more than 1000 kg during that month. The generator is considered a large-quantity generator for that month only and must manage the waste in accordance with Part 262. After that month, the generator, assuming that less than 100 kg of hazardous waste is generated, can revert back to the small-quantity generator category.

SMALL-QUANTITY GENERATORS (SQGs)

A small-quantity generator is a generator that, in a calendar month, generates less than 100 kg of nonacutely hazardous waste or less than 1 kg of an acutely hazardous waste [40 CFR 261.5(a)]. (Acutely hazardous wastes include the P-code wastes and F020, F021, F022, F023, F026, and F027 wastes.)

According to 40 CFR 261.5(b)(9), a small-quantity generator is excluded from 40 CFR Parts 262 through 270 of RCRA if (1) the waste is identified [262.11]; (2) the generator does not accumulate at any one time hazardous wastes in quantities of 1000 kg or more; and (3) the waste is either treated or disposed of on-site, or the generator ensures delivery to an off-site storage, treatment, or disposal facility. However, to be able to manage the waste, the generator or facility off-site must:

- Be permitted under Part 270 of RCRA.
- Have interim status under Part 270 of RCRA.
- Be authorized to manage hazardous waste by a state with an authorized program under Part 271 of RCRA.
- Be permitted, licensed, or registered by a state to manage municipal or industrial hazardous waste.
- Beneficially use, reuse, or legitimately recycle or reclaim the hazardous waste.
- Treat the waste prior to beneficial use or reuse or prior to legitimate recycling or reclamation.

If an SQG mixes SQG-excluded hazardous waste with a nonhazardous waste, the resultant mixture will still retain the exclusion [40 CFR 261.5(h)]. However, if an SQG mixes excluded waste with nonexcluded hazardous waste, and the resultant mixture is 100 kg or greater, the exclusion is no longer retained and is subject to full regulation [40 CFR 261.5(i)].

The SQG's waste itself is excluded from regulation, not just the generator. This means that if a transporter collects waste from multiple SQGs, the waste itself will still be excluded. The waste loses its exclusion when it is mixed with non-SQG hazardous waste. However, this exclusion does not apply when an SQG mixes a hazardous waste with any other waste that is or will be burned in an industrial furnace or boiler for energy recovery [40 CFR 261.5(b)].

If a small-quantity generator accumulates 1000 kg or more of hazardous waste on-site, the generator loses the SQG exclusion, and all of the accumulated waste is subject to full regulation under 40 CFR Part 262 [40 CFR 261.5(g)(2)]. There are no technical standards specified for accumulation units used by SQGs.

MEDIUM- AND LARGE-QUANTITY GENERATORS

Medium- and large-quantity generators (discussed separately later in this section) are similarly regulated; but, for each requirement, the large-quantity generator is more stringently regulated, as shown in Table 3-1. These two types of generators also must comply with certain require-ments that are the same for both. (The other requirements are discussed later in this section.) The similar requirements for medium- and large-quantity generators are:

- EPA identification number
- Pre-transport requirements
- Manifest system
- Land disposal restrictions
- Waste minimization
- Biennial report

EPA Identification Number

A generator may not treat, store, or dispose of hazardous waste, or offer it for transportation without an EPA identification number [40 CFR 262.12]. These 12-digit identification numbers are obtained from the state or EPA Regional Office by submitting EPA Form 8700-12, *Notification of Hazardous Waste Activity*. EPA assigns an identification number to each generation *site*. Thus, if the facility relocates, a new identification number must be obtained for the new site. If the ownership or operational control changes for a facility, a new identification number is not required, although it is recommended that the facility request a new number.

Pre-transport Requirements

The pre-transport requirements, in essence, compel generators to comply with Department of Transportation (DOT) regulations for transporting hazardous materials [40 CFR 262.30, 31, 32, and 33]. These provisions, which are described in Chapter 4, require proper:

- Packaging
- Labeling
- Marking
- Placarding

Manifest System

A generator transporting hazardous waste off-site, or offering it for trans-portation, must use the Uniform Hazardous Waste Manifest (EPA Form 8700-22) as displayed in Figure 3-1 [40 CFR 262.20(a)].

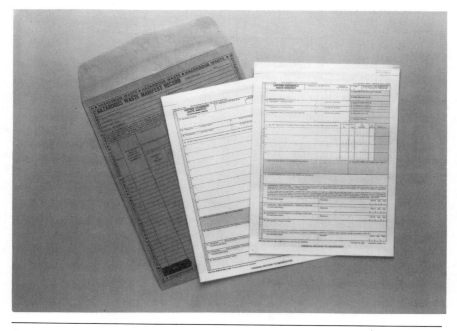

Courtesy of Lab Safety Supply, Inc., Janesville, WI.

Figure 3-1. Uniform Hazardous Waste Manifest

The Uniform Hazardous Waste Manifest is a component of a joint program between DOT and EPA. Before the joint program, a state could require the use of its own manifests, which created burdensome paperwork for transporters and generators who sent wastes outside of the state of generation. The uniform manifest, effective September 20, 1984, gave states only limited rights to require information beyond the federal requirements. The standard federal manifest has white numbered boxes and shaded lettered boxes. The shaded lettered boxes are for optional information that a state may require, while the white numbered boxes are required to be filled out by all users of a manifest. A transporter must comply only with the requirements in the state of origin and the consignment (destination) state. The transporter is not bound to comply with the state manifest requirements of the states through which the transporter travels.

The manifest, a one-page form with several carbon copies for the participants in the shipment, must identify the type and quantity of waste, the generator, the transporter, and the facility to which the waste is being shipped. The manifest must accompany the waste wherever it travels.

Each individual involved in a shipment must sign the manifest and keep one copy. When the waste reaches its final destination, the owner or operator of the designated facility signs the manifest and returns a copy to the generator to confirm arrival. Each person involved in the movement, storage, or receipt of hazardous waste requiring a manifest must retain a copy of that manifest for at least three years [40 CFR 262.40(a)]. Generators do not have to submit a copy of the manifest to EPA; however, some states require that a copy of the manifest be sent to the state.

The designated facility that signs the manifest accepts the responsibility for that shipment and cannot ship the waste back to the generator or any other facility unless the generator or facility is classified as a *designated facility,* which is a facility with interim status or a permit. Although a facility and a transporter may accept responsibility for a shipment, the generator retains indefinite liability under Section 107 of Superfund.

Manifest Acquisition Protocol

The acquisition protocol for the manifest form requires the generator to obtain the manifest from the consignment (disposal) state. However, if that state does not supply or require the use of a particular form, the manifest must be obtained from the generator's state. If the generator's state does not supply or require the use of a particular form, the generator may obtain the manifest from another source [40 CFR 262.21].

Exception Reporting

A generator who does not receive a copy of the signed manifest from the owner or operator of the designated facility within 35 days after the initial transporter accepted the waste must contact the designated facility to determine the status of the waste. If within 45 days the generator still has not received a copy of the manifest, an exception report must be filed with EPA. The *exception report* consists of a copy of the original manifest, a cover letter explaining the efforts taken by the generator to locate the waste, and the results of those efforts [40 CFR 262.42].

Land Disposal Restrictions

There are land disposal restrictions and prohibitions on certain hazardous wastes, as described in Chapter 8. Although the ultimate responsibility for compliance with land disposal restrictions is placed on the land disposal facilities, generators remain responsible for determining whether their wastes are subject to these restrictions [40 CFR 262.11(d)]. To determine if a waste is subject to these restrictions, the generator can base the determination on either knowledge of the waste, testing, or both [40 CFR 268.7(a)(1)].

If a generator determines that the waste is subject to the land disposal restrictions [40 CFR 268.7(a)(1)], but does not meet the treatment levels described in Chapter 8 (and is thus prohibited from land disposal), the generator must notify the designated facility in writing of the treatment standards and prohibition on land disposal [40 CFR 268.7(a)(1)].

If a generator determines that a waste subject to the land disposal restrictions can be land disposed of without further treatment, each shipment of that waste to a designated facility must have a notice and certification stating that the waste meets all of the applicable treatment standards [40 CFR 268.7(a)(2)]. The signed certification must state the following:

I certify under penalty of law that I personally have examined and am familiar with the waste through analysis and testing or through knowledge of the waste to support this certification that the waste complies with the treatment standards specified in 40 CFR 268 Subpart D. I believe that the information I submitted is true, accurate, and complete. I am aware that there are significant penalties for submitting a false certification, including the possibility of a fine and imprisonment.

Waste Minimization

Medium- and large-quantity generators must certify on each manifest (Item No. 16) that a program is in place to reduce the quantity and/or toxicity of the hazardous waste at that site. The generator also must describe the waste minimization program that is in place, and the results achieved by that program, in the biennial report.

Waste minimization means the reduction, to the extent feasible, of hazardous waste that is generated prior to treatment, storage, or disposal. It is defined as any source reduction or recycling activity that results in either (1) reduction of the total volume of hazardous waste, (2) reduction of the toxicity of hazardous waste, or (3) both. Practices that are considered waste minimization include recycling, source separation, product substitution, manufacturing process changes, and the use of less toxic raw materials [54 *FR* 25056, June 12, 1989].

Waste Minimization Program

EPA believes that an effective waste minimization program should include, as appropriate, each of the elements listed below [54 *FR* 25057, June 12, 1989]:

1. Top management support
   - Waste minimization as company policy.
   - Specified goals for waste minimization.
   - Commitment to recommendations.
   - Designated waste minimization coordinator.
   - Employee training.
2. Characterization of waste generation
3. Periodic waste minimization assessments
   - Comprehensive audits of entire waste process to ensure effective minimization.
   - Comprehensive analysis.
4. Technology transfer program
5. Program evaluation

Biennial Report

Each generator must prepare and submit a copy of a biennial report (EPA Form 8700-13A) by March 1 of each even-numbered year [40 CFR 262.41]. It is important to note that most states require an annual report. Information required for the biennial report includes:

- The generator's EPA identification number.
- The EPA identification number for each transporter used.
- The EPA identification number for each designated facility where hazardous waste was sent.
- A description and accounting of the quantity of hazardous waste generated.
- A report on the efforts undertaken during the year to reduce the volume and toxicity of waste generated and the reductions achieved by the generator's waste minimization program in comparison to previous years.

Medium-Quantity Generators (MQGs)

On March 24, 1986 (51 *FR* 10146), EPA removed medium-quantity generators (100–1000 kg/mo) from the existing small-quantity exclusionary provision in 40 CFR 261.5, established special requirements for hazardous waste generated by these generators, and promulgated final regulations that placed such generators under Part 262 (the standards applicable to generators of hazardous waste). EPA also promulgated specific amendments to Part 262 to exempt MQGs from some of the standards for generators of more than 1000 kg/mo.

In addition to the requirements discussed in the previous section, medium-quantity generators must comply with the requirements for:

- On-site accumulation
- Personnel training
- Preparedness and prevention
- Emergency procedures

On-Site Accumulation

Medium-quantity generators may accumulate hazardous waste on-site without a permit or interim status for up to 180 days (or 270 days if the waste will be transported over 200 miles) provided that:

- The generator does not store 6000 kg or more of hazardous waste at any time.
- Waste is accumulated in containers or tanks in compliance with specified technical standards, discussed below.
- The generator complies with the requirements for personnel training, emergency procedures, preparedness and prevention, and closure.

In accordance with 40 CFR 262.34(d)(1) and (2), each MQG accumulating hazardous waste must comply with the technical requirements for tanks or containers. Surface impoundments, waste piles, incinerators, landfills, and land treatment areas must be permitted or have interim status. Tanks or containers must be marked with the words "Hazardous Waste" and with the date when the accumulation began, to document compliance with the 180-day time limit.

Satellite Accumulation

Medium-quantity generators may accumulate up to 55 gallons of non-acutely hazardous waste or up to one quart of acutely hazardous waste in containers at *satellite accumulation areas*. The areas must be at or near any point of generation where waste initially accumulates and must be under the control of the operator of the process generating the waste. The containers must be marked with the words "Hazardous Waste," and when a container reaches the volume limit, it must be moved to the regular storage area within three days. When a container is moved to the regular storage area, the 180/270-day time limit commences.

Containers

Medium-quantity generators accumulating hazardous waste in containers must comply with Subpart I of Part 265, except for 40 CFR 265.176; this section requires ignitable and reactive wastes to be placed at least 50 feet from the facility's property boundary. In general the applicable requirements for MQGs are as follows:

- Containers must be in good condition. If a container leaks or is not in good condition, its contents must be transferred to a sound container.
- Containers must be compatible with the contents to be stored. Containers holding hazardous waste that is incompatible with other waste or other materials must be protected or physically separated.
- Containers must always be closed unless their contents are being transferred. In addition, they must always be handled in such a way as to prevent rupture or leaks.
- Container storage areas must be inspected at least weekly for signs of deterioration, corrosion, or leaks.

Tanks

Medium-quantity generators accumulating hazardous waste in a tank must comply with the following requirements as outlined in 40 CFR 265.201:

- Treatment must not generate any extreme heat, explosions, fire, fumes, mists, dusts, or gases; damage the tank's structural integrity; or threaten human health or the environment in any way.
- Hazardous wastes or treatment reagents that may cause rupture, corrosion, or structural failure must not be placed in the tank.
- At least two feet of freeboard (the distance between the top of the tank and the surface of the contents) must be maintained in an uncovered tank unless sufficient overfill containment capacity is supplied.
- Continuously fed tanks must have a waste-feed cutoff or bypass system.
- Ignitable, reactive, or incompatible wastes must not be placed into a tank unless these wastes are rendered nonignitable, nonreactive, or compatible.

- At least once each operating day, the waste-feed cutoff and bypass systems, monitoring equipment data, and waste level must be inspected. At least weekly, the construction materials and the surrounding area of the tank system must be inspected for visible signs of erosion or leakage.
- At closure, all hazardous wastes must be removed from the tank, containment system, and discharge control systems.

Personnel Training

Medium-quantity generators must ensure that all employees are thoroughly familiar with proper waste handling and emergency procedures relevant to their responsibilities during normal facility operations and emergencies [40 CFR 262.34(a)(5)(iii)].

Preparedness and Prevention

A facility must be operated and maintained in a manner that will minimize the possibility of any fire, explosion, or unplanned sudden or nonsudden release [40 CFR 262.34(d)(4) and 265.31]. An MQG also must have emergency response equipment (e.g., fire extinguishers, fire-control equipment, alarm system), maintain adequate aisle space for the unobstructed movement of emergency equipment and personnel, and make prior arrangements with local emergency response personnel.

Emergency Procedures

There must be at least one employee either at the facility or on call (i.e., available to respond to an emergency by reaching the facility within a short period of time) with the responsibility for coordinating all emergency response measures at all times. This employee is deemed the *emergency coordinator* [40 CFR 262.34(d)(5)(i)].

The emergency coordinator must respond to any emergencies that may arise and, if appropriate, institute the following emergency measures [40 CFR 262.34(d)(5)(iv)]:

- Contact the fire department and/or attempt to extinguish the fire.
- For any spill, contain the flow and commence cleanup wherever possible.
- For any fire, explosion, or release that meets a Superfund reportable

quantity (see Chapter 12) or a release that threatens human health or the environment, notify the National Response Center (1-800-424-8802).

According to 40 CFR 262.34(d)(5)(ii), the following emergency information must be posted next to facility telephones:

- The name and telephone number of the designated emergency coordinator.
- The telephone number of the fire department and appropriate emergency response organizations.
- The location of fire extinguishers, spill-control equipment, and fire alarms.

Large-Quantity Generators (LQGs)

Large-quantity generators are excluded from having to obtain a permit as a treatment, storage, or disposal facility (TSDF) provided that the generators comply with certain requirements:

- On-site accumulation
- Personnel training
- Preparedness and prevention
- Contingency plan and emergency procedures

On-Site Accumulation

A generator may accumulate hazardous waste on-site for up to 90 days without a permit or interim status provided that the facility meets certain conditions [40 CFR 262.34]:

- Storage or treatment occurs only in tanks or containers (there are no surface impoundments, waste piles, incinerators, landfills, or land treatment) and proper closure is performed.
- Tanks or containers comply with Part 265 Subpart I, Standards for Containers, and Subpart J, Standards for Tanks.
- The generator does not accept shipments of hazardous waste generated from off-site sources.
- Waste is sent to a designated facility within 90 days unless the waste is treated and rendered nonhazardous within 90 days.
- The generator complies with the requirement for Preparedness and

Prevention of Part 265, Subpart C, and Contingency Plan and Emergency Procedures of Part 265, Subpart D.

On-Site Treatment

Previously, a generator was allowed only to store waste for up to 90 days (provided that the generator complied with 40 CFR 262.34) but could not treat waste without a permit or interim status. However, on March 24, 1986 (51 *FR* 10168), EPA clarified its position by stating that treatment in a tank or container without a permit or interim status is permissible provided that the generator maintains compliance with 40 CFR 262.34. The stated reasoning behind the clarification is that allowing accumulation in a complying unit but not allowing treatment in that same unit is legally inconsistent.

Accumulation Units

LQGs accumulating hazardous waste in containers must comply with Subpart I of Part 265.

Generators accumulating hazardous waste in tanks are required to comply with most of the provisions of Subpart J of Part 265 (see Chapter 6), including:

- A one-time assessment of the tank system, including results of an integrity test.
- Installation standards for new tank systems.
- Design standards, including an assessment of corrosion potential.
- Secondary containment phase-in provisions.
- Periodic leak testing if the tank system does not have secondary containment.
- Closure of the tank system.
- Response requirements regarding leaks, including reporting to the EPA Regional Administrator the extent of any release and requirements for repairing or replacing of leaking tanks.

Owners or operators of 90-day accumulation tanks are not, however, required to prepare closure or post-closure plans or contingent closure or post-closure plans, maintain financial responsibility, or conduct waste analysis and trial tests.

Unit Marking

The date on which accumulation began must be marked on individual containers. The dating of tanks was omitted from the regulations, but some type of documentation should be kept for the purposes of demonstrating compliance with the 90-day time limit. The 90-day period starts the minute the first drop hits the tank or drum (except for satellite accumulation containers) [40 CFR 262.34(a)(2)].

Each container and tank also must have the words "Hazardous Waste" clearly marked on the unit.

Satellite Accumulation

A generator may accumulate a total of 55 gallons of hazardous waste or one quart of acutely hazardous waste in a container at or near any initial generation point. These *satellite accumulation areas* must be under the control of the operator of the process generating the waste. As soon as the 55-gallon or one-quart limit is attained, the generator has up to three days to move that container to the regular storage area. As soon as the container is at the regular storage area, the 90-day time limit starts. Containers in the satellite accumulation areas must be marked with the words "Hazardous Waste" [40 CFR 262.34(c)].

Personnel Training

Each generator must establish a training program for appropriate facility personnel. The purpose of the training requirements is to reduce the potential for errors that might threaten human health or the environment by ensuring that facility personnel acquire expertise in the areas to which they are assigned. The program also must include training for personnel to ensure facility compliance with all applicable regulations. The program must contain an initial training program as well as annual updates [40 CFR 265.16]. The content and format of the program are unspecified in the regulations. EPA accepts the use of on-the-job training as a substitute for, or supplement to, formal classroom instruction (45 *FR* 33182, May 19, 1980). However, the content, schedule, and techniques used for on-the-job training must be described in the training records maintained at the facility.

Preparedness and Prevention

Each facility must be operated and maintained in a manner that will minimize the possibility of any fire, explosion, or unplanned sudden or nonsudden release [40 CFR 265.31].

Each facility is required to have certain equipment to respond to emergencies. The equipment includes an alarm system, a communication device to contact emergency personnel (e.g., telephone), portable fire extinguishers, fire control equipment, and an adequate fire-fighting water supply system in the form of hydrants, hoses, or an auto-sprinkler system. This equipment must be routinely tested and maintained in proper working order [40 CFR 265.32]. Whenever hazardous waste is being poured, mixed, spread, or otherwise handled, all personnel involved in the operation must have immediate access to an internal alarm or emergency communication device. If there is ever just one employee at the facility while it is in operation, that employee must have immediate access to a device (e.g., radio, telephone) capable of summoning outside emergency assistance [40 CFR 265.34].

There must be adequate aisle space to allow the unobstructed movement, deployment, and evacuation of emergency equipment and personnel to any area of the facility [40 CFR 265.35]. Although the regulations do not specify the aisle space, it should be determined upon consultation with appropriate emergency organizations.

The facility must make prior arrangements with local emergency organizations (e.g., hospitals, police, fire departments) and personnel for an emergency response. The arrangements should include notification of the types of waste handled, a detailed map of the facility, a list of facility contacts, and specific agreements with various state and local emergency response organizations. Refusal of any state or local authorities to enter into such arrangements must be documented and maintained in the facility's files [40 CFR 265.37].

Contingency Plan and Emergency Procedures

Each facility must have a contingency plan, as outlined in Subpart D of Part 265, that is designed to minimize hazards in the case of a sudden or nonsudden release, fire, explosion, or similar emergency. The plan must include a description of actions that will be undertaken by facility personnel, a detailed list of emergency equipment with locations, and evacuation procedures. An owner or operator who has previously prepared a Spill Prevention, Control, and Countermeasure Plan (SPCC) in accordance with either 40 CFR Parts 112 or 300 or some other emergency or contingency plan need only amend that plan to incorporate hazardous waste management provisions that are sufficient to comply with these provisions [40 CFR 265.51 and 52].

The provisions of the plan must be carried out immediately whenever there has been a fire, explosion, or release of hazardous waste or constituents. A copy of the contingency plan must be maintained at the facility and submitted to all local police, fire, hospital, and emergency response teams. The plan also must include a list of all available emergency equipment at the facility, including the equipment's location and physical description and a brief outline of its capabilities [40 CFR 265.52 and 53].

There must be at least one employee on-site, or close by and on call, who is the designated *emergency coordinator*. The contingency plan must list current names, addresses, and phone numbers of all persons qualified as facility emergency coordinators. Whenever there is an imminent or actual emergency situation, the emergency coordinator must immediately activate the facility alarm system, notify all facility personnel, and, if needed, notify appropriate state or local agencies [40 CFR 265.55].

In the event of a release, fire, or explosion, the emergency coordinator must identify the source, character, and amount of materials involved. If any hazardous waste constituting a Superfund reportable quantity is released into the environment, the owner or operator must contact the National Response Center (1-800-424-8802) immediately [40 CFR 265.56]. (See Chapter 12 for further information on reportable quantities.)

Immediately after the incident, the emergency coordinator must provide for the treatment, storage, or disposal of any material contaminated as a result of the emergency [40 CFR 265.56(g)].

The owner or operator must report to EPA within 15 days any incident that requires the implementation of the contingency plan [40 CFR 265.56(j)].

Chapter 4

Shipping and Transportation

This chapter outlines the requirements for transporters of hazardous waste and generators who offer hazardous waste for transportation. RCRA requires generators and transporters to comply with the regulations administered by the Department of Transportation (DOT) under the Hazardous Materials Transportation Act (HMTA). Also, RCRA has additional requirements under HMTA for generators and transporters.

The information in this chapter is divided into two sections: transporters and shippers (generators). The requirements for both shippers and transporters under HMTA and RCRA are outlined in Table 4-1.

TRANSPORTERS

Under RCRA, a transporter of hazardous waste must comply with the applicable DOT requirements of 49 CFR Subchapter C [40 CFR 263.10(a)]. A *transporter* is any person engaged in the off-site transportation of hazardous waste by air, rail, highway, or water [40 CFR 260.10]. Under HMTA, transporters are known as carriers. A *carrier* is a person engaged in the transportation of passengers or property by land or water, as a common, contract, or private carrier, or civil air crate [49 CFR 171.8]. EPA has promulgated additional requirements under RCRA for persons transporting hazardous waste to ensure continuation of the "cradle to grave" system.

General Requirements Under RCRA

The transportation regulations apply to any transporter of hazardous waste except for on-site movements. A transporter who imports waste

Table 4-1. The RCRA and HMTA requirements for hazardous waste transportation.

Requirements	Agency	CFR citation
Generator/shipper:		
1. Determine if waste is hazardous	EPA	40/262.11
2. Notify EPA and obtain ID number; determine that transporter and designated TSD facility have ID numbers	EPA	40/262.12
3. Identify and classify waste according to DOT's Hazardous Materials Table	DOT	49/172.101
4. Comply with all packaging, marking, and labeling requirements	DOT	49/172-173
5. Determine whether additional shipping requirements are applicable for mode	DOT	49/174-177
6. Complete a hazardous waste manifest	EPA	40/262.20-23
7. Provide appropriate placards to transporter	DOT	49/172.506
8. Comply with record keeping and reporting	EPA	40/262.40-45
Transporter/carrier:		
1. Notify EPA and obtain ID number	EPA	40/263.11
2. Verify that shipment is properly identified, packaged, marked, labeled, and not leaking	DOT	49/174-177
3. Apply appropriate placards	DOT	49/172.506
4. Comply with the manifest requirements	EPA	40/263.20-21
5. Comply with record keeping and reporting	EPA	40/263.22
6. Take appropriate action (including cleanup) in the event of a release/spill	EPA	40/263.30-31
7. Comply with DOT incident reporting rules	DOT	49/171.15-17

Source: USEPA's *Hazardous Waste Transportation Interface - Guidance Manual, November 1981*

into the United States or places waste of different DOT shipping names into a common container is required to comply with the generator requirements of 40 CFR Part 262 [40 CFR 263.10(c)].

A transporter may not transport hazardous waste without having an EPA identification number [40 CFR 263.11], which is obtained by submitting EPA Form 8700-12 to the state, if authorized, or the EPA Regional Office. Upon receipt of a complete form, EPA (or the state) will issue the transporter a unique identification number. Transporters with either multiple terminals or vehicles should possess only one EPA identification number. Because the EPA identification number is used for a physical location, the number typically is obtained for a company's headquarters.

Manifest System

Shipments of all hazardous waste, except for small-quantity generator wastes, must be accompanied by a Uniform Hazardous Waste Manifest

[40 CFR 263.20]. The initial transporter who accepts the shipment must sign and date the manifest and present a copy of the signed manifest to the generator before leaving the property. The manifest must accompany the shipment at all times (except for railroad and water shipments).

A transporter who delivers the shipment to another transporter or to the designated facility must obtain the date of delivery and signature of the transporter or the designated facility, retain a copy of the signed manifest, and give the remaining copies of the manifest to either the next transporter or the designated facility. Each transporter must retain a copy of the signed manifest for at least three years [40 CFR 263.20].

Transfer Facilities

A transporter is allowed to store a manifested shipment at a transfer facility without a permit for up to 10 days during the normal course of transportation [40 CFR 263.12]. *Transfer facility* means any transportation related facility including loading docks, parking areas, storage areas, and other similar areas where shipments of hazardous waste are held during the normal course of transportation [40 CFR 260.10].

Delivery

The entire shipment of hazardous waste must be delivered to either the designated facility or the designated alternate facility listed on the manifest. If the waste cannot be delivered to either facility, the transporter must contact the generator immediately, obtain instructions, and revise the manifest accordingly [40 CFR 263.21].

Spills

In the case of a spill by a transporter, the appropriate authorities must be immediately notified, and the transporter must attempt to contain the spill [40 CFR 263.30]. If a government official (state, federal, local) determines that immediate cleanup is required to protect human health or the environment, that official can require appropriate action, such as removal of the waste by transporters who do not have an EPA identification number, manifest, or permit [40 CFR 263.31]. A person can receive an emergency EPA identification number or permit from a state or an EPA Regional Office.

The transporter must notify the National Response Center (800-424-

8802) [49 CFR 171.15] if the spill meets a reportable quantity under Superfund [40 CFR 302].

General Requirements Under HMTA

Carriers transporting hazardous waste are subject to the regulations for hazardous materials established by HMTA. Hazardous waste is a subset of hazardous material. Basically, all "for hire" carriers and all "in-house" carriers are subject to the same regulations. In general, the following items are the basic requirements for carriers:

- Determine the qualifications of drivers.
- Determine if the load is acceptable for shipment.
- Prepare incident reports when necessary.

Driver Qualifications

Carriers are required to ensure that their employees engaged in receiving, processing, or transporting hazardous waste are thoroughly instructed [49 CFR 174.7, 175.20, 176.13, and 177.800]. Thus, each carrier must train appropriate employees concerning the applicable HMTA regulations relevant to their job functions.

Determining the Acceptability of the Shipment

A carrier is required to ensure that a shipment of hazardous waste is prepared for transportation in accordance with Parts 171, 172, and 173 of 49 CFR [49 CFR 174.3, 175.3, 176.3, and 177.801(a)]. In general, the transporter must ensure the following:

- The shipping papers are prepared in proper format, accurate, and complete.
- The documentation matches the shipment.
- Damaged or leaking materials are not loaded.
- The shipment is properly blocked and braced to prevent movement and/or damage while in transit.
- Proper placards and identification numbers are displayed.

Incident Reports

The regulations require carriers to file reports of any accident or incident involving the spillage or unintentional release of any hazardous waste from its packaging [49 CFR 171.15 and 171.16].

At the earliest practicable moment, each carrier who transports hazardous waste must give notice to the National Response Center (800-424-8802) after any incident that occurs during the course of transportation (including loading, unloading, and temporary storage) in which, as a direct result of hazardous waste:

- A person is killed;
- A person receives injuries requiring admission to a hospital;
- Estimated carrier or other property damage exceeds $50,000;
- Fire, breakage, spillage, or suspected contamination occurs involving a shipment of radioactive material or etiologic agents;
- Fire, breakage, spillage, or suspected contamination occurs involving shipment of etiologic agents; or
- A situation exists of such a nature that, in the judgment of the carrier, it should be reported by immediate telephone report, even though it does not meet the criteria listed in this paragraph; for example, a continuing danger to life exists at the scene of the incident.

Each carrier who transports hazardous waste must report in writing, in duplicate, on DOT Form F 5800.1, to DOT within 30 days of the date of discovery, each incident that occurs during the course of transportation (including loading, unloading, or temporary storage) in which, as a direct result of the hazardous waste, any of the circumstances warranting an immediate telephone report have occurred, or there has been any unintentional release of hazardous waste from a package (including a tank) [49 CFR 171.16].

SHIPPERS

The basic purpose of the HMTA requirements for shippers (generators) is to prescribe appropriate packaging and hazard communication, such as proper classification, packaging, marking, labeling, and placarding concerning the contents being transported. The applicable requirements depend specifically on the classification of the waste to be shipped. The procedures for classifying a hazardous waste for transportation purposes under DOT are outlined in the following sections and depicted in Figure 4-1.

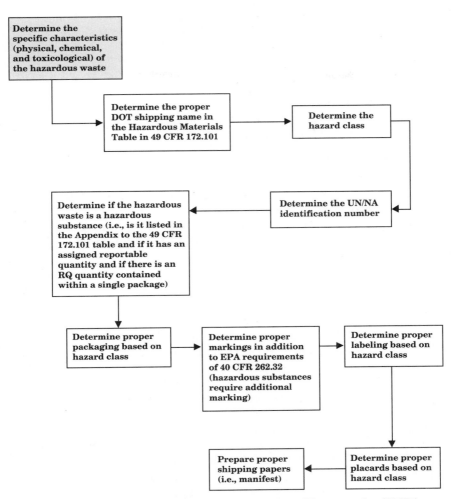

Figure 4-1. Classification Process for Hazardous Wastes under HMTA

Classification Procedure

A person who offers a hazardous waste for transportation is considered the shipper, and must comply with specific regulations for identification, classification, labeling, packaging, marking, placarding, and shipping documentation. Each of these actions is designed primarily to protect the health of humans who may be exposed to such wastes during transportation. Most of this information is contained in DOT's Hazardous Materials Table.

Each step has specific requirements, which are discussed in detail in the following pages. Briefly, the shipper must do the following:

Proper shipping name: Determine the proper shipping name of the hazardous waste based on the listings provided by DOT in the Hazardous Materials Table.
Hazard class: Select the appropriate hazard class.
Identification number: Select the identification number that corresponds to the proper shipping name and hazard class.
Labels: Determine if labels are required.
Packages: Determine the authorized packages for the hazardous waste.
Markings: Apply the required DOT and EPA markings to the package.
Placards: Determine and provide the proper placards to the transporter/carrier.
Shipping documentation: Prepare a Uniform Hazardous Waste Manifest to document the identification and classification of the waste being shipped.

The Hazardous Materials Table

The Hazardous Materials Table (HMT), found in 49 CFR 172.101, lists those materials designated by DOT as hazardous for the purposes of transportation.

To use the table specifically for hazardous wastes, one must first remember that DOT considers hazardous wastes to be a subset of hazardous materials. Thus, a hazardous waste will *always* be regarded by DOT as a hazardous material subject to certain additional requirements.

The table identifies the proper shipping names, hazard classifications, United Nations/North American identification numbers, and references for the requirements for labeling, packaging, marking, placarding, and shipping procedures. The key feature of the table is that it compiles the regulations into an index which shippers (generators) can use to readily ascertain what procedures they must follow to transport the hazardous waste.

The HMT is divided into columns that contain the various identification and classification requirements:

Column 1: Contains special notes concerning requirements for the shipping name and shipping modes (water, air).
Column 2: Contains the proper shipping names.

*These items constitute the shipping description.

Column 3: Contains the hazard classes.
Column 3a: Contains the identification numbers.
Column 4: Contains information concerning required labels.
Columns 5 and 6: Contain the packaging requirements.
Column 7: Contains requirements specifically for water shipments.

Shipping Name

The *proper shipping name* is the name appearing in the HMT ("commodity list") that most accurately describes the waste to be shipped [49 CFR 127.101]. The proper shipping name is required to determine the proper packaging, marking, labeling, and placarding requirements.

Column 2 of the HMT lists the proper shipping names in alphabetical order as designated by DOT. In selecting a proper shipping name to describe a hazardous waste, the name in the table that most accurately identifies the hazardous waste is the name to be used. Only those names listed in Roman type (nonitalics) are authorized shipping names, whereas the italicized names are to be used only as finding aids and cannot be used as shipping names.

The placement of a plus (+) sign before an entry in the commodity list in column 1 indicates that this particular entry must be used as shown. Thus, that description must be used. An entry that does not have a plus sign may not necessarily have the properties listed in the description. For example, Refrigerant gas, n.o.s., flammable gas, may be classified more accurately as a combustible gas because of the flash point. The lack of a plus sign signifies that the entry's hazard class may differ, depending on the actual characteristics of the waste to be shipped.

It is important to note that 49 CFR 172.101(c)(10) requires that if the word "waste" is not included in the shipping name in column 2 of the HMT, the proper shipping name for a hazardous waste must include the word "Waste" preceding the shipping name. For example, spent toluene used as a solvent would be: Waste Toluene.

Identification Protocol

The selection of the proper shipping name for hazardous wastes presents a difficult task for the shipper. Because hazardous wastes are typically not single-stream wastes, but are commingled waste streams, the selection of the proper shipping name should follow the hierarchial approach outlined below [49 CFR 172.101(c)(13)]. However, the most descriptive name must be used. This hierarchial approach, corresponding to a decrease in specificity, is as follows:

1. Listing by the material's specific chemical name.
2. Listing by chemical family name (n.o.s.).
3. Generic listing by the material's end-use.
4. Generic listing by the n.o.s. end-use description.
5. Generic listing by n.o.s. class description.

The chemical-specific listings are intended for single-stream wastes. For example, the proper shipping name for spent toluene from degreasing operations would be: Waste Toluene. However, if the toluene were mixed with other wastes, or if it were a solvent mixture, the above shipping name would not be correct. The name for a mixture would require another description based on the hierarchial approach. (In the case of a solvent mixture, it would probably be the last descriptor contained in number 5; e.g., Waste Flammable liquid, n.o.s.).

If the waste to be shipped is not specifically listed by name, the chemical family can be used. It is important to note that if the specific name is listed, it must be used. For example, for butyl alcohol, Butyl alcohol would have to be used instead of Alcohol, n.o.s. Examples of chemical family names include:

- Alcohol, n.o.s.
- Alkaline liquid, n.o.s.
- Chlorate, n.o.s.

The next step is to identify the waste according to its end-use or purpose; that is, the entry that best describes the purpose of the material rather than its chemical composition. Examples of end-use descriptions include:

- Compound, cleaning, liquid
- Dye intermediate, liquid
- Engine starting fluid

The next step is the generic n.o.s. end-use description. The description is less specific than the end-use description without the n.o.s. designation as described above. Examples of generic n.o.s. end-use descriptions include:

- Insecticide, liquid, n.o.s.
- Refrigerant gas, n.o.s.
- Drugs, n.o.s.

The final and least specific description is based on the generic listing by the n.o.s. hazard classification. These listings do not identify the material itself, but the hazard associated with the material. Examples of generic n.o.s. listings include:

- Flammable solid, n.o.s.
- Combustible liquid, n.o.s.
- Oxidizer, n.o.s.

Hazardous Substances

Hazardous substances are those substances designated under Section 101(14) (codified in 40 CFR 302) of the Comprehensive Environmental Response, Compensation, and Liability Act (CERCLA). It is important to note that every hazardous waste under RCRA is classified as a hazardous substance under CERCLA. Hazardous substances are those substances that pose special hazards when released into the environment. CERCLA establishes reporting requirements when an amount of a hazardous substance is released at or greater than its reportable quantity. (The Clean Water Act also has reporting requirements for hazardous substances released into U.S. waters.)

DOT's role in regulating the hazardous substances is tied to EPA's role. That is, DOT has no role in determining what is or is not a hazardous substance or the appropriate reportable quantity for materials designated as hazardous substances. This authority is vested in EPA by CERCLA. DOT regulates CERCLA hazardous substances by establishing two additional requirements for hazardous substances being shipped: a notation of "RQ" before or after the shipping description on the shipping paper (i.e., manifest) and marking of the package.

For a substance to be designated as a *hazardous substance* under DOT [49 CFR 171.8], it must meet the following requirements:

- It is listed as a hazardous substance in the Appendix to 49 CFR 172.101.
- It is in a quantity, in one package, that equals or exceeds the reportable quantity (RQ) listed in the Appendix to 49 CFR 172.101. (Thus, it is based on a per package basis.)
- If the substance is in a mixture or solution, its concentration (by weight) must equal or exceed the concentration that is shown in Table 4-2 corresponding to the RQ identified for the substance in the Appendix to 49 CFR 172.101.

Hazard Class

The proper classification of the hazards exhibited by the waste to be shipped is an important aspect of the DOT regulations. This classification

Table 4-2. Reportable quantities in mixtures and
solutions.

	Concentration by weight	
RQ in pounds (kilograms)	Percent	ppm
5,000 (2,270)	10	100,000
1,000 (454)	2	20,000
100 (45.4)	0.2	2,000
10 (4.54)	0.02	200
1 (0.454)	0.002	20

further determines the requirements for packaging, labeling, and any special requirements that must be met by shippers (generators) and carriers (transporters). The hazard class is specified for each designated proper shipping name contained in column 3 of the HMT. The designated hazard classes are contained in Table 4-3. Although the classifications used by RCRA and DOT may appear to be similar, they differ, and close attention should be paid to the selection of the appropriate hazard class. For example, a D001 ignitable waste under RCRA has a flash point of less than 140°F. However, under HMTA a RCRA ignitable waste might be a flammable liquid (<100°F) or a combustible liquid (100–200°F), depending on the waste's flash point.

Multiple Hazards

In those instances where a hazardous waste is not specifically listed in the HMT, or a waste would fit into multiple hazard classes, the generator must evaluate the waste against the criteria for all of the hazard classes. The selection of the appropriate hazard class is based on a priority listing provided in 49 CFR 173.2 and described below.

A hazardous waste having more than one hazard must be classed according to the following ranking, in descending order of hazards:

1. Radioactive material (except for small quantities)
2. Poison A
3. Flammable gas
4. Nonflammable gas
5. Flammable liquid
6. Oxidizer
7. Flammable solid
8. Corrosive material (liquid)
9. Poison B

Table 4-3. The DOT hazard classes.

Flammable liquid: Any liquid with a flash point below 100°F as determined by tests listed in 49 CFR 173.115(d). Exceptions are listed in 49 CFR 173.115(a).

Combustible liquid: Any liquid having a flash point at or above 100°F and below 200°F as determined by the tests listed in 49 CFR 173.115(d). Exceptions are listed in 49 CFR 173.115(b).

Flammable solid: Any solid material, other than an explosive, liable to cause fires through friction or retained heat from manufacturing or processing, or which can be ignited readily creating a serious transportation hazard because it burns vigorously and persistently [49 CFR 173.150].

Oxidizer: A substance such as chlorate, permanganate, inorganic peroxide, or a nitrate that yields oxygen readily to stimulate the combustion of organic matter [49 CFR 173.151].

Organic peroxide: An organic compound containing the bivalent —O—O— structure, and which may be considered a derivative of hydrogen peroxide where one or more of the hydrogen atoms have been replaced by organic radicals. Exceptions are listed in 49 CFR 173.151(a).

Corrosive: Liquid or solid that causes visible destruction or irreversible alterations in human skin tissue at the site of contact. Liquids that severely corrode steel are included [49 CFR 173.240(a)].

Flammable gas: A compressed gas, as defined in 49 CFR 173.300(a), that meets certain flammability requirements [49 CFR 173.300(b)].

Nonflammable gas: A compressed gas other than a flammable gas.

Irritating material: A liquid or solid substance that on contact with fire or when exposed to air gives off dangerous or intensely irritating fumes. Poison A materials are excluded [49 CFR 173.381].

Poison A: Extremely dangerous poison gases or liquids. Very small amounts of these gases or vapors of these liquids, mixed with air, are dangerous to life [49 CFR 173.326].

Poison B: Substances, liquids or solids (including pastes and semi-solids), other than Poison A or irritating materials, that are known to be toxic to humans. In the absence of adequate data on human toxicity, materials are presumed to be toxic to humans if they are toxic to laboratory animals exposed under specified conditions [49 CFR 173.343].

Etiologic agents: A viable microorganism, or its toxin, that causes or may cause human disease. These materials are limited to agents listed by the Department of Health and Human Services [49 CFR 173.386, 42 CFR 72.3].

Radioactive material: A material that spontaneously emits ionizing radiation having a specific activity greater than 0.002 microcurie per gram (μCi/g). Further classifications are made within this category according to levels of radioactivity [49 CFR 173, Subpart I].

Explosive: Any chemical compound, mixture, or device, the primary or common purpose of which is to function by explosion, unless such compound, mixture, or device is otherwise classified [49 CFR 173.50]. Explosives are divided into three classes:

Class A explosives are detonating explosives [49 CFR 173.53].

Table 4-3. (*Continued*)

Class B explosives generally function by rapid combustion rather than detonation [49 CFR 173.88].

Class C explosives are manufactured articles, such as small arms ammunition, that contain restricted quantities of Class A and/or Class B explosives, and certain types of fireworks [49 CFR 173.100].

Blasting agent: A material designed for blasting, but so insensitive that there is very little probability of ignition during transport [49 CFR 173.114(a)].

ORM (Other Regulated Material): Any material that does not meet the definition of the other hazard classes. ORMs are divided into five classes:

ORM-A is a material that has an anesthetic, irritating, noxious, toxic, or other similar property and can cause extreme annoyance or discomfort to passengers and crew in the event of leakage during transportation [49 CFR 173.500(a)(1)].

ORM-B is a material capable of causing significant damage to transport vehicle or vessel if leaked. This class includes materials that may be corrosive to aluminum [49 CFR 173.500(a)(2)].

ORM-C is a material that has other inherent characteristics not described as an ORM-A or ORM-B, but which make it unsuitable for shipment unless properly identified and prepared for transportation. Each ORM-C material is specifically named in the Hazardous Materials Table in 49 CFR 172.101 [49 CFR 173.500(a)(3)].

ORM-D is a material such as a consumer commodity that, although otherwise subject to regulation, presents a limited hazard during transportation due to its form, quantity, and packaging [49 CFR 173.500(a)(4)].

ORM-E is a material that is not included in any other hazard class, but is subject to the requirements of this subchapter. Material, in this class include some hazardous wastes and hazardous substances [49 CFR 173.500(a)(5)].

---

10. Corrosive material (solid)
11. Irritating material
12. Combustible liquid packaged in containers over 110 gallons in capacity
13. ORM-B
14. ORM-A
15. Combustible liquid packaged in containers with a capacity of 110 gallons or less
16. ORM-E

For example, a listed hazardous waste is listed because it is toxic and also has a flash point of 96°F. In this case, the waste exhibits the hazards associated with the Poison B hazard class and the Flammable liquid hazard class. In accordance with the hazard class ranking described below, the appropriate hazard class for this waste is Flammable liquid.

ORM-E Classifications

Because DOT's hazardous material regulations program predated RCRA, many of the existing requirements and designations are derived from the "traditional" acute transportation hazards such as fires and explosions. Although many of the RCRA hazardous wastes fall within these traditional hazard classifications, some of the wastes do not. Therefore, DOT created a new category, Other Regulated Material-E (ORM-E).

It should be noted, however, that most hazardous wastes will fit under the traditional hazard classifications (e.g., Flammable liquid, Poison B, Corrosive). Thus, one should guard against using the ORM-E classification too liberally. It should be used only when no other hazard classification is appropriate.

Identification Number

The identification number is based on a United Nations/North America (UN/NA) number that consists of the prefix "UN" or "NA" followed by a four-digit number. The UN/NA numbers for each assigned hazardous waste are located in column 3a of the Hazardous Materials Table. The UN/NA numbers are used on shipping papers and transport vehicles, either on a separate orange panel or on the placard. The UN numbers are based on an international system developed by the United Nations Committee of Experts on the Transport of Dangerous Goods. The NA numbers identify materials not recognized for international shipment by the UN Committee except for transport between the United States and Canada.

Shipping Descriptions

The shipping description combines the proper shipping name, hazard class, and identification number. The proper shipping description is used for marking and shipping paper documentation.

There are required modifications to the shipping name for hazardous wastes contained in 49 CFR 172.101(c) and 172.203. These modifications are outlined below.

A mixture or solution of a DOT listed hazardous material and a non-hazardous material may be described by using the proper shipping name of the listed hazardous material, if:

- The mixture or solution is not specifically listed elsewhere in the HMT;

Table 4-4. Proper shipping names requiring technical name(s).

Proper shipping names	
Acid liquid, n.o.s.	Irritation agent, n.o.s.
Alcohol, n.o.s.	Nonflammable gas, n.o.s.
Alkaline liquid, n.o.s.	Organic peroxide, liquid or solution,
Cement, adhesive, n.o.s.	n.o.s.
Combustible liquid, n.o.s.	ORM-A, n.o.s.
Compressed gas, n.o.s.	ORM-B, n.o.s.
Corrosive liquid, n.o.s.	ORM-E, n.o.s.
Corrosive liquid, poisonous, n.o.s.	Oxidizer, corrosive, liquid, n.o.s.
Corrosive solid, n.o.s.	Oxidizer, corrosive, solid, n.o.s.
Dispersant gas, n.o.s.	Oxidizer, n.o.s.
Etching acid, liquid, n.o.s.	Oxidizer, poisonous, liquid, n.o.s.
Etiologic agent, n.o.s.	Oxidizer, poisonous, solid, n.o.s.
Flammable gas, n.o.s.	Poisonous liquid or gas, flammable, n.o.s.
Flammable liquid, corrosive, n.o.s.	Poisonous liquid or gas, n.o.s.
Flammable liquid, n.o.s.	Poisonous liquid, n.o.s.
Flammable liquid, poisonous, n.o.s.	Poison B liquid, n.o.s.
Flammable solid, corrosive, n.o.s.	Poisonous solid, corrosive, n.o.s.
Flammable solid, n.o.s.	Poisonous solid, n.o.s.
Flammable solid, poisonous, n.o.s.	Poison B, solid, n.o.s.
Hazardous substance, liquid or solid, n.o.s.	Pyrophoric liquid, n.o.s.
Infectious substance, human, n.o.s.	Pyroforic liquid, n.o.s.
Insecticide, dry, n.o.s.	Refrigerant gas, n.o.s.
Insecticide, liquid, n.o.s.	Water reactive solid, n.o.s.

- The hazard class of the mixture or solution is the same as that of the hazardous material; and
- The qualifying word "mixture" or "solution," as appropriate, is added as part of the proper shipping name. For instance, a solution of acetone, mineral oil, and water, meeting the definition of a flammable liquid, may be described as "Acetone solution, flammable liquid" [49 CFR 172.101(c)(11)].

Unless otherwise excepted, if the hazardous waste is described by one of the shipping descriptions listed in Table 4-4, the technical name of the hazardous waste must be entered in parentheses in association with the basic description. For example, "Waste corrosive, n.o.s. (Capryl chloride) UN1760" or "Waste corrosive liquid, n.o.s., UN1760 (contains capryl chloride)." The word "contains" may be used in association with the technical name [49 CFR 172.203(k)]. *Technical name* means the scientific designation of a chemical in accordance with the nomenclature system developed by the International Union of Pure and Applied Chemistry or the Chemical Abstract Registry Service rules of nomenclature, or a name currently recognized in the Registry of Toxic Effects of Chemical Substances. The term does not include trade names [49 CFR 171.8].

If the hazardous waste is a mixture or solution of two or more hazardous wastes, the technical names of at least two of the components most predominately contributing to the hazards of the mixture or solution must be entered; for example, "Flammable liquid, corrosive, n.o.s. (Methanol, Potassium hydroxide), UN 2924" [49 CFR 172.203(k)(12)].

If the shipping name for a hazardous substance does not reveal the name of the regulated constituent, the EPA waste code number of the regulated constituent must be included in parentheses [49 CFR 172.202(c)].

Poisons

If a hazardous waste meets the definition of a poison, and the poison is not disclosed in the shipping name or class entry, the word "Poison" must be contained in the shipping description [49 CFR 172.203(m)(1)].

If the technical name of the compound or principal constituent that causes a waste to meet the definition of poison is not included in the proper shipping name for the waste, the technical name must be included in the shipping description; for example, "Waste motor fuel antiknock compound (Tetraethyl lead), Poison B, UN1649" or "Waste motor fuel antiknock compound, Poison B, UN1649 (Tetraethyl lead)" [49 CFR 172.203(m)(2)]. In addition, if the waste meets the criteria of an inhalation hazard of 49 CFR 173.3a(b)(2), the words "Poison–Inhalation Hazard" must be contained in the shipping description.

Packaging

The RCRA regulations [40 CFR 262.30] require all generators of hazardous wastes to transport their wastes in packaging that complies with the DOT shipping and packaging regulations in Parts 173, 178, and 179 of Title 49. Part 173 of the regulations addresses the general requirements for shipments and packaging of hazardous wastes, while Parts 178 and 179 outline the specifications for both shipping containers and tank cars, respectively.

As with most other DOT requirements for hazardous waste, the selection of the container hinges upon the determination of the proper shipping description. In column 5 of the Hazardous Materials Table

(HMT), the regulatory references for the required packaging are listed. Also in this column, exceptions to packaging requirements are listed. Exceptions are for limited quantities of specified materials.

The DOT regulations on the packaging of hazardous wastes are specific and do not provide a great deal of discretion to the maker of that packaging or the shipper in varying these specifics. The regulations key the packaging to the proper shipping description. The entries in the alphabetical commodity list lead to the specific sections referencing authorized packaging.

DOT specification packaging (i.e., that packaging to which DOT specification numbers are assigned and for which there are exceedingly detailed construction and quality control requirements) are set forth in 49 CFR Part 178, and Part 179 for tank cars.

The specifications detail what is minimally (not nominally) required in the construction and arrangement of given packaging. For some products, particularly in smaller quantities, no detailed specifications are prescribed in the regulations. Note, however, that all packaging must satisfy the general packaging requirements contained in 49 CFR 173.24, entitled "Standard Requirements for All Packages." There have been many enforcement cases brought under this section, which pertains to such things as the compatibility of the product with the packaging materials, legibility of markings, general integrity of the packaging, common marking requirements, and so forth.

Marking

Marking means placing on the outside of a shipping container one or more of the following: the descriptive name, instructions, caution, and/or weight. Marking also includes any required specification marks on the inside or outside shipping container but is separate from labeling and placarding [49 CFR 172.300].

Shippers (generators) are required to mark all packages of hazardous wastes with a capacity of 110 gallons or less with the proper shipping name, the UN/NA identification number, and the name and address of either the shipper or the designated facility [49 CFR 172.301]. For each hazardous substance present in a reportable quantity in one package (having a capacity of less than 110 gallons) it is necessary to have the RQ designation marked before or after the shipping name. If the proper shipping name of the hazardous substance does not identify the hazardous substance by name, the *technical name* of the hazardous substance must be placed in parentheses in association with the shipping name [49 CFR 172.324].

Packages (including overpacks) containing liquid hazardous waste must be marked THIS SIDE UP or THIS END UP, and an arrow symbol on the outside packaging must be included to show the correct position for the package (49 CFR 172.312).

EPA's Marking Requirements

In addition to the DOT requirements, EPA also requires special markings for packages of hazardous wastes [40 CFR 262.32(b), 262.34(a)(2), and 262.34(a)(3)]. A generator accumulating hazardous waste in compliance with the 90- or 180/270-day limit provisions of 40 CFR 262.34 must mark the container with the words "Hazardous Waste" and with the date upon which each period of accumulation begins. In addition, before offering hazardous waste for transportation off-site, a generator must mark each container of 110 gallons or less with the following words:

HAZARDOUS WASTE—Federal Law Prohibits Improper Disposal. If found, contact the nearest police or public safety authority or the U.S. Environmental Protection Agency.

Generator's Name and Address _____ .
Manifest Document Number _____ .

The standard yellow label shown in Figure 4-2, commonly used by generators, combines the DOT and EPA marking requirements for hazardous waste.

Labels

Labels are 4-inch-by-4-inch colored diamonds that provide symbolic representations of the hazards associated with a particular material. The labels are shown in Figure 4-3. Column 4 of the HMT indicates which materials require labels. Shipments of limited quantities of certain hazardous materials may not require labeling; these exceptions are referenced in column 5a of the HMT under packaging exceptions. The labels, when required, must be printed or affixed near the marked shipping name [49 CFR 172.406] and must meet the required color scheme (not depicted in Figure 4-3).

Labels are not required for any material classed as ORM-A, ORM-B, ORM-C, ORM-D, or ORM-E, or a package containing a combustible liquid if the package does not contain any other material classed as a hazardous material that requires labeling [49 CFR 172.400(b)(8) and 172.400(b)(9)].

```
////////////////////////

HAZARDOUS WASTE
FEDERAL LAW PROHIBITS IMPROPER DISPOSAL.

IF FOUND CONTACT THE NEAREST POLICE
PUBLIC SAFETY AUTHORITY OR THE
U.S. ENVIRONMENTAL PROTECTION AGENCY.

PROPER DOT
SHIPPING NAME_____ UN OR NA#_____

GENERATOR INFORMATION:

NAME _____

ADDRESS _____

CITY _____ STATE _____ ZIP _____

EPA                          EPA
ID NO. _____   WASTE NO. _____

ACCUMULATION                 MANIFEST
START DATE _____   DOCUMENT NO. _____

CAUTION:
THIS CONTAINER HOLDS HAZARDOUS OR TOXIC WASTE.

HANDLE WITH CARE!
© Copyright Science Related Materials Inc., Janesville, WI 53547
```

Courtesy of Lab Safety Supply, Inc., Janesville, WI.

Figure 4-2. Standard Yellow Hazardous Waste Label

Multiple Labeling

Pursuant to 49 CFR 172.402(a), DOT has established criteria where multiple labeling is required. This section requires each package containing a material meeting the definition of more than one hazard class to be labeled as follows:

- A material classed as an Explosive A, Poison A, or Radioactive material that also meets the definition of another hazard class must be labeled as such.
- A Poison B liquid that also meets the definition of a Flammable liquid must be labeled POISON and FLAMMABLE LIQUID.
- A material classed as an Oxidizer, Flammable solid, or Flammable liquid that also meets the definition of Poison B must be labeled POISON in addition to the class label.

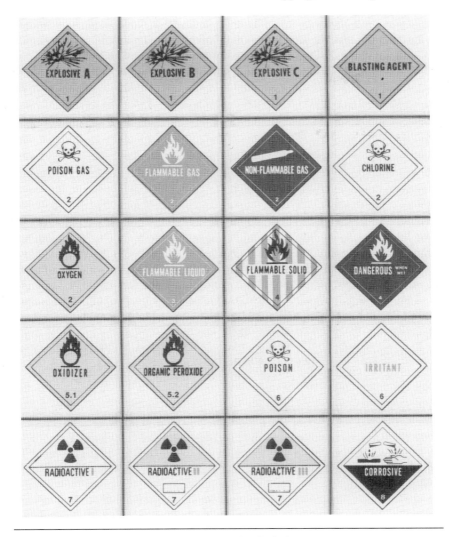

Figure 4-3. DOT Labels

- A material classed as a Flammable solid that also meets the definition of a Water reactive material must have both the FLAMMABLE SOLID and DANGEROUS WHEN WET labels affixed.
- A material classed as a Corrosive material that also meets the definition of a Poison B must be labeled with a POISON label in addition to the CORROSIVE label.

- A material classed as a Poison B, Oxidizer, or Flammable liquid that also meets the definition of a Corrosive material must be labeled with a CORROSIVE label in addition to the class label.
- A material meeting the inhalation hazard criteria contained in 49 CFR 173.3a(b)(2) must be labeled with a POISON label in addition to any other label(s) unless it already has a POISON label.

Placards

Placards are large, diamond-shaped color-coded signs that are placed on the outside of transport vehicles indicating the hazards of the cargo. The DOT placards, shown in Figure 4-4, are similar to the labels (the required colors schemes are not depicted).

All motor vehicles, rail cars, and freight containers carrying *any* hazardous waste meeting a hazard class identified in Table 4-5 or *any* hazardous waste over 1000 pounds of those hazard classes identified in Table 4-6 must be placarded. Placarding is not required for etiologic agents, ORM-A, ORM-B, ORM-C, ORM-D, ORM-E, or limited-quantity shipments [49 CFR 172.500(b)(2)]. A transport vehicle that contains two or more classes of materials requiring different placards specified in Table 4-6 in one vehicle may be placarded DANGEROUS instead of using separate placards. However, when the gross weight of *all* hazardous wastes listed in Table 4-6 is less than 1000 pounds, no placard is required for those materials.

Placarding hazardous wastes is the joint responsibility of the shipper (generator) and the carrier (transporter). Shippers who offer a hazardous waste for transport by highway must provide the carrier with the placards required for the waste prior to or at the time when it is offered for transport, unless the carrier's vehicle is already properly placarded [49 CFR 172.500(a)].

Shipping Documentation

Pursuant to 49 CFR 172.205 and 40 CFR 262.20, a person who offers, transports, transfers, or delivers a hazardous waste must use a Uniform Hazardous Waste Manifest, EPA Form 8700-22, as shown in Figure 3-1.

The Uniform Hazardous Waste Manifest is a component of a joint program between DOT and EPA. The standard federal manifest has white numbered boxes and shaded lettered boxes. The shaded lettered boxes are for optional information that a state may require, while the white

Figure 4-4. DOT Placards

Table 4-5. DOT placarding table 1.

If the transport vehicle or freight container contains any material classed (described) as:	The transport vehicle or freight container must be placarded on each side and each end:
Class A explosives	EXPLOSIVES A (1)[1]
Class B explosives	EXPLOSIVES B (2)[2]
Poison A	POISON GAS (4)[1]
Flammable solid (DANGEROUS WHEN WET label only)	FLAMMABLE SOLID W (12)[3]
Radioactive material	RADIOACTIVE (16)[4]
Radioactive material:	
Uranium hexafluoride, fissile (containing >1.0% U^{235})	RADIOACTIVE (16)[4,5] and CORROSIVE (17)[6]
Uranium hexafluoride, low specific activity (1.0% or less U^{235})	RADIOACTIVE (16)[4,5] and CORROSIVE (17)[6]

[1]See §172.510(a).

[2]EXPLOSIVES B placard not required if the freight container, motor vehicle, or rail car contains class A explosives and is placarded EXPLOSIVES A as required.

[3]FLAMMABLE SOLID "W" placard is required only when the DANGEROUS WHEN WET label is specified in §172.101 for a material classed as a Flammable solid.

[4]Applies only to any quantity of packages bearing the RADIOACTIVE YELLOW III label. (See § 172.403.)

[5]See §173.403, for full-load shipments of radioactive materials meeting the definition of low specific activity when transported pursuant to §173.425(b).

[6]CORROSIVE placard not required for shipments of less than 1000 pounds gross weight.

numbered boxes are required to be filled out by all users of a manifest. A transporter must comply only with the requirements in the state of origin and the consignment (destination) state. A transporter is not bound to comply with the state manifest requirements of the states through which the transporter travels (49 *FR* 10492, March 20, 1984).

The manifest, a one-page form with carbon copies for the participants in the shipment, must identify the type and quantity of waste, the generator, the transporter, and the facility to which the waste is being shipped. The manifest must accompany the waste wherever it travels. When the waste reaches its final destination, the owner or operator of the designated facility signs the manifest and returns a copy to the generator to confirm the arrival. The transporter must retain a copy of that manifest for at least three years.

Emergency Response Information

Under 49 CFR 172.600, a new section has been added to the Hazardous Materials Communication Regulations. The new section is 49 CFR 172.600—Emergency Response Information.

Table 4-6. DOT placarding table 2.

If the transport vehicle or freight container contains 1000 lbs. or more of a material classed (described) as:	The transport vehicle or freight container must be placarded on each side and each end:
Class C explosives	DANGEROUS (18)[1, 9]
Blasting agents	BLASTING AGENTS (3)[9, 10]
Nonflammable gas	NONFLAMMABLE GAS (2)[8]
Nonflammable gas (chlorine)	CHLORINE (7)[7]
Nonflammable gas (fluorine)	POISON (15)
Nonflammable gas (O_2, cryogenic liquid)	OXYGEN (8)[2]
Flammable gas	FLAMMABLE GAS (5)[8]
Combustible liquid	COMBUSTIBLE (10)[3, 4]
Flammable liquid	FLAMMABLE (9)
Flammable solid	FLAMMABLE SOLID (11)[5]
Oxidizer	*OXIDIZER (13)[9, 10]
Organic peroxide	ORGANIC PEROXIDE (14)
Poison B	POISON (15)
Corrosive material	CORROSIVE (17)[6]
Irritating material	DANGEROUS (18)

[1]Applies only to a Class C explosive required to be labeled with an EXPLOSIVE C label.
[2][Reserved]
[3]COMBUSTIBLE placard required only when material classed as a combustible liquid is transported in a packaging having a rated capacity of more than 110 gallons, a cargo tank, or a tank car.
[4]A FLAMMABLE placard may be used on a cargo tank or portable tank during transportation by highway, rail or water, and on a compartmented tank car containing materials classed as Flammable liquid and Combustible liquid. However, no EMPTY placard may be displayed on an "empty" Combustible liquid tank car.
[5]Except when offered for transportation by water, a FLAMMABLE placard may be displayed in place of a FLAMMABLE SOLID placard except when a DANGEROUS WHEN WET label is specified for the material in §172.101. (See table 1. this section.)
[6]See §173.245(b) of this subchapter for authorized exceptions.
[7]CHLORINE placard required only for a packaging having a rated capacity of more than 110 gallons; the NON-FLAMMABLE GAS placard for packagings having a rated capacity of 110 gallons or less.
[8]A NON-FLAMMABLE GAS placard is not required on a motor vehicle displaying a FLAMMABLE GAS placard.
[9]BLASTING AGENTS, OXIDIZER, and DANGEROUS placards need not be displayed if a freight container, motor vehicle, or rail car also contains Class A or Class B explosives and is placarded EXPLOSIVES A or EXPLOSIVES B as required.
[10]Except for shipments by water, OXIDIZER placard need not be displayed if a freight container, motor vehicle, or rail car also contains blasting agents and is placarded BLASTING AGENT as required.

This section requires new pieces of information. First, a copy of an Emergency Response Information Form must be attached to each hazardous material or waste shipping document, outlining the following items:

1. DOT basic description of the hazardous materials
2. Immediate health hazards
3. Risks
4. Immediate precautions to be taken

5. Immediate methods for handling small or large fires
6. Methods for handling small or large leaks
7. Preliminary first aid required

The Emergency Response Information Form must be prepared by the shipper or generator. However, a copy of the actual DOT Emergency Response Guide may be attached to the shipping document instead. To determine the particular Emergency Response Guide required for each hazardous material shipment offered by the shipper, check the UN or NA identification number in the basic description. Then cross-reference this in the *DOT Emergency Response Guide*.

Emergency Response Guides and Information Forms may be stapled or attached to shipping documents, or they may be glued or affixed to the back of the shipping document.

A telephone number must be provided with each individual shipment of hazardous waste. If one telephone number provides all the emergency response information for all hazardous materials or waste listed on a document, then enter the words EMERGENCY CONTACT, followed by that telephone number, somewhere on the face of the shipping document. If more than one telephone number is provided on a shipping document, then list each individual telephone number after the DOT Basic Description.

The telephone number may be the number of any person or organization capable of, and accepting responsibility for, providing emergency response and accident information 24 hours a day, 7 days a week. That can be an employee or officer of the shipper or generator, or it can be an organization such as CHEMTREC.

Chapter **5**

General Standards for Waste Management Facilities

This chapter outlines the requirements for owners and operators of hazardous waste management facilities. These requirements are divided into sections addressing the general facility standards, groundwater monitoring, closure activities, and financial requirements for hazardous waste management facilities.

APPLICABILITY

Any person who treats, stores, or disposes of hazardous waste is considered an owner or operator of a treatment, storage, or disposal facility (TSDF) (also referred to as a hazardous waste management facility or a designated facility) and is subject to the requirements of Part 264 or 265 *unless* excluded by 40 CFR 264/265.1.

Treatment is any method, technique, or process, including neutralization, designed to change the physical, chemical, or biological character or composition of any hazardous waste so as to neutralize such waste, or so as to recover energy or material resources from the waste, or so as to render such waste nonhazardous or less hazardous; safer to transport, store, or dispose of; or amenable to recovery, amenable to storage, or reduced in volume [40 CFR 260.10].

Storage is the holding of hazardous waste for a temporary period, at the end of which the hazardous waste is treated, disposed of, or stored elsewhere [40 CFR 260.10].

Disposal is the discharge, deposit, injection, dumping, spilling, leaking, or placing of any solid waste or hazardous waste into or on any land or water so that such solid waste or hazardous waste or any constituent thereof may enter the environment or be emitted into the air or discharged into any waters, including groundwaters [40 CFR 260.10].

Exclusions

As stated in 40 CFR 264.1(g) and 265.1(c), the following persons or activities are excluded from the requirements of Parts 264 and 265:

- Facilities that are state-approved to exclusively handle small-quantity generator waste (<100 kg/mo).
- A totally enclosed treatment facility as defined in 40 CFR 260.10. It is important to note that the exemption is for the unit itself, effluent is not excluded. In addition, a totally enclosed treatment facility must meet the following according to OSWER Directives 9432.01(83) and 9432.02(84):
  1. Completely contained on all sides
  2. Pose negligible potential for escape of constituents to the environment
  3. It is connected directly to a pipeline or similar totally enclosed device to an industrial production process.
- A generator accumulating hazardous waste in compliance with 40 CFR 262.34.
- A farmer disposing of waste pesticides in compliance with 40 CFR 262.51.
- The management of wastes in an elementary neutralization unit or a wastewater treatment unit as defined in 40 CFR 260.10.
- A person engaged in the immediate treatment or containment of a discharge of hazardous waste.
- A transporter storing manifested waste at a transfer facility in compliance with 40 CFR 262.30.
- The addition of absorbent material to waste or the addition of waste to absorbent material.

Although these persons or activities are for the most part excluded from Parts 264 and 265, there are regulatory references to these Parts for some of these persons or activities. For example, generators accumulating hazardous waste on-site must comply with specified sections of Part 265. (See 40 CFR 262.34 for these references.)

Part 264 versus Part 265

The basic difference between Part 265 (interim status standards) and Part 264 (final operating standards) is that the interim status standards were written for facilities treating, storing, or disposing of RCRA hazardous waste when the Phase I regulations first went into effect on November 19, 1980. Congress wanted EPA to establish interim standards that would allow facilities to continue to operate as though they had a permit while EPA developed the more stringent Part 264 standards for new and existing facilities. A facility received interim status by filing a RCRA 40 CFR 3010 notification (EPA Form 8700-12, *Notification of Hazardous Waste Activity*) by August 26, 1980, and a Part A permit application by November 19, 1980. (Refer to Chapter 7 for a more detailed discussion of interim status.) An owner or operator who qualified for and obtained interim status remains subject to the Part 265 standards until the final administrative disposition of the facility's permit application is made. The Part 265 standards are self-implementing, whereas the Part 264 standards are part of the conditions of a permit as discussed in Chapter 7.

GENERAL FACILITY STANDARDS

The general facility standards are applicable to all RCRA hazardous waste management facilities unless specifically excluded. The general facility standards are found in Subpart B of Parts 264 and 265 and are essentially the same for both permitted and interim status facilities. Any differences are noted in the following text. The general facility standards are separated into sections:

- Notification and record keeping requirements
- General waste handling requirements
- Preparedness and prevention
- Contingency plan and emergency procedures
- Manifest system

Notification and Record Keeping

This section addresses the requirements for:

- EPA identification number
- Required notices
- Record keeping

- Operating log
- Biennial report

EPA Identification Number

An owner or operator of a hazardous waste management facility must have an EPA identification number to accept hazardous waste from off-site sources. The EPA identification number is obtained by submitting EPA Form 8700-12. Many facilities also are generators because of the derived-from rule; therefore their site-specific EPA identification number also must include generator status [40 CFR 264/265.11].

Required Notices

Before transferring ownership or operational control of a hazardous waste management facility during its operating life, or of a land disposal facility during its post-closure care period, the owner or operator must notify the new owner or operator in writing of the requirements of Subtitle C of RCRA. However, even if the old owner or operator fails to comply with this requirement, the new owner or operator is still required to comply with all of the applicable RCRA regulations [45 *FR* 33179, May 19, 1980 and 40 CFR 264.12(c) and 265.12(b)].

Importing Hazardous Waste

Hazardous waste management facilities receiving waste from a foreign source must notify the EPA Regional Office of the shipment at least four weeks before receiving the shipment. Subsequent shipments from the same foreign source containing the same waste do not require notification [40 CFR 264/265.12(a)].

It is important to note that when importing hazardous wastes into the United States, the importer, who must be a U.S. citizen, must comply with Section 13 of the Toxic Substances Control Act (TSCA). This section requires all importers of *chemical substances* (see Chapter 16 for definition) to certify either that the shipment is in compliance with all applicable rules and regulations under TSCA, or that it is not subject to TSCA. Hazardous wastes that are not subject to TSCA under Section 13 (i.e., materials that are not included under the definition of chemical substance) are active pesticide ingredients, drugs, cosmetics, and nuclear materials. In determining whether a material is in compliance with TSCA, there are two primary concerns: (1) every chemical component in the waste stream must be an "existing chemical," meaning that the chemical must be included in EPA's TSCA Chemical Substances Inventory, and (2) none of the chemical components of the waste stream can be prohibited from importation. It should be noted that a material must be a hazardous waste to be subject to RCRA, whereas a material must be defined as a chemical substance to be subject to TSCA. Hazardous waste is a subset of chemical substances. Regulatory information pertaining to the import status of chemical substances under TSCA can be obtained from EPA's TSCA Assistance hotline at 202-554-1404.

Record Keeping

All records that are required to be maintained for the various regulations must be made available to any EPA-designated inspector upon request. Unless otherwise specified, all records must be maintained for at least three years after the recorded activity ceases. In addition, a copy of all records containing waste locations and their quantities must be submitted at closure, if applicable.

Operating Log

An owner or operator must maintain a written operating record (log) at the facility until closure [40 CFR 264/265.73]. The contents of the operating record must include the following:

- Description of waste received and method, quantity, and date of treatment, storage, or disposal.
- Location and quantity of all hazardous waste at the facility (landfills require a map).
- Records and results of waste analyses.
- Details of any instances requiring implementation of the contingency plan.
- Records and results of inspections.
- Results of required groundwater monitoring analyses.
- Waste minimization statement if applicable.
- Closure cost estimates.
- Post-closure cost estimates (land disposal facilities only).
- Notices to generators (Part 264 only).

Biennial Report

The owner or operator must submit a biennial report before March 1 of each even-numbered year [40 CFR 264/265.75]. It is important to note that most states require annual reporting. The required contents of the report are:

- The facility's EPA identification number.
- The EPA identification number of each generator that sent waste to the facility.
- The quantity and description of each hazardous waste received.
- The method of treatment, storage, or disposal for each waste.
- The most recent closure and post-closure cost estimate.
- A signed statement certifying the accuracy of the information.

General Waste Handling Requirements

This section addresses the following waste handling requirements:

- Security
- Personnel training
- General waste analysis
- Unstable waste handling
- Facility inspections
- Location standards

Security

An owner or operator must either establish a security system or upgrade an existing system to prevent unknowing entry and to minimize unauthorized entry of any person or livestock onto the active portion of a facility. Either a 24-hour surveillance system or an access barrier around the active portion of a facility is required. A fence with locked gates is considered an access barrier. Signs must be prominently displayed along the periphery of the active portion, warning that entering the active portion is potentially hazardous [40 CFR 264/265.14].

Personnel Training

Each facility must establish a training program for appropriate facility personnel [40 CFR 264/265.16]. *Facility personnel* means all persons who work at, or oversee the operations of a hazardous waste facility, and whose actions or failure to act may result in noncompliance with the requirements of 40 CFR 264 or 265 [40 CFR 260.10]. The purpose of the training requirements is to reduce the potential for errors that might threaten human health or the environment by ensuring that facility personnel acquire expertise in the areas to which they are assigned. In addition to the RCRA requirements, the Occupational Safety and Health Administration (OSHA) has recently established personnel training requirements for facility personnel involved in hazardous waste operations.

RCRA Requirements

The personnel training requirements under RCRA are:

- Facility personnel must successfully complete a training program that ensures the facility's compliance with the requirements of RCRA.
- The training program must be directed by a person trained in hazardous waste management procedures.
- The training program must be designed to ensure that facility personnel are able to respond adequately during an emergency situation.
- Facility personnel must successfully complete the program within six months of their assignment.
- Facility personnel must take part in an annual review of the training program.
- The owner or operator must maintain documentation at the facility.

The contents and format for the program are unspecified in the regulations. EPA accepts the use of on-the-job training as a substitute for, or supplement to, formal classroom instruction (45 *FR* 33182, May 19, 1980). However, the content, schedule, and techniques used for on-the-job training must be described in the training records required to be maintained at the facility and will be subject to approval during the permitting process.

OSHA Requirements

On March 6, 1989 (54 *FR* 92921), OSHA promulgated a final rule for the protection of the health and safety of employees engaged in hazardous waste operations.

Only some of these regulations, 20 CFR 1910.120(p), are applicable to hazardous waste management facilities. Guidance on health and safety also is contained in the *Occupational Safety and Health Guidance Man-*

ual for Hazardous Waste Site Activities, NIOSH/OSHA/USCG/EPA, 1985.

The major elements of the OSHA regulations regarding employees at RCRA hazardous waste management facilities, include:

Safety and health program: Each employer must develop and implement a written safety and health program for its employees involved in hazardous waste operations. The program must identify, evaluate, and control safety and health hazards for the purpose of employee protection.

Hazard communication: Employees, contractors, and subcontractors are to be informed of the degree and nature of any safety and health hazards specific to the work site.

Medical surveillance program: A medical surveillance program must be instituted for employees involved in hazardous waste operations. Examinations are to be conducted prior to an assignment, annually, upon an employee's termination, and as soon as possible where an employee has symptoms that may indicate an exposure.

Decontamination program: Decontamination procedures must be developed and implemented for employees. The purpose of this program is to minimize the contact of contaminated personnel and equipment with uncontaminated equipment and personnel.

New technology program: A program for developing and implementing procedures must be instituted for the introduction of effective new technologies and equipment developed for the improved protection of employees. These new technologies may include use of foams, absorbents, adsorbents, neutralizers, and so forth.

Material handling program: At facilities where drums or containers will be handled by employees, a special material handling program must be developed. The purpose of this program is to ensure that employees handle drums properly.

Training program: A training program that includes both initial (24 hours) and refresher (8 hours annually) training must be provided to employees before they are permitted to engage in hazardous waste operations that could expose them to hazardous substances, safety, or health hazards, as shown in Table 5-1. A written certificate attesting that they have successfully completed the program is required.

Emergency Response Program

In addition to the health and safety program, each employer must establish an emergency response plan [29 CFR 1910.120(p)(8)]. Many of

Table 5-1. Personnel training requirements.

Applicable Staff		
General site employees	____	**24** hours of initial or equivalent
	____	**8** hours annual refresher
Site emergency response personnel	____	Trained to level of competency
	____	Annual refresher

the requirements may already be addressed by the facility's Preparedness and Prevention and Contingency Plan and its Emergency Procedures program. The emergency response plan must be part of the required written safety and health plan. The plan must address:

- Pre-emergency planning and coordination with outside parties.
- Personnel roles, lines of authority, and communication.
- Emergency recognition and prevention.
- Safe distances and places of refuge.
- Site security and control.
- Evacuation routes and procedures.
- Decontamination procedures.
- Emergency medical treatment and first aid.
- Emergency alerting and response procedures.
- Critique of response and follow-up.
- Personal protective equipment and emergency equipment.

The employees must be trained specifically for the emergency response procedures before an employee is called upon to perform in an emergency [29 CFR 1910.120(p)(8)(iii)]. This training must include the elements of the emergency response plan discussed above, standard operating procedures, and personal protective equipment to be worn during emergency operations.

General Waste Analysis

An owner or operator of a hazardous waste management facility must obtain a detailed analysis of representative samples of any waste before that waste is managed. Beyond the general waste analysis requirements, the regulations for each specific unit (e.g., surface impoundment, incinerators, land treatment area) addressed in Chapter 6 include additional waste analysis requirements that are appropriate for that unit [40 CFR 264/265.13(a)]. The general waste analysis requirements distinguish between two types of hazardous waste management facilities: on-site and off-site facilities.

Waste Analysis Plan

Each facility must prepare and maintain a waste analysis plan to implement the waste analysis requirements. The objective of a waste analysis plan is to describe the procedures that will be undertaken to obtain sufficient information about a waste to ensure that a facility will handle the waste in accordance with its permit or interim status requirements. The waste analysis plan establishes the hazardous waste sampling and analysis procedures that the facility must follow. These objectives are the same for both on-site and off-site facilities. However, because on-site facilities are better acquainted with the waste generation process and its characteristics, off-site facilities are required to conduct more frequent checks on wastes than on-site facilities.

The regulations do not specify a format for waste analysis plans. However, when preparing a plan, an owner or operator should consult EPA's *Waste Analysis Plans: A Guidance Manual*, October 1984, EPA/530-SW-84-012.

Unstable Waste Handling Requirements

Ignitable, reactive, and incompatible wastes must be handled in such a way as to ensure the prevention of accidental ignition or reaction. While ignitable or reactive wastes are being handled, smoking and operations involving open flames (e.g., welding activities) must be limited to specially designed locations. "No Smoking" signs must be conspicuously placed wherever there is a potential hazard from ignitable or reactive wastes [40 CFR 264/265.17].

Facility Inspections

An owner or operator must inspect the facility for deterioration, malfunction, and any operating error that may cause a release or a threat of a release [40 CFR 264/265.15(a)]. The owner or operator is required to develop and follow an inspection schedule written for that facility based on the facility's critical processes, equipment, and structures, and on the potential for failure and the rate of any processes that may promote deterioration.

If the owner or operator finds any malfunctioning equipment or structures, the equipment or structure must be repaired or replaced immediately [40 CFR 264/265.15(c)]. The inspections must be logged and maintained in the facility's operating record for at least three years [40 CFR 264/265.15(d)].

Location Standards

Site-specific location standards based solely on hydrogeologic considerations are nonexistent although the groundwater protection standards, as well as general design and operating requirements, contain performance standards that implicitly involve hydrologic and geologic factors. Current regulations do not provide the legal basis to deny a RCRA permit based on sensitive locations, such as vulnerable groundwater formations, although a RCRA Section 7003 order can be used if there *may* be an imminent threat to health or the environment. (See Chapter 10 for further explanation of this topic.)

Currently, the only location restrictions are:

- The facility must be at least 200 feet from an active (during the last 10,000 years) Holocene fault.
- Facilities in a 100-year floodplain must be designed to prevent washout from 100-year floods.

Facilities are not allowed in a 100-year floodplain unless one of the three following conditions is met:

- The facility is protected, using dikes or equivalent measures, from washout during a 100-year flood.
- All hazardous wastes can be removed to safe ground prior to flooding.
- It can be demonstrated that no adverse effects to human health or the environment will occur should flood waters reach the hazardous wastes.

New facilities in active fault zones are prohibited. However, only those facilities that will be located in certain political jurisdictions listed in Appendix VI to 40 CFR Part 264 are required to demonstrate compliance with these standards. These jurisdictions include areas in Alaska, Arizona, and Colorado, and the entire state of California.

In addition to a location that satisfies the floodplain and seismic standards, Executive Order 11990 (Protection of Wetlands) must be considered for facilities located on federally owned lands that may potentially have an impact on wetlands in the event of a facility failure.

More stringent location standards, as mandated by HSWA, are expected to be issued in 1992. The purpose of these standards will be to create national requirements for the location of hazardous waste management facilities. These requirements will be contained under Subpart Z to Part 264 and will include location restrictions based on proximity to populations, vulnerable hydrogeology, seismic zones, 100-year floodplains, poor foundation areas, subsidence-prone areas, landslide-prone areas, wetlands, and karst terranes (limestone areas with fissures, sinkholes, underground streams, and caverns).

For further information concerning current location standards, consult EPA's *Permit Writer's Guidance Manual for Hazardous Waste Land Storage and Disposal Facilities*, February 1985.

Preparedness and Prevention

A facility must be operated and maintained in a manner that will minimize the possibility of any fire, explosion, or unplanned sudden or nonsudden release. These requirements, found in 40 CFR, Subpart C of Part 264 and Part 265, require a facility to address:

- Required equipment
- Aisle space
- Outside assistance

Required Equipment

The facility is required to possess certain equipment. This equipment includes an alarm system, a communication device to contact emergency personnel (e.g., telephone, air horn), portable fire extinguishers, fire control equipment, and an adequate fire-fighting water supply system in the form of hoses, hydrants, or automatic sprinkler systems. This equipment must be routinely tested and maintained in proper working order [40 CFR 264/265.32].

Aisle Space

There must be adequate aisle space to allow the unobstructed movement (i.e., deployment and evacuation) of emergency equipment and personnel to any area of the facility. The regulations do not specify the aisle space; this should be determined upon consultation with local emergency organizations [40 CFR 264/265.34].

Outside Assistance

Facilities must make prior arrangements with local emergency organizations and personnel for an emergency response. The arrangements should include notification of the types of waste handled, detailed layout of the facility, facility contacts, and specific agreements with various state and local emergency response organizations. Refusal of any state or local authorities to enter into such arrangements must be documented and noted in the facility's operating record [40 CFR 264/265.37].

Contingency Plan and Emergency Procedures

Each facility must prepare a contingency plan designed to minimize hazards in the case of a sudden or nonsudden release, fire, explosion, or similar emergency. If the owner or operator has previously prepared a Spill Prevention, Control, and Countermeasure Plan (SPCC) in accordance with either 40 CFR Part 112 or 300 or some other emergency or contingency plan, that plan needs only to be amended to incorporate hazardous waste management provisions that are sufficient to comply with these requirements. The provisions of the plan must be carried out immediately whenever there is a fire, an explosion, or a release of hazardous waste or constituents [40 CFR 264/265.51].

A copy of the contingency plan must be maintained at the facility and submitted to all local police, fire department, hospitals, and emergency response teams [40 CFR 264/265.52]. The plan also must be submitted by interim status facilities to EPA upon request. Permitted facilities would already have submitted the plan as part of their permit application. The contents of the plan must include:

- A description of the planned response actions that will be undertaken in the event of an emergency.
- Information on any arrangements with local and state organizations to provide emergency response support when needed.

- A list of current names, addresses, and phone numbers of all persons qualified as emergency coordinators. There must be at least one employee on-site or close by and on call who is the designated *emergency coordinator*.
- A list of all available emergency equipment located at the facility, including the location and a physical description of each item and a brief outline of the equipment's capabilities.

The contingency plan must be amended:

- Whenever there are revisions to applicable interim status regulations.
- Whenever there are revisions to a facility's permit.
- If the plan fails in an emergency.
- If there are changes in the emergency equipment at the facility.
- If there are changes in the person(s) qualified to act as facility emergency coordinator.
- If there are changes in the facility design, construction, operation, maintenance, or other circumstances that materially increase the potential for fire, explosions, or releases of hazardous waste or change the response requirements in an emergency situation.

Emergency Procedures

In accordance with 40 CFR 264/265.56, whenever there is an imminent or an actual emergency situation, the emergency coordinator must:

- Immediately activate the facility alarm system, notify all facility personnel, and, if needed, notify appropriate state or local agencies.
- Institute measures to prevent the spread of fires and explosions to other wastes at the facility.
- Immediately assess the possible hazards to the environment and to human health outside the facility.
- Immediately after the emergency, provide for the treating, storing, or disposing of any contaminated material as a result of the emergency.
- In the event of a release, fire, or explosion, identify the source, character, and amount of materials involved. If any hazardous substances are released into the environment constituting a Superfund reportable quantity, the owner or operator must immediately contact the National Response Center at 800-424-8802. (See Chapter 12 for further explanation of this topic.)

The owner or operator must submit a written report to EPA, within 15 days, for any incident that requires implementation of the contingency plan [40 CFR 264/265.56(j)].

The written report must include:

- Name, address, and telephone number of the owner or operator and the facility.
- Date, time, and type of accident (e.g., fire, explosion).
- Name and quantity of materials involved.
- The extent of injuries.
- An assessment of actual or potential hazards to human health or the environment.
- Estimated quantity and disposition of recovered material following the incident.

Manifest System

The manifest requirements are applicable only to facilities accepting hazardous waste from off-site sources. A *facility representative* must sign and date each copy of the manifest, giving one copy to the transporter immediately. Within 30 days, a signed copy of the manifest must be sent to the generator, and a copy of the manifest must be retained for at least three years in the facility's files [40 CFR 264/265.71]. If a shipment is initiated from a hazardous waste management facility, the facility must comply with the Part 262 generator standards, which require that the receiving facility be a *designated facility*.

Manifest Discrepancies

A *manifest discrepancy* is a significant difference between the type or quantity of waste received and the type or quantity of waste described on the manifest. *Significant discrepancies* include variations of 10 percent or more by weight of bulk waste, any variation in piece count (e.g., one drum), or a difference in waste description [40 CFR 264/265.72(a)]. Upon discovery of a significant discrepancy involving information contained in the manifest, the owner or operator must reconcile it with the generator or transporter verbally. If the discrepancy is not resolved within 15 days after receipt of the waste, the owner or operator must notify EPA in writing, describing the discrepancy [40 CFR 264/265.72].

Unmanifested Waste Report

If a facility receives a shipment of unmanifested waste that is not excluded by 40 CFR 261.5, the owner or operator must prepare and submit to EPA an unmanifested waste report (EPA Form 8700-13B) [40 CFR 264/265.76].

GROUNDWATER MONITORING

The goal of the groundwater monitoring program is to detect, identify, and clean up any releases of hazardous waste or constituents from land disposal units that have entered the underlying groundwater in sufficient quantities to cause a "significant" change in groundwater quality.

The interim status regulations under Part 265 establish a two-stage groundwater program designed to detect and characterize the release of any hazardous waste or constituents, whereas the Part 264 regulations establish a three-stage program designed to detect, evaluate, and clean up groundwater contamination from land disposal units.

Groundwater Monitoring at Interim Status Units

Applicability

Owners or operators of interim status hazardous waste management facilities with land treatment areas, landfills, waste piles, and/or surface impoundments must have a groundwater monitoring program capable of evaluating the impact of the facility on the quality of the groundwater underlying the site [40 CFR 265.90(a)].

The groundwater monitoring program is to be carried out during the *active life* of the hazardous waste management unit, which includes the closure and post-closure period. The post-closure period uses 30 years as a baseline, but this time period can be reduced or extended by EPA when appropriate [40 CFR 265.117(a)(1)].

Waivers

Some facilities may qualify for a partial or complete waiver [40 CFR 265.90(c)] of the monitoring requirements if the owner or operator can demonstrate that there is a low potential for hazardous waste (or waste constituents) to migrate from the facility via the underlying groundwater to surface water or water-supply wells. Only a small percentage of interim status facilities would be expected to qualify for a waiver of all monitoring requirements based on the underlying hydrogeology. The owner or operator claiming such a waiver must keep a detailed written demonstration, certified by a qualified geologist or geotechnical engineer at the facility [40 CFR 265.90(c)].

Pursuant to 40 CFR 265.90(k), the written demonstration must establish the following:

1. The potential for migration of hazardous waste or hazardous waste constituents from the facility to the underlying groundwater by an evaluation of:
   - A water balance of precipitation, evapotranspiration, runoff, and infiltration.
   - Unsaturated zone characteristics (i.e., geologic materials, physical properties, and depth to groundwater).
2. The potential for hazardous waste or hazardous waste constituents that enter the underlying groundwater to migrate to a water supply well or surface water, by an evaluation of:
   - Saturated zone characteristics (i.e., geologic materials, physical properties, and rate of groundwater flow).
   - The proximity of the facility to water supply wells or surface water.

An additional waiver from the groundwater monitoring program is made for surface impoundments used solely to neutralize corrosive wastes. Such a waiver is based not on hydrogeologic factors but on the premise and documentation that only corrosive wastes will be added to the impoundment, and that the neutralization occurs so rapidly that the waste is no longer corrosive if it migrates out of the impoundment. This waiver also must be certified by "a qualified professional" and maintained at the facility [40 CFR 265.90(e)].

Sampling and Analysis Plan

The owner or operator must develop and follow a groundwater sampling and analysis plan for each monitoring system [40 CFR 265.92(a)]. This plan must be maintained at the facility. Owners or operators also must simultaneously prepare and maintain an outline of a *groundwater quality assessment program* [40 CFR 265.93(a)].

The contents of the sampling and analysis plan must include procedures and techniques for:

- Sample collection
- Sample preservation
- Sample shipment
- Analytical procedures
- Chain-of-custody control

The chain-of-custody program should include sample labels, sample seals, a field log book, a chain-of-custody record, sample analysis request sheets, and a laboratory log book. A detailed description of each element, including sample forms, is available in EPA's *Test Methods for Evaluating Solid Waste: Physical/Chemical Methods*, SW-846.

In accordance with 40 CFR 265.93(a), an *outline* of the groundwater quality assessment program must describe a more comprehensive program than the detection monitoring program. This outline will form the basis of the groundwater quality assessment program if hazardous waste or constituents enter the underlying groundwater. The outline must describe procedures that are capable of determining:

- Whether hazardous waste or constituents have entered the groundwater.
- The rate and extent of migration of hazardous waste or constituents in the groundwater.
- The concentration of hazardous waste or constituents in the groundwater.

Monitoring System

A groundwater monitoring system must be installed in a manner that will yield good-quality groundwater samples for analysis. The monitoring wells must be cased in a manner that maintains the integrity of the monitoring well bore hole. This casing must be screened or perforated and, if necessary, packed with sand or gravel to enable sample collection at depths where appropriate aquifer flow zones exist. The annular space (the space between the bore hole and the well casing) above the selected sampling depth must be sealed with a suitable material, such as bentonite slurry or grout [40 CFR 265.91(a)].

If a facility has more than one hazardous waste management unit, a separate groundwater monitoring system is not necessarily required, provided that the system is adequate to detect any discharge from any of the units. The *waste management area* in this situation would be described by an imaginary line that surrounds all of the units [40 CFR 265.91(b)].

Upgradient Wells

A minimum of one monitoring well must be installed hydraulically upgradient from the waste management area. The number, location, and
depth of the well(s) must be sufficient to yield samples that are representative of the background groundwater quality in the uppermost aquifer
and are not affected by the facility [40 CFR 265.91(a)(1)].

Downgradient Wells

A minimum of three monitoring wells must be installed hydraulically
downgradient of the waste management area. Their number, location,
and depth must ensure the immediate detection of any statistically significant amounts of hazardous waste or hazardous waste constituents
that migrate from the facility to the uppermost aquifer [40 CFR
265.91(a)(2)].

In general, the required minimum number of upgradient and downgradient wells (four) typically is not sufficient to detect contamination.
There are many conditions that can complicate the detection of contaminants in the groundwater. Large multicomponent waste management
areas consisting of several landfills, surface impoundments, or land treatment zones would require a greater number of monitoring wells than the
minimum. The minimum number of wells would be adequate only for a
small unit in which the contaminants and hydrogeology were simple and
well documented.

Detection Monitoring

Detection monitoring, the first stage in the interim status groundwater
monitoring program, is a program developed to determine whether a land
disposal unit has released hazardous waste or constituents into the underlying groundwater in quantities sufficient to cause a significant change
in groundwater quality.

Facilities not qualifying for a waiver from the groundwater monitoring
program are required to install a basic detection monitoring system [40
CFR 265.92(b)]. For one year, the facility owner or operator must conduct quarterly sampling of wells upgradient and downgradient of the
facility to account for seasonal variation. The owner or operator must
analyze samples for:

- Drinking water suitability
- Groundwater quality

- Indicators of groundwater contamination
- Groundwater elevation

The first year of monitoring is intended to establish baseline information (background data) on the underlying groundwater for future statistical comparison, as outlined in Figure 5-1.

Alternate Groundwater Monitoring Program

If an owner or operator assumes or knows that a statistically significant increase (or pH decrease) in one or more of the specified indicator parameters could occur, the owner or operator may install, operate, and maintain an *alternate groundwater monitoring program* [40 CFR 265.90(d)], which allows facilities, suspected or known to be discharging hazardous waste or waste constituents to groundwater, to enter immediately into the assessment phase rather than delay the assessment program a year by doing detection monitoring and background comparisons. An owner or operator who chooses the alternate groundwater monitoring program must submit to EPA a groundwater assessment plan as outlined in 40 CFR 265.93(d)(3).

Monitoring Parameters

To determine if a release has occurred during detection monitoring, the owner or operator must compare monitoring data from downgradient wells to background concentration levels established at the end of the first year for drinking water suitability, groundwater quality, and indicator parameters based on quarterly measurements.

The *parameters of drinking water suitability*—substances used to assess the suitability of the aquifer as a drinking water supply [40 CFR 265.92(b)(1)]—are:

- Arsenic
- Barium
- Cadmium
- Chromium
- Coliform bacteria
- 2,4-D
- Endrin
- Fluoride
- Gross alpha
- Gross beta
- Lead

- Lindane
- Mercury
- Methoxychlor
- Nitrate
- Radium
- Selenium
- Silver
- Toxaphene
- 2,4,5-TP (Silvex)

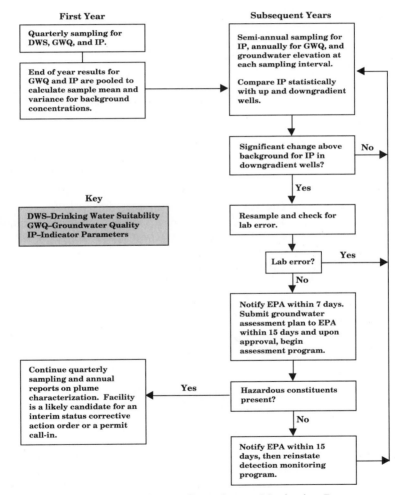

Figure 5-1. Interim Status Groundwater Monitoring Program

Within 15 days of completing each quarterly analysis, the owner or operator must report to EPA the concentrations of drinking water suitability parameters [40 CFR 265.94(a)(2)(i)]. It must be noted in the report if any of these constituents exceed the levels established in Appendix III to 40 CFR Part 265. After the first year, the owner or operator is not required to analyze for drinking water suitability. However, the first year's data will have to be submitted if an assessment plan is required [40 CFR 265.93(d)(3)(iii)].

The *parameters of groundwater quality*—substances used to assess the suitability of the groundwater for other nondrinking purposes [40 CFR 265.92(b)(2)]—are:

- Chloride
- Iron
- Manganese
- Phenols
- Sodium
- Sulfate

During the first year, the owner or operator must establish the initial background concentrations based on quarterly measurements. After the first year, the owner or operator must analyze samples of both upgradient and downgradient wells annually for groundwater quality. Although there is no requirement for the statistical evaluation of these parameters, the data are to be used as a basis for comparison if a groundwater quality assessment program is implemented as required by 40 CFR 265.93(d).

The *indicator parameters,* which are measurements used as gross indicators of whether contamination has occurred [40 CFR 265.92(b)(3)], are:

- pH
- Specific conductance
- Total organic carbon (TOC)
- Total organic halogen (TOX)

During the first year, for each quarterly sampling, at least four replicate measurements must be obtained for each sample from the upgradient well(s); then the initial background arithmetic mean and variance must be determined by pooling the replicate measurements for the respective indicator parameter concentrations. For the downgradient wells, initial background concentrations must be obtained based on quarterly sampling [40 CFR 265.92(c)(2)]. After background values have been established from the first year, subsequent comparisons of both upgradient and downgradient indicator parameter values are made with the initial background values of the upgradient well only.

In subsequent years of monitoring, all monitoring wells must be sampled for indicator parameters semiannually. A mean and variance, based on four replicate measurements, must be determined for each of the indicator parameters.

By March 1 of each calendar year, the concentrations of each of the indicator parameters (as well as the groundwater elevations) must be reported to EPA for each monitoring well. Each monitoring well must be compared statistically with its initial background arithmetic mean and variance of each indicator parameter derived from the first year's quarterly sampling of the upgradient well, and subsequent means and variances of each indicator parameter derived from all wells, including the upgradient well [40 CFR 265.93(b)]. The comparison must consider each of the wells individually in the monitoring system.

Statistical Comparisons

Pursuant to 40 CFR 265.93(b), the owner or operator must use the Student's t-test to determine statistically significant changes in the concentrations of an indicator parameter in groundwater samples compared to the initial background concentration of that indicator parameter. There are different types of Student's t-test available. The interim status regulations, however, do not require the use of a specific method.

The comparison must consider individually each of the wells in the monitoring system. For three of the indicator parameters (specific conductance, total organic carbon, and total organic halogen) a single-tailed Student's t-test must be used at the 0.01 level of significance for increases over background. The test for pH uses a two-tailed test because pH increases or decreases can be significant.

Significant Changes

If the comparison for any of the *downgradient wells* shows a significant increase (or any change in pH), the affected wells must be resampled and samples split into two (duplicates) for a qualitative check for possible laboratory error. The samples may be split into four replicates and another t-test run, but this is not required [40 CFR 265.93(c)(2)].

If this resampling indicates that the change was due to laboratory error, the owner or operator should continue with the detection monitoring program [40 CFR 265.93(d)(1)]. However, if resampling shows that the significant change was not a result of laboratory error, the owner or operator must notify EPA within 7 days that contamination may have occurred. Within 15 days of that notification, the owner or operator must submit to EPA a groundwater quality assessment plan, based on the required assessment outline, certified by a qualified geologist or a geotechnical engineer [40 CFR 265.93(d)(1)].

If the comparison for the *upgradient wells* shows a significant increase (or pH decrease), the owner or operator must submit this information to EPA without a qualitative laboratory check pursuant to 40 CFR 265.94(a)(2)(ii). The groundwater quality assessment phase is not triggered when there is a significant change in upgradient wells. The owner or operator must, however, submit this information to EPA [40 CFR 265.93(c)(1)].

If a facility never detects a statistically significant increase in any of the wells for the indicator parameters, and an assessment plan is never done, detection monitoring for groundwater quality and indicator parameters continues on an annual and a semiannual basis, respectively, through closure and throughout the post-closure period.

Assessment Monitoring

If a significant change in water quality is discovered during the detection monitoring phase, the owner or operator must undertake a more comprehensive groundwater monitoring program called *assessment monitoring*.

Because parameters used in detection monitoring are nonspecific, a statistically significant change in a parameter may not necessarily signify leakage into the aquifer. Thus, the first step is to determine whether hazardous waste constituents have indeed migrated into the groundwater. Then, the owner or operator must determine the vertical and horizontal concentration profiles of all hazardous waste constituents in the plume(s) emanating from the waste management area. In addition, the owner or operator must establish the rate and extent of contaminant migration [40 CFR 265.93(d)(3)].

The information developed during assessment monitoring is used by EPA to evaluate the need for corrective action at the facility. If corrective action is necessary, EPA may issue an enforcement order compelling corrective action under Section 3008(h) prior to or in conjunction with the issuance of a permit (see Chapter 9 for further information).

Assessment Monitoring Plan

Owners or operators required to conduct plume characterization activities for the assessment program are required to have a *written* assessment monitoring plan. According to 40 CFR 265.93(d)(3), the required elements of the plan include:

- Number, location, and depth of wells.
- Sampling and analytical methods to be used.
- Evaluation procedures of groundwater data.
- A schedule of assessment monitoring implementation.

If the assessment confirms that hazardous constituents have entered the groundwater, the owner or operator must continue the assessment on a quarterly basis until final closure of the facility or until a permit is issued [40 CFR 265.93(d)(7)]. If the initial assessment confirming contamination was performed during post-closure, no subsequent quarterly monitoring is required [40 CFR 265.93(d)(7)(ii)]. However, this type of facility would be a likely candidate for a post-closure permit or an interim status corrective action order. In applying for a post-closure permit, the owner or operator would be required to conduct a comprehensive groundwater characterization program to generate the information that is required for the permit application found in 40 CFR 270.14(c)(8).

By March 1 of each calendar year, the owner or operator must submit to EPA a report containing the results of the facility's assessment program, which must include the calculated (or measured) rate of migration of the hazardous waste or hazardous waste constituents for the reporting period.

If this assessment confirms that no hazardous constituents have entered the groundwater, EPA must be notified within 15 days of the determination with a written report. The owner or operator may then reinstate the detection monitoring program or enter into a consent agreement with EPA to follow a revised protocol designed to avoid false triggers [40 CFR 265.93(d)(6)].

Groundwater Monitoring at Permitted Units

Introduction

Whereas the principal objective of the Part 265 groundwater monitoring program is to identify and assess releases from land disposal units, the objective of the Part 264 groundwater monitoring program (for existing facilities) is to establish site-specific monitoring programs to characterize any leachate and to ensure that corrective action is taken to prevent leachate migration beyond the waste management area. To achieve this goal, the regulations establish a three-step program designed to detect,

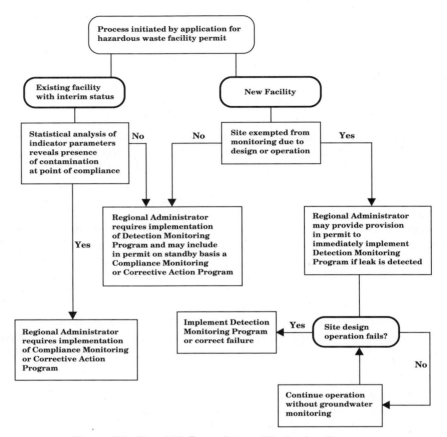

Figure 5-2. Part 264 Groundwater Monitoring Program

evaluate, and clean up groundwater contamination arising from leaks or discharges from regulated units, as outlined in Figure 5-2. A *regulated unit* is any land disposal unit that accepted waste after July 26, 1982. *All* regulated units are subject to the Subpart F, Part 264, groundwater monitoring requirements [40 CFR 265.90(a)]. Thus even interim status units will at some point have to comply with the Part 264 groundwater monitoring requirements.

Applicability

An interim status facility must comply with the Part 265 requirements until the final administrative disposition is made concerning the facility's permit. When a permit is issued for a unit, the owner or operator is then subject to the conditions of the permit, which are based on the Part 264 standards. Thus, an interim status unit that is a regulated unit follows the Part 265 groundwater monitoring program requirements only until a permit is issued [40 CFR 264.3].

The groundwater protection requirements of Part 264 define a general set of responsibilities that the owner or operator must meet; however, the specific requirements are tailored to the individual facility through its permit. The permit provisions concerning groundwater are based on 40 CFR 264.90 through 264.100 and 40 CFR 270.14(6), (7), and (8).

The nature of the monitoring program in the permit will depend on the information available at the time of permitting. The key question is whether a regulated unit has begun to leak. For new units this is not an issue. For existing units, there should be a reliable base of information that can be used to determine whether hazardous constituents have entered the groundwater.

Variances

There are four variances from the Part 264 groundwater monitoring requirements available to owners and operators [40 CFR 264.90(b)]. These variances, which are applied for through the submittal of the Part B permit application (see Chapter 7 for further information), are as follows:

1. EPA finds that a regulated unit is an engineered structure, does not receive or contain free liquids or wastes containing free liquids, is designed and operated to exclude liquid, precipitation, and other run-on and run-off, has both inner and outer layers of containment enclosing the waste, and has a leak detection system built into each containment layer; and the owner or operator will provide continuing operation and maintenance of the leak detection systems throughout the facility's "active life," and to a reasonable degree of certainty, will not allow hazardous constituents to migrate beyond the outer containment layer prior to the end of the post-closure period [40 CFR 264.90(b)(2)].

2. EPA finds, pursuant to 40 CFR 264.280(d), that the treatment zone of a land treatment unit does not contain hazardous constituents above background levels.

3. EPA finds that there is no potential for migration of liquid from regulated units to the uppermost aquifer during the facility's active life [40 CFR 264.90(b)(4)].

4. The unit is a waste pile and is operated in compliance with 40 CFR 264.250(c) (a waste pile that is enclosed).

General Requirements

The facility must have a sufficient number of wells representing the background water quality not affected by leakage from a waste management unit and represent the water quality passing the point of compliance [40 CFR 265.97(a)]. (The point of compliance is addressed in the section on detection monitoring addressed later in this section.)

If the facility has more than one regulated unit, separate groundwater monitoring systems are not necessarily required, provided that the system is adequate for all units. The *waste management area* would be described by an imaginary line circumscribing all of the regulated units [40 CFR 264.97(b)].

The sampling program must ensure a reliable indication of groundwater quality. The program also must include chain-of-custody control, sample collection procedures, sample preservation and shipment, and analytical procedures [40 CFR 264.97(d)].

Statistical Analysis

To determine if a regulated unit is affecting the groundwater quality, statistical analysis of the monitoring results is required. Whereas the interim status groundwater monitoring program requires the use of the Student's t-test, the Part 264 program provides for five options. An owner or operator must choose, for each of the chemical parameters and hazardous constituents listed in the permit, one or more of the statistical methods described below. In determining which statistical test is appropriate, the owner or operator should consider the theoretical properties of the test, the data available, the site hydrogeology, and the fate and transport characteristics of potential contaminants at the unit. EPA will review and, if appropriate, approve the proposed statistical methods and sampling procedures when issuing the permit.

EPA has identified the following statistical methods that an owner or operator can use [40 CFR 264.97(h)]:

1. A parametric analysis of variance (ANOVA) followed by multiple comparisons procedures to identify statistically significant evidence of contamination. The method must include estimation and testing of the contrasts between each compliance well's mean and the background mean levels for each constituent.
2. An analysis of variance (ANOVA) based on ranks followed by multiple comparisons procedures to identify statistically significant evidence of contamination. The method must include estimation

and testing of the contrasts between each compliance well's median and the background median levels for each constituent.

3. A tolerance or prediction interval procedure in which an interval for each constituent is established from the distribution of the background data, and the level of each constituent in each compliance well is compared to the upper tolerance or prediction limit.

4. A control chart approach that gives control limits for each constituent.

5. Another statistical test method submitted by the owner or operator and approved by the EPA Regional Administrator.

For further information concerning the requirements and applicability of each test for groundwater monitoring, consult EPA's *Statistical Analysis of Ground-Water Monitoring Data at RCRA Facilities*, April 1989.

Detection Monitoring

Detection monitoring, the first stage of the Part 264 groundwater monitoring program, requires the sampling for *indicator* parameters to determine if the unit is leaking.

Indicator parameters, established in the permit, may include specific conductance, total organic carbon, total organic halogen, waste constituents, or reaction products. The selected parameters, established in the permit, are determined by considering:

- The types, quantities, and concentrations of constituents in waste at the regulated unit.
- The mobility, stability, and persistence of waste constituents and reaction products in the underlying unsaturated zone.
- The detectability of the parameters.
- The concentration or values and coefficients of variation of the parameters in the groundwater background.

Detection monitoring is implemented at facilities where no hazardous constituents are known to have migrated from the facility to the groundwater. Applicants who are seeking permits for new facilities and for interim status facilities that have not been triggered into the assessment phase would generally qualify for the detection monitoring phase. Facilities that are in the assessment program of Part 265 would not start with detection monitoring but with compliance monitoring [40 CFR 264.91(a)(1)].

The detection monitoring program, like its interim status counterpart, is based on one year of background groundwater monitoring. The background, or upgradient wells, must be sampled on a quarterly basis for one year. The permittee then routinely monitors for a selected set of indicator parameters specified in the permit rather than the four indicator parameters used in the Part 265 program.

The number and types of samples (to be specified in the permit) collected to establish background levels must be appropriate for the form of statistical test employed [40 CFR 264.97(g)].

Values from the upgradient wells are used to establish background levels during the first year of monitoring only. However, the downgradient wells (at the point of compliance) must continue to be monitored after the first year. The regulations do not explicitly require continued monitoring of the upgradient wells, but the permit may.

In accordance with 40 CFR 264.98(h), if it is determined that there is significant change above background levels for any of the indicator parameters, the owner or operator must:

- Notify EPA, in writing within seven days, of those indicators that have changed.
- Run a complete Appendix IX (see Appendix E of this book) scan of all of the monitoring wells to determine the chemical composition of the leachate.
- Establish a background level for each Appendix IX constituent found at each well.
- Submit a Class 3 permit modification application to EPA within 90 days to establish a compliance monitoring program.
- Submit an engineering feasibility plan for a corrective action program.

The owner or operator can, within 90 days, attempt to demonstrate that a source other than the regulated unit is the cause of the increase, or that there is an error in sampling or analysis. EPA must be notified while the owner or operator is attempting to demonstrate these options [40 CFR 264.98(i)].

Compliance Monitoring

The goal of the compliance monitoring program is to ensure that the leakage of hazardous constituents (Appendix IX of Part 264 and Appendix E of this book) into the groundwater does not exceed designated levels. The framework for a compliance monitoring program is established by incorporating a groundwater protection standard into the permit.

Groundwater Protection Standard

The *groundwater protection standard* (GWPS), established in the permit, is a standard that places a constituent-based limit on the leachate from a regulated unit, which is measured at the point of compliance. In other words, the GWPS is used to determine if and when corrective action is required. The *point of compliance* is a vertical plane located at the hydraulically downgradient limit of the waste management area, which extends down into the groundwater underlying the regulated unit that is specified in the permit [40 CFR 264.95].

EPA will establish the groundwater protection standard in the facility's permit when hazardous constituents have entered the groundwater from a regulated unit. A groundwater protection standard is not established at a regulated unit where groundwater contamination has not been detected [40 CFR 264.92].

The GWPS consists of four elements, each of which is specified in the permit:

1. A listing of selected Appendix VIII (Part 261) hazardous constituents that could reasonably have been derived from the waste at the facility and that are present in the groundwater. The burden of demonstrating that a particular constituent could not reasonably be derived from the waste, or is incapable of posing a substantial present or potential hazard to human health or the environment, lies with the owner or operator in accordance with 40 CFR 264.93(a) and (b).
2. The establishment of concentration limits for each hazardous constituent, listed in accordance with the above. Where possible, concentration limits must be based on well-established numerical concentration limits so as to prevent degradation of water quality unless the owner or operator can demonstrate that a higher limit will not adversely affect public health or the environment [40 CFR 264.94(a)].

   The concentration limits are set at one of the following:
   • Maximum contaminant levels (MCLs)
   • Alternate concentration limits (ACLs)
   • Background levels
   (Background levels are generally not used because the GWPS is implemented only when contamination is detected. Thus, ACLs and MCLs would typically be less stringent for the owner or operator than background levels.)
3. The establishment of the point of compliance.
4. The establishment of the compliance period during which the GWPS applies. The compliance period is to be a number of years equal

to the active life of the waste management area, including the closure period [40 CFR 264.99].

The compliance period, however, may extend beyond the post-closure period if corrective action has been initiated but not completed. If the owner or operator is engaged in corrective action, the compliance period is extended until the owner or operator can demonstrate that the groundwater protection standard has not been exceeded for three consecutive years [40 CFR 264.96(c)].

Alternate Concentration Limits

Alternate concentration limits (ACLs) generally may be established when the levels of hazardous constituents in the groundwater are found above background. An ACL can be established provided that it will not pose a substantial or potential hazard to human health or the environment as long as the ACLs are not exceeded at the point of compliance. The ACL demonstration must justify all claims regarding the potential effects of groundwater contaminants on human health and the environment. In terms of human considerations, the regulations require assessments of toxicity, exposure pathways, and exposed populations [40 CFR 264.94(b)].

There are three basic policy guidelines established (OSWER 481.00-6c) for ACLs at facilities with "usable" groundwater:

1. Groundwater contaminant plumes should not increase in size or concentration above allowable health or environmental exposure levels.
2. Increased facility property holdings should not be used to allow a greater ACL.
3. ACLs should not be established so as to contaminate off-site groundwater above allowable health or environmental exposure levels.

The information required to be considered in establishing ACLs [40 CFR 264.94(b)] is:

1. Potential adverse effects on groundwater quality, considering:
   - The physical and chemical characteristics of the waste in the regulated unit, including its potential for migration.
   - The hydrogeologic characteristics of the facility and surrounding land.
   - The quantity of groundwater and the direction of groundwater flow.

- The proximity and withdrawal rates of groundwater users.
- The current and future uses of groundwater in the area.
- The existing quality of groundwater, including other sources of contamination and their cumulative impact on the groundwater quality.
- The potential for health risks caused by human exposure to waste constituents.
- The potential damage to wildlife, crops, vegetation, and physical structures caused by exposure to waste constituents.
- The persistence and permanence of potential adverse effects.

2. Potential adverse effects on hydraulically connected surface water quality, considering:
   - The volume and physical and chemical characteristics of the waste in the regulated unit.
   - The hydrogeologic characteristics of the facility and surrounding land.
   - The quantity and quality of groundwater and the direction of groundwater flow.
   - The patterns of rainfall in the region.
   - The proximity of the regulated unit to surface waters.
   - The current and future uses of surface waters in the area and any water quality standards established for those surface waters.
   - The existing quality of surface water, including other sources of contamination and the cumulative impact on surface water quality.
   - The potential for health risks caused by human exposure to waste constituents.
   - The potential damage to wildlife, crops, vegetation, and physical structures caused by exposure to waste constituents.
   - The persistence and permanence of the potential adverse effects.

Requirements during Compliance Monitoring

A facility that is in the compliance monitoring phase must continue the program for the active life of the facility, including closure [40 CFR 264.99(a)(4) and 264.96]. During post-closure, the facility may switch back to detection monitoring, but this will occur only if the levels in compliance monitoring have consistently reached background. Otherwise, the facility must remain in compliance monitoring.

In accordance with 40 CFR 264.99(a), during the compliance monitoring program, the owner or operator must:

- Determine whether the regulated units are in compliance with the groundwater protection standard.

- Determine the concentration of constituents at the point of compliance point as determined by the permit, but ast least semi-annually.
- Determine the groundwater flow rate and direction at least annually.
- Conduct a complete Appendix IX scan at least annually to determine if there are any new constituents at the point of compliance.

According to 40 CFR 264.99(i), if it is determined that the groundwater protection standard is being exceeded at any monitoring well during compliance monitoring, the owner or operator must:

- Notify EPA in writing within 7 days.
- Submit a Class 3 permit modification application to EPA within 180 days to establish a corrective action program.
- Prepare a plan for a groundwater monitoring program that will demonstrate the effectiveness of the corrective action program.

Corrective Action

The goal of the corrective action is to bring the facility back into compliance with its groundwater protection standard [40 CFR 264.100].
The elements of the corrective action program include:

- Implementation of corrective measures to remove or treat the constituents as specified by the permit.
- The time period for implementing the corrective action program as specified in the permit.
- Termination of the corrective action program only upon demonstration of the facility's meeting the groundwater protection standard.
- Submittal of a written report semiannually to EPA on the effectiveness of the corrective action program.

In conjunction with a corrective action program, the owner or operator must implement a groundwater monitoring program at least as effective as the compliance monitoring program (in determining compliance with the groundwater protection standard) to demonstrate the effectiveness of the corrective action program [40 CFR 264.100(d)]. Corrective action will continue until the owner or operator can demonstrate that the groundwater protection standard has not been exceeded for a period of three consecutive years [40 CFR 264.96(c) and 264.100(f)].

Once contamination has been reduced below the concentration limits set in the GWPS, the facility may discontinue corrective action measures and monitoring, and return to the compliance monitoring program [40 CFR 264.100(f)].

CLOSURE AND POST-CLOSURE

The primary purpose of closure and post-closure is to ensure that all hazardous waste management facilities are closed in a manner that to the extent necessary (1) protects human health and the environment and (2) controls, minimizes, or eliminates post-closure escape of hazardous waste, hazardous constituents, leachate, contaminated precipitation run-off, or waste decomposition products, to the ground or atmosphere [40 CFR 264/265.111]. The closure and post-closure requirements are divided into general standards applicable to all hazardous waste management facilities (addressed in the following sections) and technical standards specific to the type of waste management unit (addressed in Chapter 6).

All waste management units are subject to the closure requirements; land-based units (e.g., landfills, surface impoundments, waste piles) that do not *clean close* are subject to the post-closure care requirements.

Closure Requirements

Closure is the act of securing a hazardous waste management facility pursuant to the closure requirements [40 CFR 270.2]. It is the period after which wastes are no longer accepted and during which the owner or the operator completes all treatment, storage, and disposal operations. The owner or the operator may conduct partial closure of a facility. *Partial closure* is closure of a hazardous waste management unit at a facility that contains other operating hazardous waste management units. Closure of the last unit constitutes *final closure* of the facility.

Closure Plan

All hazardous waste management facilities must prepare and maintain a written closure plan that outlines the procedures to complete closure [40 CFR 264/265.112]. The plan must identify steps necessary to perform partial or final closure at any time during the facility's active life. (An example outline of a typical closure plan is shown in Table 5-2.) The necessary steps of closure include:

- A description of how each hazardous waste management unit will be closed in accordance with applicable closure performance standards.
- A description of how final closure of the entire facility will be con-

Table 5-2. Contents of a typical closure plan.

Activities to be described in closure plan	Regulatory citation
Facility description	40 CFR 264/265.111
Partial closure activities	40 CFR 264/265.112(b)(1)
Final closure activities based on the maximum extent of operations	40 CFR 264/265.112(b)(2)
Treating, removing, or disposing of the maximum amount of inventory	40 CFR 264/265.112(b)(3)
Facility decontamination	40 CFR 264/265.112(b)(4) and 264/265.114
Final cover*	40 CFR 264/265.112(b)(5), 264/265.228, 264/265.258, 264/265.280, and 264/265.310
Groundwater monitoring*	40 CFR 264/265.112(b)(5)
Ancillary closure activities (e.g., leachate management, gas monitoring, run-on and run-off control)	40 CFR 264/265.112(b)(5)
Survey plat*	
Closure certification	40 CFR 264/265.116
Closure (final and partial) schedule	40 CFR 264/265.115
	40 CFR 264/265.112(b)(6)
*May not be required.	

Source: OSWER Directive 9476.00-5.

ducted, including a description of the maximum extent of the operation that will remain unclosed during the facility's active life.
• An estimate of the maximum inventory of hazardous wastes on-site at any time during the active life of the facility. The estimate of the maximum inventory (OSWER Directive 9476.00-5) of wastes should include:
   – The maximum amount of hazardous wastes, including residues, in all treatment, storage, and disposal units.
   – The maximum amount of contaminated soils and residues from drips and spills from routine operations.
   – If applicable, the maximum amount of hazardous wastes from manufacturing/process areas and raw material/product storage and handling areas.

- A description of the steps needed to remove or decontaminate all hazardous waste residues from any of the facility components, equipment, or structures.
- A sampling and analysis plan for testing surrounding soils to determine the extent of decontamination required to meet closure standards.
- A description of all other activities during closure, including groundwater monitoring, leachate collection, and precipitation control.
- A schedule for closure of each hazardous waste management unit and for final closure of the facility.
- The expected year of closure.

Permitted storage surface impoundments and waste piles that do not have liners that meet the requirements of 40 CFR 264.221(a) and 264.251(a) and permitted and interim status tanks without secondary containment (assuming that they are not exempt) must prepare closure plans that describe activities necessary to conduct closure under two sets of conditions. The first plan must describe how the unit will be closed by removing all hazardous waste and hazardous constituents. The second is a *contingent closure plan* that outlines the closure activities to be undertaken if the owner or operator cannot remove all hazardous waste and constituents from the unit and must be closed as a landfill.

A copy of the closure plan, including all revisions to the plan, must be kept at the facility until closure is certified to be complete [40 CFR 264/265.112(a)]. The plan must be furnished to EPA upon request, including a request by mail. In addition, for facilities without *approved* plans, the plan must be provided on the day of a site inspection to any duly designated representative of EPA [40 CFR 265.112(a)]. An owner or an operator who intends to clean close a unit must include specific details of how he or she expects to make the necessary demonstration of removal and/or decontamination. Specific details that are required include sampling protocols, schedules, and the cleanup levels that will be used as a standard for assessing whether removal or decontamination is achieved (52 *FR* 8706, March 19, 1987).

Amendments to the Closure Plan

Facilities operating under interim status may amend the closure plan at any time prior to notification of partial or final closure. A written request for approval of any amendments to an *approved* closure plan (approval of closure plans is discussed below) must be submitted to EPA [40 CFR 265.112(c)(2) and (3)].

As shown in Table 5-3, the owner or the operator of a facility with

Table 5-3. Amending closure plans for interim status units.

Units without approved closure plans		Units with approved closure plans
	Voluntary Amendments	
May amend the plan at any time prior of closure		Must submit a written request to EPA to amend the plan
	Mandatory Amendments*	
Must amend the plan at least 60 days prior to facility design and operation		Must submit the modified plan at least 60 days prior to the proposed change in facility design and operation
Must amend the plan no later than 60 days after an unexpected event has occurred that has affected the plan		Must submit the modified plan no later than 60 days prior to an unexpected event
Must amend the plan no later than 30 days after an unexpected event that occurs during the closure period		Must submit the modified plan no later than 30 days after an unexpected event that occurs during the closure period.

*A closure plan must be amended whenever changes in operating plans or facility design affect the closure plan; whenever there is a change in the expected year of closure (if applicable); or, in conducting closure activities, unexpected events require a modification of the closure plan.

either an approved or a nonapproved plan must amend the closure plan whenever:

- Changes occur in the facility design or operations that affect the closure plan.
- A change in the expected year of closure occurs.
- Unexpected events occur during closure.

The plan must be amended at least 60 days prior to a proposed change or no later than 60 days after an unexpected change occurs. If an unexpected change occurs during closure, the plan must be amended within

30 days [40 CFR 265.112(c)(3)]. For example, if a surface impoundment or waste pile originally intended to clean close but cannot, and instead must close with waste in place (e.g., landfill), the closure plan must be amended within 30 days.

Notification of Closure

The owner or the operator must submit the closure plan to EPA at least 180 days prior to the expected date on which closure will begin for the first land disposal unit (i.e., surface impoundment, waste pile, land treatment, or landfill unit). An owner or an operator of a facility that has only incinerators, tanks, or container storage units must submit the closure plan at least 45 days before the expected date of the commencement of closure as listed in Table 5-4 [40 CFR 264/265.112(d)].

The *expected date of closure* must be either within 30 days after the date on which any hazardous waste management unit receives the known final volume of hazardous wastes, or, if the hazardous waste management unit will be receiving additional hazardous wastes, no later than one year after the date when the unit received the most recent volume of hazardous waste [40 CFR 264/265.112(d)(2)]. However, this date can be extended upon approval by EPA.

If the facility's interim status is terminated for reasons other than the issuance of a permit, the owner or the operator must submit a closure plan within 15 days unless the facility is issued either a judicial decree or a compliance order to close [40 CFR 265.112(d)(3)].

Facilities that have *approved* closure plans must notify EPA at least 60 days prior to closure for any land disposal unit, or 45 days for facilities with only container storage, tank, or incinerator units [40 CFR 264/265.112(d)].

Closure Plan Approval

Owners and operators of interim status facilities must submit their plans (closure and, if required, post-closure) for review and approval to EPA prior to final closure of the facility or closure of the first land disposal unit, as shown in Figure 5-3.

A permitted facility was to have included the closure plan as part of the permit application [40 CFR 270.14(13)]. When the permit is issued, the closure plan, which is now a condition of the permit, is the *approved* closure plan.

EPA must approve, modify, or disapprove a closure plan for interim status facilities (permitted facilities would have had their closure plan

Table 5-4. Closure notification requirements.

Facility type		Notification requirement
Permitted and interim status facilities with approved plans		
Partial closure	Disposal units _____	60 days
	Nondisposal units (tank, incineration, container storage) _____	No notification required
Final closure	Disposal unit _____	60 days
	Nondisposal unit _____	45 days
Interim status facilities without approved plans		
Partial closure	Disposal unit	180 days and submittal of closure and post-closure plan
	Nondisposal unit	No notification required
Final closure	Disposal unit	180 days and submittal of closure and post-closure plan
	Nondisposal unit	45 days and submittal of closure plan

Source: OSWER Directive 9476.00-5.

approved upon issuance of the permit) within 90 days of its receipt. Upon receipt of a closure plan, EPA will provide the owner or the operator and the public the opportunity to submit written comments or requests for modifications to the plan, and a public hearing may be held if one is requested [40 CFR 265.112(d)(4)].

If the plan is not approved, EPA must provide a detailed written statement to the owner or the operator with the reasons for disapproval. The owner or the operator then has 30 days after receiving the written statement to modify the plan or submit a new one. EPA must approve or modify the new or resubmitted plan within 60 days. If EPA modifies

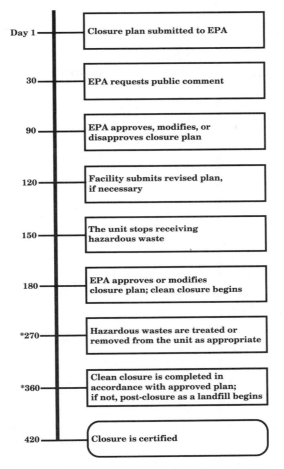

Day 1	Closure plan submitted to EPA
30	EPA requests public comment
90	EPA approves, modifies, or disapproves closure plan
120	Facility submits revised plan, if necessary
150	The unit stops receiving hazardous waste
180	EPA approves or modifies closure plan; clean closure begins
*270	Hazardous wastes are treated or removed from the unit as appropriate
*360	Clean closure is completed in accordance with approved plan; if not, post-closure as a landfill begins
420	Closure is certified

*A longer time period may be granted by EPA pursuant to 40 CFR 265.113.
Source: OSWER Directive 9476.00-5.

Figure 5-3. Approximate Timeframe for Clean Closure of Interim Status Units

this plan, the modified plan becomes the *approved* closure plan [40 CFR 265.112(d)(4)].

There are, however, no provisions under RCRA that allow an owner or an operator to appeal the final closure plan issued by EPA. The owner or the operator would have to pursue other legal avenues outside of the RCRA regulations to appeal provisions in a final closure plan.

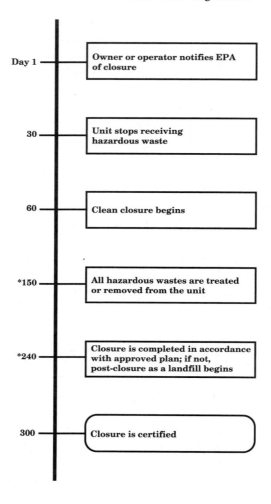

Day 1	Owner or operator notifies EPA of closure
30	Unit stops receiving hazardous waste
60	Clean closure begins
*150	All hazardous wastes are treated or removed from the unit
*240	Closure is completed in accordance with approved plan; if not, post-closure as a landfill begins
300	Closure is certified

*A longer time period may be granted by EPA pursuant to 40 CFR 264.113.
Source: OSWER Directive 9476.00-5.

Figure 5-4. Approximate Timeframes for Clean Closure of Permitted Units

Closure Period

As shown in Figure 5-3 for interim status units and Figure 5-4 for permitted units, within 90 days after receiving the final volume of hazardous waste or 90 days after approval of the closure plan, whichever is later, all hazardous waste must be treated, disposed of, or removed. The owner or the operator has an additional 90 days to complete decontaminating the facility, dismantling equipment, and so forth. Thus, closure must be completed within 180 days after final receipt of hazardous waste or plan approval. However, a time extension can be granted by EPA under specified conditions (outlined below) no later than 30 days prior to the expiration of either the initial 90 days or the total 180-day period [40 CFR 264/265.113].

The conditions for a time extension during closure include:

- The required closure activities will, if necessary, take longer than the applicable 90 or 180 days.
- The facility has the capacity to receive additional wastes.
- There is reasonable likelihood that a person other than the owner or the operator will recommence operation of the site.
- Closure of the facility would be incompatible with continued operation of the site.

An approval of a time extension for closure is contingent on whether the owner or the operator has taken and will continue to take all steps necessary to prevent threats to human health and the environment.

Cleanup Requirements

During partial or final closure, all contaminated liners, equipment, structures, and subsoils must be removed and properly disposed of or decontaminated; or the unit must be closed as a landfill [40 CFR 264/265.114]. EPA interprets "contaminated subsoils" to include contaminated groundwater (53 *FR* 9944, March 28, 1988). During the closure process, all hazardous wastes, waste residues, contaminated subsoils, groundwater, and equipment must be managed as a hazardous waste unless the material is delisted (if it was a listed waste), or the waste does not exhibit a characteristic of hazardous waste. This means that even though contaminated material at a surface impoundment is not (by definition) a hazardous waste, it must be removed, but it can be managed as a Subtitle D waste, subject to state rules and regulations [40 CFR 264/265.114].

To satisfy the closure requirements, it may be necessary to create new treatment, storage, or disposal units. There is no exclusion from the permitting requirements because a facility is subject to the closure requirements, as the Part 264 standards are applicable to new units added during closure as well as to new operating units. However, a Class 2 permit modification (for tanks, containers, and some waste piles) or a Class 3 permit modification (for landfills, surface impoundments, incinerators, and waste piles) may be sought to create these units. Interim status facilities, however, may add new units if the addition constitutes an allowable change to a facility during interim status. According to 40 CFR 270.72(c), changes in processes or addition of processes may be allowed if a revised Part A permit application and justification are submitted, and EPA approves the change. (See Chapter 9 for further explanation.) In addition, a facility probably will become a generator during the closure and cleanup process, subject to the Part 262 generator standards, and it must comply accordingly.

Clean Closure

At closure, owners and operators of hazardous waste management units can choose between removing/decontaminating all hazardous wastes and waste residues (*clean closure*) and terminating further regulatory responsibility under RCRA for the unit; or closing the unit with hazardous waste or waste residue remaining in place (*dirty closure*) and instituting post-closure care similar to that of landfills.

Previously, owners and operators of interim status facilities attempting a clean closure were required to remove wastes from a unit to the point that wastes were no longer *hazardous*. The criteria for this determination depended on whether the wastes in the unit were hazardous because they were listed or because they exhibited a hazardous waste characteristic. Thus, if a surface impoundment contained ignitable hazardous waste only, the owner or the operator could cease the removal of material if that material no longer exhibited the ignitability characteristic. In addition, the responsibility of the owner or the operator under Subtitle C of RCRA ceased at the time of certification of clean closure (45 *FR* 33203, May 19, 1980). Consequently, the clean-closure standard allowed facilities to be relieved of their RCRA responsibility even though there may have been contamination remaining (assuming that the contamination was not defined as a hazardous waste).

To address this contamination, EPA promulgated final regulations on March 19, 1987 (52 *FR* 8704), and on December 1, 1987 (52 *FR* 45788), that significantly strengthened the clean-closure requirements for interim status units. The interim status requirements now are nearly identical to the Part 264 requirements. An important aspect of these regulations is that they are applicable to *any* land disposal unit that received waste after July 26, 1982, or certified closure after January 26, 1983. Thus, even if a unit previously clean closed successfully, the facility owner or operator will have to demonstrate (as discussed below) that the unit has met the Part 264 clean-closure requirements (52 *FR* 45795, December 1, 1987).

For example, on June 13, 1983, an owner of a surface impoundment (which was used to treat ignitable waste only) clean closed the surface impoundment in accordance with the approved closure plan. The owner of the impoundment ceased removing contaminated subsoils at the point where the soil did not exhibit the ignitability characteristic in accordance with 40 CFR 265.228(b). However, the recent changes to the closure rules (52 *FR* 8704 and 52 *FR* 45788) now require that owner either to remove *all* wastes and waste residues (i.e., hazardous constituents) from the previously closed impoundment to attain a clean closure or to close the impoundment similar to a landfill and commence the post-closure care period.

Remove and Decontaminate Requirement

EPA interprets *remove* and *decontaminate* to indicate the amount of removal or decontamination that obviates the need for post-closure care (52 *FR* 8706, March 19, 1987). This means that an owner or an operator must remove all hazardous waste or waste residue (i.e., all hazardous constituents) that pose a "substantial present or potential threat to human health or the environment." EPA intends to review site-specific demonstrations submitted by the owner or operator to determine if the removal or decontamination is sufficient. The closure demonstrations submitted must document that any contaminants left in the soil and/or groundwater, surface water, or atmosphere, in excess of EPA-recommended limits or factors, based on *direct contact* (i.e., fate and transport considerations are not allowed) through inhalation or ingestion, will not result in a threat to human health or the environment. *EPA-recommended limits or factors* are those that have undergone peer review by EPA. At the present time, these include Maximum Contaminant Levels, Federal Water Quality Criteria, Verified Reference Doses, Carcinogenic Slope Factors, and Health Assessment Documents, as shown in Table 5-5. The most current levels associated with these criteria are available from EPA's Integrated Risk Information System. (Contact EPA's Office of Research and Development in Cincinnati, Ohio at 513-569-7595 for further information.) If no EPA-recommended exposure limit exists for a particular constituent, then the owner or the operator must either remove the constituent to background levels, submit data of sufficient quality for EPA to determine the environmental and health effects of the constituent in accordance with TSCA [40 CFR Parts 797 and 798], or follow closure and post-closure requirements similar to landfills (52 *FR* 8706, March 19, 1987).

Table 5-5. Clean closure cleanup levels.

Media	EPA-recommended limits or factors
Ground Water	MCLs;* if nonexistent, oral Rfds* for oral noncarcinogenic constituents and CSFs* for carcinogens. Carcinogens must be in risk range of 10^{-4} to 10^{-6}, with 10^{-6} as the point of departure.
	If above limits or factors are nonexistent, can use either natural background levels or conduct testing in compliance with TSCA to develop a health-based standard. If background levels are elevated, may use detection limit.
Surface Water	If surface water is used as a drinking water source, use MCLs; if nonexistent, use oral RfDs and CSFs. Use Ambient Water Quality Criteria (WQC) to determine if protective of the environment (aquatic species).
Soil	Use oral RfDs and CSFs.
Air	National Ambient Air Quality Standards (NAAQS); if nonexistent, use inhalation RfDs and CSFs.

*MCL = maximum contaminant level; RfD = reference dose; CSF = carcinogenic slope factor

Clean Closure of a Regulated Unit

Previously, it was interpreted that a unit that clean closed was no longer subject to Part 265 (i.e., post-closure care). However, on March 28, 1986 (51 *FR* 10716), EPA asserted its opinion that an interim status disposal unit that clean closes after July 26, 1982, is required to obtain a post-closure permit. If the unit also is a regulated unit, it is subject to the Part 264 groundwater regulations when a post-closure permit is issued.

EPA's rationale for this opinion is that the clean-closure standards [40 CFR 265.228(b)] state "that provided the cleanup standards are met, the impoundment is not further subject to this Part [Part 265]." It is not stated that the unit is excluded from the Part 270 permit requirements, or the Part 264 groundwater requirements. EPA is stating that congressional intent was for all regulated units to be subject to the Part 264 groundwater regulations regardless of a successful clean closure. However, EPA will allow an interim status unit to be relieved of any further requirements of RCRA if the owner or the operator can demonstrate that any further cleanup is unnecessary; otherwise, a unit that has clean closed can be required to obtain a post-closure permit. A permit application will, however, trigger the 3004(u) corrective action provision to address releases from solid waste management units (hazardous waste management units are a subset of these units) at the entire facility. If a permitted surface impoundment, tank system, or waste pile clean closes, it is no longer subject to RCRA because it already has a permit and has been operating under the Part 264 groundwater program.

Equivalency Demonstration

The demonstration that an interim status unit was clean closed in accordance with the Part 264 requirements may be accomplished by either submitting a Part B permit application for a post-closure permit or by petitioning EPA for an equivalency demonstration under 40 CFR 270.1(c)(5). The *equivalency demonstration* is a petition that attempts to demonstrate that a post-closure permit (i.e., further cleanup) is not required because the owner or the operator has met the applicable Part 264 closure standards for that unit (52 *FR* 45795, December 1, 1987). The demonstration submitted by the owner or the operator, at a minimum, must contain sufficient information for identifying the type and location of the unit, the unit boundaries, the waste that had been managed in the unit, and the extent of waste and soil removal or decontamination undertaken at closure. Relevant groundwater monitoring and soil sampling data also should be submitted to demonstrate that any Appendix VIII and Appendix IX constituents that remain at closure are below levels posing a threat to human health and the environment. The demonstration may use data developed at the time of closure. If insufficient data are available to support the demonstration, new data may have to be collected for the determination (OSWER Directive 9476.00-18).

EPA must make a determination as to whether the unit has met the removal or decontamination requirements within 90 days of receiving a demonstration as outlined in Figure 5-5. EPA also must provide for a 30-day public comment period. If EPA finds that the closure did not meet the applicable cleanup requirements (i.e., hazardous constituents above EPA recommended limits or factors remain), they must provide a written statement of the reasons why the closure was not successful. The owner or the operator can submit additional information in support of the demonstration within 30 days after receiving such a written statement. EPA must review this additional information and make a final determination within 60 days. If EPA determines that the closure does not meet the Part 264 standards, the owner or the operator must submit a Part B permit application containing all the applicable information required in Part 270, including groundwater monitoring information.

Dirty Closure

An owner or an operator who either chooses not to conduct a clean closure or fails to do so must provide post-closure care similar to that of a landfill [40 CFR 264/264.310], including:

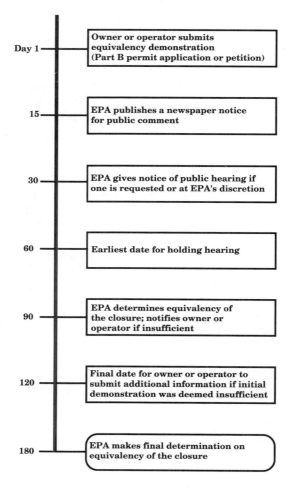

Source: OSWER Directive 9476.00-18.

Figure 5-5. Equivalency Demonstration Process

- Eliminating all free liquids by either removing the liquid wastes/residues from the impoundment or solidifying them.
- Stabilizing the remaining waste and waste residues to a bearing capacity sufficient to support a final cover.
- Installing a final cover that provides long-term minimization of infiltration into the closed unit, functions with minimum maintenance, promotes drainage, and minimizes erosion.
- Performing post-closure care and groundwater monitoring.

There are unit-specific standards that provide specific instructions. In addition, the general closure performance standard [40 CFR 264/265.111] applies to activities that are not otherwise addressed by the process-specific standards but are necessary so that the facility is closed in a manner that will ensure protection of human health and the environment. For example, under the closure performance standard, an owner or an operator can be required to install source control (e.g., leachate collection and run-on/run-off control) that is not otherwise specifically required (OSWER Directive 9476.00-13).

Certification of Closure

Within 60 days of the completion of closure for each individual land disposal *unit* at a facility, or within 60 days of closure completion for an incinerator, tank, or container storage *facility,* a certification prepared by the owner or the operator and a qualified, independent, registered professional engineer must be submitted to EPA. The owner or the operator must certify that the facility or unit was closed in accordance with the approved facility closure plan. Within 60 days after receiving the closure certification, EPA will notify the owner or the operator in writing that under RCRA said owner or operator is no longer required to maintain financial assurance for closure for that particular unit or facility unless EPA has reason to believe that closure has not been done in accordance with the closure plan [40 CFR 264/265.115].

Closure Notices

Within 60 days of the closure certification, the owner or the operator must submit a written record to the local zoning authority and EPA. The record must specify the type, quantity, and location of hazardous waste disposed of in each cell [40 CFR 264/265.119(a)].

Within 60 days of closure certification, a permanent notation must [40 CFR 264/265.119(b)] be made on the deed, stating that:

- Hazardous waste management occurred on the property.
- Its use is restricted under RCRA.
- The survey plat and other applicable information are available at the local zoning authority.

A certification by the owner or the operator that the notification was placed on the deed, and a copy of the deed, must be submitted to EPA.

If the owner or the operator or any subsequent owner desires to remove any waste from the closed facility, a modification to the approved post-closure plan must be obtained. A notation indicating that waste was removed may be added to the deed at a later time [40 CFR 264/265.119(c)].

Post-closure Requirements

Units at which hazardous wastes or residues will remain after partial or final closure are subject to post-closure requirements. Owners or operators of hazardous waste management units must conduct certain monitoring and maintenance activities during the post-closure care period, which begins with the certification of closure and continues for 30 years; however, this date may be extended or reduced by EPA as appropriate [40 CFR 264/265.117].

All land disposal units that close after July 26, 1982, are subject to the post-closure requirements and are required to obtain a post-closure permit except for clean closed units [40 CFR 270.1(c)]. Thus, an interim status unit that is a regulated unit closing after July 26, 1982, and entering its post-closure period can be required to obtain a post-closure permit at any time during its post-closure care period.

If that facility receives a post-closure permit, it is then subject to both the 40 CFR 264.100 corrective action requirements for groundwater and the 3004(u) provisions (the latter being initiated by the permit application), which may require corrective action for any solid waste management unit (SWMU) at the entire facility, regardless of when the SWMU closed. [See Chapter 9 for further explanation of 3004(u).]

Post-closure Plan

Facilities with land disposal units must prepare and maintain a written post-closure plan at the facility. Until the final closure of a facility without an approved post-closure plan, a copy of the most current plan must be furnished to EPA upon request [40 CFR 264/265.118].

The post-closure plan must describe the frequency of monitoring and maintenance activities to be conducted after closure of each disposal unit. The plan should include provisions for the kinds of monitoring and maintenance activities that reasonably can be expected during the post-closure care period. It should be noted that any subsequent use of the property may not allow any disturbance of the integrity of the final cover, containment system, or monitoring system [40 CFR 264/265.118(b)]. Because of difficulty in predicting what may be required, the plan should include a range of alternatives, thus avoiding a potential permit modification.

The post-closure plan must include:

- A description of the planned groundwater monitoring requirements, including the frequency of sampling.
- Information and documentation concerning the integrity of the cap and final cover or other containment systems.
- A description of the planned maintenance activities for the cap, containment, and monitoring equipment.
- The name and address of the facility contact person overseeing post-closure care.

Amendments to the Plan

The plan may be amended by the owner or operator at any time during the active life or post-closure care period. An owner or an operator with an *approved* post-closure plan must submit a written request to EPA for authorization to modify the approved plan. The plan must be amended whenever operating plans or facility designs affect the post-closure plan, whenever any event occurs that affects the plan, and at least 60 days before a change in operations or 60 days after an unexpected event. If the plan needs to be amended and the facility has a permit, a Class 2 permit modification must be sought [40 CFR 264/265.118(d)].

Approval of the Plan

The plan for an interim status facility (a permitted facility is already approved) must be submitted at least 180 days before the owner or operator expects to begin partial or final closure of the first hazardous waste disposal unit. Facilities that intend to clean close are not required to have a post-closure plan. However, if an owner or an operator intended to clean close but cannot, and must close as a landfill, the owner or the operator must submit the post-closure plan within 90 days of making that determination [40 CFR 265.118(e)].

Upon receipt of a post-closure plan, EPA will provide the owner or the operator and the public the opportunity to submit written comments or requests for modifications to the plan. EPA must approve, modify, or disapprove a post-closure plan within 90 days of its receipt. A public hearing may be held if one is requested and with the discretion of EPA.

If EPA does not approve the plan, a detailed written statement must be provided to the owner or the operator with the reasons for disapproval. The owner or the operator then has 30 days after receiving the written statement to modify the plan or submit a new one. EPA must approve or modify the new or resubmitted plan within 60 days. If EPA modifies this plan, the modified plan becomes the *approved* post-closure plan [40 CFR 265.118(f)]. All post-closure activities must conform to the approved post-closure plan.

Post-closure Certification

Within 60 days after the completion of the post-closure care period for each hazardous waste disposal unit, the owner or the operator must submit, by registered mail, a certification stating that post-closure care was performed in accordance with the approved post-closure plan. The certification must be signed by both the owner or the operator and an independent, qualified, registered professional engineer [40 CFR 264/ 265.120].

FINANCIAL RESPONSIBILITY REQUIREMENTS

The financial responsibility requirements were established to ensure that funds are available to pay for properly closing a facility, for maintaining post-closure care at disposal facilities, and for compensation to third parties for bodily injury and property damage caused by sudden and nonsudden accidents related to the facility's operation. Federal- and state-owned facilities are exempt from these requirements [40 CFR 264/ 265.140(c)]. However, this exclusion does not cover county or municipally owned facilities (45 *FR* 33199, May 19, 1980).

Two programs are addressed under the financial responsibility regulations: financial assurance and liability coverage.

Financial Assurance

The purpose of the financial assurance requirements is to ensure that there are sufficient funds for the proper closure and post-closure care of a hazardous waste management facility.

The owner or the operator must have a detailed written estimate for *facility* closure and post-closure (if applicable) in current dollars. These cost estimates are used to determine the level of financial assurance required. The closure cost estimate, based on the closure plan, must equal the cost of final closure at the point during the active life when closure would be the most expensive and based on third-party costs (i.e., contractor costs), not on the use of facility personnel. The costs may not take into account value from any salvageable materials, equipment, or wastes [40 CFR 264/265.142].

The key activities to be included in the closure cost estimate include:

- Waste inventory management
  - Transportation to off-site TSDF
  - On-site treatment or disposal
- Facility decontamination
- Monitoring activities
- Final cover installation
- Maintenance of security program
- Survey plat
- Closure certification

The key activities to be included in the post-closure cost estimate include:

- Monitoring
- Leachate management
- Routine maintenance
- Filing post-closure notices
- Maintenance of security program
- Post-closure certification

The closure and post-closure cost estimate must be revised yearly to account for inflation [40 CFR 264/265.142(b) and 264/265.144(b)]. This revision is based on the annual inflation factor, a value that may be obtained from either EPA's RCRA/Superfund hotline (800-424-9346) or by dividing the latest annual implicit price deflator for the gross national product by the previous annual deflator. The deflators are published by the U.S. Department of Commerce in its *Survey of Current Business*.

The cost estimate must be updated:

- Within 30 days after the close of the firm's fiscal year for facilities using the financial test or corporate guarantee.
- Within 60 days of the anniversary of the date when the first cost estimate was made for all other financial mechanisms.

The post-closure cost estimate must be in current dollars and based on the annual cost required for proper post-closure maintenance according to the post-closure plan. The annual cost is then multiplied by the established post-closure care period. Facilities with land-based units that intend to clean close are not required to maintain a post-closure cost estimate [40 CFR 264/265.144(a)].

Financial Assurance for Closure and Post-closure

Each owner or operator must establish financial assurance for the proper closure and post-closure care (if applicable) of the facility and must choose from the following options:

- Trust fund
- Letter of credit
- Insurance
- Financial test and corporate guarantee
- Surety bond guaranteeing payment into a trust fund
- Surety bond guaranteeing performance of closure (Part 264 only)

These options may be used individually or in combinations. The owner or the operator can substitute another form of financial assurance at any time, provided that EPA approval is granted [40 CFR 264/265.143(g) and 264/265.145(f)].

Trust Fund

A *trust* is an arrangement in which one party, the grantor, transfers money to another party, the trustee, who manages the money for the benefit of one or more beneficiaries. For the purposes of this section, the facility owner or operator is the grantor; the financial institution is the trustee; and EPA is the beneficiary. These trusts are irrevocable; they cannot be altered or terminated by the owner or operator without the consent of EPA and the financial institution. The trust is established when the trust agreement is signed by the grantor and the financial institution.

For permitted facilities, payments must be made annually over the term of the initial RCRA permit (i.e., 10 years). For interim status facilities, payments are made annually over 20 years or the remaining operating life of the facility, whichever is shorter. The operating life of the facility is determined by using the expected year of closure, which should be identified in the closure plan. If the facility subsequently receives a permit, the pay-in period is adjusted accordingly [40 CFR 264/265.143(a)].

After the pay-in period is complete, more payments must be made if the closure cost estimate increases or inflation factoring shows that a greater amount is needed. However, if the amount in the trust fund is greater than needed for closure, the owner or the operator may submit to EPA a written request to release excess money. After partial or final closure has begun, a request for reimbursement for closure expenditures may be submitted to EPA using itemized bills.

Surety Bond

A *surety bond* is a bond guaranteeing performance of an obligation, such as closure and/or post-closure. If an owner or an operator uses a surety bond or a letter of credit, a standby trust fund (essentially the same as the trust fund) must be established. In most cases, a standby trust fund is established with an initial nominal fee agreed on by the owner or the operator and the trustee. Further payments into this fund are not required until the standby trust is funded by a surety company as required. The surety company must be listed as an acceptable surety in *Circular 570* of the U.S. Department of the Treasury.

If an administrative order is issued to compel closure or closure is required by an appropriate court order, the amount equal to the penalty sum must be placed into the standby trust fund within 15 days of issuance.

Letter of Credit

A *letter of credit* is an agreement by the issuing institution that it will make available to the beneficiary (EPA) a specific sum of money during a specific time period on behalf of its customer (facility owner or operator). The letter of credit must be irrevocable and issued for one year. The letter must have an automatic extension unless the issuing institution notifies both EPA and the facility owner or operator at least 120 days prior to the expiration date that the letter will not be extended. The letter of credit also must establish a standby trust fund.

If the facility fails to perform final closure in accordance with the approved closure plan, EPA may draw upon the letter of credit to ensure proper closure.

Insurance

Insurance is basically a contract through which one party guarantees another party monies (usually a prespecified amount) to perform the closure in return for premiums paid.

Financial Test and Guarantee

The financial test is one of the means that can be used to provide financial assurance. The test includes three criteria: the firm must have a net worth of at least $10 million in the United States, a ratio of total liabilities to net worth not greater than 3 to 1, and net working capital in the United States at least twice the amount of the cost estimates to be covered. The firm has to demonstrate these characteristics in quarterly, unconsolidated, audited reports. A firm meeting the financial test also can guarantee the closure and post-closure obligations of another entity by meeting the corporate guarantee. This guarantee is used primarily by parent firms to guarantee the obligations of their subsidiaries.

Liability Coverage

On April 16, 1982 (47 *FR* 16546), EPA promulgated regulations requiring owners and operators to demonstrate liability coverage during the operating life of a facility for bodily injury and property damage to third parties resulting from facility operations. Under the liability coverage regulations [40 CFR 264/265.147], owners and operators of all hazardous waste management facilities are required to demonstrate, on an owner/operator (per firm) basis, adequate liability coverage. This means that even if a firm has multiple hazardous waste management facilities, the coverage stays the same.

Liability coverage is required for nonsudden accidental occurrences in the amount of $3 million per occurrence and $6 million annual aggregate, exclusive of legal defense costs. An *accidental occurrence* is an accident that is neither expected nor intended. A *nonsudden accidental occurrence* is an accidental occurrence that takes place over a period of time and involves continuous or repeated exposure, such as a hazardous waste leaching into groundwater. Liability coverage also is required for sudden accidental occurrences in the amount of $1 million per occurrence with an annual aggregate of at least $2 million, exclusive of legal defense costs. A *sudden accidental occurrence* is an accidental occurrence that is not continuous or repeated, such as a fire or an explosion.

First-dollar coverage is required; that is, the amount of any deductible must be covered by the insurer, with right of reimbursement from the insured. Liability coverage must be continuously provided for a facility until the certification of closure is received by EPA. The coverage options include financial responsibility, which can be demonstrated through a financial test, corporate guarantee, liability insurance, or a combination of the three.

Chapter 6

Technical Standards for Waste Management Units

In addition to the general standards applicable to all hazardous waste management facilities, RCRA establishes technical operating requirements that are unique to each type of waste management unit.

INTRODUCTION

Generally, it is not the process that is regulated per se, but the type of unit through which the process occurs. For example, a facility may employ many processes that occur in tanks to treat various wastes; however, the facility will generally comply with the same standards for all of the tanks (assuming they are all basically similar) regardless of which process is being employed.

The hazardous waste management units that are addressed by RCRA are:

- Container storage units
- Tank systems
- Surface impoundments
- Waste piles
- Land treatment areas
- Landfills
- Incinerators
- Thermal treatment units
- Chemical, physical, and biological treatment units

161

- Miscellaneous units
- Underground injection wells

CONTAINER STORAGE UNITS

A *container* is any portable device in which a material is stored, transported, treated, disposed of, or otherwise handled [40 CFR 260.10].

Container Management

A container storing waste must always be closed unless hazardous waste is being removed or added. A container must not be opened, handled, or stored in a way that might cause the contents to leak. If a container leaks or is in poor condition, the contents of that container must be placed into a sound container [40 CFR 264/265.171].

The owner or the operator must inspect the area(s) where containers are stored, at least weekly, for leaks and corrosion or other indications of potential container failure. Results of these inspections are to be recorded in the facility's operating log [40 CFR 264/265.174].

Containers holding ignitable or reactive wastes must be stored at least 50 feet from the facility's property boundary [40 CFR 264/265.176].

Waste must be compatible with the container, and waste cannot be placed in an unwashed container if it previously held an incompatible waste. Incompatible wastes cannot be placed into the same container. A container storing waste that is incompatible with other materials must be separated from these materials by a physical structure (e.g., dike or wall) or removed from the area [40 CFR 264/265.172].

Closure for Interim Status Units

At closure, all hazardous wastes and residues must be removed from the storage area. Remaining containers, liners, bases, and contaminated soil must be removed or decontaminated [40 CFR 265.11].

Additional Requirements for Permitted Units

In addition to the above requirements, a permitted container storage unit, in accordance with 40 CFR 264.175, must have a containment system that includes:

- An impervious flooring that will allow the collection of any leakage.
- Flooring that is sloped to collect any leaks or spills.
- A containment area that has sufficient capacity to contain 10 percent of the volume of all containers or the volume of the largest container, whichever is greater.
- A system to prevent precipitation run-on into the containment system unless the containment system has excess containment capacity.
- A collection and removal system for any released waste.

Container storage areas that store wastes that have no *free liquids* (i.e., wastes that pass the Paint Filter Test, Method 9095) are not required [40 CFR 264.175(c)] to have a containment system as described in the above paragraph, provided that:

- The storage area is sloped to drain and remove any liquid resulting from precipitation.
- The containers are elevated or protected from contact with any accumulation.

The dioxin-containing wastes (F020, F021, F022, F023, F026, F027, and F028) must have a containment system that complies with the storage requirements for liquid wastes regardless of whether free liquid is present [40 CFR 264.175(d)].

Closure

At closure, all hazardous wastes and residues must be removed. Remaining containers, liners, bases, and contaminated soil must be either removed or decontaminated [40 CFR 264.178].

TANK SYSTEMS

The regulations contained in Subpart J of Parts 264 and 265 are applicable to *tank systems*, which include the tank, all associated ancillary equipment, and the containment system. A *tank* is a stationary device, designed to contain an accumulation of hazardous waste, that is constructed primarily of nonearthen materials (e.g., wood, steel, plastic) that provide structural support [40 CFR 260.40]. *Ancillary equipment* is any device, including, but not limited to, piping, fittings, flanges, valves, and pumps, used to distribute, meter, or control the flow of hazardous waste from its point of generation to a storage or treatment tank(s), between hazardous waste storage and treatment tanks to a point of disposal on-site, or to a point of shipment for disposal off-site [40 CFR 260.10].

On July 14, 1986 (51 *FR* 25422), EPA promulgated sweeping regulatory changes to the existing hazardous waste tank regulations contained in Subpart J. These regulations established new and revised standards for *accumulation tank systems* (i.e., for on-site generators regulated under 40 CFR 262.34), interim status tank systems, and permitted tank systems.

EPA's regulatory program for hazardous waste tank systems includes these key objectives:

- To maintain the integrity of the primary containment system for both new and existing tank systems.
- To require the proper installation of new tank systems.
- To outline the installation of secondary containment with leak detection capabilities for new and existing tank systems.
- To implement a program for adequate response to releases from tank systems.
- To ensure the proper operation, maintenance, and inspection of tank systems.
- To implement a program to ensure proper closure and post-closure care for tank systems.

Special Requirements for Medium-Quantity Generators

Medium-quantity generators (generators of 100 to 1000 kg/mo) accumulating waste in a tank need only to comply with the following requirements pertaining to tank systems [40 CFR 262.34(d)(3)]:

- Treatment must not generate any extreme heat, explosions, fire, fumes, mists, dusts, gases; or damage the tank's structural integrity; or threaten human health or the environment in any way.
- Hazardous wastes or reagents that may cause corrosion, erosion, or structural failure must not be placed into the tank.
- At least two feet of freeboard must be maintained in an uncovered tank unless sufficient containment capacity is supplied.
- Continuously fed tanks must have a waste-feed cutoff or bypass system.
- No ignitable, reactive, or incompatible wastes are to be placed into a tank unless these wastes are rendered nonignitable, nonreactive, or compatible.
- At least once each operating day, the waste-feed cutoff and bypass systems, monitoring equipment data, and waste level must be inspected.

- At least weekly, construction materials and the surrounding area of the tank system must be inspected for possible corrosion, leaks, or visible signs of erosion.
- At closure, all hazardous wastes must be removed from the tank, containment system, and discharge control systems.

Accumulation Tanks for On-Site Generators

Owners and operators of 90-day accumulation tanks, that accumulate hazardous waste in accordance with 40 CFR 262.34, are required to comply with most of the provisions of Subpart J of Part 265, including:

- A one-time assessment of the integrity of the tank system.
- Installation standards for new tanks.
- Design standards, including an assessment of corrosion potential.
- Secondary containment phase-in provisions.
- Closure.
- Periodic leak testing if the tank system does not have secondary containment.
- Additional response requirements regarding leaks, including reporting to the EPA Regional Administrator on the extent of any release as well as repairing or replacing leaking tanks.

However, owners or operators of 90-day accumulation tanks are not required to prepare closure or post-closure plans, prepare contingent closure or post-closure plans, maintain financial responsibility, or conduct waste analysis and trial tests [40 CFR 262.34(a)(1) and 265.201].

Interim Status Tanks

Interim status tank systems without secondary containment (which eventually must be retrofitted) were required to have written assessment of the tanks' integrity completed and on file at the facility by January 12, 1988 [40 CFR 265.191]. If a tank contains a solid waste that subsequently becomes a hazardous waste (i.e., is newly listed), the assessment must be conducted within 12 months of the listing. The assessment, certified by an independent, qualified, registered professional engineer, must determine the adequacy of the tank's design and ensure that it will not rupture, collapse, or fail, based on the following considerations:

- The tank design standards.
- Hazardous characteristics of the waste.

Table 6-1. Regulatory deadlines for providing secondary containment.

Tank description	Regulatory deadline
All existing tank systems (regardless of age) used to store or treat EPA hazardous waste numbers: F020, F021, F022, F023, F026, or F027.	January 12, 1989
Tank systems used to store or treat a waste that is defined as hazardous after January 12, 1987	Within two years after the date that the waste is listed as hazardous waste (to determine secondary containment deadline, substitute the date handled material becomes a hazardous waste for "January 12, 1987" in the following deadline descriptions)
Existing tank systems of known and documented age	Within two years after January 12, 1987, or when the tank system has reached 15 years of age, whichever comes later
Existing tank systems for which the age cannot be documented	Within 8 years of January 12, 1987, but if the age of the facility is greater than 7 years, secondary containment must be provided by the time the facility reaches 15 years of age or within 2 years of January 12, 1987, whichever comes later
New tank systems after July 14, 1986	Prior to putting the tank system into service

- Existing corrosion protection.
- Documented age of the tank.
- Results of a leak test (tank tightness test), internal inspection, or other integrity test results.

All tanks without secondary containment that cannot be entered for inspection must undergo a leak test. If the assessment indicates that the tank is leaking or is unfit for use, it must be taken out of service immediately [40 CFR 265.191(b)(5)(i)].

Secondary Containment

Existing tanks were required to have secondary containment, including leak-detection capability, by January 12, 1989, or the date when the tank system reached 15 years of age, whichever is later, as shown in Table

6-1. If the age of the tank system cannot be documented, secondary containment must be provided by January 12, 1995. However, for a facility older than 7 years, secondary containment was to be provided by January 12, 1989, or when the facility reaches 15 years of age, whichever is later. Documentation may include a bill of sale, an installation certification, or dated engineering drawings of the system [40 CFR 265.193(a)].

If a tank handles hazardous waste that does not contain any free liquids and is situated inside a building on an impermeable floor, it is not subject to the secondary containment section [40 CFR 265.190(a)].

The containment system must be designed to prevent any migration of wastes or liquids into the soil, groundwater, or surface water, as well as capable of detecting and collecting any released waste [40 CFR 265.193]. At a minimum, the containment system must be:

- Constructed or lined with compatible materials that have sufficient strength and thickness to prevent failure from pressure gradients, weather, waste contact, and daily operational stress.
- Able to prevent failure from settlement, compression, or uplift.
- Provided with a leak-detection system that will detect the presence of any waste released within 24 hours of release.
- Sloped or designed to drain and remove any liquids resulting from leaks, spills, or precipitation.

In accordance with 40 CFR 265.193(d), each tank system must use one or more of the following containment devices:

- Liner system
- Vault system
- Double-walled tank
- Alternative design approved by EPA

Liner System

A liner system must be:

- Free of gaps and cracks.
- Able to contain 100 percent of the volume of the largest tank contained in the system.
- Designed and operated to prevent run-on or precipitation from a 25-year, 24-hour rainfall event.
- Designed to completely surround the tank and to cover all surrounding earth that may come into contact with any released waste.

Vault System

A vault system must be:

- Designed for 100 percent containment capacity of the largest tank.
- Designed or operated to prevent precipitation run-on from a 25-year, 24-hour rainfall event.
- Constructed with chemically resistant waterstops at all joints.
- Constructed with an impermeable, compatible lining or coating.
- Constructed with an outside moisture barrier to prevent migration of moisture into the vault.

Double-Walled Tanks

A double-walled tank must be:

- Designed as an integral structure so that any release will be contained by the outer shell.
- Protected from corrosion if constructed of metal.
- Provided with a built-in continuous (interstitial) leak detection system capable of detecting a leak within 24 hours of a release.

Ancillary Equipment

A tank system's ancillary equipment must be provided with secondary containment (e.g., trenches, jacketing, double-walled piping), except for the following devices, provided that a daily inspection is conducted:

- Welded joints, flanges, or connections.
- Sealless or magnetic coupling pumps.
- Aboveground piping.
- Pressurized aboveground piping systems with automatic shutoff devices.

Variances

A variance from secondary containment requirements may be granted if the owner or the operator can demonstrate that alternative design and operating practices, together with the location characteristics, will prevent the migration of any hazardous waste or constituents into the groundwater or surface water at least as effectively as secondary containment. The considerations involved in assessing a variance are listed in 40 CFR 264/265.193(g).

General Operating Requirements

The following requirements [40 CFR 265.194] are general operating requirements applicable to tank systems:

- Incompatible wastes or reagents must not be placed into the tank system.
- No ignitable, reactive, or incompatible wastes are to be placed into a tank unless these wastes are rendered nonignitable, nonreactive, or compatible.
- The tank must have spill prevention (e.g., check valves) and overfill prevention controls.
- The tank must maintain sufficient freeboard (distance between the top of the tank and the surface of the waste) to prevent overtopping by precipitation or wind action.

Inspections

At least once each operating day the owner or the operator must inspect:

- Aboveground portions of the tank to detect corrosion or releases.
- Data gathered from monitoring and leak-detection equipment.
- Construction materials and surrounding areas of the tank system for visible erosion or releases.
- Overfill and spill control equipment (Part 265 and 90-day accumulation tanks only); permitted tanks must develop a schedule that will be specified in the permit for inspection of the spill control equipment.

Waste Analysis

If a tank is going to be used to hold any waste that is substantially different, or uses a process to treat a waste that is substantially different from the previous contents or treatment action, both a waste analysis and a trial test must be conducted [40 CFR 265.200].

Leaks or Spills

Any tank that has a release or is unfit for service must immediately be taken out of service. The flow of incoming waste must be stopped immediately, and the tank contents must be removed within 24 hours or as soon as possible. If the release is confined to the containment system, the contents must be removed [40 CFR 265.196].

Any release from a tank system into the environment meeting a Superfund reportable quantity must be reported immediately. (See Chapter 12 for further discussion.) In addition, within 30 days of the detection of a release, a report containing the following information must [40 CFR 265.196(d)(3)] be submitted to EPA:

- Likely route of migration.
- Characteristics of surrounding soils.
- Results of any monitoring or sampling conducted (must be sent as soon as available).
- Proximity to downgradient drinking water, surface water, and human populations.
- Description of response actions taken or planned unless the tank system is repaired prior to its return to service.

For all major repairs, the owner or operator must submit a certification to EPA prior to the tank's being placed into service. The certification, verifying the adequacy of the tank's repairs, must be performed by an independent, qualified, registered professional engineer [40 CFR 265.196(f)].

Closure

At closure, the owner or the operator must remove or decontaminate all waste residues, contaminated containment system components, contaminated soils, and contaminated structures and equipment [40 CFR 265.197(a)].

If the owner or the operator cannot clean close the tank system or demonstrate that decontamination or removal of all soils is practicable, the system must be closed as a landfill [40 CFR 265.197(b)].

New Tank Systems

New tank systems must be designed, installed, and operated in compliance with the new tank standards. These standards require an assessment by an independent, qualified, registered professional engineer regarding the adequacy of the tank's structural support, foundation, seams, connections, and pressure control. This assessment must ensure that the tank will not fail, collapse, or rupture [40 CFR 264.192].

The owner or the operator of a tank must ensure that proper handling procedures are followed to prevent damage during the tank's installation.

Before a new tank system is covered or enclosed, a qualified installation inspector must examine the system for weld breaks, punctures, scrapes in the protective coating, cracks, corrosion, or any other structural damage, inadequate construction, or improper installation procedures. New tanks, including their ancillary equipment, must be tested for tightness prior to being covered or enclosed. Written documentation of these inspections and assessments must be obtained and kept at the facility.

SURFACE IMPOUNDMENTS

A *surface impoundment* is a facility or part of a facility that is a natural topographic depression, man-made excavation, or diked area formed primarily of earthen materials (although it may be lined with man-made materials), which is designed to hold an accumulation of liquid wastes or wastes containing free liquids and is not an injection well. Examples of surface impoundments are holding, storage, settling, and aeration pits; ponds; and lagoons [40 CFR 260.10].

For regulatory purposes, including the land disposal ban, it is important to make the regulatory distinction between a tank and a surface impoundment because of their structural similarities. If all the surrounding earthen material is removed from a unit and the unit maintains its structural integrity, it is a tank. However, if the unit does not maintain its structural integrity without support from surrounding earthen material, it is a surface impoundment [Regulatory Interpretation Letter (RIL) No. 110].

Interim Status Requirements

Any unit that is new or is an expansion or replacement of an interim status surface impoundment requires a double-liner system in compliance with the minimum technological requirements of HSWA. Existing interim status surface impoundments also must have been retrofitted to comply with the minimum technological requirements by November 8, 1988 [40 CFR 265.221].

General Operating Requirements

An impoundment must have at least two feet of freeboard (the space between the surface of the waste and the top of the containment device), which must be inspected daily to ensure compliance. The surface impoundment, including the dike and surrounding vegetation, must be inspected at least weekly to detect any leaks, deterioration, or failures in the impoundment [40 CFR 265.222].

Ignitable or reactive waste may not be placed into the impoundment unless the waste is treated so that it no longer retains its hazardous characteristic, or is managed in such a way as to prevent ignition or reaction [40 CFR 265.229].

All earthen dikes must have a protective cover, such as grass, shale, or rock, to minimize wind and water erosion as well as to preserve the structural integrity of the dike [40 CFR 265.233].

Waste Analysis

In addition to the waste analysis program required by the general facility standards contained in 40 CFR 264/265.13, whenever an impoundment is to be used to chemically treat a waste different from that previously treated, or to employ a substantially different method to treat the waste, the owner or the operator of the impoundment must conduct waste analyses and treatment tests (bench or pilot scale) or obtain written, documented information on similar treatment of similar waste under similar conditions to show that this treatment will not create any extreme heat, fire, explosion, violent reactions, toxic mists, fumes, gases, or dusts, or damage the structural integrity of the impoundment. The documentation or test results must be entered into the facility's operating record [40 CFR 265.225].

Closure

At closure, the owner or the operator may elect to remove or decontaminate at the impoundment *all* standing liquids, waste and waste residues, the containment system (e.g., liner), and underlying and surrounding contaminated soil and groundwater, or to close the impoundment as a landfill [40 CFR 265.228].

If the owner or the operator can demonstrate that *all* of the materials were removed or decontaminated as described, the impoundment will no longer be subject to 40 CFR Part 265. Removal of the underlying and surrounding contaminated soil must include the removal of any contaminated groundwater. This is known as a *clean closure* or closure by removal, as discussed in Chapter 5. However, if a clean closure cannot be attained, the closure plan must be modified and approved to close the surface impoundment as a landfill. A post-closure permit will be required, and when an owner or operator applies for a permit, selected

RCRA corrective action provisions [3004(u)] will be necessary, as discussed in Chapter 9.

Requirements for Permitted Surface Impoundments

All permitted surface impoundments must have a liner for all portions of the impoundment. The liner must be constructed in such a manner as to prevent any migration of wastes to the surrounding environment. Any new unit or expansion or replacement of a surface impoundment must have a double-liner system that is in compliance with the minimum technological requirements of HSWA. The double-liner requirement may be waived if the unit is a monofill that handles only foundry wastes that are hazardous solely because of the characteristic of toxicity, and it has at least one liner [40 CFR 264.221].

General Operating Requirements

Ignitable or reactive wastes may not be placed into the impoundment unless the waste no longer retains the ignitable or reactive characteristic [40 CFR 264.229].

The impoundment must be inspected weekly to detect any possible leakage [40 CFR 264.226(a)]. If the dike leaks or the level of liquid suddenly drops without known cause, the impoundment must be taken out of service, in which case the waste inflow must be discontinued, any surface leakage must be contained, and the leak must be immediately stopped. If the leak cannot be stopped, the contents must be removed. If any leakage enters the leak-detection system, EPA must be notified, in writing, within seven days. The impoundment cannot be placed back into service until all repairs are completed [40 CFR 264.227].

If the waste is removed from it, the unit is out of service. To reuse that unit, it must be retrofitted with a double liner meeting minimum technological requirements. Removing the waste and then reusing the unit is considered *replacement*.

Closure

If the impoundment is clean closed, it is no longer subject to RCRA. However, if it cannot clean close, it must be closed as a landfill subject to post-closure care and maintenance [40 CFR 264.228].

WASTE PILES

A *waste pile* is a noncontainerized accumulation of solid, nonflowing waste [40 CFR 260.10]. Any expansion or replacement of an existing waste pile or the creation of a new pile must comply with the minimum technological requirements of HSWA [40 CFR 265.254].

Interim Status Requirements

A waste pile operating under interim status must comply with the following requirements:

- The pile must be protected from wind dispersion [40 CFR 265.251].
- The pile must be located on an impermeable base [40 CFR 265.253].
- No liquid may be placed on the pile [40 CFR 265.253].
- The waste pile must be separated from other potentially incompatible materials [40 CFR 265.257].
- A run-on control and collection system must be installed and able to prevent a flow onto the active portion of the pile from a peak discharge from a 25-year storm, and the pile must be protected from precipitation (i.e., have a roof) and run-on [40 CFR 265.253].
- No ignitable or reactive wastes may be placed on the pile. However, once a waste is treated and no longer retains a hazardous waste characteristic, it may be placed onto the pile [40 CFR 265.256].

Waste Analysis

In addition to the waste analysis requirements of the general facility standards contained in 40 CFR 265.13, the owner or the operator must analyze a representative sample of the waste from each incoming shipment before adding the waste to a pile, unless the only wastes that the facility receives are amenable to piling and are compatible with each other. The waste analysis must be capable of differentiating between the types of hazardous wastes that the owner or the operator places on the pile to protect against inadvertent mixing of incompatible wastes [40 CFR 265.252].

Closure

All contaminated soil, groundwater, liners, equipment, and structures must be removed or decontaminated in accordance with the closure plan.

If not all materials are removed or decontaminated (i.e., clean closure does not occur), the pile must be closed as a landfill [40 CFR 265.258].

Requirements for Permitted Waste Piles

A permitted waste pile must have the following [40 CFR 264.251]:

- A liner on a supporting base or foundation that prevents the migration of any waste vertically or horizontally.
- A leachate collection and removal system, situated above the liner, that is maintained and operated to remove all leachate.
- A run-on control system able to collect and control the water from at least a 24-hour, 25-year storm.
- Inspections weekly and after any storm.

Any ignitable or reactive waste must be rendered nonignitable or non-reactive before being placed onto the pile.

Closure

The owner or operator must remove or decontaminate all equipment, structures, liners, groundwater, and soils in accordance with the closure plan. If the unit cannot clean close, it must be closed similar to a landfill [40 CFR 264.258].

LAND TREATMENT AREAS

Land treatment is the process of using the land or soil as a medium to simultaneously treat and dispose of hazardous waste. Land treatment is used primarily for petroleum wastes.

General Operating Requirements

Hazardous waste must not be placed on the land unless the waste can be made less hazardous or nonhazardous by biological degradation or chemical reactions in the soil. A treatment demonstration must be conducted prior to the application of wastes to verify that the hazardous constituents will be treated by the process [40 CFR 264.271 and 265.272].

Monitoring, according to a written plan, must be conducted on the soil beneath the treatment area, and the resulting data must be compared to data obtained on the background concentrations of constituents in untreated soils to detect any vertical migration of hazardous wastes or constituents [40 CFR 264/265.278].

Waste Analysis

In addition to the waste analysis requirements of the general standards contained in 40 CFR 264/265.13, waste analyses must be conducted [40 CFR 264.272 and 265.273] prior to placement of wastes in or on the land to determine the concentrations of:

- Any substance in the waste whose concentration meets or exceeds the levels in Table I of 40 CFR 261.4 (rendering the waste toxic by characteristic).
- Hazardous waste constituents (Appendix VIII).
- Arsenic, cadmium, lead, and mercury (if food-chain crops are grown on the land).

The growing of food-chain crops is prohibited in a treated area containing arsenic, cadmium, lead, mercury, and other hazardous constituents unless it is demonstrated that those constituents would not be transferred to the food portion of the crop, or they occur in concentrations less than those observed in identical groups grown on untreated soil in the same region [40 CFR 264/265.276].

Closure

During the closure period, the owner or the operator must continue operating practices that are designed to maximize degradation, transformation, and immobilization of the wastes at the land treatment area. Operating practices designed to maximize treatment include tilling of the soil, control of soil pH and moisture content, and fertilization. These practices generally must be continued throughout the closure period. In addition, the owner or the operator must continue those practices that were designed to minimize precipitation run-off from the treatment zone and to control wind dispersion (if needed) during the closure period [40 CFR 264/265.280].

Proper closure of a land treatment area includes the placement of a vegetative cover that is capable of maintaining growth without extensive maintenance. A vegetative cover consists of any plant material established on the treatment zone to provide protection against wind or water erosion or to aid in the treatment of hazardous constituents.

LANDFILLS

Landfilling historically has been the preferred means of disposing of hazardous waste. However, the U.S. Congress took the position that the existing requirements for land disposal were inadequate to protect human health and the environment, and through HSWA it discouraged land disposal. This includes the land disposal ban (discussed in Chapter 8) as well as other land disposal restrictions (e.g., prohibiting liquids in landfills and waste containing free liquids).

The problems that hazardous waste landfills have presented can be divided into two broad classes, which are addressed in the interim status requirements. The first class includes fires, explosions, production of toxic fumes, and similar problems resulting from the improper management of ignitable, reactive, and incompatible wastes. Owners and operators are required to conduct waste analyses to provide enough information for proper management. Mixing of incompatible wastes is prohibited in landfill cells, and ignitable and reactive wastes may be landfilled only when they are rendered nonignitable or nonreactive.

The second type of problem is the contamination of surface water and groundwater. To prevent contamination, there are required operational controls such as prohibiting the placement in a landfill of bulk, noncontainerized liquid hazardous wastes; nonhazardous liquid waste; or hazardous waste containing free liquids. This prevents the formation of hazardous leachate. An exemption on disposing of nonhazardous liquids may be obtained if the only reasonably available disposal method for such liquids is a landfill or unlined surface impoundment. Like surface impoundments and waste piles, a new landfill unit (including expansions or replacements) must install two or more liners and a leachate collection system (one collector above and one between the liners) in compliance with the minimum technological requirements of HSWA.

Other measures incorporated in the interim status regulations are diversions of precipitation run-on away from the active portion of the landfill, proper closure (including a cover) and post-closure care to control erosion and the infiltration of precipitation, and crushing or shredding of most landfilled containers so that they cannot later collapse with resultant subsidence and cracking of the cover. In addition, the regulations require the collection of precipitation and other run-off from the landfill to control surface water pollution. The segregation of wastes such as acids, which would mobilize, solubilize, or dissolve other wastes or waste constituents such as heavy metals, also is required.

Closure and Post-Closure

A final cover must be placed over a landfill at closure. The closure plan must address the functions as well as specify the design of the final cover. It is necessary to place an appropriate cover on a landfill to control the infiltration of moisture that could increase leaching and to prevent erosion or escape of contaminated soil.

There are specific requirements [40 CFR 264/265.310] regarding the type, depth, permeability, and number of soil layers required for the final cover. The requirements also list a minimum set of technical factors that the owner or the operator must consider in addressing the control objectives. These factors, with regard to cover design characteristics, include cover materials, surface contours, porosity and permeability, thickness, slope, run length of slope, and vegetation type. The cover design should take into account the number of soil compaction layers and the indigenous vegetation. It should avoid or make allowances for deep-rooted vegetation and should prevent water from pooling. The final cover design in many instances can simply be the placement, compaction, grading, sloping, and vegetation of on-site soils, or it could be a complex design such as a combination of compacted clay or a membrane liner placed over a graded and sloped base and covered by topsoil and vegetation.

INCINERATORS

An *incinerator* is any enclosed device using controlled flame combustion that neither meets the criteria or classification as a boiler nor is listed as an industrial furnace [40 CFR 260.10].

Interim Status Requirements

The interim status requirements are primarily general operating standards with some performance standards (except for the incineration of dioxin wastes, which have strict performance standards).

Exemptions

Under the interim status requirements, there are specified waste streams exempted from the incinerator requirements except for the closure requirements [40 CFR 265.340(b)]. For the owner or the operator to operate under an exemption, it must be documented that the exempted waste stream would not reasonably be expected to contain any of the Appendix VIII hazardous constituents and would be classified as one of the following wastes:

- A listed hazardous waste solely because it is ignitable, corrosive, or both.
- A listed hazardous waste solely because it is reactive for reasons other than its ability to generate toxic gases, vapors, or fumes that will not be burned when other hazardous wastes are present in the combustion zone.
- A characteristic hazardous waste solely because it is ignitable, corrosive, or both.
- A characteristic hazardous waste solely because it is reactive for reasons other than its ability to generate toxic gases, vapors, or fumes that will not be burned when other hazardous wastes are present in the combustion zone.

General Operating Requirements

During the start-up and shutdown phase of the incinerator, the owner or the operator must not feed hazardous waste into the unit unless the incinerator is at steady-state (normal) conditions of operation, including steady-state operating temperature and air flow [40 CFR 265.345].

The incinerator and all associated equipment (e.g., pumps, valves, conveyors) must be inspected at least daily for leaks, spills, fugitive emissions, and all emergency shutdown controls and alarm systems to assure proper operation. Instruments relating to combustion and emission control must be monitored at least every 15 minutes. If needed, corrections must be made immediately to maintain steady-state combustion [40 CFR 265.347].

Waste Analysis

In addition to the waste analysis required under 40 CFR 265.13 of the general standards, the owner or the operator must sufficiently analyze any hazardous waste that has not been previously burned in the incinerator. The purpose of the additional waste analysis requirements is to establish steady-state operating conditions, which include waste and auxiliary fuel feed and air flow requirements, and to determine the type of pollutants that might be emitted [40 CFR 265.341]. At a minimum, the analysis must determine:

- Heating value of the waste.
- Halogen and sulfur content of the waste.
- Concentrations of lead and mercury in the waste unless there is written documentation showing that these elements are not present.

Closure

At closure, all hazardous waste and hazardous waste residues must be removed from the incinerator. Hazardous waste residues include, but are not limited to, ash, scrubber waters, and scrubber sludges. Because incinerators typically also have regulated storage areas, appropriate cleanup of these units must be addressed as well [40 CFR 265.351].

Requirements for Permitted Incinerators

For permitted incinerators, each permit specifies the hazardous waste that is allowed to be incinerated and the operating conditions required for each waste feed. When an owner or an operator wishes to burn wastes for which operating conditions have not been set in a permit, either a permit modification must be secured or, if the burn is to be of short duration and for the specific purposes listed in 40 CFR 122.27(b), a temporary trial burn permit must be obtained.

There are three general performance standards [40 CFR 264.343] applicable to incinerators subject to the Part 264 provisions:

- A 99.99 percent destruction and removal efficiency (DRE) is required for each principal organic constituent specified in the permit.
- Incinerators burning hazardous waste containing more than 0.5 percent chlorine must remove 99 percent of the hydrogen chloride from their exhaust gas.
- Particulate matter must not exceed 180 mg per dry standard cubic meter of gas emitted through the stack.

Mobile Incinerators

Under RCRA, a mobile incinerator must obtain a permit for each site where it intends to operate. This is because a mobile incinerator meets the definition of a new facility. The owner or the operator can submit trial burn data from previous operations in lieu of data from the anticipated site.

When applying for a permit for a mobile incinerator, the applicant should use the model permit application and permit developed for the first permitted mobile treatment site, EPA Office of Research and Development's mobile incinerator at the Denny Farm Site in Missouri (OSWER Directive 9527-02).

Trial Burns

Compliance with the standards for incinerators burning hazardous waste initially must be established through the performance of a *trial burn,* which is a test of an incinerator's ability to meet all applicable performance standards when burning a waste under a specific set of operating conditions. During the trial burn, the applicant tests the incinerator's ability to destroy the hazardous waste or wastes to be treated at the facility. Generally, the goal in conducting the trial burn is to identify the most efficient conditions, or range of conditions, under which the incinerator can be operated in compliance with the performance standards.

General Operating Requirements

During start-up or shutdown phases of the incinerator, hazardous wastes must not be fed into the incinerator unless it is operating within the specified conditions of operation (e.g., temperature, air feed rate) contained in the permit. The incinerator must be operated with a functioning system that can automatically cut off the waste feed to the incinerator when required to do so [40 CFR 264.345(c)].

Waste feed mixtures must be specified in the facility's permit. For each waste feed mixture identified, the permit will specify the principal organic hazardous constituents (POHCs) that must be destroyed or removed as required by the appropriate performance standard. Thus, identification of those waste feed constituents to which the performance standard will be applied is central to the application of the regulatory program. EPA designates specific POHCs, rather than all hazardous constituents of the waste, that are the most difficult to destroy. This approach ensures that less stable hazardous organic constituents also are destroyed [40 CFR 264.342(b)].

Inspections and Monitoring

The incinerator and all associated equipment (e.g., pumps, valves, and conveyors) must be inspected at least daily for leaks, spills, and fugitive emissions, and all emergency waste feed cutoff controls and alarm systems must be inspected to verify proper operation [40 CFR 264.347(b)].

At a minimum, the following monitoring must be done [40 CFR 264.347(a)] while the unit is incinerating hazardous waste:

- Combustion temperature, waste feed rate, and air feed rate must be checked on a continuous basis.
- Carbon monoxide must be continuously monitored at a point in the incinerator downstream of the combustion zone and prior to release to the atmosphere.
- As specified by the permit, or upon request by EPA, sampling and analysis of the waste and exhaust emissions can be required, to verify that the specified performance standards are achieved.

Data obtained from inspections or monitoring must be recorded and maintained in the facility's operating log.

Closure

At closure, all hazardous waste and hazardous waste residues must be removed from the incinerator. Hazardous waste residues include, but are not limited to, ash, scrubber waters, and scrubber sludges. Because incinerators typically also have regulated storage areas, appropriate closure of these units must be addressed as well [40 CFR 264.351].

THERMAL TREATMENT UNITS

Thermal treatment is the treatment of hazardous waste in a device that uses elevated temperature as the primary means to change the chemical, physical, or biological character or composition of the waste. By comparison, incineration uses controlled flame combustion to oxidize a waste, which is more closely associated with destruction rather than treatment.

Several methods of thermal treatment, such as molten salt pyrolysis, calcination, and wet air oxidation, are regulated under this subsection. Owners or operators who thermally treat hazardous wastes (other than incinerators) must operate the unit by following most of the requirements that are applied to an incinerator. However, the thermal treatment standards prohibit open burning of hazardous waste except for the detonation of explosives such as outdated military ordnances.

Only interim status standards are available for these units. The Part 264 standards for the units are addressed in the Subpart X standards for miscellaneous units.

CHEMICAL, PHYSICAL, AND BIOLOGICAL TREATMENT UNITS

Treatment, although most frequently conducted in tanks, surface impoundments, and land treatment areas, also can occur in other types of equipment by such processes as centrifugation, reverse osmosis, ion exchange, and filtration. Because the processes are frequently waste-specific, EPA has not developed detailed regulations for any particular type of process or equipment. Instead, general requirements have been established to ensure safe containment of hazardous wastes. In most respects, these other treatment methods are very similar to using tanks for treatment; therefore, they are essentially regulated in the same way. The requirements that must be met include avoiding equipment or process failure that could pose a hazard, restricting the use of reagents or wastes that could cause equipment or a process to fail, and installing safety systems in continuous flow operations to stop the waste inflow in case of a malfunction.

Only interim status standards are available for these units. The Part 264 standards for these units are addressed by the Subpart X standards for miscellaneous units.

MISCELLANEOUS UNITS

Introduction

A *miscellaneous unit* is a hazardous waste management unit in which hazardous waste is treated, stored, or disposed of, and which is not a container, tank, surface impoundment, waste pile, land treatment area, landfill, incinerator, boiler, industrial furnace, or underground injection well [40 CFR 260.10].

Previously, EPA promulgated standards for specific units, but some hazardous waste management technologies were not covered by the existing Part 264 standards. Thus, owners or operators of facilities utilizing these technologies were not able to obtain the necessary RCRA operating permits for these units. To rectify this problem, EPA promulgated (52 *FR* 46946, December 10, 1987) a new set of standards under the heading of Subpart X of Part 264, Standards for Miscellaneous Units. These standards are applicable to owners and operators of new and existing miscellaneous units.

General Operating Requirements

A miscellaneous unit must be located, designed, constructed, operated, and closed in a manner that will ensure protection of human health and the environment. So that the requirements will be met, permit conditions must incorporate the requirements under Subparts I through O of Part 264 that are appropriate for the unit to be permitted. In addition, the principal hazardous substance migration pathways must be protected. These pathways are:

- Wetlands
- Soil
- Groundwater
- Surface water
- Air

UNDERGROUND INJECTION WELLS

EPA has estimated that in 1987, approximately 10 percent (30 million metric tons) of RCRA regulated hazardous waste (primarily liquids) was disposed of in underground injection wells. These wells are regulated primarily by the Underground Injection Control (UIC) program established under Part C of the Safe Drinking Water Act (SDWA). SDWA has established five classes of injection wells. These are:

Class I—   Wells that are used to inject liquid wastes, including hazardous waste, below the lowermost underground of drinking water. (*Underground sources of drinking water* are those currently serving as a public drinking water supply or those which have the potential to serve as a public drinking water supply and have less than 10,000 mg/l total dissolved solids.) Less than 1 percent of all injection wells are Class I. Of these wells, 34 percent inject hazardous waste.

Class II— Wells used in oil and gas production, primarily the injection of produced brine, injection for enhanced recovery, and hydrocarbon storage.

Class III— Wells that are used to inject fluids for the extraction of minerals.

Class IV— Wells, which are currently banned, used to inject hazardous or radioactive waste into or above an underground source of drinking water.

Class V— Wells, currently unregulated, that are used for purposes not identified in the first four classes of wells.

Class I UIC wells that are used to dispose of hazardous waste must have authorization under SDWA and RCRA. Although the UIC program under SDWA regulates an injection well below the wellhead, all Class I UIC wells that inject hazardous waste must also be authorized under RCRA as a hazardous waste management facility. They are eligible for interim status and must comply with 40 CFR 265.430. In addition, Class I UIC wells are eligible for a permit-by-rule under 40 CFR 270.60(b), explained further in Chapter 7. Class I UIC wells that apply for a permit-by-rule will then be subject to the corrective action requirements established under 3004(u) of RCRA which is discussed in Chapter 9. In addition, Class I UIC wells are subject to the applicable requirements of the land disposal restrictions program discussed in Chapter 8.

Similar to RCRA, the SDWA UIC program allows for a state to operate the UIC program with oversight from the federal government. A state that operates the program in lieu of the federal government is classified as having *primacy*. Texas and Louisiana, which contain 73 percent of all Class I hazardous waste wells, have primacy.

Chapter 7

Permits and Interim Status

An owner or operator of a hazardous waste treatment, storage, or disposal facility (TSDF) is required to obtain a permit to legally operate. A qualified facility that does not yet have a permit may operate under interim status. Permits stipulate the required administrative and technical performance standards for the facilities in the form of permit conditions.

INTRODUCTION

Because all hazardous waste management facilities are required to obtain a permit, with some exceptions (see below), that is the key to implementing the Subtitle C program. On the effective date of the RCRA regulations (November 19, 1980), the treatment, storage, or disposal of hazardous waste was prohibited unless the operations were authorized by a RCRA permit or excluded. However, this provision obviously would have created a disastrous situation for the Nation's hazardous waste management program as it existed then. Therefore, Congress established interim status provisions. A facility with interim status is considered to be operating under a permit until such time as EPA takes final administrative action on the facility's permit application. The permit procedures, as well as operation during interim status regulations, are contained in 40 CFR Part 270.

Exclusions

The following persons or processes are excluded from the requirement to obtain either a permit or interim status to operate under RCRA:

- Facilities that are state approved to exclusively handle small-quantity generator waste (less than 100 kg/mo).
- Facilities that meet the definition of a totally enclosed treatment facility in 40 CFR 260.10.
- A generator accumulating waste in compliance with 40 CFR 262.34.
- A farmer disposing of waste pesticides from his or her own use in compliance with 40 CFR 262.51.
- An elementary neutralization unit or a wastewater treatment unit as defined in 40 CFR 260.10.
- A person engaged in the immediate treatment or containment of a discharge of hazardous waste.
- A transporter storing manifested waste at a transfer facility in compliance with 40 CFR 262.30.
- The addition of absorbent material to waste or vice versa.

Relationship with NEPA

EPA has determined that RCRA permits are not subject to the environmental impact statement (EIS) provisions of Section 102(2)(C) of the National Environmental Policy Act (NEPA) [40 CFR 124.9(b)(6)]. EPA has asserted (45 *FR* 33173, May 19, 1980) that RCRA permit requirements are the functional equivalent of an EIS; thus, an EIS is not required.

INTERIM STATUS

Interim status is the statutorily conferred authorization for a hazardous waste management facility to operate pending issuance or denial of its RCRA permit. The interim status provisions, contained in 40 CFR Part 265, allow a facility to operate legally. The facility is considered to be operating under a permit until EPA takes final administrative action on that facility's permit application.

Originally, the requirements for obtaining interim status included establishing that a facility was in existence on November 19, 1980, filing a Section 3010 notification, and filing a Part A permit application. The HSWA provisions changed the interim status eligibility requirements; previously a facility had to have existed on November 19, 1980, but HSWA changed the in-existence requirement to the effective date of a regulatory or statutory change. For example, a facility is managing a solid waste. If EPA lists that particular waste as a hazardous waste, the facility is then eligible for interim status (unless the facility has a permit for which a modification is required), provided that the facility notified EPA (Section 3010) and a Part A permit application are filed by the date specified in the rule. Thus, any facility in existence on the effective date of a new regulation is eligible for interim status provided that interim status was not previously terminated for that facility.

Part A Permit Application

The Part A permit application is a request for interim status for existing facilities and the initial permitting step for new facilities. A standardized form (EPA Form 3510-1) is used, which requires general information about a facility, including:

- Name of the owner or the operator and the facility address, including longitudinal and latitudinal coordinates.
- The activities to be conducted that require a RCRA permit.
- The facility's design capacity.
- Description of the processes for treating, storing, or disposing of hazardous wastes.
- Description of the facility's processes generating hazardous waste.
- A scale drawing of the facility, including photographs.
- A detailed description of hazardous wastes to be handled.
- A topographic map.
- A listing of all federal environmental permits obtained or applied for by the facility.

EPA may issue a Notice of Deficiency (NOD) to any owner or operator of an existing hazardous waste management facility who submits a deficient Part A permit application. The owner or operator has 30 days after being notified to explain or amend the application before being subject to EPA enforcement. After such notification and opportunity for response, EPA will determine if that facility qualifies for interim status (OSWER Directive 9528:50-1A).

Operation during Interim Status

A facility must comply with the applicable requirements contained in 40 CFR Part 265 as discussed in Chapters 5 and 6. (Chapter 5 addresses general facility requirements, whereas Chapter 6 addresses unit-specific requirements.)

A facility is subject to the Part 265 standards only until it receives its final permit. On the day the final permit is issued, the facility is subject to the conditions specified in its permit, which are based on the Part 264 standards.

A facility that has had its interim status terminated must meet the Part 265 standards, including those for closure, post-closure, and financial responsibility. A technical amendment to the interim status regulations, which was published in the November 21, 1984 *Federal Register* (49 *FR* 46094), clarified that interim status standards are applicable to facilities whose interim status is terminated until their closure and post-closure requirements are fulfilled. Thus, even if a facility no longer has interim status (and thus can no longer manage hazardous waste), the facility must comply with all applicable regulations under interim status until it is satisfactorily closed.

Operational Requirements

There are specific operational constraints (beyond the operating standards of interim status of Part 265) established for interim status facilities. These operational constraints, contained in 40 CFR 270.71 and 270.72, are:

- A facility may not treat, store, or dispose of any hazardous waste not specified in the facility's Part A permit application.
- A facility may not employ processes not specified in the Part A permit application.
- A facility may not exceed the design capacities that were specified in the Part A permit application.
- A facility may not make any changes to the facility during interim status that constitute reconstruction of that facility. (*Reconstruction* is a capital investment exceeding 50 percent of the capital cost of a comparable new hazardous waste management facility.) However, changes that are prohibited under this provision do not include changes to treat or store in containers or tanks hazardous wastes subject to the land disposal prohibitions imposed by Part 268, provided that such changes are made solely for the purpose of complying with Part 268.

These changes (except reconstruction) are allowed under certain conditions. New wastes can be handled simply by submitting a revised Part A permit application. The process and design capacity changes require a revised Part A permit application, written justification for a change, and state or federal approval [40 CFR 270.72].

A change of ownership or operational control of a facility is allowed if the facility submits a revised Part A at least 90 days prior to the change. The previous owner or operator must comply with the financial requirements until the new owner or operator can demonstrate compliance with the financial requirements to EPA. The new owner or operator must comply with the financial requirements within six months of the change.

HAZARDOUS WASTE MANAGEMENT PERMITS

Permits are issued by EPA, an authorized state, or both. Currently, under HSWA, until states receive HSWA authorization, all permits are handled as a joint issuance provided that the state has the authority to implement pre-HSWA provisions. A joint permit may be issued in two ways: there can be one complete permit with signatures of both the State Director and the EPA Regional Administrator on the same document; or the second option is issuance of two incomplete permits, one signed by EPA and the other signed by the state. In either situation, signatures by EPA and the state are necessary to provide the facility with authority to operate under RCRA. If a single permit is issued, it is important to have a clear understanding of which provisions stem from federal authorities and which from state authorities. This distinction will enable a permittee to determine the appropriate authority to approach when appealing a given permit condition. If the state has no authorization, EPA issues the permit.

The actual permit consists simply of written approval of the completed permit application. The permit requires the applicant to adhere to all statements made in the application and may include conditions (e.g., corrective action) with which the applicant must comply.

Standards Applicable to All Permits

Under 40 CFR 270.30, the following conditions apply to all RCRA permits and are incorporated into the permits either expressly or by reference:

- Compliance with all conditions of the permit.
- Proper operation and maintenance, including the operation of backup or auxiliary units when necessary to achieve compliance.

- Halting production when necessary to ensure compliance, and taking all reasonable steps to minimize releases to the environment.
- Providing all relevant information requests by EPA regarding facility operation, including the reporting of any noncompliance that may endanger health or the environment within 24 hours of the time when the owner or the operator becomes aware of such conditions. (*Note:* A notice of anticipated noncompliance does not suspend or negate any permit condition.)
- Allowing authorized representatives to inspect the facility upon presentation of credentials.
- Maintaining and reporting all records and monitoring information necessary to document and verify compliance, including data such as continuous-strip chart recordings from monitoring instruments.
- Reporting all planned changes and anticipated periods of noncompliance.

EPA's Omnibus Permit Authority

Section 3005(c)(3) of RCRA gives the permit-issuing agency (state or federal) broad authority concerning permit conditions. This section reads: "Each permit issued under this Section [3005] shall contain such terms and conditions as the Administrator [or state] determines necessary to protect human health and the environment."

This provision allows the issuing agency to impose permit conditions beyond those contained in the Subtitle C regulations as may be necessary to protect human health and the environment from risks posed by a particular facility. For example, this authority could be used if a facility adversely affected vulnerable groundwater because of a lack of adequate location standards.

Permit Shield Provision

The regulations provide that compliance with a RCRA permit during its term constitutes compliance with the statute. The purpose of the shield provision is to protect permittees who are in full compliance with their permit yet may not be in full compliance with other provisions under RCRA. The permit shield provision protects the permittee from enforcement action brought by EPA and states as well as civil actions from citizen groups. However, this provision does not provide a defense to an imminent hazard action under Section 7003 of RCRA (45 *FR* 33428, May 19, 1980).

Permit-by-Rule

To avoid duplicative permitting, EPA has established the permit-by-rule program. A *permit-by-rule* is essentially an amendment to an existing federal environmental permit stating that a facility or activity is deemed to have a RCRA permit if it meets specified requirements. Those eligible for a permit-by-rule are:

- Publicly owned treatment works (POTWs) that have a permit under the National Pollutant Discharge Elimination System (NPDES) under the Clean Water Act (CWA).
- Persons with ocean dumping permits under the Marine Protection, Research, and Sanctuaries Act (MPRSA).
- Permitted Underground Injection Control (UIC) facilities under the Safe Drinking Water Act (SDWA).

The specified requirements for obtaining a permit-by-rule for the above activities are contained in 40 CFR 270.60.

Permit Application Process

The necessary steps in the permitting process, regulated under Parts 124 and 270, are depicted in Figure 7-1.

The basic steps in the permitting process are as follows:

1. The owner or the operator of a hazardous waste management facility completes and submits both Parts A and B of a RCRA permit application.
2. EPA conducts an administrative and technical review of the permit application for completeness. EPA may issue a notice of deficiency and request additional information.*
3. If it is required, the applicant prepares and submits additional information.
4. EPA again reviews the original and any additional submittals and notifies the applicant, in writing, that the application is complete.
5. EPA prepares a draft permit or issues a notice of intent to deny the application.

---

*At *any time* during the process, a Notice of Deficiency (NOD) may be issued to the permittee for deficient information. The permit applicant then must either submit the requested information, withdraw the application, or face possible denial of the permit.

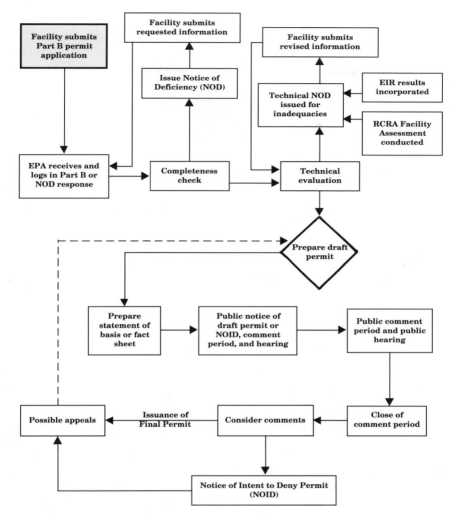

Figure 7-1. Permit Process

6. EPA sends copies of the document prepared in Step 5 to the applicant and simultaneously notifies the public. The notice is to allow for public and applicant comment.
7. If a public hearing is requested, it will be scheduled and announced at least 30 days prior to the hearing date.
8. EPA prepares and issues a final permit decision.

Part B Permit Application

Owners and operators of hazardous waste management facilities are required to submit a permit application that address the design, operation, maintenance, and closure of the facility as outlined in 40 CFR Part 270. The permit application is divided into two parts, A and B.

If the operator of a facility submits the permit application, the owner of the facility also must sign it; if the owner fails to sign the application, then a RCRA permit cannot be issued (OSWER Directive 9523.01). Both the owner and the operator are the "permittees" on the permit; however, it is common for the operator to assume responsibility for meeting permit conditions. Both the owner and the operator are liable during the facility's operating life. Both the owner and the operator are liable during closure and post-closure of the facility, unless the closure and post-closure plans specify that the owner of the facility is becoming the operator as well as the owner. This action would be accompanied by a permit modification and relieve the original operator from liability (under RCRA) during the closure and post-closure period.

Confidentiality

An applicant may claim information in the permit application as confidential in compliance with Part 2 of 40 CFR, which sets forth the general requirements and procedures for EPA's handling of confidential information. 40 CFR 270.12 requires that the permit applicant attach a cover sheet, use a stamp, or type a notice of confidentiality on each page of the information, or otherwise identify its confidential portion(s). Whenever possible, the applicant should separate the information contained in the application into confidential and nonconfidential sections and submit them under separate cover letters.

If there is a public request for information under the Freedom of Information Act, before releasing any information for which a claim of confidentiality has been made EPA will give the applicant an opportunity to substantiate the claim, and then will determine whether the information warrants confidential treatment. If it is considered confidential by EPA, such information will not be released.

Contents of the Application

There is no standard form for the Part B permit application. It is a document prepared by the permit applicant that addresses each point of concern specified in 40 CFR 270.22, and it may be presented in several ways. The actual application format is left to the discretion of the applicant. However, EPA suggests, in its *Permit Applicant's Guidance Manual for Land Disposal, Treatment, and Storage Facilities*, a general format for the submission of a Part B permit application, as follows:

PART I—GENERAL INFORMATION REQUIREMENTS

- A copy of the Part A permit application.
- General description of the facility.
- The process codes (from Part A) that identify the type of units for which the permit is required.
- Chemical and physical analysis of hazardous waste to be handled and a copy of the waste analysis plan.
- Security description for the active portion of the facility.
- General inspection schedule and description of the procedures, including the specific requirements for particular units.
- Preparedness and prevention documentation.
- Contingency plan documentation.
- Documentation of preventive procedures, structures, and equipment for control of unloading hazards, waste run-off, water supply contamination, effects of equipment failure and power outages, and undue personnel exposure to wastes.
- Documentation of prevention of accidental ignition or reaction, including specific requirements for particular unit types.
- Facility traffic documentation.
- Facility location documentation.
- Personnel training program documentation.
- Closure plan documentation, including specific requirements for particular unit types.
- Post-closure plan, when applicable, including specific requirements for particular unit types.
- Documentation for deed notice.
- Closure cost estimate and documentation of financial assurance mechanism.
- Post-closure cost estimate and documentation of financial assurance mechanism.
- Documentation of insurance.
- Topographical map showing contours with 0.5- to 2.0-meter intervals, map scale, map date, 100-year floodplain area, surface waters including intermittent streams, surrounding land uses, wind rose, north orientation, legal boundaries of facility, access control, injection and withdrawal wells, buildings and other structures, utility areas, barriers for drainage or flood control, and location of operating

units, including equipment cleaning areas. Each hazardous waste management unit should be shown on the map with a unique identification code and the associated process code from the Part A.

PART II—SPECIFIC INFORMATION REQUIREMENTS

The information contained in this section depends on the particular type of unit for which the permit is required. Refer to Subparts I, J, K, L, M, N, O, and X of Part 264 for the appropriate unit specific information requirements.

PART III—ADDITIONAL INFORMATION REQUIREMENTS

- Summary of groundwater monitoring data obtained during the interim status period.
- Identification of aquifers beneath the facility.
- Delineation of waste management area and point of compliance for groundwater monitoring on topographic map.
- Description of any existing plume of contamination in the groundwater.
- Detailed groundwater monitoring program description.
- Detection monitoring program description, if applicable.
- Compliance monitoring program description, if applicable.

PART IV—INFORMATION REQUIREMENTS FOR SOLID WASTE MANAGEMENT UNITS

- Location of SWMUs on topographic map.
- Type of SWMU (e.g., pile, landfill).
- Dates of operation.
- An inventory of all wastes managed at the SWMU.
- Information on release of hazardous waste or constituents.
- Dimensions and structured descriptions.

PART V—EXPOSURE INFORMATION REPORT

The Hazardous and Solid Waste Amendments (Section 3019) require all permit applications submitted after August 7, 1985, to be accompanied by an exposure information report. The major goals of this report are to identify human exposures to past releases from subject units and potential exposures from future releases that may be mitigated by specific permit conditions.

The three elements needed to assess a complete exposure pathway for a past release are: (1) a confirmed release of hazardous constituents, (2) migration of constituents off-site, and (3) population known (or suspected) to have come into contact with the contaminated media. The pathways of concern include groundwater, air, surface water, subsurface gas, soil, and food-chain contamination.

Administrative and Technical Review

When EPA receives a RCRA permit application, it reviews the application for administrative and technical completeness. The completeness review generally takes 60 days for existing facilities and 30 days for new ones.

If the application is incomplete, EPA will request the missing information through a Notice of Deficiency (NOD) letter, which details the information needed to complete the application and specifies the date for submission of the data. EPA can issue a warning letter to accompany the NOD, requiring submission of the necessary information within a specified additional period of time. If an applicant fails or refuses to correct the deficiencies in the application, the permit may be denied, and appropriate enforcement actions may be taken under statutory provisions including RCRA Section 3008 (OSWER Directive 9521.01).

EPA will determine when the application is complete. This determination, however, is not necessarily a determination that the application is free of deficiencies. During detailed review of the application and drafting of the permit conditions, it may become necessary for the applicant to clarify, modify, or supplement provisions previously submitted before a draft permit is granted or a decision to deny is made.

Technical Review

The purpose of the technical review is to determine whether a specific facility should be granted a permit; in other words, to determine if the facility has satisfied all the siting, design, and operation criteria, as well as closure, post-closure, and financial requirements.

The steps of the technical review include:

- Preliminary review
- Site visit
- Verification of accuracy
- Compliance assessment

The *preliminary review* involves primarily a secondary completeness check to ensure that the applicant has responded adequately to any previous notices of deficiency.

The *site visit* enables the permit reviewer/writer to inspect the facility and its hazardous waste management units to ensure that the permit application accurately reflects the stated conditions.

The *verification of accuracy* involves a check on the reasonableness of data and the accuracy of computations. It also requires a professional assessment of information, assumptions, and methodology presented to identify weaknesses that may require a response from the permit applicant.

The *compliance assessment,* conducted concurrently with the accuracy verification step, is a process intended to ensure that the permitted operations will be in compliance with Part 264.

Upon completion of the technical review, EPA tentatively decides whether to issue or deny a RCRA permit. If the tentative decision is to issue the permit, EPA prepares a draft permit. EPA also must prepare a fact sheet or a statement of basis for the public, which explains in simple language each condition included in the draft permit and the reasons for each condition. The draft permit, prepared primarily for public review, contains tentative conditions.

Permit Compliance Schedules

Permit compliance schedules can be used to allow facilities to construct or install equipment that is not mandated under Part 265 but is required under Part 264. However, a permit compliance schedule cannot be used to satisfy the information requirements under Part 270. A permit compliance schedule must be specific and enforceable, give for public notice and comment, and give the applicant additional time only when it is legitimately needed (OSWER Directive 9524.01).

Draft Permit

A draft permit functions only as a tentative decision on the issuance, modification, reissuance, or termination of a permit. It is only a proposal, subject to change based on comments received during the public comment period and hearing. The draft permit must be accompanied by a statement of basis or a fact sheet (described below), and must be based on the administrative record. When public notice of the draft permit is given, as required by 40 CFR 124.10(a), the comment period on the permit application begins. It is during this time that interested persons must raise all issues. Failure to do so can limit the ability to raise an issue on appeal.

Public Comment

In accordance with 40 CFR 124.10(a), public notice must be given whenever:

- A permit application has been tentatively denied.
- A draft permit has been prepared.
- An informal public hearing has been scheduled.
- An appeal has been granted by EPA regarding a final permit decision.

EPA must issue a public notice identifying the applicant and the facility and must state where copies of the draft permit and other related information may be obtained (e.g., statement of basis or fact sheet). The notice must be circulated in local newspapers for major permits and mailed to various agencies and parties expressing interest.

Public notice provides interested persons a minimum of 45 days to comment on the draft permit. If written opposition to EPA's intent to issue a permit and a request for a hearing are received during the comment period, a public hearing may be held. Notification of the hearing is issued at least 30 days prior to the scheduled date, and the public comment period is extended until the close of the public hearing.

Statement of Basis and Fact Sheet

The statement of basis and the fact sheet, which must accompany the public notice of the draft permit, briefly set forth the principal facts and the significant factual, legal, methodological, and policy questions considered in preparing the draft permit.

The fact sheet must be prepared for all *major facilities* (i.e., land disposal facilities and incinerators) and for those facilities that EPA finds are "the subject of widespread public interest or raise major issues" [40 CFR 124.8].

Both documents must include the following information:

- A description of the activity that requires the draft permit.
- The type and quantity of wastes that are proposed to be or are being treated, stored, or disposed of.
- Reasons why any requested variances or alternatives to required standards do or do not appear justified.

- A description of the procedures used in reaching a final decision on the draft permit, including:
  - The extent of the public comment period.
  - Procedures for requesting a hearing.
  - Any other procedures in which the public can participate.
- Name and telephone number of a person to contact.

After the close of the public comment period (which includes the public hearing period), EPA must either grant or deny the permit application. In either case, the applicant and those persons submitting questions and those requesting notification must be notified of the decision, and must be given information regarding appeal procedures.

Permit Issuance

Final RCRA permits become effective 30 days after the date of the public notice of decision to issue a final permit unless a later date is specified in the permit, or the conditions of 40 CFR 124.15(b) are met. At the time when the final RCRA permit is issued, EPA also issues a response to any significant public comments received and indicates any provisions of the draft permit that have been changed and the reasons for the changes. The response to comments becomes part of the administrative record.

Permit Duration

A permit may be issued for any length of time up to ten years. All land disposal permits must be reviewed every five years and modified if necessary. However, a permit can be terminated at any time if noncompliance with any condition of the permit occurs, any false information was included in the application, or the facility's activity endangers human health or the environment.

Permit Denial

A permit may be issued or denied for one or more units at a facility without simultaneous issuance or denial of a permit to all of the units at the facility [40 CFR 270.1(c)(4)]. (The interim status of any unit for which a permit has not been issued or denied does not affect the issuance or denial of a permit for any other unit at a facility.)

If EPA tentatively decides to deny a RCRA permit, a notice of intent to deny a permit is prepared. This notice is considered a type of draft permit and follows the same procedures as any other draft permit. These procedures include preparation of a statement of basis or a fact sheet containing reasons supporting the tentative decision to deny the permit, public notices of the denial, acceptance of comments, a possible hearing, preparation of a final decision, and possible receipt of a request for appeal.

A permit may be denied for the following reasons:

- The facility cannot meet the requirements set forth in 40 CFR Part 264.
- Activities at the facility would endanger human health or the environment.
- An applicant is believed not to have fully disclosed all relevant facts in the application or during the RCRA permit issuance process.
- An applicant has misrepresented relevant facts.
- The application did not fully meet the requirements of Part 270 (e.g., did not have the signature(s) of both the owner and the operator).

Permit Appeals

An owner or an operator wanting to appeal a permit denial must follow the procedures in 40 CFR 124.19, which addresses recourse for permit denial. This section contains procedures for informal hearings.

Persons who submitted comments on the draft RCRA permit or participated in any public hearing are allowed 30 days after the final permit decision to file a notice of appeal and a petition for review with the EPA Administrator in Washington, DC, who will review and then grant or deny the petition within a reasonable time. If the Administrator decides to conduct a review, the parties are given the opportunity to file briefs in support of their positions. Within the 30-day period, the Administrator may, on his or her own motion, decide to review the decision to grant or deny a hearing. The Administrator then notifies the parties and schedules a hearing. On review, the Administrator has several options regarding the final decision. It may be summarily affirmed without opinion, modified, set aside, or remanded for further proceedings. This petition for review is a prerequisite for judicial review of the Administrator's final decision.

Permit Modifications

The permit establishes a facility's operating conditions for hazardous waste management. However, over time, the facility may need to modify the permit to improve equipment, employ new management techniques, conduct corrective action, or make changes in response to new standards. Recognizing this, EPA established procedures for modifying permits.

Requirements

Previously, there were two types of permit modifications, major and minor. Any modification that was not classified as minor was considered a major modification. Major modifications required public notice and comment as well as the issuance of a draft permit, which was a lengthy process.

On September 28, 1988 (53 *FR* 37912), EPA revised the regulations governing permit modifications contained in 40 CFR 270.41 and 270.42 to incorporate a process that better accommodates the different types of modifications. The revisions provide both owners and operators and EPA more flexibility to change specified permit conditions, expand public notification and participation opportunities, and allow for expedited approval if no public concern exists regarding a proposed change.

The program establishes procedures that apply to changes facility owners and operators may want to make at their facilities. EPA has categorized selected permit modifications into three classes and established administrative procedures for approving modifications in each of these classes.

Appendix I to 40 CFR 270.42 (see Appendix F of this book) contains a list of specific modifications and assigns them to Class 1, 2, or 3 designations, which may be described as follows:

- Class 1 permit modifications address routine and administrative changes.
- Class 2 permit modifications primarily address improvements in technology and management techniques.
- Class 3 permit modifications deal with major changes to a facility and its operations.

EPA has established procedures [40 CFR 270.42(d)] for a permittee wishing to make a permit modification covering an activity that does not have a predesignated class: submit a Class 3 modification request or alternatively ask EPA for a determination that Class 1 or 2 modification procedures should apply. In making this determination, EPA will consider the similarity of the requested modification to listed modifications and also will apply the general definitions of Class 1, 2, and 3 modifications.

Class 1 Modifications

Class 1 modifications are those that do not substantially alter the permit conditions or significantly affect the overall operation of the facility. They cover changes that are necessary to correct minor errors in the permit, to upgrade plans and records maintained by the facility, or to make routine changes to the facility or its operation. Generally, these modifications include the correction of typographical errors; necessary updating of names, addresses, or phone numbers identified in the permit or its supporting documents; updating of sampling and analytical methods to conform with revised EPA guidance or regulations; updating of certain types of schedules identified in the permit; replacement of equipment with functionally equivalent equipment; and replacement of damaged groundwater monitoring wells.

The approval procedures for Class 1 modifications are specified in 40 CFR 270.42(a). There are two categories of Class 1 modifications: those that do not require prior EPA approval and those that do.

Under the procedures, the permittee may, at any time, put into effect any Class 1 modification that does not require prior EPA approval. The permittee is required to notify EPA by certified mail or by any other means that establishes proof of delivery within seven calendar days of making the change. The notice must specify the change being made to the permit conditions or documents referenced in the permit and explain briefly why it was necessary.

The permittee also is required to notify, by mail, persons on the *facility mailing list* within 90 days of making the modification. [EPA is required under 40 CFR 124.10(c)(viii) to compile and maintain a mailing list for each RCRA permitted facility. The list must include all persons who have asked in writing to be on the list (e.g., in response to public solicitations from EPA). Also, it generally includes both local residents in the vicinity of the facility and statewide organizations that have expressed interest in receiving such information on permit modifications.]

The approval procedure is analogous to the former minor modification procedure; that is, a Class 1 permit modification requiring prior EPA approval (see Appendix F) may be made only with the prior written approval of EPA. In addition, upon approval of such a request, the permittee must notify persons on the facility mailing list of the decision within 90 calendar days after it is made.

There are no time-frame requirements for EPA action concerning a decision. However, 40 CFR 270.42(a)(3) allows a permittee to elect to follow the Class 2 process (instead of the Class 1 process). The Class 2 process assures that a decision will be made on the modification request within established time frames (usually 90 to 120 days).

Although the permittee may make most Class 1 modifications without EPA approval or prior public notice, under 40 CFR 270.42(a)(iii) the public may ask the permitting agency to review any Class 1 modification.

In the event that such a review is conducted, and EPA denies a Class 1 modification request, EPA must notify the permittee in writing of its ruling, and the permittee is required to comply with the original permit conditions.

Class 2 Modifications

Class 2 modifications cover changes that are necessary to enable a permittee to respond, in a timely manner, to:

- Common variations in the types and quantities of the wastes managed under the facility permit.
- Technological advancements.
- Regulatory changes, where such changes can be implemented without substantially altering the design specifications or management practices prescribed by the permit.

Class 2 modifications include increases of 25 percent or less in a facility's non-land-based treatment or storage capacity, authorizations to treat or store new wastes that do not require different unit design or management practices, and modifications to improve the design of hazardous waste management units or improve management practices.

Under 40 CFR 270.42(b)(1), a permittee who wishes to make a Class 2 modification is required to submit to EPA a modification request describing the exact change to be made to the permit conditions. The permittee also must submit supporting documents that identify the modification as a Class 2 modification, explain why it is needed, and provide the applicable information required by 40 CFR 270.13 through 270.21, 270.62, and 270.63.

Under 40 CFR 270.42(b)(2), the permittee must notify persons on the facility mailing list and appropriate units of state and local government, and publish a notice in a local newspaper regarding the modification request.

The following information is required in the notice [40 CFR 270.42(b)(2)]:

- Announcement of a 60-day comment period during which interested persons may submit written comments to the permitting agency.
- Announcement of the date, time, and place for an informational public meeting.
- Name and telephone number of the permittee's contact person, whom the public can contact for information on the request.
- Name and telephone number of an agency contact person, whom the public can contact for information about the permit, the modification request, applicable regulatory requirements, permit modification procedures, and the permittee's compliance history.
- Information on viewing copies of the modification request and any supporting documents.
- A statement that the permittee's compliance history during the life of the permit is available from the agency's contact person. Also, 40 CFR 270.42(b)(2) requires the permittee to submit to the permitting agency evidence that this notice was published in a local newspaper and mailed to persons on the facility mailing list.

The permittee also must make a copy of the permit modification request and supporting documents accessible to the public in the vicinity of the permitted facility (e.g., at a public library, local government agency, or location under control of the owner).

Under 40 CFR 270.42(b)(6)(i), EPA must make one of the following five decisions within 90 days of receiving the modification request:

- Approve the request with or without changes.
- Deny the request.
- Determine that the modification request must follow the procedures for Class 3 modifications.
- Approve the request, with or without changes, as a temporary authorization having a term of up to 180 days.
- Notify the permittee that it will make a decision on the request within 30 days.

If the permitting agency notifies the permittee of a 30-day extension for a decision (or if it fails to make any of the decisions), it must, by the 120th day after receiving the modification request, make one of the following decisions:

- Approve the request, with or without changes.
- Deny the request.

- Determine that the modification request must follow the procedures for Class 3 modifications.
- Approve the request as a temporary authorization for up to 180 days.

In accordance with 40 CFR 270.42(b)(6)(vii), EPA is allowed to extend the deadlines for action on a Class 2 request with the written consent of the permittee. This option may be useful if EPA requests additional information from the permittee, or the permittee wishes to conduct additional public meetings.

If, however, EPA fails to make one of the four decisions listed above by the 120th day, the activities described in the modification request, as submitted, are authorized for a period of 180 days as an "automatic authorization" without EPA action. However, at any time during the term of the automatic authorization, EPA may approve or deny the permit modification request. If EPA does so, this action will terminate the automatic authorization. If EPA has not acted on the modification request within 250 days of receipt of the modification request (i.e., 50 days before the end of the automatic authorization), under 40 CFR 270.42(b)(6)(iv) the permittee must notify persons on the facility mailing list within 7 days, and make a reasonable effort to notify other persons who submitted written comments, that the automatic authorization will become permanent unless EPA acts to approve or deny it.

If EPA fails to approve or deny the modification request during the term of the automatic authorization, the activities described in the modification request become permanently authorized without EPA action on the day after the end of the term of the automatic authorization. However, if the owner or operator fails to notify the public when EPA has not acted on an automatic authorization 50 days before its termination date, the clock on the automatic authorization will be suspended. The permanent authorization will not go into effect until 50 days after the public is notified. Until the permanent authorization becomes effective, EPA may approve or deny the modification request at any time. In addition, the owner or the operator will be subject to potential enforcement action. This permanent authorization lasts for the life of the permit unless modified later by the permittee [40 CFR 270.42] or EPA [40 CFR 270.41]. This procedure for automatic authorization is commonly referred to as the "default" provision.

Class 3 Modifications

Class 3 modifications cover changes that substantially alter the facility or its operations. Generally, they include:

- Increases in the facility's land-based treatment, storage, or disposal capacity.
- Increases of more than 25 percent in the facility's non-land-based treatment or storage capacity.
- Authorization to treat, store, or dispose of wastes not listed in the permit that require changes in unit design or management practices.
- Substantial changes to landfill, surface impoundment, and waste pile liner and leachate collection/detection systems.
- Substantial changes to the groundwater monitoring systems or incinerator operating conditions.

The first steps in the application procedures for Class 3 modifications are similar to the procedures for Class 2. Under 40 CFR 270.42(c)(1), the permittee must submit a modification request to EPA indicating the change to be made to the permit, identifying the change as a Class 3 modification, explaining why the modification is needed, and providing applicable information required by 40 CFR 270.13 through 270.21, 270.62, and 270.63. As with Class 2 modifications, the permittee is encouraged to consult with EPA before submitting the modification request.

The permittee must notify persons on the facility mailing list and local and state agencies concerning the modification request. This notice must occur not more than 7 days before and not more than 7 days after the date of submission. The notice must contain the same information as the Class 2 notification, including an announcement of a public informational meeting. The meeting must be held no fewer than 15 days after and no fewer than 15 days before the end of the comment period [40 CFR 270.42(c)(2)].

After the conclusion of the 60-day comment period, the permitting agency then initiates the permit issuance procedures of 40 CFR Part 124 for the Class 3 modification. Thus, the permitting agency will prepare a draft permit modification, publish a notice, allow a 45-day public comment period on the draft permit modification, hold a public hearing on the modification if requested, and issue or deny the permit modification.

Temporary Authorizations

EPA can grant a temporary authorization, without prior public notice and comment, for a permittee to conduct activities necessary to respond promptly to changing conditions [40 CFR 270.42(e)]. An EPA-issued temporary authorization may be obtained for activities that are necessary to:

- Facilitate timely implementation of closure or corrective action activities.
- Allow treatment or storage in tanks or containers of restricted wastes in accordance with Part 268.
- Avoid disrupting ongoing waste management activities at the permittee's facility.
- Enable the permittee to respond to changes in the types or quantities of wastes being managed under the facility's permit.
- Carry out other changes to protect human health and the environment.

Temporary authorizations can be granted for any Class 2 modification that meets these criteria, or for a Class 3 modification that is necessary to:

- Implement corrective action or closure activities.
- Allow treatment or storage in tanks or containers of restricted waste.
- Provide improved management or treatment of a waste already listed in the permit when necessary to avoid disruption of ongoing waste management, to allow the permittee to respond to changes in waste quantities, or to facilitate other changes to protect human health and the environment.

A temporary authorization will be valid for a period of up to 180 days. The term of the temporary authorization will begin at the time of its approval by EPA or at some specified effective date shortly after the time of approval. The authorized activities must be completed at the end of the authorization.

POST-CLOSURE PERMITS

A permit is required for a hazardous waste management unit during its active life and the closure period. In addition, a post-closure permit is required for any unit closing after January 26, 1983 [40 CFR 2701.1(c)].

If a facility currently has an operating permit, there is no separate permit for post-closure care. A separate post-closure permit is intended for interim status units that close without an operating permit. Thus, if a surface impoundment loses its interim status or voluntarily closes under interim status, EPA can request ("call in") the facility's Part B permit application for a post-closure permit. Failure to submit a Part B on time or the submission of incomplete information is grounds for the termination of a facility's interim status.

The information required for post-closure permits is generally less than the standard operating permit. At a minimum, an owner or an operator must submit the following information:

- The post-closure plan.
- A copy of the post-closure inspection schedule.
- Location information, including a delineation of the floodplain area.
- Documentation of the notice in the deed.
- Cost estimate for post-closure.
- A copy of the financial mechanism to be used.
- Exposure information.
- Groundwater data and a demonstration of compliance with Part 264 Subpart F.
- Information pertaining to the Section 3004(u) corrective action provision (e.g., location and type of SWMUs).
- Demonstration of financial responsibility for corrective action, if required.

RESEARCH, DEMONSTRATION, AND DEVELOPMENT PERMITS

HSWA provides EPA with authority to issue permits for research, development, and demonstration (RD&D) treatment activities. EPA has authority to issue permits independent of existing regulations relating to hazardous waste treatment processes. EPA is directed to include certain provisions in each permit as well as any other requirements deemed necessary to protect human health and the environment [40 CFR 270.65].

The EPA Administrator is authorized to issue RD&D permits for innovative and experimental treatment technologies or processes for which permit standards have not been established under Part 264. The Administrator may establish permit terms and conditions for the RD&D activities as necessary to protect human health and the environment. The statute allows the Administrator to select the appropriate technical standards for each RD&D activity to be permitted. EPA is required to address construction (if appropriate), limit operation for not longer than one year, and place limitations on the waste that may be received to those types and quantities of wastes deemed necessary to conduct the RD&D activities. The permit must include the financial responsibility requirements currently in EPA's regulations and other such requirements as necessary to protect human health and the environment. Other possible requirements include, but are not limited to, provisions regarding monitoring, operation, closure, remedial action, testing, and information reporting.

EPA may decide not to permit an RD&D project if it determines that the project, even with restrictive permit terms and conditions, may threaten human health or the environment.

EMERGENCY PERMITS

If EPA finds that an imminent and substantial endangerment to human health or the environment exists, a temporary emergency permit may be issued [40 CFR 270.61]. This permit may be issued to:

- A nonpermitted facility to allow treatment, storage, or disposal of hazardous waste.
- A permitted facility to allow treatment, storage, or disposal of wastes not covered by an effective permit.

The permit may be oral or written. If it is oral, a written emergency permit is suppose to be sent to the facility within five days. The conditions of an emergency permit [40 CFR 270.61] are that it:

- Shall not exceed 90 days.
- Shall specify the types of wastes to be received and their methods of handling (e.g., disposal or treatment).
- Can be terminated at any time by EPA.
- Shall be accompanied by a public notice.
- Shall incorporate, to the greatest extent possible, all applicable standards in Parts 264 and 266.

Chapter 8

Land Disposal Restrictions

The Hazardous and Solid Waste Amendments of 1984 (HSWA) established a strong statutory presumption against land disposal by prohibiting the continued land disposal of hazardous wastes beyond specified dates unless such disposal is determined by EPA to be protective of human health and the environment.

OVERVIEW

In its enactment of HSWA, Congress stated explicitly that "reliance on land disposal should be minimized or eliminated, and land disposal, particularly landfills and surface impoundments, should be the least favored method for managing hazardous wastes" [RCRA Section 1002(b)(7)].

The statute requires EPA to set levels or methods of treatment, if any, that substantially diminish the toxicity of the waste or substantially reduce the likelihood of migration of hazardous constituents from the waste so that short-term and long-term threats to human health and the environment are minimized. Wastes that meet the treatment standards established by EPA are not prohibited from land disposal.

The land disposal restrictions, codified in 40 CFR Part 268, place stringent controls on the land disposal of hazardous wastes. *Land disposal* is defined to include, but not be limited to, any placement of hazardous waste in a landfill, surface impoundment, waste pile, injection well, land treatment facility, salt dome formation, or underground mine or cave [40 CFR 268.2]. *Placement* means movement of hazardous waste into or onto a land disposal unit. The following are three examples of what constitutes placement: (1) wastes are removed from a unit and put into another unit; (2) wastes are removed from a unit, treated in a second unit, and redeposited in the original unit or a third unit; and (3) a treatment unit is constructed within a larger land disposal unit, and material is excavated from the land disposal unit, treated in the newly constructed treatment unit, and then redeposited in the land disposal unit. EPA also considers placement of hazardous wastes in concrete vaults or bunkers intended for disposal purposes as a type of waste management subject to the land disposal restrictions. However, waste consolidation within a unit, *in situ* waste treatment (provided the wastes were not moved from another unit), and capping of wastes in place do not constitute placement. In addition, EPA does not consider open burning and detonation to be methods constituting land disposal and has concluded that the land disposal restrictions program is not applicable in these instances (51 *FR* 40580, November 7, 1986). HSWA required EPA to establish treatment standards for each of seven groups of hazardous wastes by specific dates. These dates, referred to as the statutory deadlines, are expected to eventually restrict the land disposal of all hazardous wastes, as outlined in Table 8-1.

The land disposal restrictions contain requirements for testing, treatment, storage, notification, certification of compliance, and record keeping. The regulations also contain variances from the restrictions.

Applicability

The land disposal restrictions are applicable only to wastes identified as hazardous. According to the applicability provisions set forth in 40 CFR 268.1(a), "This part identifies hazardous wastes that are restricted from land disposal and defines those limited circumstances under which an otherwise prohibited waste may continue to be land disposed." Consequently, if the waste cannot be identified as a hazardous waste under RCRA, then the regulations of Part 268 do not apply, including the certification requirement.

It is important to note that the land disposal restrictions apply prospectively to wastes that are land disposed *after* the effective date of the restrictions (i.e., the land disposal restrictions do not require that wastes land-disposed prior to the effective date of the restrictions be removed and treated). If restricted wastes land-disposed prior to the applicable effective date were to be removed from the disposal unit, subsequent placement of such wastes in or on the land would be subject to the applicable prohibitions and treatment provisions.

RCRA does not impose an absolute ban on the land disposal of haz-

Table 8-1. Statutory deadlines for the land disposal restrictions.

Waste	Statutory deadline
Spent solvent and dioxin-containing wastes	November 8, 1986
California lists wastes	July 8, 1987
First third wastes	August 8, 1988
Spent solvent, dioxin-containing and California list soil and debris from CERCLA/RCRA corrective actions	November 8, 1988
Second third wastes	June 8, 1989
Third third wastes	May 8, 1990
Newly identified wastes	Within 6 months of identification as a hazardous waste

ardous waste. A waste may be excluded from the ban under the following circumstances [40 CFR 268.1(c)]:

- The waste meets treatment standards established by EPA under Section 3004(m) of RCRA.
- A nationwide extension to the effective date is granted because of a lack of available treatment capacity.
- EPA grants a site-specific variance that demonstrates that there will be no migration of hazardous constituents from the disposal unit for as long as the waste remains hazardous.
- An individual extension to an effective date is granted based on the characteristics of a specific waste.
- Untreated waste may be treated in a surface impoundment that complies with the minimum technological requirements (i.e., double liner with leachate collection and removal system) if the treatment residues that are hazardous are removed within a year of placement in the impoundment.

Restricted versus Prohibited Wastes

Restricted wastes are hazardous wastes that are subject to the prohibitions on land disposal (53 *FR* 31208, August 17, 1988). A waste becomes restricted under the land disposal restrictions on its statutory deadline.

Thus, the universe of restricted wastes includes all wastes for which the statutory land disposal restriction deadline has passed, including those wastes that may currently be land-disposed of because of an extension or a variance, or by meeting the applicable treatment standard, as well as those that are currently banned from land disposal.

Prohibited wastes are a subset of restricted wastes, a prohibited waste being a restricted waste that is currently banned from land disposal (53 *FR* 31208-9, August 17, 1988). This would include all wastes that do not meet the applicable treatment standards for which the applicable land disposal restriction date has passed, and for which no variances or extensions have been granted.

Responsibility to Comply

The owner or the operator of the disposal facility has the ultimate responsibility for verifying that only wastes meeting the treatment standards are land-disposed. The owner or the operator of the land disposal facility must maintain documentation to demonstrate that the wastes are in compliance with the applicable treatment standards.

Generators who send wastes directly to land disposal or treatment facilities have the obligation to certify in writing that restricted wastes, including any residuals from the treatment of restricted wastes, meet the applicable treatment standards [40 CFR 262.11(d) and 268.7]. Because of the derived-from rule [40 CFR 261.3(c)(2)(i)], all residuals resulting from the treatment of the original listed waste are likewise considered to be listed wastes, and thus must meet the treatment standards if these residuals are to be disposed of in or on the land (53 *FR* 31142, August 17, 1988).

Reclamation of Restricted Wastes

Restricted wastes may continue to be recovered or reclaimed. However, while the reclamation operation itself is exempt from regulation under RCRA, storage of restricted wastes prior to reclamation is still subject to the provisions specified in 40 CFR 268.50. Still bottoms and other residues from reclamation of restricted wastes remain subject to the land disposal restrictions if they meet the definition of hazardous waste.

Schedule of Restrictions

Congress set forth a schedule of land disposal restrictions in HSWA. The statute automatically prohibited (hammer provision) the land disposal of hazardous wastes if EPA failed to set a treatment standard by the statutory deadline.

The statute also required EPA to make determinations on prohibiting land disposal, within the indicated timeframes, for the following:

- At least one-third of all ranked and listed hazardous wastes by August 8, 1988 (the "First Third").
- At least two-thirds of all ranked and listed hazardous wastes by June 8, 1989 (the "Second Third").
- All remaining ranked and listed hazardous wastes and all hazardous wastes identified by a characteristic by May 8, 1990 (the "Third Third").

EPA promulgated this schedule on May 28, 1986 (51 *FR* 19300), under 40 CFR 268.10, 11, and 12. The schedule was based on a ranking of the listed hazardous wastes by intrinsic hazard and volume generated. High-volume hazardous wastes with a high intrinsic hazard were scheduled first, and low-volume wastes with a lower intrinsic hazard were scheduled last.

The wastes included in the First Third were:

F006, F007, F008, F009, and F019.

K001, K004, K008, K011, K013, K014, K015, K016, K017, K018, K020, K021, K022, K024, K030, K031, K035, K036, K037, K044, K045, K046, K047, K048, K049, K050, K051, K052, K060, K061, K062, K069, K071, K073, K083, K085, K086, K087, K099, K101, K102, K103, K104, and K106.

P001, P004, P005, P010, P011, P012, P015, P016, P018, P020, P030, P036, P037, P039, P041, P048, P050, P058, P059, P063, P068, P069, P070, P071, P081, P082, P084, P087, P089, P092, P094, P097, P102, P105, P108, P110, P115, P120, P122, and P123.

U007, U009, U010, U012, U016, U018, U019, U022, U029, U031, U036, U037, U041, U043, U044, U046, U050, U051, U053, U061, U063, U064, U066, U067, U074, U077, U078, U086, U089, U103, U105, U108, U115, U122, U124, U129, U130, U133, U134, U137, U151, U154, U155, U157, U158, U159, U171, U177, U180, U185, U188, U192, U200, U209, U210, U211, U219, U220, U221, U223, U226, U227, U228, U237, U238, U248, and U249.

The wastes included in the Second Third were:

F010, F011, F012, and F024.

K009, K010, K019, K025, K027, K028, K029, K038, K039, K040, K041, K042, K043, K096, K097, K098, and K105.

P002, P003, P007, P008, P014, P026, P027, P029, P040, P043, P044, P049, P054, P057, P060, P072, P074, P085, P098, P104, P106, P107, P111, P112, P113, and P114.

U002, U003, U004, U005, U008, U011, U014, U015, U020, U021, U023, U025, U026, U028, U032, U035, U047, U049, U057, U058, U059, U060, U062, U070, U073, U080, U083, U092, U093, U094, U097, U098, U099, U101, U106, U107, U109, U110, U111, U114, U116, U119, U127, U128, U131, U135, U138, U140, U142, U143, U144, U146, U147, U149, U150, U161, U162, U163, U164, U165, U168, U169, U170, U171, U172, U173, U174, U176, U177, U178, U179, U189, U193, U196, U203, U205, U206, U208, U213, U214, U215, U216, U217, U218, U235, U239, and U244.

All remaining listed hazardous wastes and the characteristic wastes were placed in the Third Third.

For any waste listed after November 8, 1984, EPA must make a determination on land disposal within six months of the listing. However, there is no automatic prohibition (hammer) on land disposal of such wastes if EPA fails to meet this deadline.

Treatment Standards

By each statutory deadline, EPA promulgated treatment standards for the applicable hazardous wastes (restricted wastes). Wastes that meet these treatment standards may be directly land-disposed. Wastes that do not meet these standards must be treated before they are placed in a land disposal unit.

EPA set one of three types of treatment standards for restricted wastes:

- A concentration level to be achieved prior to disposal (the most common type of treatment standard);
- A specified technology to be used prior to disposal; or
- A "no land disposal" designation when the waste is no longer generated, is totally recycled, or is not currently being land-disposed, or when no residuals are produced from treatment.

All three types of treatment standards are established based on the best demonstrated available technology (BDAT) identified for that waste. Dilution, however, is not normally considered an allowable treatment method. As stated in 40 CFR 268.3, "No generator, transporter, handler, or owner or operator of a treatment, storage, or disposal facility shall in any way dilute a restricted waste or the residual from treatment of a restricted waste as a substitute for adequate treatment to achieve compliance with Subpart D of this part.'' However, treatment that necessarily involves some degree of dilution (such as biological treatment or steam stripping) is acceptable. Also, mixing wastes together prior to treatment is not considered dilution. Dilution is prohibited if it is conducted in lieu of adequate treatment for purposes of attaining the applicable treatment standards.

If a new technology is shown to be more effective in reducing the concentration of hazardous constituents in the waste (or the waste extract) than the existing technology upon which the treatment standard has been based, EPA can revise the treatment standard.

Wherever possible, EPA establishes treatment standards as performance standards rather than requiring a specific treatment method. In such cases, any method (other than inappropriate solidification practices that would be considered dilution to avoid adequate treatment) that can meet the treatment standard is acceptable. Solidification may, nonetheless, be a necessary prerequisite to land disposal to comply with the prohibition against free liquids in landfills [40 CFR 264/265.314]. When EPA has specified a technology as the treatment standard, the applicable wastes must be treated by using the specified technology.

Analysis Requirements

The regulations specify the analytical method to be used for each designated waste. For example, the solvent- and dioxin-containing wastes are required to use the toxicity characteristic leaching procedure (TCLP). However, some restricted wastes (e.g., California wastes) require a total composition analysis instead of an extract analysis. Thus, in some cases, the TCLP is inappropriate.

Documentation

The generator may identify the applicable treatment standard based on waste analysis data, knowledge of the waste, or both. Where this determination is based solely on the generator's knowledge of the waste, the generator is required to maintain in the facility files all supporting data used to make this determination.

If a generator determines that the waste does not meet the specified treatment levels (and is thus prohibited from land disposal), the generator must so notify the designated facility in writing.

According to 40 CFR 268.7(a)(1), the notice must contain the:

- EPA hazardous waste number.
- Corresponding treatment standard.
- Waste analysis data (where applicable).
- Manifest number associated with the shipment of waste.

If a generator determines that a restricted waste can be land-disposed of without further treatment, each shipment of that waste to a designated facility must have a notice and certification stating that the waste meets all of the applicable treatment standards [40 CFR 268.7(a)(1)]. Because a recycler is a treatment facility, a generator must notify the recycler. The signed certification must state the following:

> I certify under penalty of law that I have personally examined the waste through analysis and testing or through knowledge of the waste to support this certification that the waste complies with the treatment standards specified in 40 CFR 268.32 or RCRA Section 3004(d). I believe that the information submitted is true, accurate, and complete. I am aware that there are significant penalties for submitting a false certification, including the possibility of a fine or imprisonment.

Documentation that must be maintained by an off-site disposal facility includes:

- Waste analysis data obtained through testing of the waste.
- A copy of the notice and certification required by the owner or operator of a treatment facility under 40 CFR 268.7(b)(1) and (2).
- A copy of the notice and certification required by the generator in cases where the wastes meet the treatment standard and can be land-disposed without further treatment [40 CFR 268.7(a)(2)].
- Records of the quantities (and date of placement) for each shipment of hazardous waste placed in the unit under an extension of the effective date (a case-by-case extension or a two-year extension of the effective date) or a no-migration petition and a copy of the notice under 40 CFR 268.7(a)(3).

Variances

Generators or owners and operators of hazardous waste management facilities may petition EPA for a variance from a treatment standard. Wastes may be granted a variance due to physical and chemical characteristics that are significantly different from those of the wastes evaluated by EPA in setting the treatment standards. For example, in some cases, it may not be possible to treat a restricted waste to the applicable treatment standards [40 CFR 268.44(a)].

The available variances from the land disposal restrictions are:

- Nationwide variances
- No-migration petitions
- Case-by-case extensions

In accordance with 40 CFR 268.44(g), during the petition review process the applicant is required to comply with all restrictions on land disposal under Part 268 once the effective date for the waste has been reached.

Nationwide Variances

If the capacity of alternative treatment, recovery, or disposal facilities is insufficient for a particular waste or group of wastes nationwide, EPA can grant a nationwide extension to the effective date of the restriction and has done so. The purpose of the extension is to allow time for the development of this capacity. This extension may not exceed a period of two years beyond the applicable statutory deadline for the waste.

No-Migration Petitions

A facility owner or operator can petition EPA to allow continued land disposal of a specific waste at a specific site. The applicant must demonstrate that the waste can be contained safely in a particular type of disposal unit so that no migration of any hazardous constituents occurs from the unit for as long as the waste remains hazardous. If EPA grants the petition, the waste is no longer prohibited from land disposal in that specific unit at that site [40 CFR 268.6(a)]. However, a successful demonstration of "no-migration" is difficult. Owners and operators of land treatment areas treating petroleum wastes and wood preservative wastes are most apt to be granted a no-migration petition.

The statutory standard for the evaluation of no-migration petitions requires that the petitioner demonstrate, to a reasonable degree of certainty, that there will be no migration of hazardous constituents from the disposal unit or injection zone for as long as the wastes remain hazardous [RCRA Section 3004(d)].

EPA is requiring applicants to submit petitions directly to the EPA Administrator. Where possible, EPA intends to process Part B permit applications and no-migration petitions concurrently. However, if the review of Part B applications or no-migration petitions may be unduly delayed by concurrent reviews, EPA typically will process such applications separately. Applications for no-migration petitions are reviewed at EPA headquarters, whereas EPA regional offices or authorized states are responsible for issuing Part B permits. EPA headquarters coordinates reviews with appropriate regional and state staff responsible for reviewing Part B applications for the same facility [40 CFR 268.6(c)].

Case-by-Case Extensions

Any person who generates or manages a restricted hazardous waste may submit an application to the EPA Administrator for a case-by-case extension of the applicable effective date. The applicant must demonstrate that:

- He or she has made a good-faith effort to contract with a treatment, storage, or disposal facility.
- A binding contract has been entered into to construct or otherwise provide alternative capacity.
- This alternative capacity cannot reasonably be made available by the applicable effective date because of circumstances beyond the applicant's control.

There is no deadline for submitting these applications to EPA. However, case-by-case extensions cannot extend beyond 48 months from the date of the statutory land disposal restriction [40 CFR 268.5(e)].

Storage

The storage of hazardous wastes restricted from land disposal is prohibited except where storage is needed to accumulate sufficient quantities to allow for proper recovery, treatment, or disposal [40 CFR 268.50(a)].

Owners and operators of hazardous waste management facilities may store restricted wastes as needed to accumulate sufficient quantities to allow for proper recovery, treatment, or disposal. However, when storage lasts beyond one year, the owner or the operator bears the burden of proving, in the event of an enforcement action, that such storage is used solely for the purpose of accumulating sufficient quantities to allow for proper recovery, treatment, or disposal. For periods less than or equal to one year, the burden of demonstrating whether or not a facility is in compliance with the storage provisions lies with EPA [40 CFR 268.50(b)]. These facilities may store restricted wastes in containers and tanks only if each container or tank is clearly marked to identify its content and the date when the hazardous waste entered storage [40 CFR 268.50(a)(2)].

PHASE I—SOLVENT AND DIOXIN-CONTAINING WASTES

Applicability

On November 7, 1986 (51 *FR* 40572), EPA promulgated Phase I of the land disposal ban. This rule set out the regulatory framework for implementing the land disposal prohibitions and promulgated treatment standards for specified solvent and dioxin wastes.

The wastes under Phase I, the solvent- and dioxin-containing wastes, are those wastes numbered F001, F002, F003, F004, F005, F020, F021, F022, F023, F026, F027, and F028.

Solvents Wastes

A *solvent waste* must meet the following criteria to be covered by the solvent listings (i.e., EPA hazardous waste codes F001, F002, F003, F004, and F005):

- The solvent waste must have been used for its *solvent* properties, that is, to solubilize (dissolve) or mobilize other constituents.
- The solvent waste must be defined as hazardous (i.e., spent). A solvent is considered *spent* when it has been used and is no longer fit for use without being regenerated, reclaimed, or otherwise reprocessed.
- If it is a spent solvent mixture or blend, it must contain, before use, a total of 10 percent or more (by volume) of one or more of the solvents listed in F001, F002, F004, or F005.

The treatment levels are specified in Table 8-2. The generator must use the TCLP to determine if these standards have been met. For the purposes of defining applicability of the treatment standards for wastewaters containing F001–F005 spent solvents, wastewaters are defined as solvent–water mixtures containing total organic carbon (TOC) of one percent or less. Wastewaters containing greater than one percent TOC must meet the treatment standard for all "other spent solvent wastes."

Treatment standards for solvent-containing wastewater were based on either a combination of biological treatment, steam stripping, and acti-

Table 8-2. Constituents contained in solvent waste extract.

Constituent	Wastewater(mg/L)	All other wastes(mg/L)
Acetone	0.050	0.590
n-Butyl alcohol	5.00	5.00
Carbon disulfide	1.05	4.81
Carbon tetrachloride	0.05	0.96
Chlorobenzene	0.15	0.05
Cresols (cresylic acid)	2.82	0.75
Cyclohexanone	0.125	0.75
1,2-Dichlorobenzene	0.65	0.125
Ethyl acetate	0.05	0.75
Ethylbenzene	0.05	0.053
Ethyl ether	0.05	0.75
Isobutanol	5.00	5.00
Methanol	0.25	0.75
Methylene chloride	0.20	0.96
Methylene chloride (pharmaceutical)	2.7	0.96
Methyl ethyl ketone	0.05	0.75
Methyl isobutyl ketone	0.05	0.33
Nitrobenzene	.066	0.125
Pyridine	0.12	0.33
Tetrachloroethylene	0.079	0.05
Toluene	1.12	0.33
1,1,1-Trichloroethane	1.05	0.41
Trichloroethylene	0.062	0.091
Trichlorofluoromethane	0.05	0.96
1,1,2-Trichloro-1,2,2-trifluoroethane	1.05	0.96
Xylene	0.05	0.15

vated carbon technologies or on the technologies individually. The treatment standards for all other spent solvent wastes were based on incineration.

If dilution is a legitimate step in a properly operated treatment process (e.g., if a waste is mixed with other wastes prior to incineration), or if a treatment method includes the addition of reagents to physically or chemically change the waste (and does not merely dilute hazardous constituents into a larger volume of waste so as to lower the constituent concentration), then dilution is allowed.

Dioxin-Containing Wastes

The regulations apply to the designated dioxin-containing wastes. Those hazardous wastes identified as the dioxin-containing wastes are hazardous waste codes F020, F021, F022, F023, F026, F027, and F028. The treatment standards for the dioxin wastes are outlined in Table 8-3.

Table 8-3. Constituents contained in dioxin waste extract.

Constituent	Concentration
HxCDD - All Hexachlorodibenzo-*p*-dioxins	<1 ppb
HxCDF - All Hexachlorodibenxofurans	<1 ppb
PeCDD - All Pentachlorodibenzo-*p*-dioxins	<1 ppb
PeCDF - All Pentachlorodibenzofurans	<1 ppb
TCDD - All Tetrachlorodibenzo-*p*-dioxins	<1 ppb
TCDF - All Tetrachlorodibenzofurans	<1 ppb
2,4,5-Trichlorophenol	<0.05 ppm
2,4,6-Trichlorophenol	<0.05 ppm
2,3,4,6-Tetrachlorophenol	<0.10 ppm
Pentachlorophenol	<0.01 ppm

PHASE II—THE CALIFORNIA WASTES

Applicability

The *California list wastes,* so named because the State of California initiated land disposal restrictions, are shown in Table 8-4. The associated treatment levels also are specified in the table. The concentrations expressed in Table 8-4 are determined by means of a total composition analysis rather than an extract analysis using the TCLP.

To be subject to Phase II of the land disposal prohibitions, a waste must meet the following criteria:

- It must be listed or identified as a RCRA hazardous waste.
- It must contain a California list constituent at or above the concentrations specified in Table 8-4.

Table 8-4. The California list wastes.

Constituent	Level*
Free cyanides	1,000 mg/L
Arsenic	500 mg/L
Cadmium	100 mg/L
Chromium	500 mg/L
Lead	500 mg/L
Mercury	20 mg/L
Nickel	134 mg/L
Selenium	100 mg/L
Thallium	130 mg/L
PCBs	50 ppm
Corrosive wastes	<2.0 pH

*A waste is a California list waste if it is a liquid and it meets or exceeds any of these levels.

- Its physical form must be liquid. [However, a California waste (except for halogenated organic compound wastes) can be transformed into a solid and thus be land-disposed.]

Wastes Containing HOCs

All liquid and nonliquid hazardous waste containing halogenated organic compounds (HOCs) in total concentration greater than or equal to 1,000 mg/kg, except for dilute halogenated compound wastewaters, such as HOC–water mixtures that contain primarily water and have less than 10,000 mg/L HOCs, must be incinerated in accordance with existing RCRA regulations. However, HOC wastewaters need not be incinerated, but they must be treated to the 1,000 mg/L prohibition level.

For the purposes of the prohibition on land disposal, EPA has defined the HOCs that must be included in the calculation as any compounds having a carbon–halogen bond, as listed in Appendix III to Part 268. The Appendix III list is contained in Table 8-5.

Wastes with Polychlorinated Biphenyls

Because polychlorinated biphenyls (PCBs) by themselves are not defined as hazardous waste, a waste containing PCBs at or above 50 ppm will

Table 8-5. List of halogenated organic compounds.

Volatiles	
Bromodichloromethane	1,1-Dichloroethylene
Bromomethane	Trans-1,2-Dichloroethene
Carbon tetrachloride	1,2-Dichloropropane
Chlorobenzene	Trans-1,3-Dichloropropen
2-Chloro-1,3-butadiene	cis-1,3-Dichloropropene
Chlorodibromomethane	Iodomethane
Chloroethane	Methylene chloride
2-Chloroethyl vinyl ether	1,1,1,2-Tetrachloroethane
Chloroform	1,1,2,2-Tetrachloroethane
Chloromethane	Tetrachloroethene
3-Chloropropene	Tribromomethane
1,2-Dibromo-3-chloropropane	1,1,1-Trichloroethane
1,2-Dibromomethane	1,1,2-Trichloroethane
Dibromomethane	Trichloroethene
trans-1,4-Dichloro-2-butene	Trichloromonofluoromethane
Dichlorodifluoromethane	1,2,3-Trichloropropane
1,1-Dichloroethane	Vinyl chloride
1,2-Dichloroethane	

Table 8-5. (*Continued*)

Semivolatiles

Bis(2-chloroethoxy)ethane
Bis(2-chloroethyl)ether
Bis(2-chloroisopropyl)ether
p-Chloroaniline
Chlorobenzilate
p-Chloro-m-cresol
2-Chloronapthalene
2-Chlorophenol
3-Chloropropionitrile
m-Dichlorobenzene
o-Dichlorobenzene
p-Dichlorobenzene
3,3'-Dichlorobenzidine
2,4-Dichlorophenol
2,6-Dichlorophenol
Hexachlorobenzene

Hexachlorobutadiene
Hexachlorocyclopentadiene
Hexachloroethane
Hexachloropropene
4,4'-Methylenebis(chloroaniline)
Pentachlorobenzene
Pentachloroethane
Pentachloronitrobenzene
Pentachlorophenol
Pronamide
1,2,4,5-Tetrachlorobenzene
2,3,4,6-Tetrachlorophenol
1,2,4-Trichlorobenzene
2,4,5-Trichlorophenol
2,4,6-Trichlorophenol
Tris(2,3-dibromopropyl)phosphate

Organochlorine Pesticides

Aldrin
alpha-BHC
beta-BHC
delta-BHC
gamma-BHC
Chlordane
DDD
DDE
DDT
Dieldrin

Endosulfan I
Endosulfan II
Endrin
Endrin aldehyde
Heptachlor
Heptachlor epoxide
Isodrin
Kepone
Methoxychlor
Toxaphene

Phenoxyacetic Acid Herbicides

2,4-Dichlorophenoxyacetic acid
Silvex
2,4,5-T

Polychlorinated Biphenyls

Aroclor 1016
Aroclor 1221
Aroclor 1232
Aroclor 1242

Aroclor 1248
Aroclor 1254
Aroclor 1260
PCBs N.O.S.

Dioxins and Furans

Hexachlorodibenzo-p-dioxins
Hexachlorodibenzofuran
Pentachlorodibenzo-p-dioxins
Pentachlorodibenzofuran

Tetrachlorodibenzo-p-dioxins
Tetrachlorodibenzofuran
2,3,7,8-Tetrachlorodibenzo-p-dioxin

be subject to the land disposal ban only if the PCBs are either mixed with a listed hazardous waste or exhibit a characteristic of hazardous waste.

Liquid hazardous wastes containing PCBs at concentrations greater than or equal to 50 ppm must be treated in accordance with the existing Toxic Substances Control Act (TSCA) disposal regulations in 40 CFR Part 761. These regulations require that PCB wastes be either incinerated or burned in a high-efficiency boiler.

Chapter 9

Corrective Action

The primary objective of the RCRA corrective action program is to clean up releases of hazardous waste or hazardous constituents from RCRA hazardous waste management facilities. The RCRA permitting process is the driving force for corrective action.

OVERVIEW

Prior to the Hazardous and Solid Waste Amendments (HSWA), EPA had limited authority in requiring corrective action at interim status facilities. It had to pursue lengthy legal action or attempt to issue the facility a permit, because a permitted facility has strict requirements concerning corrective action.

However, HSWA established three new corrective action authorities for interim status hazardous waste management facilities that greatly strengthened EPA's authority (permitted facilities are governed under Part 264.100). The corrective action programs are:

- *Prior Releases* [§3004(u)]
- *Interim Status Corrective Action Orders* [§3008(h)]
- *Beyond Facility Boundaries* [§3004(v)]

Prior Releases

Scope and Applicability

The prior release program, also known as the Section 3004(u) program, requires corrective action for releases of hazardous waste or hazardous constituents from any solid waste management unit (SWMU) or hazardous waste unit (which is a subset of solid waste management units) at a RCRA hazardous waste management facility [40 CFR 264.101]. The corrective action program is initiated through the permitting process; that is, an owner or an operator must implement this program when applying for a RCRA permit.

Definitions

A *facility* is the entire facility as defined in 40 CFR 260.10. Thus, even if a permit is being sought for a unit only, the owner or the operator must address possible releases from all waste management units at the facility under this program.

The term *release* refers to the Superfund definition contained in Section 101(22):

> *Release* means any spilling, leaking, pumping, pouring, emitting, emptying, discharging, injecting, escaping, leaching, dumping, or disposing into the environment, but excludes (A) any release which results in exposure to persons solely within a workplace, with respect to a claim which such persons may assert against the employer of such persons, (B) emissions from the engine exhaust of a motor vehicle, rolling stock, aircraft, vessel, or pipeline pumping station engine, (C) release of source, byproduct, or special nuclear material from a nuclear incident, as those terms are defined in the Atomic Energy Act of 1954, if such release is subject to requirements with respect to financial protection established by the Nuclear Regulatory Commission under Section 170 of such Act, or, for the purposes of Section 104 of this title or any other response action, any release of source byproduct, or special nuclear material from any processing site designated under Section 102(a)(1) or 302(a) of the Uranium Mill Tailings Radiation Control Act of 1978, and (D) the normal application of fertilizer.

The terms *hazardous waste* and *hazardous constituent* mean any waste identified as a RCRA hazardous waste (listed or characteristic) and any Part 261, Appendix VIII hazardous constituent. Thus, a nonhazardous waste can release a hazardous constituent and trigger corrective action.

A *solid waste management unit* is any discernible waste management unit at a RCRA facility from which hazardous waste or hazardous constituents might migrate, irrespective of whether the unit was intended for the management of solid and/or hazardous waste. Thus, if a facility is seeking a RCRA permit and has nonhazardous waste management units (or units that accepted waste prior to November 19, 1980) on-site, the owner or the operator must address those units for possible corrective action. Even though some units are currently exempt from permit standards (e.g., wastewater treatment units, elementary neutralization units), they are considered SWMUs under this provision.

According to OSWER Directive 9502.00-6c, the solid waste management unit definition includes:

- Containers, tanks, surface impoundment, container storage areas, waste piles, land treatment units, landfills, incinerators, underground injection wells, and other physical, chemical, and biological units, including units defined as *regulated units*.
- Recycling units, wastewater treatment units, and other units that EPA has generally exempted from standards applicable to waste management units.
- Areas associated with production processes at facilities that have become contaminated by routine, systematic, and deliberate discharges of waste or constituents.

One-time spills of hazardous waste or constituents are subject to 3004(u) only if the spill occurred from a solid waste management unit. A spill that cannot be linked to a discernible solid waste management unit is not itself a SWMU. Likewise, leakage from product storage and other types of releases associated with production processes would not be considered a SWMU, unless those releases were routine, systemic, and deliberate (50 *FR* 28712, July 15, 1985). Routine and systemic releases constitute, in effect, management of wastes; the area at which this activity has taken place can thus reasonably be considered a solid waste management unit. "Deliberate" does not require a showing that the owner or operator knowingly caused a release of hazardous waste or constituents. Rather, the term deliberate was included to indicate EPA's intention not to exercise its Section 3004(u) authority against one-time, accidental spills that cannot be linked to a SWMU. An example of this type of release would be an accidental spill from a truck at a RCRA facility (OSWER Directive 9502.00-6c).

Implementation

The 3004(u) provision is initiated when an owner or an operator applies for a permit. The application can be for an operating permit or a post-closure permit. It is important to note that it is the application of a permit that triggers corrective action, and not the issuance of a permit. Thus, even if a permit is denied, the 3004(u) provisions would be applicable. 40 CFR 270.14(c) requires specified information concerning solid waste management units to be included in the Part B permit application. New facilities seeking a permit that were not previously engaged in hazardous waste operations also would be subject to the provisions. Section 3004(u) states that corrective action is required "for all releases of hazardous waste or constituents from any solid waste unit at a treatment, storage, or disposal facility seeking a permit . . . under Subtitle C of RCRA . . . regardless of the time at which waste was placed in such unit. . . ." Therefore, any solid waste management unit located on a site that is involved in a permit application is subject to corrective action even if there has never been any previous authorization for hazardous waste activity at the site.

Section 3004(u) states that corrective action for a facility shall be required as a condition of each permit issued after November 8, 1984. Because a permit modification is not equivalent under 40 CFR 270.41 to the issuance of a permit, a facility that is seeking a modification to a permit issued prior to November 8, 1984, is not required to address the corrective action requirements of 3004(u). A facility permit being reviewed for reissuance, however, is subject to the 3004(u) corrective action provisions.

A facility that is not required to obtain a permit under Section 3005(c) of RCRA will not have to comply with Section 3004(u) (e.g., a surface impoundment that clean closes). However, if EPA found a release of hazardous waste, or hazardous constituents from hazardous or solid waste, it could order corrective action under the interim status corrective action order authority in Section 3008(h). Section 3008(h) orders may be issued both before, during, and after closure.

The owner or the operator must submit the following information in the Part B permit application concerning SWMUs [40 CFR 270.14(c)]:

- The location of the unit(s) on the required topographical map.
- Designation of type of unit (e.g., landfill, impoundment).
- General dimensions and structural description (supplying any available drawings).
- The dates of operation.
- Specification of all wastes that have been managed at each unit.

Interim Status Corrective Action Orders

EPA also has authority to order facilities to undertake corrective action outside the permitting process for interim status facilities. As authorized by Section 3008(h) of HSWA, EPA can require corrective actions or other measures necessary to protect human health and the environment whenever there is or has been a release of hazardous wastes or hazardous constituents from an interim status facility. Such orders also may revoke or suspend a facility's interim status and/or assess penalties of up to $25,000 per day for noncompliance with previous corrective action orders.

Section 3008(h) authorizes the EPA Administrator to issue corrective action orders to address releases of hazardous wastes into the environment from facilities *authorized* to operate under interim status [§3005(e) of RCRA]. This authority extends to include those facilities that should have had interim status but failed to notify EPA under Section 3010 of RCRA or failed to submit a Part A application (OSWER Directive 9901.1). For example, facilities with closed units may remain in interim status indefinitely, and thus are potentially subject to enforcement action under Section 3008(h).

The authority under Section 3008(h) is not confined to addressing releases from solid waste management units as 3004(u). Thus, one-time spills and other types of contamination at facilities can be addressed under Section 3008(h). In addition, 3004(u) is initiated only when an owner or an operator is applying for a permit, whereas 3008(h) has no such limitations for interim status facilities.

Beyond Facility Boundaries

Owners and operators of permitted and interim status hazardous waste management units are required to institute corrective action beyond the facility's boundary when necessary to protect human health and the environment, unless the owner or the operator is denied access to adjacent property despite the best efforts of the owner or operator (52 *FR* 45790, December 1, 1987). In determining *best efforts,* EPA considers case-by-case circumstances; however, at a minimum, the effort should include a certified letter to the adjacent property owner (52 *FR* 45790, December 1, 1987).

Even if permission from the adjacent landowner is denied (despite the best efforts of the owner or the operator), the facility is not necessarily relieved of its responsibility to undertake corrective measures to address releases that have migrated beyond the facility boundary. EPA can require the facility to implement on-site corrective measures in an attempt to clean up releases beyond its boundary. Any corrective measures will be based on their feasibility and appropriateness, according to case-by-case circumstances, considering hydrogeologic conditions and other relevant factors (52 *FR* 45790, December 1, 1988).

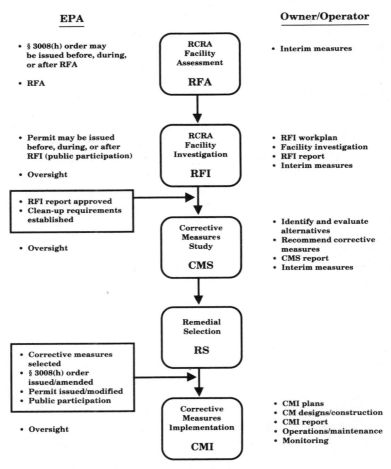

EPA   Owner/Operator

- § 3008(h) order may
  be issued before, during,
  or after RFA

- RFA

- Permit may be issued
  before, during, or after
  RFI (public participation)

- Oversight

- RFI report approved
- Clean-up requirements
  established

- Oversight

- Corrective measures
  selected
- § 3008(h) order
  issued/amended
- Permit issued/modified
- Public participation

- Oversight

RCRA Facility Assessment — **RFA**

RCRA Facility Investigation — **RFI**

Corrective Measures Study — **CMS**

Remedial Selection — **RS**

Corrective Measures Implementation — **CMI**

- Interim measures

- RFI workplan
- Facility investigation
- RFI report
- Interim measures

- Identify and evaluate
  alternatives
- Recommend corrective
  measures
- CMS report
- Interim measures

- CMI plans
- CM designs/construction
- CMI report
- Operations/maintenance
- Monitoring

Source: OWPE RCRA Corrective Active Handbook (EPA).

Figure 9-1. Corrective Action Process

CORRECTIVE ACTION PROCESS

The 3004(u) program consists of five phases, as outlined in Figure 9-1:

1. *RCRA Facility Assessment (RFA).* The RFA is an investigation conducted by EPA to identify possible hazardous waste or hazardous constituent releases.

2. *RCRA Facility Investigation (RFI).* If the RFA determines that there is a suspected release, the owner or operator must conduct an RFI, which characterizes the nature and extent of the release.

3. *Corrective Measures Study (CMS)*. If the RFI determines that a corrective action is necessary, a CMS is performed to determine the most effective cleanup alternative.
4. *Remedy Selection*. After the CMS, EPA then selects a suitable remedy and either incorporates it into the permit or issues a corrective action order specifying the remedy and the time when it must be implemented.
5. *Corrective Measures Implementation (CMI)*. After the remedy has been selected, the corrective measures are implemented.

Note: Throughout the corrective action process, EPA has the authority to initiate an Interim Measure (IM) (e.g., requiring the immediate cleanup of a unit, constructing a fence, or segregating wastes). IMs primarily are used when there is an immediate threat to human health and the environment.

The RCRA corrective action program has been modeled after the Superfund remedial action program. A comparison of these two programs is outlined in Figure 9-2.

RCRA Facility Assessment

The RCRA facility assessment (RFA), previously known as the preliminary assessment/site investigation, is conducted for each facility seeking a RCRA permit (OSWER Directive 9502.00-6c). The purpose of the RFA is to identify solid waste management units and potential releases of hazardous wastes or hazardous constituents from hazardous and solid waste management units.

Under the RFA process, EPA does the following:

- Identifies and gathers information on releases at RCRA facilities.
- Evaluates solid waste management units for releases to all media (e.g., groundwater, surface water, soil, and air) and releases from regulated units to media other than groundwater.
- Makes a preliminary determination regarding releases of concern and the need for further action, such as an RFI or an IM (e.g., constructing a dike around the release until a more permanent solution is feasible).

EPA is responsible for conducting RFAs. Typically, EPA uses contractors to assist them in conducting these investigations, but EPA retains overall responsibility. However, in some cases, the facility owner or

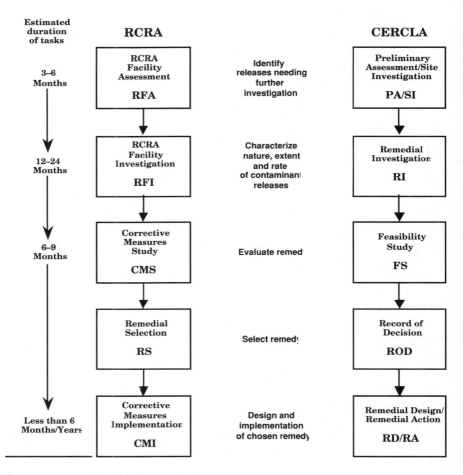

Figure 9-2. Comparison of RCRA Corrective Action and CERCLA Remedial Process

operator is requested to conduct certain sampling activities (OSWER Directive 9502.00-5).

The RFA identifies potential releases from solid waste management units and hazardous waste management units that need to be cleaned up. EPA uses the information gathered in the RFA to determine if further investigation is necessary, to assess potential risk to human health and the environment, and to require an immediate cleanup if warranted.

The RFA consists of three basic stages:

- Preliminary review
- Visual site inspection
- Sampling visit

The RFA begins with a preliminary review of pertinent information concerning the facility. During the preliminary review, EPA collects and evaluates information, such as state and facility files, inspection reports, monitoring reports, and information collected during interviews with people familiar with the facility. In the visual site inspection, an EPA representative tours the facility and looks for evidence of solid waste management units and releases, fills in data gaps identified in the preliminary review, and determines the need for a sampling visit, an interim measure, or an RFI.

During the sampling visit, which is the optional part of the RFA, EPA conducts sampling to fill data gaps found during the preliminary review and visual site inspection. The data gathered during this stage of the corrective action process are limited compared to the data gathered during the RFI.

One of the primary goals of the RFA is to identify releases or potential releases from solid waste management units. When determining the potential for releases from a solid waste management unit, EPA considers such factors as unit characteristics, waste characteristics (e.g., some wastes migrate more quickly than others), pollution-migration pathways (the paths a pollutant may follow when it is released from a unit), evidence of a release, and exposure potential. These factors are evaluated separately to detect releases to each medium, including groundwater, surface water, air, subsurface gas (such as methane generated in landfills), and soil.

The findings of the RFA will have one or more results:

- No further action will be required if there is no evidence of a release.
- A RCRA facility investigation by the owner or the operator will be required if the information collected indicates that a release exists and further information is needed.
- Interim corrective measures by the owner or the operator will be required if EPA determines that expedited action is necessary to protect human health or the environment.

RCRA Facility Investigation

The RCRA facility investigation (RFI), which is analogous to the remedial investigation in the Superfund program, is the second phase of the corrective action process. If the RFA indicates that a release has occurred, or if there is a significant potential for a release, EPA requires the owner or the operator of a facility to conduct an RFI, with EPA overseeing the entire process. Generally, permit applicants are required to set out a schedule for the RFI as part of the permit application, which when issued, will make the RFI a condition of the permit.

The RFI characterizes solid waste management units, the nature and extent of releases of hazardous wastes or constituents from these units, the environmental setting, and the potentially exposed population and affected environment; also it determines the need for an IM or a CMS and whether wastes have migrated beyond the facility boundary. The general requirements include the identification of each solid waste management unit, the types of investigation required for each medium, and the level of detail required. The schedule of compliance also may include constituent concentration levels that, if exceeded, would require the owner or the operator to proceed to the next step of the corrective action process, the CMS, which determines the most suitable cleanup option.

The RFI uses a phased approach, whereby data are collected and analyzed and then used to revise future sampling criteria for more specific sampling if necessary. The phased approach ensures that all data are incorporated into future portions of the investigation; it is especially important when little is known about the site and the actual location of the unit, or when a release needs to be verified.

The RFI is divided into media-specific investigations, one each for groundwater, surface water, soil, air, and subsurface gas. The unit characteristics, waste characteristics, and release characteristics, and how they affect the potential for and the extent of the exposure, are assessed. In addition, each of the media-specific investigations takes into account the unique characteristics of each medium (e.g., the groundwater investigation measures the rate, direction, and flow of groundwater and the depth to the water table, whereas the soil investigation studies surface features and the erosion potential of the soil).

Corrective Measures Study

If the need for a corrective measure is identified during the RFI process, the owner or the operator is required to conduct a corrective measures study (CMS), which will probably require a permit modification. The purpose of the CMS is to identify and recommend specific corrective measures that will adequately correct the release. (The CMS process is analogous to a feasibility study under the Superfund program.)

The CMS can range from a highly focused study of a single treatment technology to a complex study of several cleanup options. The feasibility and the effectiveness of each cleanup technology are examined. The selected corrective action must protect human health and the environment, meet cleanup levels specified by EPA, and minimize any further releases. The level of the cleanup is important, as it determines if the cleanup will be protective of human health and the environment. Any wastes removed during the cleanup must be managed according to the EPA rules and regulations discussed throughout this book.

A corrective measures study typically includes:

- Evaluation of performance, reliability, ease of implementation, and potential impacts of the remedy, including safety impacts, cross media impacts, and control of exposure to any residual contamination.
- Assessment of the effectiveness of potential remedies in achieving adequate control of sources and cleanup of hazardous waste and constituents released from SWMUs.
- Assessment of the time required to begin and complete the remedy.
- Estimation of the costs of remedy implementation.
- Assessment of the institutional requirements, such as state or local permit requirements, or other environmental or public health requirements that may substantially affect implementation of the remedy.

The CMS also evaluates any possible impacts that a corrective action might cause, such as cross-media contamination (e.g., when groundwater containing a volatile organic is run through an air stripper treatment system, volatile organics are typically transferred from the groundwater to the air).

Because sites differ, EPA has not established national uniform standards for cleanup *per se*. *EPA-recommended limits or factors* (discussed in Chapter 5 in the section on closure) generally are used as cleanup levels. These factors are health-based levels (e.g., MCLs, RfDs, and CSFs). As in most other EPA programs, carcinogens must be cleaned up until the risk range of 10^{-4} to 10^{-6} exists, with 10^{-6} as the point of departure. Site-specific factors also are used to determine cleanup levels. These factors include groundwater use (i.e., drinking water), depth of contamination, mobility and persistence of contaminants, and potential receptors.

Upon completion and receipt of the corrective measures study, EPA evaluates its adequacy. If the plan is deficient, EPA either modifies the plan or requires the owner or the operator to make the appropriate modifications before approval of the remedy selection.

Remedy Selection

The corrective measures study presents corrective action alternatives with a preferred alternative. The remedy selection process requires the evaluation of a number of factors before a remedy is selected and the corrective measures implementation phase begins.

The selected remedy must:

- Be protective of human health and the environment.
- Attain the cleanup standards.
- Control the sources of releases to reduce or eliminate threats to human health and the environment.
- Comply with the applicable hazardous waste management regulations.

A remedy that meets the above standards also must meet the following technical standards:

- Long-term reliability and effectiveness.
- Reduction of toxicity, mobility, and/or volume.
- Short-term effectiveness.
- Implementability.

Corrective Measures Implementation

The purpose of the corrective measures implementation (CMI) phase is to design, construct, operate, maintain, and monitor the performance of selected corrective measures.

The implementation of corrective measures is the actual cleanup process. The selected corrective measure is implemented by the owner or the operator, with close supervision by EPA; and the cleanup is conducted until concentration levels set by EPA are attained. The facility is monitored during and after the CM process to ensure that all wastes or constituents have been cleaned up and will not be released over time.

The corrective measures can be implemented through compliance schedules contained in the facility's permit, which will probably require a permit modification and subsequent public involvement. On June 22, 1987 (52 *FR* 2344), EPA promulgated amendments to allow the information related to detailed corrective action planning, required by 40 CFR 270.14(c)(7), (c)(8)(iii), and (c)(8)(iv), to be developed at EPA's discretion, after the issuance of a permit, through the use of compliance schedules.

The owner or the operator is required to obtain advanced written authorization from EPA waiving submittal of the corrective action information if it is issued in compliance schedules. This waiver applies only to the design of the corrective action program and not to information required to assess the need or the extent of the corrective action.

Public Participation

Public participation under RCRA is generally limited to the permit application process and permit modification requests. Because the corrective action program is implemented through permits, it is here that the public has the opportunity to participate.

At the time when the permit application is submitted, a mailing list must be prepared by EPA for the community in which the facility is located [40 CFR 124.10(c)(1)(viii)]. The list serves as a communication tool to enable EPA to reach interested members of the public with announcements of meetings, hearings, events, reports, and documents.

After developing a draft permit, EPA is required to provide public notice that a draft permit has been prepared and is available for public review [40 CFR 124.6]. A 45-day public comment period on the draft permit must follow the public notice. The comment period for the draft permit provides the public an opportunity to comment on corrective action conditions contained in the permit. In most cases, requirements for the RFI will be included in the schedule of compliance in the draft permit.

Chapter 10

Enforcement and State Authorization

It is the intent of RCRA [Section 1003(a)(7)] to establish a viable state–federal partnership to carry out the provisions of RCRA and ultimately to assist the states in operating the Nation's waste management program in lieu of the federal government. For a state to operate the program, its program must be *equivalent* to the federal program, be *consistent* with the federal and other state programs, and provide for adequate enforcement.

RCRA'S ENFORCEMENT PROVISIONS

The purpose of any enforcement program, including RCRA's, is to compel compliance with a set of regulations. The RCRA enforcement program has many tools, both legal and administrative, to help or force compliance with the regulations. The effectiveness of the hazardous waste management regulatory program under RCRA depends on whether or not the regulated community complies with the requirements. Close monitoring of facility activities and legal action when noncompliance exists are a necessity. Monitoring allows EPA to determine which facilities are out of compliance and to evaluate the effectiveness of enforcement programs.

Compliance Inspections

The primary means of collecting valuable monitoring data is the facility compliance inspection, which is a formal visit to a facility to review records, obtain samples, and determine the facility's compliance with the requirements by observing facility operations. Various acts provide the authority for EPA, an authorized state, or representatives (e.g., contractors) of either to enter any facility that has handled hazardous waste for inspection to examine the facility's records and to obtain samples of the wastes.

Section 3007 of RCRA authorizes EPA employees and their representatives (including EPA contractors) to enter at reasonable times any establishment where hazardous wastes are or have been generated; or from which they have been transported; or where they have been treated, stored, or disposed of. This authorization includes allowance to inspect the facility, obtain samples, and obtain and copy records and information related to hazardous wastes (OSWER Directive 9938.0). Authorized officers, employees, and representatives, including authorized contractors, are allowed to enter any portion of a facility that is being or has been used to generate or manage *hazardous wastes*. The specific objective of the inspection does not have to be written in any form, but the inspection must strictly deal with the generation, management, or transportation of hazardous waste (OSWER Directive 9938.0).

The main purpose of any inspection is to determine whether the facility is operating in accordance with the terms of its permit, in compliance with interim status standards, or in compliance with other applicable regulations.

An inspection typically consists of the following steps:

1. Before visiting the facility, the inspector reviews the facility's permit or other records to identify any problems that may be encountered.
2. The inspector enters the facility, identifies him- or herself, and describes the nature of the inspection. An opening conference is held with the owner or the operator to describe the information and samples to be gathered.
3. The facility is inspected. The inspection includes examination of facility records, possible collection of samples, and observation of the facility, including any hazardous waste management operations. The inspector also may observe all associated activities, such as unloading of wastes, lab work, and safety procedures. The inspector may use field notebooks, checklists, and photographs to document the visit.
4. The inspector holds a closing conference with the owner or the operator to respond to questions about the inspection and provide additional information.
5. The inspector prepares a report summarizing the results of the inspection, including the results of sampling. Violations are docu-

mented in the report. The entire process usually lasts from one day to one week.

Any records, reports, or other information obtained from an inspection is available to the public, unless a claim of confidentiality is asserted under EPA's business confidentiality regulations, contained in 40 CFR Part 2.

Prior to the Hazardous and Solid Waste Amendments (HSWA), RCRA did not mandate inspections of facilities. Because there were too few inspections to effectively monitor compliance with the regulations, HSWA requires that all federal- or state-operated facilities be inspected annually. Furthermore, EPA must inspect all privately owned facilities at least once every two years. Facilities also may be inspected at any time if there is reason to suspect that a violation has occurred or is occurring.

Enforcement Options

Two situations may cause a RCRA enforcement action to be initiated: (1) a facility is found to be out of compliance with applicable Subtitle C regulations; or (2) a facility is found to present a substantial threat to human health or the environment.

EPA considers both the owner(s) and the operator of a facility to be responsible for regulatory compliance. For this reason, EPA may initiate an enforcement action against either the owner, the operator, or both. Normally, the compliance order is issued to the person responsible for the daily operations at the facility because that person is most likely to be in a position to correct the problems. If the operator is unable or unwilling to rectify the problems, then EPA may issue a separate compliance order to the owner.

There are several types of enforcement action available under RCRA, including:

- Administrative actions
- Civil actions
- Criminal actions

Administrative Actions

An *administrative action* is a nonjudicial enforcement action taken by EPA or a state under its own authority. These actions require less preparation than a lawsuit (civil action). Two types of administrative actions exist, informal actions and administrative orders. Both constitute an enforcement response outside of the court system.

Informal Actions

An *informal administrative action* is any communication from EPA or a state that notifies a facility that it is not in compliance with a specified provision of the regulations. EPA uses notices of violations and warning letters. If the owner or the operator does not take steps to comply within a certain time period after receiving a communication, a more formal action can be taken.

For more serious violations, EPA or the state can use a warning letter setting out specific actions to be taken to bring the facility back into compliance. A warning letter also sets out the enforcement actions that will follow if the facility fails to take the required steps.

A warning letter generally contains the following information:

- Identification, citation, and explanation of the violation.
- A deadline for achieving full compliance with the appropriate regulatory or statutory requirements.
- A statement indicating that continued noncompliance beyond a particular date would generally result in the issuance of a Section 3008 compliance order or other enforcement action, including the assessment of civil penalties of up to $25,000 per day per violation.
- The name and telephone number of an EPA contact person.

Administrative Orders

When a violation is detected that is more severe than those requiring an informal action, EPA or the state can give an administrative order. Issued directly under the authority of RCRA, an administrative order imposes enforceable legal requirements. Orders can be used to force a facility to comply with specific regulations; to initiate corrective action; to conduct monitoring, testing, and analysis; or to address a threat to human health or the environment. Four types of orders can be issued under RCRA:

- Compliance orders
- Corrective action orders
- Monitoring and analysis orders
- Imminent endangerment orders

Compliance Orders

Section 3008(a) of RCRA authorizes the use of an order requiring any person who is not complying with a requirement thereunder to take steps to come into compliance. A compliance order may require immediate compliance or may set out a timetable to be followed to move toward compliance. The order can include a penalty of up to $25,000 for each day of noncompliance and can suspend or revoke the facility's permit or interim status. When an agency issues a compliance order, the person who receives the order can request a hearing on any of its factual provisions. If no hearing is requested, the order will become final 30 days after it is issued.

Corrective Action Orders

Section 3008(h) of HSWA authorizes the use of an order requiring corrective action at a facility when there has been a release of a hazardous waste or constituents into the environment, as discussed in Chapter 9. Such orders can be issued to require corrective action regardless of when waste was placed in the unit. In addition, the orders can suspend interim status and impose penalties of up to $25,000 for each day of noncompliance.

Monitoring and Analysis

If EPA or the state finds that a substantial hazard to human health or the environment exists at a facility, a monitoring and analysis order under Section 3013(a) can be issued. This order is used to evaluate the extent of the problem through monitoring, analysis, and testing. It can be issued to either the current owner of the facility or to a past owner if the facility is not currently in operation.

A Section 3013(a) order requires the person to whom the order was issued to submit to EPA, within 30 days of the issuance of the order, a proposal for carrying out the required monitoring, testing, analysis, and reporting. The EPA Administrator may, after providing the person an opportunity to confer with EPA, require that he or she carry out the proposal, as well as make any modifications in the proposal that the EPA Administrator deems reasonable to ascertain the nature and extent of the hazard. EPA may commence a civil judicial action against any person who fails or refuses to comply with a Section 3013(a) order. Such an action is brought in the U.S. district court in which the defendant is located, resides, or is doing business. The court may not only require compliance with the order but also may assess a civil penalty of up to $5,000 for each day during which such failure or refusal occurs.

Imminent Endangerment Orders

Prior to HSWA, in any situation in which an imminent and substantial endangerment to human health or the environment was caused by the handling of hazardous wastes, the responsible agency could order persons contributing to the problem to take steps to rectify the situation [RCRA Section 7003]. Although this language implied that only those currently contributing to the endangerment could be ordered to clean up the problem, Section 7003 was almost always interpreted to include past contributors as well. HSWA validated this interpretation by allowing EPA to bring actions against past or present generators, transporters, or owners or operators of a site. Violation of a Section 7003 order can result in fines of up to $5,000 per day. Evidence possessed to support the issuance of a RCRA Section 7003 order must show that the "handling, storage, treatment, transportation, or disposal of any solid or hazardous waste *may present* an imminent and substantial endangerment to health or the environment." The words "may present" indicate that Congress established a standard of proof that does not require a certainty. The evidence is not required to demonstrate that an imminent and substantial endangerment to public health or the environment definitely exists. Instead, an order may be issued if there is sound reason to believe that such an endangerment may exist.

Civil Actions

A *civil action* is a formal lawsuit, filed in court against an individual or a facility that either has failed to comply with some regulatory requirement or administrative order or has contributed to a threat to human health or the environment. Civil actions are generally reserved for situations that present repeated or significant violations or serious threats to the environment. (The U.S. Department of Justice represents EPA in any civil or criminal prosecution or defense.)

RCRA provides authority for filing four types of civil actions:

- Compliance action
- Corrective action
- Monitoring and analysis action
- Imminent hazard action

Frequently, several of the civil action authorities are used together in the same lawsuit. This is likely to happen when a facility has been issued an administrative order for violating a regulatory requirement, has ignored that order, and is in continued noncompliance. In this circumstance, a lawsuit can be filed that seeks penalties for violating the original requirement, penalties for violating the order, and a court order requiring future compliance with the requirement and the administrative order.

Compliance Action

EPA or an authorized state can file a lawsuit to force a person to comply with applicable RCRA regulations. The court also can impose a penalty of up to $25,000 per day for noncompliance.

Corrective Action

In a situation in which there has been a release of hazardous waste from a facility, EPA or a state can sue to have the court order the facility to correct the problem and take any necessary response measures. The court also can suspend or revoke a facility's interim status as a part of its order.

To exercise the corrective action authority, EPA must first have information that there is or has been a release at the facility. Additional sources that may provide information on releases include: inspection reports, RCRA facility assessments, RCRA Part A and Part B permit applications, responses to Section 3007 information requests, information obtained through Section 3013 orders, notifications required by Section 103 of CERCLA, information-gathering activities conducted under Section 104 of CERCLA, or citizens' complaints corroborated by supporting information.

Monitoring and Analysis Action

If EPA or a state has issued a monitoring and analysis order under Section 3013 of RCRA, and the facility to which the order was issued fails to comply, EPA or a state can sue to get a court to require compliance with the order. In this type of case, the court can levy a penalty of up to $5,000 for each day of noncompliance with the order.

Imminent Hazard Action

As with a Section 7003 administrative order, when any facility or person has contributed or is contributing to an imminent hazard to human health or the environment, EPA or a state can sue the person or facility and request the court to require that person or facility to take action to remove the hazard or remedy any problem. If an agency had first issued an administrative order, the court also can impose a penalty of up to $5,000 for each day of noncompliance with the order.

Criminal Actions

A *criminal action suit* is an action that can result in the imposition of fines or imprisonment. There are seven instances identified in Section 3008 of RCRA that carry criminal penalties. Six of the seven criminal acts carry a penalty of up to $50,000 per day or up to five years in jail. Stated briefly, these acts are the *knowing:*

- Transportation of hazardous waste to a nonpermitted facility.
- Treatment, storage, or disposal of hazardous waste without a permit or in violation of a condition of a permit.
- Omission of required information from a label or manifest.
- Generation, storage, treatment, or disposal of hazardous waste without compliance with RCRA's record keeping and reporting requirements.
- Transportation of hazardous waste without a manifest.
- Export of hazardous waste without the consent of the receiving country.

The seventh criminal act is the *knowing* transportation, treatment, storage, disposal, or export of any hazardous waste in such a way that another person is placed in imminent danger of death or serious bodily injury. This act carries a possible penalty of up to $250,000 or 15 years in prison for an individual or a $1 million fine for a corporation.

Priority Classification Scheme

The RCRA enforcement program employs several terms to define priorities for enforcement response and to assess penalties (OSWER Directive 9900.0-1A). The program classifies individual violations into one of two classes:

- *Class I Violation:* a violation that results in a release or serious threat of release of hazardous waste to the environment or involves failure to assure that groundwater will be protected, that proper closure and post-closure activities will be undertaken, or that hazardous waste will be destined for and delivered to permitted or interim status facilities.
- *Class II Violation:* any violation of RCRA requirements that does not meet the criteria listed above for Class I violations.

Note: The two-class system replaces the previous three-class system.

RCRA Violators

A RCRA handler is classified according to the nature of its collection of violations and various additional factors, such as compliance history. The RCRA enforcement program establishes three categories of violators: high-, medium-, and low-priority violators.

High-Priority Violator

A *high-priority violator* is a handler who has either:

- Substantially deviated from RCRA statutory or regulatory requirements;
- Deviated from conditions of a permit, order, or decree by not meeting the requirements in a timely manner or failing to perform the required actions;
- Caused a substantial likelihood of exposure to hazardous waste or has caused actual exposure; or
- Is a chronic or recalcitrant violator.

High-priority violators are the violators who merit the most stringent and immediate enforcement response. The goal of any enforcement action against a high-priority violator is to impose sanctions that will compel a rapid return to compliance, penalize the violator, recover economic gains the violator may have accrued, and deter other members of the regulated community from violating the law. Once a violation discovery is made, it is expected that within 90 days a formal administrative action will be taken, or a referral will be made for judicial action.

Medium-Priority Violator

A *medium-priority violator* is a handler with one or more Class I violations who does not meet the criteria for a high-priority violator. Handlers with only Class II violations also may be medium-priority violators when the compliance official believes that an administrative order is the appropriate response. The appropriate response is either the issuance of an administrative order or a less formal response that results in compliance within 90 days of violation discovery. The issuance of an administrative order with penalties is the preferred response.

Low-Priority Violator

A *low-priority violator* is a handler who has only Class II violations and is not a medium- or high-priority violator. A low-priority violator normally will receive a notice of violation or a warning letter as the initial response within 60 days of violation discovery.

Imposing Fines

EPA uses the *RCRA Civil Penalty Policy* for assessing administrative penalties under RCRA. The penalty policy is a matrix table used to derive potential fines for a violation after several factors are considered. The purpose of the policy is to assure that RCRA civil penalties are assessed in a fair and consistent manner, that the penalties are appropriate for the violation committed, that economic incentives for noncompliance are eliminated, that persons are deterred from committing violations, and that compliance is achieved (OSWER Directive 9900.1).

EPA Action in Authorized States

States with authorized programs have the primary responsibility for ensuring compliance with the RCRA program requirements. Nevertheless, Section 3008 of RCRA specifically provides EPA with the authority to take enforcement action in authorized states under certain conditions. EPA will take enforcement actions in an authorized state when the state asks EPA to do so or fails to take timely and appropriate action.

If the state has failed to issue an order or complete a referral within 90 days after the discovery of a high-priority violator (or 60 days after deciding to issue an order to a Class I violator), the EPA Regional Office notifies the state that EPA intends to take action. The EPA Regional

Office also may choose to assess a penalty against a high-priority violator if the state's action failed to include one. The Memorandum of Agreement (MOA) or Grant Agreement (GA) between EPA and each state should set out the mechanism by which notice will be provided. The EPA Regional Office may need to conduct its own case development inspection and prepare additional documentation before initiating an action. If the state has made reasonable progress in returning the facility to compliance or in processing an enforcement action, EPA may delay a response.

Citizen Suits

Section 7002 of RCRA authorizes any citizen to commence a civil action (suit) against:

- Any person or government agency alleged to be in violation of any permit, standard, regulation, condition, requirement, or order that has become effective under RCRA.
- Any past or present generator, transporter, or owner or operator of a facility who has contributed to or is contributing to a condition that may present an imminent and substantial endangerment to human health or the environment.
- The EPA Administrator where there is alleged failure of the Administrator to perform any act or duty under RCRA that is not a discretionary action.

The right of citizens to bring suits under Section 7002 is limited in certain situations, as follows:

- No suit may be brought if the EPA Administrator or a state has commenced, and is "diligently prosecuting," an enforcement action against the alleged violator.
- Suits are not allowed to be used to impede the issuance of a permit or the siting of a facility (except by state and local governments).
- Transporters are protected from citizen suits in response to incidents arising after delivery of waste.
- A facility actively engaged in a removal action under CERCLA may not be sued.

Before filing a suit under this provision, a citizen must give a 60-day notice to EPA, to the state in which the alleged violation occurred, and to the alleged violator.

If a citizen is suing a past or present generator presenting a substantial endangerment under Section 7002(a)(1)(B), a 90-day notice must be given to EPA, to the state in which the alleged violation occurs, and to the alleged violator.

There is no prescribed format for the notification. A simple, concise letter (certified) stating the alleged violation(s), the alleged violator, the location of the alleged violator, and the intent to file suit is sufficient. The notice to EPA should be sent to:

The Administrator
U.S. Environmental Protection Agency
401 M Street, SW
Washington, DC 20460

The suit must be brought in the district court for the district in which the alleged violation or endangerment occurred. If a person is bringing suit against the EPA Administrator, the suit may be brought in either the district court in which the alleged violation occurred or the District Court of the District of Columbia. In addition, whenever action is brought against a past or present contributing generator, the plaintiff must serve a copy of the suit to the Attorney General of the United States and to the EPA Administrator.

The court, in issuing any final order in any action brought under Section 7002, may award costs of litigation (including reasonable attorney and expert witness fees) to the prevailing or substantially prevailing party, whenever the court determines such an award is appropriate.

STATE AUTHORIZATION

It is the intent of RCRA to have the Nation's hazardous waste management program administered by the states with only minimal oversight from the federal government. The program elements and the process necessary for states to obtain the responsibility for the Subtitle C program involve developing a state hazardous waste program and approval by EPA as outlined in Part 271. Because EPA's hazardous waste regulations were developed in stages, the states have been given the opportunity to implement a phased approach to the Subtitle C program, which allows the state eventually to operate the program. Before HSWA, a state could obtain *interim authorization* (Phase I) for a program that was *substantially equivalent* to the federal program. Interim authorization allowed a state to administer Parts 260, 261, 262, 263, and 265. A state also could obtain authorization to administer specific permitting programs (Phase II). For example, a state that had Phase II, component A could write permits for tanks and container storage units only; component B was for incinerators; and component C was for land disposal units. However, under HSWA, in states with only interim authorization as of January 31, 1986, the program reverted back to full EPA control. Since that date, states have had to seek final authorization for the complete program, that is, the complete Subtitle C program as it was *before* the enactment of HSWA. Any state that had final authorization prior to HSWA must obtain authorization specifically for HSWA. Until a state has HSWA authorization, EPA will administer the HSWA provisions.

Program Elements

Any state that seeks final authorization for its hazardous waste program must submit to the EPA Administrator an application consisting of the following elements:

- A letter from the state's governor requesting program approval.
- Copies of all applicable state statutes and regulations, including those governing state administrative procedures.
- A description of the program.
- Statement by the state's attorney general.
- A Memorandum of Agreement (MOA).

Program Description

As the name implies, the program description submitted to EPA must detail the state hazardous waste program [40 CFR 271.6]. It must include descriptions of:

- The scope, structure, coverage, and processes of the state program.
- The state agency or agencies that will have responsibility for running the program.
- The state-level staff who will carry out the program.
- The state's compliance tracking and enforcement program.
- The state's manifest system.
- The estimated costs involved in running the program and an item- ization of the sources and amounts of funding available to support the program's operation.

If a state chooses to develop a program that is more stringent and/or extensive than the one required by federal law, the description should address those parts of the program that go beyond what is required under Subtitle C.

Attorney General's Statement

Any state that wants to assume the responsibility for Subtitle C must demonstrate to EPA that the laws of the state provide adequate authority to carry out all aspects of the state program. This demonstration comes in the form of a statement written by the state's attorney general. The statement includes references to the statutes, regulations, and judicial decisions that the state will rely on in administering its program [40 CFR 271.1].

Memorandum of Agreement

Although a state with an authorized program assumes primary responsibility for administering Subtitle C, EPA still retains some responsibilities and oversight powers in relation to the state's execution of its program. The Memorandum of Agreement (MOA) between the State Director and the EPA Regional Administrator outlines the nature of these responsibilities and oversight powers and the level of coordination between the state and EPA in operating the program [40 CFR 271.8(b)]. The MOA includes provisions for:

- Specification of the frequency and contents of reports that the state must submit to EPA.
- Coordination of compliance monitoring activities between the state and EPA.
- Joint processing of permits for those facilities that require a permit from both the state and EPA under different programs.
- Specification of those types of permit applications that will be sent to the EPA Regional Administrator for review and comment.

States with Different Programs

A state with final or interim authorization may be more stringent or broader in scope than EPA. A requirement is *broader in scope* if it increases the regulated community; for example, a state regulates a non-hazardous waste such as asbestos as a hazardous waste. A requirement is *more stringent* if it is stricter than its federal equivalent; for example, a state may require annual reporting by a generator instead of the biennial reporting required by the federal program.

The distinction between broader and more stringent state requirements is significant because EPA may enforce a more stringent state requirement, but not state requirements that are broader in scope. Section 3008(a)(2) of RCRA allows EPA to enforce any provision of an authorized state's approved program. More stringent state requirements fall into this category. State provisions that are broader in scope are not part of the federally approved RCRA program, according to 40 CFR 271.1(i), and therefore are not enforceable by EPA. [See Program Implementation Guidance (PIG) 84-1 and 82-3.]

Revising State Programs

As federal and state statutory or regulatory authority relating to RCRA is modified or supplemented, it often is necessary to revise the state program accordingly. Such revisions can be initiated by the state or required because of changes in the federal program [40 CFR 271.21].

If a state decides to revise its program, it must notify EPA and submit a modified program description, an MOA, and any other documentation EPA deems necessary. The revisions become effective upon approval by EPA [40 CFR 271.21(b)].

State programs also must be revised in response to changes in the federal program. Because state programs must be as stringent as the federal program, changes will be required. If the state is able to modify its program without passing a statutory amendment, the program must be revised within one year of the date of federal promulgation (*Federal Register* publication date). However, if a state statutory amendment is required, the state is given two years to revise its program [40 CFR 271.21].

The Hazardous and Solid Waste Amendments

Although authorized states have one, or in some cases, two years to modify their programs, the federal government can enforce the HSWA provisions in an authorized state until the state receives administrative approval to do so.

In certain circumstances states are not required to have their program reauthorized before being able to enforce new federal requirements resulting from HSWA. Any state that has final authorization for the pre-HSWA program may submit to EPA evidence that its program contains requirements that are substantially equivalent to any requirement created by HSWA. Such a state may request interim authorization for HSWA.

Delisting

A state is not required to have a delisting program to obtain EPA authorization for its hazardous waste regulatory program. However, if a state does have provisions to delist a hazardous waste, the program must conform to the federal delisting program (OSWER Directive 9433.00-1).

Radioactive Mixed Wastes

For a state to obtain and maintain authorization for its hazardous waste regulatory program, the state must have the authority to regulate the hazardous components of a radioactive mixed waste. *Radioactive mixed wastes* are wastes that contain hazardous wastes subject to RCRA and low-level radioactive wastes subject to the Atomic Energy Act (51 *FR* 24504, July 3, 1986).

Program Reversion

Authorized state programs are continually subject to review. If EPA finds that a state's program no longer complies with the appropriate regulatory requirements, EPA may withdraw program approval. Such circumstances include a failure to:

- Issue permits that conform to the regulatory requirements.
- Inspect and monitor activities subject to regulation.
- Comply with terms of the MOA.
- Take appropriate enforcement action.

In some cases (e.g., when there is a lack of sufficient resources), states with approved hazardous waste management programs may voluntarily transfer the programs back to EPA. In such a case, the appropriate EPA Regional Office will administer the RCRA program in the state.

PART II

Superfund

The Comprehensive Environmental Response, Compensation, and Liability Act (CERCLA), commonly known as Superfund,* provides the federal government with broad authority to respond to emergencies involving uncontrolled releases of hazardous substances, to develop long-term solutions for the most serious hazardous waste sites, and to arrange for the restoration of damaged natural resources. Superfund also establishes liabilities for responsible parties involving the release of hazardous substances, as well as outlining a claims procedure for parties who have cleaned up sites.

RCRA, a system of cradle-to-grave regulation of hazardous waste enacted in 1976, required EPA to regulate the management of hazardous waste. However, it was soon realized that EPA lacked the authority to respond quickly to a release or threatened release of hazardous substances (the term *hazardous substances* includes RCRA hazardous wastes). It also was apparent that the government's authority under RCRA was not adequate to clean up the type of hazardous waste site discovered at the Love Canal in Niagara Falls, New York. In addition, EPA did not have the authority to force responsible parties to remediate the environmental problems caused by releases of hazardous substances.

At Love Canal in 1978, President Jimmy Carter declared a state of emergency in a neighborhood where long-buried chemical wastes were seeping into homes, and incidences of adverse health effects were reported. Intense public attention triggered the discovery of thousands of

*The Comprehensive Environmental Response, Compensation, and Liability Act amended by the Superfund Amendments and Reauthorization Act are collectively referred to as Superfund in this book.

257

dumpsites throughout the Nation and mobilized the Administration and Congress. Because of intense public pressure, Congress hastily wrote and passed CERCLA, which incorporated under one statute those federal authorities responsible for responding to releases of hazardous substances, whether they be intentional, accidental, or continuous releases or a one-time spill.

A principal thrust of Superfund is to arrange for or compel potentially responsible parties (PRPs) to clean up hazardous waste sites. Superfund provides EPA with the authority and funding to initiate cleanup activities or to require others to undertake immediate cleanup without first having to determine who is liable. If the responsible party cannot be found or is bankrupt, money from the Hazardous Substance Response Trust Fund (the Superfund) can be used. If a responsible party refuses to clean a site, EPA can do so with federal monies and sue the responsible party for treble damages.

To finance these actions, the act established a $1.6 billion Hazardous Substance Response Trust Fund. The monies for this fund were generated from a tax on specified feedstock chemicals; however, Superfund's taxing authority ceased on October 1, 1985. Although the statute was still in effect, without money, CERCLA would have been short-lived; but, on October 17, 1986, President Ronald Reagan signed the Superfund Amendments and Reauthorization Act of 1986 (SARA). The basic principles of Superfund, including requiring PRPs to finance cleanups, did not change. However, this new reauthorization changed the cleanup approach and standards, as well as allowing for more public involvement throughout the cleanup process. SARA also provided for an $8.5 billion fund derived from various taxes.

Under CERCLA, few regulations have been promulgated. Instead of mandating EPA to promulgate regulations, Congress simply stated the requirements, with no action necessarily required by EPA. Thus, because of a lack of legal clarification through the rulemaking procedure, the courts have supplied many of the legal interpretations through case law.

Most of the information disseminated by EPA pertaining to Superfund has been in the form of policies and memos instead of regulations, and until recently there was no tracking system for the Superfund policies. This situation has presented a major problem for the regulated community, as well as other interested parties, trying to stay informed about policies and procedures related to Superfund actions. However, the policies and memos pertaining to Superfund have been incorporated into the OSWER (Office of Solid Waste and Emergency Response) Directive System, and further information on that system can be obtained from the RCRA/Superfund hotline' (800-424-9346 or 202-382-3000).

In writing the reauthorization of Superfund, Congress simply put into statutory language many of the policies and procedures that had been established by EPA. Thus, many of the provisions contained in SARA are not necessarily new but have been adopted as statutory requirements.

Relationship with Other Laws

The Resource Conservation and Recovery Act

No clear line distinguishes when Superfund or RCRA is solely applicable in a given situation because many provisions of the statutes overlap. It is generally perceived that Superfund addresses past activities and RCRA current activities; however, this generalized distinction can be altered by such factors as financial viability, type of waste managed, waste management practice, and dates of actions. In general, if a facility comes under the purview of RCRA, EPA will not pursue Superfund actions for that facility (51 *FR* 21057, June 10, 1986). For example, RCRA generally cannot be applied to a facility that disposed of hazardous wastes and ceased this practice before November 19, 1980 (the effective date of Phase I of the RCRA regulations); therefore, that facility would be subject to Superfund. However, if the facility managed waste after November 19, 1980, it would be subject to RCRA. But if a RCRA corrective action order cannot be issued, or the facility cannot financially pursue corrective action measures, Superfund may be applied.

It is generally advantageous for a facility owner or operator to be under the purview of Superfund rather than RCRA. Site-specific Superfund response actions are based primarily on performance standards that are to be cost-effective and technologically attainable. This means that a site under Superfund must be cleaned up to specified levels using any means technically and economically feasible and without requiring federal, state, or local environmental permits. RCRA, on the other hand, stipulates the cleanup levels, as well as the means to perform a cleanup, regardless of cost-effectiveness. In addition, cleanup operations under RCRA usually classify a site as a hazardous waste management facility, requiring the site to obtain appropriate permits and to comply with applicable standards of RCRA 40 CFR Parts 260 through 270. The requirements that must be adhered to under RCRA could have negative economic implications, delay response actions, stultify innovative and experimental technologies, and fan public opposition.

National Environmental Policy Act

Section 102(2)(C) of the National Environmental Policy Act (NEPA) requires that environmental impact statements be prepared for "all major actions significantly affecting the quality of the human environment.'' This requirement exists unless Congress has specifically exempted a federal action from NEPA, or the entity follows procedures that serves as a "functional equivalent" of an impact statement.

Superfund does not contain a NEPA exemption; however, EPA has asserted that the Superfund process performs as a functional equivalent to the EIS process under NEPA. This opinion, dated September 1, 1982, from Robert M. Perry, Associate Administrator, Office of General Counsel to Rita Lavelle, Assistant Administrator for Office of Solid Waste and Emergency Response, states that under the functional equivalent exception, an agency with expertise in environmental matters is not obligated to comply with the formal EIS process prior to taking a particular action if two criteria are met. First, the agency's authorizing statute must provide "substantive and procedural standards that ensure full and adequate consideration of environmental issues" [*Environmental Defense Fund, Inc. v. EPA*, 489 F.2d 1247, 1257 (D.C. Cir. 1973)]. Second, the agency must afford an opportunity for public participation in the evaluation of environmental factors prior to arriving at a final decision (*Portland Cement Association v. Ruckelshaus, supra*, 486 F.2d at 386). The opinion further states that: "it must be stressed that remedial actions do not automatically qualify for the functional equivalent exception to §102(2)(C) of NEPA. Rather, the availability of the exception is contingent upon structuring remedial actions to satisfy the requirements for environmental assessment and public participation underlying the exception. If EPA complies with the procedures for environmental evaluation contained in the NCP and provides for public comment during the decisionmaking process, a strong argument can be made that the exception is applicable. However, if these precautions are not taken, there is a considerable risk that a court will find remedial actions to be subject to the EIS requirements."

To date, no organization has successfully challenged an EPA-led Superfund cleanup on the basis of insufficient compliance with NEPA. However, it is important to note that federal agencies other than EPA would probably not qualify under the functional equivalence exemption and would, therefore, be required to comply with NEPA.

Chapter **11**

Key Definitions Under Superfund

This chapter contains key regulatory definitions of Superfund terms used throughout Part II. These definitions are listed in Section 101 of CERCLA and 40 CFR 300.6 and are marked accordingly.

Act of God means an unanticipated grave natural disaster or other natural phenomenon of an exceptional, inevitable, and irresistible character, the effects of which could not have been prevented or avoided by the exercise of due care or foresight [§101(1)].

Administrator means the Administrator of the United States Environmental Protection Agency [CERCLA §101(2)].

Alternative Water Supplies includes, but is not limited to, drinking water and household water supplies [CERCLA §101(34)].

Applicable Requirements means those Federal requirements that would be legally applicable, whether directly, or as incorporated by a Federally authorized State program, if the response actions were not undertaken pursuant to CERCLA section 104 or 106 [40 CFR 300.6].

Barrel means forty-two United States gallons at sixty degrees Fahrenheit [CERCLA §101(3)].

Claim means a demand in writing for a sum certain [CERCLA §101(4)].

Claimant means any person who presents a claim for compensation under this Act [CERCLA §101(5)].

Coastal Waters, for the purposes of classifying the size of discharges, means the waters of the coastal zone except for the Great Lakes and specified ports and harbors on inland rivers [40 CFR 300.6].

Contractual Relationship means

(A) for the purpose of Section 107(b)(3), includes, but is not limited to, land contracts, deeds or other instruments transferring title or possession, unless the real property on which the facility concerned is located was acquired by the defendant after the disposal or placement of the hazardous substance on, in, or at the facility, and one or more of the circumstances described in clause (i), (ii), or (iii) is also established by the defendant by a preponderance of the evidence:

(i) At the time the defendant acquired the facility the defendant did not know and had no reason to know that any hazardous substance which is the subject of the release or threatened release was disposed of on, in, or at the facility.

(ii) The defendant is a government entity which acquired the facility by escheat, or through any other involuntary transfer or acquisition, or through the exercise of eminent domain authority by purchase or condemnation.

(iii) The defendant acquired the facility by inheritance or bequest.

In addition to establishing the foregoing, the defendant must establish that he or she has satisfied the requirements of section 107(b)(3)(a) and (b).

(B) To establish that the defendant had no reason to know, as provided in clause (i) of subparagraph (A) of this paragraph, the defendant must have undertaken at the time of acquisition all appropriate inquiry into the previous ownership and uses of the property consistent with good commercial or customary practice in an effort to minimize liability. For purposes of the preceding sentence the court shall take into account any specialized knowledge or experience on the part of the defendant, the relationship of the purchase price to the value of the property if uncontaminated, commonly known or reasonably ascertainable information about the property, the obviousness of the presence or likely presence of contamination at the property, and the ability to detect such contamination by appropriate inspection.

(C) Nothing in this paragraph or in Section 107(b)(3) shall diminish the liability of any previous owner or operator of such facility who would otherwise be liable under this Act. Notwithstanding this paragraph, if the defendant obtained actual knowledge of the release or threatened release of a hazardous substance at such facility when the defendant owned the real property and then subsequently transferred ownership of the property to another person without disclosing such knowledge, such defendant shall be liable under section 107(a)(1) and no defense under section 107(b)(3) shall be available to such defendant.

(D) Nothing in this paragraph shall affect the liability under this Act of a defendant who, by any act or omission, caused or contributed to the release or threatened release of a hazardous substance which is the subject of the action relating to the facility [CERCLA §101(35)].

Damages means damages for injury or loss of natural resources as set forth in Section 107(a) or 111(b) of this Act [CERCLA §101(6)].

Drinking Water Supply means any raw or finished water source that is or may be used by a public water system (as defined in the Safe Drinking Water Act) or as drinking water by one or more individuals [CERCLA §101(7)].

Environment means (A) the navigable waters, the waters of the contiguous zone, and the ocean waters of which the natural resources are under the exclusive management authority of the United States under the Fishery Conservation and Management Act of 1976, and (B) any other surface water, ground water, drinking water supply, land surface or subsurface strata, or ambient air within the United States or under the jurisdiction of the United States [CERCLA §101(8)].

Facility means (A) any building, structure, installation, equipment, pipe or pipeline (including any pipe into a sewer or publicly owned treatment works), well, pit, pond, lagoon, impoundment, ditch, landfill, storage container, motor vehicle, rolling stock, or aircraft, or (B) any site or area where a hazardous substance has been deposited, stored, disposed of, or placed, or otherwise come to be located; but does not include any consumer product in consumer use or any vessel [CERCLA §101(9)].

Feasibility Study is a process undertaken by the lead agency (or responsible party if the responsible party will be developing a cleanup proposal) for developing, evaluating, and selecting remedial actions which emphasizes remedial data analysis. The feasibility study is generally performed concurrently and in an interdependent fashion with the remedial investigation. In certain situations, the lead agency may require potentially responsible parties to conclude initial phases of the remedial investigation prior to initiation of the feasibility study. The feasibility study process uses data gathered during the remedial investigation. These data are used to define the objectives of the response action and to broadly develop remedial action alternatives. Next, an initial screening of these alternatives is required to reduce the number of alternatives to a workable number. Finally, the feasibility study involves a detailed analysis of a limited number of alternatives which remain after the initial screening stage. The factors that are considered in screening and analyzing the alternatives are public health, economics, engineering practicality, environmental impacts, and institutional issues [40 CFR 300.6].

Federally Permitted Release means

(A) discharges in compliance with a permit under section 402 of the Federal Water Pollution Control Act,

(B) discharges resulting from circumstances identified and reviewed and made part of the public record with respect to a permit issued or modified under section 402 of the Federal Water Pollution Control Act and subject to a condition of such permit,

(C) continuous or anticipated intermittent discharges from a point source, identified in a permit or permit application under section 402 of the Federal Water Pollution Control Act, which are caused by events occurring within the scope of relevant operating or treatment systems,

(D) discharges in compliance with a legally enforceable permit under section 404 of the Federal Water Pollution Control Act,

(E) releases in compliance with a legally enforceable final permit issued pursuant to section 3005 (a) through (d) of the Solid Waste Disposal Act from a hazardous waste treatment, storage, or disposal facility when such permit specifically identifies the hazardous substances and makes such substances subject to a standard of practice, control procedure or bioassay limitation or condition, or other control on the hazardous substances in such releases,

(F) any release in compliance with a legally enforceable permit issued under section 102 or section 103 of the Marine Protection, Research, and Sanctuaries Act of 1972,

(G) any injection of fluids authorized under Federal underground injection control programs or State programs submitted for Federal approval (and not disapproved by the Administrator of the Environmental Protection Agency) pursuant to part C of the Safe Drinking Water Act,

(H) any emission into the air subject to a permit or control regulation under section 111, section 112, title I part C, title I part D, or State implementation plans submitted in accordance with section 110 of the Clean Air Act (and not disapproved by the Administrator of the Environmental Protection Agency), including any schedule or waiver granted, promulgated, or approved under these sections,

(I) any injection of fluids or other materials authorized under applicable State law (i) for the purpose of stimulating or treating wells for the production of crude oil, natural gas, or water, (ii) for the purpose of secondary, tertiary, or other enhanced recovery of crude oil or natural gas, or (iii) which are brought to the surface in conjunction with the production of crude oil or natural gas and which are reinjected,

(J) the introduction of any pollutant into a publicly owned treatment works when such pollutant is specified in and in compliance with applicable pretreatment standards of section 307(b) or (c) of the Clean Water Act and enforceable requirements in a pretreatment program submitted by a State or municipality for Federal approval under section 402 of such Act, and

(K) any release of source, special nuclear, or by-product material, as those terms are defined in the Atomic Energy Act of 1954, in compliance with a legally enforceable license, permit, regulation, or order issued pursuant to the Atomic Energy Act of 1954 [CERCLA §101(10)].

Fund or *Trust Fund* means the Hazardous Substance Response Trust Fund established by section 221 of CERCLA [40 CFR 300.6].

Ground Water means water in a saturated zone or stratum beneath the surface of land or water [CERCLA §101(11)].

Guarantor means any person, other than the owner or operator, who provides evidence of financial responsibility for an owner or operator under this Act [CERCLA §101(13)].

Hazardous Substance means

(A) any substance designated pursuant to section 311(b)(2)(A) of the Federal Water Pollution Control Act,

(B) any element, compound, mixture, solution, or substance designated pursuant to section 102 of this Act,

(C) any hazardous waste having the characteristics identified under or listed pursuant to section 3001 of the Solid Waste Disposal Act (but not including any waste the regulation of which under the Solid Waste Disposal Act has been suspended by Act of Congress),

(D) any toxic pollutant listed under section 307(a) of the Federal Water Pollution Control Act,

(E) any hazardous air pollutant listed under section 112 of the Clean Air Act, and

(F) any imminently hazardous chemical substance or mixture with respect to which the Administrator has taken action pursuant to section 7 of the Toxic Substances Control Act. The term does not include petroleum, including crude oil or any fraction thereof which is not otherwise specifically listed or designated as a hazardous substance under subparagraphs (A) through (F) of this paragraph, and the term does not include natural gas, natural gas liquids, liquefied natural gas, or synthetic gas usable for fuel (or mixtures of natural gas and such synthetic gas) [CERCLA §101(14)].

Indian Tribe means any Indian tribe, band, nation, or other organized group or community, including any Alaska Native village but not including any Alaska Native regional or village corporation, which is recognized as eligible for the special programs and services provided by the United States to Indians because of their status as Indians [CERCLA §101(36)].

Lead Agency means the Federal agency (or State agency operating pursuant to a contract or cooperative agreement executed pursuant to section 104(d)(1) of CERCLA) that has primary responsibility for coordinating response actions under this Plan. A Federal lead agency is the agency that provides the OSC or RPM as specified elsewhere in this Plan. In the case of a State as lead agency, the State shall carry out the same responsibilities delineated for OSCs/RPMs in this Plan (except coordinating and directing Federal agency response actions) [40 CFR 300.6].

Liable or *Liability* under this title shall be construed to be the standard of liability which obtains under section 311 of the Federal Water Pollution Control Act [CERCLA §101(32)].

Management of Migration means actions that are taken to minimize and mitigate the migration of hazardous substances or pollutants or contaminants and the effects of such migration. Management of migration actions may be appropriate where the hazardous substances or pollutants or contaminants are no longer at or near the area where they were originally located or situations where a source cannot be adequately identified or characterized. Measures may include, but are not limited to, provision of alternative water supplies, management of a plume of contamination, or treatment of a drinking water aquifer [40 CFR 300.6].

National Contingency Plan means the national contingency plan published under section 311(c) of the Federal Water Pollution Control Act or revised pursuant to section 105 of this Act [CERCLA §101(31)].

Natural Resources means land, fish, wildlife, biota, air, water, ground water, drinking water supplies, and other such resources belonging to, managed by, held in trust by, appertaining to, or otherwise controlled by the United States (including the resources of the fishery conservation zone established by the Fishery Conservation and Management Act of 1976), any State or local government, or any foreign government [CERCLA §101(16)].

Navigable Waters or *Navigable Waters of the United States* means the waters of the United States, including the territorial seas [CERCLA §101(15)].

Offshore Facility means any facility of any kind located in, on, or under any of the navigable waters of the United States, and any facility of any kind which is subject to the jurisdiction of the United States and is located in, on, or under any other waters, other than a vessel or a public vessel [CERCLA §101(17)].

On-Scene Coordinator (OSC) means the Federal official predesignated by the EPA or USCG to coordinate and direct Federal responses under Subpart E and removals under Subpart F of this Plan; or the DOD official designated to coordinate and direct the removal actions from releases of hazardous substances, pollutants, or contaminants from DOD vessels and facilities [40 CFR 300.6].

Onshore Facility means any facility (including, but not limited to, motor vehicles and rolling stock) of any kind located in, on, or under, any land or nonnavigable waters within the United States [CERCLA §101(18)].

Operable Unit is a discrete part of the entire response action that decreases a release, threat of release, or pathway of exposure [40 CFR 300.6].

Otherwise Subject to the Jurisdiction of the United States means subject to the jurisdiction of the United States by virtue of United States citizenship, United States vessel documentation or numbering, or as provided by international agreement to which the United States is a party [CERCLA §101(19)].

Owner or Operator means

(A) (i) in the case of a vessel, any person owning, operating, or chartering by demise, such vessel, (ii) in the case of an onshore facility or an offshore facility, any person owning or operating such facility, and (iii) in the case of any facility, title, or control of which was conveyed due to bankruptcy, foreclosure, tax delinquency, abandonment, or similar means to a unit of State or local government, any person who owned, operated, or otherwise controlled activities at such facility immediately beforehand.

(B) In the case of a hazardous substance which has been accepted for transportation by a common or contract carrier and except as provided in section 107(a)(3) or (4) of this Act, (i) the term *owner or operator* shall mean such common carrier or other bona fide for hire carrier acting as an independent contractor during such transportation, (ii) the shipper of such hazardous substance shall not be considered to have caused or contributed to any release during such transportation which resulted solely from circumstances or conditions beyond his control.

(C) In the case of a hazardous substance which has been delivered by a common or contract carrier to a disposal or treatment facility and except as provided in section 107(a)(3) or (4)(i) the term *owner or operator* shall not include such common or contract carrier, and (ii) such common or contract carrier shall not be considered to have caused or contributed to any release at such disposal or treatment facility resulting from circumstances or conditions beyond its control.

(D) The term *owner or operator* does not include a unit of State or local government which acquired ownership or control involuntarily through bankruptcy, tax delinquency, abandonment, or other circumstances in which the government involuntarily acquires title by virtue of its function as sovereign. The exclusion provided under this paragraph shall not apply to any State or local government which has caused or contributed to the release or threatened release of a hazardous substance from the facility, and such a State or local government shall be subject to the provisions of this Act in the same manner and to the same extent, both procedurally and substantively, as any nongovernmental entity, including liability under section 107 [CERCLA §101(20)].

Person means an individual, firm, corporation, association, partnership, consortium, joint venture, commercial entity, United States Government, State, municipality, commission, political subdivision of a State, or any interstate body [CERCLA §101(21)].

Plan means the National Oil and Hazardous Substances Pollution Contingency Plan published under section 311(c) of the CWA and revised pursuant to section 105 of CERCLA [40 CFR 300.6].

Pollutant or Contaminant, as defined by section 104(a)(2) of CERCLA, shall include, but not be limited to, any element, substance, compound, or mixture, including disease causing agents, which after release into the environment and upon exposure, ingestion, inhalation, or assimilation into any organism, either directly from the environment or indirectly by ingesting through food chains, will or may reasonably be anticipated to cause death, disease, behavioral abnormalities, cancer, genetic mutation, physiological malfunctions (including malfunctions in reproduction), or physical deformation in such organisms or their offspring. The term does not include petroleum, including crude oil and any fraction thereof which is not otherwise specifically listed or designated as a hazardous substance under section 101(14) (A) through (F) of CERCLA, nor does it include natural gas, liquefied natural gas, or synthetic gas of pipeline quality (or mixtures of natural gas and synthetic gas). For purposes of Subpart F of this Plan, the term pollutant or contaminant means any pollutant or contaminant which may present an imminent and substantial danger to public health or welfare [40 CFR 300.6].

Release means any spilling, leaking, pumping, pouring, emitting, emptying, discharging, injecting, escaping, leaching, dumping, or disposing into the environment, including the abandonment or discarding of barrels, containers, and other closed receptacles containing any hazardous substance or pollutant or contaminant, but excludes (A) any release which results in exposure to persons solely within a workplace, with respect to a claim which such persons may assert against the employer of such persons, (B) emissions from the engine exhaust of a motor vehicle, rolling stock, aircraft, vessel, or pipeline pumping station engine, (C) release of source, byproduct, or special nuclear material from a nuclear incident, as those terms are defined in the Atomic Energy Act of 1954, if such release is subject to requirements with respect to financial protection established by the Nuclear Regulatory Commission under section 170 of such Act, or for the purposes of section 104 of this title or any other response action, any release of source byproduct, or special nuclear material from any processing site designated under section 102(a)(1) or 302(a) of the Uranium Mill Tailings Radiation Control Act of 1978, and (D) the normal application of fertilizer [CERCLA §101(22)].

Relevant and Appropriate Requirements are those Federal requirements that, while not "applicable," are designed to apply to problems sufficiently similar to those encountered at CERCLA sites that their application is appropriate. Requirements may be relevant and appropriate if they would be "applicable" but for jurisdictional restrictions associated with the requirement [40 CFR 300.6].

Remedial Investigation is a process undertaken by the lead agency (or responsible party if the responsible party will be developing a cleanup proposal) which emphasizes data collection and site characterization. The remedial investigation is generally performed concurrently and in an interdependent fashion with the feasibility study. However, in certain situations, the lead agency may require potentially responsible parties to conclude initial phases of the remedial investigation prior to initiation of the feasibility study. A remedial investigation is undertaken to determine the nature and extent of the problem presented by the release. This includes sampling and monitoring, as necessary, and includes the gathering of sufficient information to determine the necessity for and proposed extent of remedial action. Part of the remedial investigation involves assessing whether the threat can be mitigated or minimized by controlling the source of the contamination at or near the area where the hazardous substances or pollutants or contaminants were originally located (source control remedial actions) or whether additional actions will be necessary because the hazardous substances or pollutants or contaminants have migrated from the area of their original location (management of migration) [40 CFR 300.6].

Remedial Project Manager (RPM) means the Federal official designated by EPA (or the USCG for vessels) to coordinate, monitor, or direct remedial or other response activities under Subpart F of this Plan; or the Federal official DOD designates to coordinate and direct Federal remedial or other response actions resulting from releases of hazardous substances, pollutants, or contaminates from DOD facilities or vessels [40 CFR 300.6].

Remedy or *Remedial Action* means those actions consistent with permanent remedy taken instead of or in addition to removal actions in the event of a release or threatened release of a hazardous substance into the environment, to prevent or minimize the release of hazardous substances so that they do not migrate to cause substantial danger to present or future public health or welfare or the environment. The term includes, but is not limited to, such actions at the location of the release as storage; confinement; perimeter protection using dikes, trenches, or ditches; clay cover; neutralization; cleanup of released hazardous substances or contaminated materials; recycling or reuse; diversion; destruction; segregation of reactive wastes; dredging or excavations; repair or replacement of leaking containers; collection of leachate and runoff; on-site treatment or incineration; provision of alternative water supplies; and any monitoring reasonably required to assure that such actions protect the public health and welfare and the environment. The term includes the costs of permanent relocation of residents and businesses and community facilities where the President determines that, alone or in combination with other measures, such relocation is more cost-effective than and environmentally preferable to the transportation, storage, treatment, destruction, or secure disposition off-site of hazardous substances, or may otherwise be necessary to protect the public health or welfare; the term includes off-site transport and off-site storage, treatment, destruction, or secure disposition off-site of hazardous substances and associated contaminated materials [CERCLA §101(24)].

Remove or *Removal* means the cleanup or removal of released hazardous substances from the environment, such actions as may be necessary taken in the event of the threat of release of hazardous substances into the environment, such actions as may be necessary to monitor, assess, and evaluate the release or threat of release of hazardous substances, the disposal of removed material, or the taking of such other actions as may be necessary to prevent, minimize, or mitigate damage to the public health or welfare or to the environment, which may otherwise result from a release or threat of release. The term includes, in addition, without being limited to, security fencing or other measures to limit access, provision of alternative water supplies, temporary evacuation and housing of threatened individuals not otherwise provided for, action taken under section 104(b) of this Act, and any emergency assistance which may be provided under the Disaster Relief Act of 1974 [CERCLA §101(23)].

Respond or *Response* means remove, removal, remedy, and remedial action. All such terms (including the term "removal" and "remedial action") include enforcement activities related thereto [CERCLA §101(25)].

Source Control Action is the construction or installation and start-up of those actions necessary to prevent the continued release of hazardous substances or pollutants or contaminants (primarily from a source on top of or within the ground, or in buildings or other structures) into the environment [40 CFR 300.5].

Source Control Maintenance Measures are those measures intended to maintain the effectiveness of source control actions once such actions are operating and functioning properly such as the maintenance of landfill caps and leachate collection systems [40 CFR 300.5].

Territorial Sea and *Contiguous Zone* shall have the meaning provided in section 502 of the Federal Water Pollution Control Act [CERCLA §101(30)].

Transport or *Transportation* means the movement of a hazardous substance by any mode, including pipeline (as defined in the Pipeline Safety Act), and in the case of a hazardous substance which has been accepted for transportation by a common or contract carrier, the term *transport* or *transportation* shall include any stoppage in transit which is temporary, incidental to the transportation movement, and at the ordinary operating convenience of a common or contract carrier, and any such stoppage shall be considered as a continuity of movement and not as the storage of a hazardous substance [CERCLA §101(26)].

United States and *State* include the several States of the United States, the District of Columbia, the Commonwealth of Puerto Rico, Guam, American Samoa, the United States Virgin Islands, the Commonwealth of the Northern Marianas, and any other territory or possession over which the United States has jurisdiction [CERCLA §101(27)].

Vessel means every description of watercraft or other artificial contrivance used, or capable of being used, as a means of transportation on water [CERCLA §101(28)].

Chapter 12

Reporting Requirements

This chapter deals with two reporting requirements: reportable quantities of spills and notification of hazardous waste management facilities. The reporting of spills is mandated by Superfund, SARA Title III, the Clean Water Act, and the Hazardous Materials Transportation Act.

SPILL REPORTING

Four separate statutes address the reporting of releases that present a potential threat to human health or the environment:

- Comprehensive Environmental Response, Compensation, and Liability Act (CERCLA or Superfund)
- Title III of the Superfund Amendments and Reauthorization Act (SARA Title III)
- Hazardous Materials Transportation Act (HMTA)
- Clean Water Act (CWA)

The Clean Water Act was the original statute dealing with emergency notification of releases; however, it was limited to releases to water. The enactment of Superfund expanded the reporting requirements to releases into the environment, which includes land, water, and air.

HMTA addresses releases that may cause a threat to public health during transportation-related incidents. SARA Title III, which was enacted as a direct result of the Bhopal, India disaster, was designed to address acutely hazardous release.

The regulatory requirements under these statutes overlap, but Superfund is considered the focal point for the emergency release notification regulations. Hence, the requirements under each of these statutes have been slowly modeled and tied into Superfund, thus alleviating conflicts and overlapping requirements. It is anticipated that this process will continue.

Superfund Reportable Quantities

The Comprehensive Environmental Response, Compensation, and Liability Act established broad federal authority to deal with releases or threats of releases of hazardous substances from vessels and facilities.

Superfund requires the reporting of a release of a hazardous substance into the environment at or above the designated reportable quantity. *Hazardous substances* under CERCLA [Section 101(14)] are simply a compilation of substances regulated under other specified federal environmental statutes. The referenced substances include:

- Hazardous air pollutants under Section 112 of the Clean Air Act.
- Hazardous wastes under RCRA.
- Toxic pollutants (priority pollutants) under Section 307(a) of the Clean Water Act.
- Hazardous substances under Section 311 of the Clean Water Act.
- Substances designated as an imminent hazard under Section 7 of TSCA. (To date, there have been no such designations.)

It is important to note that petroleum is specifically excluded from the definition of hazardous substance under Superfund.

Reportable Quantities

In addition to all listed hazardous substances, Section 102(a) authorizes EPA to designate a reportable quantity (RQ) for any nondesignated hazardous substance that may present substantial danger when released into the environment.

Currently, there are approximately 720 Superfund hazardous substances. These substances and their designated RQs are listed in 40 CFR Part 302. Each such designated substance automatically receives an RQ of one pound until it is superseded by regulation establishing a different RQ. Section 102(a) authorizes EPA to adjust an RQ, through rulemaking when appropriate. EPA adjusts RQs based on a substance's intrinsic physical, chemical, and toxicological properties. The intrinsic properties include aquatic toxicity, mammalian toxicity (oral, dermal, and inhalation), ignitability, reactivity, chronic toxicity, and potential carcinogenicity. EPA ranks each intrinsic property (except for carcinogenicity potential) on a five-tier scale that has an RQ level for each tier. The five-tier scale uses RQ levels of 1, 10, 100, 1000, and 5000 pounds, previously established by the Clean Water Act (44 *FR* 50776, August 29, 1979). Each substance is evaluated for its carcinogenicity potential. A low, medium, or high carcinogenicity potential receives a corresponding RQ level of 1, 10, or 100 pounds. At the end of this ranking process, a substance is assigned the lowest RQ from the evaluations, provided that the RQ is protective of human health and the environment.

Reporting Requirements

Section 103 of Superfund requires any person in charge of a facility that has a release of a reportable quantity to report that release immediately to the National Response Center, which is a 24-hour hotline (800-424-8802) operated by the U.S. Coast Guard (USCG). When a call is received, the duty officer requests information, including the identity, location, and nature of the release; the identity of the transporter or owner of the facility or vessel; the nature of any injuries or property damage; and other relevant information. The National Response Center relays the release information directly to either the predesignated on-scene coordinator (OSC) at the appropriate EPA Regional Office, or to the appropriate USCG District Office. This notification is a trigger for informing the government of a release so that appropriate federal personnel can evaluate the need for a federal removal or remedial action and, if warranted, pursue any action in a timely fashion. Federal personnel evaluate all reported releases, but they will not necessarily initiate a removal or remedial action in response to all reported releases because a release of a hazardous substance does not necessarily pose a hazard to public health or the environment. Many considerations other than the quantity released affect the government's decision concerning whether and how it should undertake a response action pursuant to the National Contingency Plan (NCP) with respect to a particular release. The location of the release, its proximity to drinking-water supplies, the likelihood of exposure to nearby populations, response actions taken by responsible parties, and other factors must be assessed by the federal OSC on a case-by-case basis.

It is important to note that, unless specifically exempted from Superfund, a party responsible for a release of a hazardous substance is liable for the costs of cleaning up that release and for any natural resource damages caused by the release, even if the release is not subject to the notification requirements of Section 103. The fact that a release of a hazardous substance is properly reported, or that it is not subject to the notification requirements of Section 103, does not preclude EPA or other appropriate government agencies from undertaking response actions, seeking reimbursement from responsible parties, or pursuing an enforcement action against responsible parties.

Note: It is strongly recommended that the NRC be contacted concerning a release without necessarily determining if it meets an RQ. This is because the determination can be very difficult especially during an emergency. It is important to note that no facility has ever been cited for reporting a release that did not meet an RQ whereas there have been numerous citations for failure to report where a release does meet an RQ.

Determination Period

A reportable quantity is determined within a 24-hour period. Thus if a substance with a reportable quantity of 10 pounds were releasing one pound per hour, it would have to be reported as soon as it met the RQ because the spill would release a reportable quantity within the 24-hour time period. If the release rate had been 0.25 pound per hour, the release would not have to be reported because the spill would not equal the reportable quantity of 10 pounds within 24 hours. This does not mean that, if there is a reportable spill, the notification can be delayed until the 24-hour time period elapses. The spill must be reported *immediately* upon meeting the reportable quantity.

Into-the-Environment Requirement

A release must be *into the environment* (i.e., air, land, surface water, groundwater) for it to be reportable. A spill in a contained building that met a reportable quantity would not require reporting. However, if that same spill were then vented to the outside, and the amount of vented material met the designated reportable quantity, it would be reportable. A facility's boundaries are irrelevant for reporting requirements; the requirements depend on whether the release is into the environment. It is important to note that the disposal of hazardous substances at a disposal facility in compliance with EPA regulations is not subject to the Superfund notification requirements (50 *FR* 13461, April 4, 1985). However, spills or releases that occur during or prior to disposal and constitute a reportable quantity must be reported.

Mixture Rule

EPA applies the *mixture rule,* previously developed under Section 311 of the Clean Water Act, to releases of mixtures and solutions containing hazardous substances. This rule provides that releases of mixtures and solutions are subject to reporting only when a component hazardous substance is released in a quantity equal to or greater than its reportable quantity [40 CFR 302.6(b)]. Reportable quantities of different substances are not additive under the mixture rule. Thus, releasing a mixture containing half an RQ of one substance and half an RQ of another substance does not require reporting. For example, toxaphene has a reportable quantity of one pound. If there is a formulation with 10 percent toxaphene and 90 percent inert ingredient, 10 pounds of the formulated pesticide would have to be released to constitute a one-pound reportable toxaphene release. If the exact proportions are unknown, then one pound of the formulation is the appropriate reportable quantity.

Federally Permitted Release

Reporting of a federally permitted release is not required under Superfund. However, to qualify for this exclusion, the release must be in compliance with the facility's enforceable permit. Section 101(10) defines releases that qualify as *federally permitted*. For example, a facility has a National Pollutant Discharge Elimination System (NPDES) permit allowing a maximum daily discharge of one pound of bromoform. If the facility discharges two pounds of bromoform through its NPDES-regulated outfall, it must report this release to the National Response Center. The facility is legally allowed to release only one pound of bromoform, which has an RQ of one pound.

Continuous Release

Under Superfund there is no distinction between episodic or continuous releases exceeding the reportable quantity. However, Section 103(f)(2) sets forth a reduced reporting requirement for certain releases. "Releases that are continuous, stable in quantity and rate, and [for which] notification has been given under Section 103 for a period sufficient to establish the continuity, quantity, and regularity of the release are subject to less frequent reporting requirements." However, there are five kinds of notification for a continuous release [40 CFR 302.8], which are: (1) initial telephone notification to the NRC; (2) initial written notification within 30 days of the telephone conversation to the appropriate EPA regional office; (3) a written follow-up report to EPA on the first anniversary of the initial written notification; (4) immediate notification of a change in the source or composition of the release or of previously submitted information; and (5) immediate notification of any *statistically significant increase* in the release.

Public Notice

Any owner or an operator who has a release of a hazardous substance must so notify the potentially affected parties by publication in the local newspaper. This is a statutory requirement [Section 111(g)]. There has been no further clarification on this provision offered by EPA.

Penalties

Section 103(b) authorizes penalties, including criminal sanctions, for persons in charge of vessels or facilities who fail to report releases of hazardous substances that equal or exceed a reportable quantity. Section 109 of SARA amended Superfund by increasing the maximum penalties and years of imprisonment. Any person who, as soon as he or she has knowledge of a reportable release, fails to report the release immediately, or who knowingly submits any false or misleading information, shall upon conviction be subject to fines of not more than $250,000 for individuals (or $500,000 for an organization) and/or imprisonment for not more than three years.

SARA Title III Reportable Quantities

In 1986, Congress passed the Emergency Planning and Community Right-to-Know Act (EPCRA) as Title III of the Superfund Amendments and Reauthorization Act (SARA). It is commonly referred to as Title III because it appears as the third part of another law, the Superfund Amendments and Reauthorization Act (SARA). Even though Title III is a part of Superfund, it is a free-standing act.

Section 304 of EPCRA requires a facility to notify state and local authorities of a *reportable quantity* of an *extremely hazardous substance* released into the environment. There are approximately 360 chemicals listed by EPA in 40 CFR, Part 355, Appendix A, that are designated as extremely hazardous substances. A release of a reportable quantity of an extremely hazardous substance requires notification of the release to local authorities. This differs from Superfund, which requires notification to federal authorities of releases of *hazardous substances*. However, because some of the Superfund hazardous substances also are SARA Title III extremely hazardous substances, a facility may have a dual reporting requirement, to both the local and the federal government.

HMTA Reportable Quantities

Under the Hazardous Materials Transportation Act (HMTA), release of a designated *hazardous substance* is subject to reporting. Hazardous substances under HMTA are those substances designated as Superfund hazardous substances.

For a substance to be designated as a *hazardous substance* under DOT [49 CFR 171.8], it must meet the following requirements:

- It is listed as a hazardous substance in the Appendix to 49 CFR 172.101.
- It is in a quantity, in *one* package, that equals or exceeds the reportable quantity (RQ) listed in the Appendix to 49 CFR 172.101. (Thus, its reporting is on a per package basis.)
- If the substance is in a mixture or solution, its concentration (by weight) must equal or exceed the concentration that is shown in Table 4-2, corresponding to the RQ identified for the substance in the Appendix to 49 CFR 172.101.

If a carrier/transporter is involved in an incident where release of a reportable quantity of a hazardous substance occurs, the transporter must notify the National Response Center immediately.

Clean Water Act Reporting Requirements

The Clean Water Act (CWA) was the first statute addressing the reporting of releases of substances that may present a threat to the environment. The act addressed the release of designated *hazardous substances* and *oil* into or upon the navigable waters of the United States [40 CFR 117.11(a)]. (These hazardous substances, listed in Table 117.3 of 40 CFR 117.3, also are Superfund listed hazardous substances [40 CFR 302.4].) *Navigable waters* means water of the United States, including the territorial seas. This term includes all of the following:

- All waters that are currently used, were used in the past, or may be susceptible to use in interstate or foreign commerce, including all waters subject to the ebb and flow of the tide.
- Interstate waters, including interstate wetlands.

- All other waters such as intrastate lakes, rivers, streams (including intermittent streams), mud flats, sand flats, and wetlands, the use, degradation or destruction of which would affect or could affect interstate or foreign commerce including any such waters:
  - Which are or could be used by interstate or foreign travelers for recreation or other purposes.
  - From which fish or shellfish are or could be taken and sold in interstate or foreign commerce.
  - Which are used or could be used by industries in interstate commerce.
- All impoundments of waters otherwise defined as navigable waters.
- Tributaries of waters identified in the above example, including adjacent wetlands.
- Wetlands adjacent to the above-identified waters. *Wetlands* are those areas that are inundated or saturated by surface water or groundwater at a frequency and duration sufficient to support, and that under normal conditions do support, a prevalence of vegetation typically adapted for life in saturated soil conditions. Wetlands generally include play lakes, swamps, marshes, bogs, and similar areas such as sloughs, prairie potholes, wet meadows, prairie river overflows, mud flats, and natural ponds.

Petroleum

Whereas Superfund specifically excludes petroleum [Section 101(14)] from the reporting requirements, CWA specifically requires the reporting of certain oil releases. *Oil* means oil of any kind or in any form, including, but not limited to, petroleum, fuel oil, sludge, oil refuse, and oil mixed with wastes other than dredged spoil [40 CFR 110.1(a)].

Under 40 CFR 110, EPA has established requirements for certain discharges of oil. Oil discharges, into or upon U.S. waters, that must be reported to the NRC include those that:

- Cause a sheen to appear on the surface of the water;
- Violate applicable water quality standards; or
- Cause a sludge or emulsion to be deposited beneath the surface of the water or upon the adjoining shorelines.

NOTIFICATION OF HAZARDOUS WASTE MANAGEMENT FACILITIES

Whereas Section 103(a) of Superfund addresses current releases, Section 103(c) addresses past releases, including the discovery of contamination at an existing facility.

Section 103(c) requires any person who owns or operates, or who at the time of disposal owned or operated, a facility at which RCRA hazardous wastes are or have been stored, treated, or disposed of, to notify EPA of the facility's existence. This requirement is for RCRA hazardous wastes only; it does not include other hazardous substances. This provision is applicable regardless of when the activity occurred. There are nine exclusions from reporting under Section 103(c):

1. A generator accumulating hazardous waste for less than 90 days in compliance with 40 CFR 262.34.
2. Totally enclosed treatment facilities as defined in 40 CFR 260.10.
3. Wastewater treatment tanks as defined in 40 CFR 260.10.
4. Farmers disposing of waste pesticides from their own use.
5. Facilities that disposed of less than 55 gallons on-site.
6. Incidental spillage and leakage (*de minimis* losses).
7. Inactive storage facilities that no longer store wastes.
8. Persons filing or who have filed a RCRA Section 3010 notification as a hazardous waste management facility.
9. Any person who has filed a Part A permit application under RCRA.

Note: Exclusions 8 and 9 are not applicable if a contaminated area is found that was not identified on the forms.

The statutory language appears to indicate that after June 9, 1981, a facility would no longer be subject to this provision. However, EPA's Office of General Counsel has consistently provided the RCRA/Superfund hotline with the interpretation that Section 103(c) is an ongoing reporting requirement.

In summary, the presence of hazardous wastes at a facility means that unless the facility is exempted, a notification is required. Thus, it is necessary to determine (1) if the material is a RCRA hazardous waste; (2) if the facility has previously made a notification; and (3) if the facility meets any of the exclusions. If the facility must notify EPA, notification must be done as soon as possible using the prescribed form (46 *FR* 22155, April 15, 1981).

Information received pursuant to Section 103(c) notifications is placed in the Comprehensive Environmental Response, Compensation, and Liability Information System (CERCLIS, formerly ERRIS). CERCLIS is a database with an inventory of potential Superfund sites that currently numbers about 32,000. CERCLIS also functions as a tracking system for the status of Superfund sites throughout the remedial process.

Chapter 13

Response Actions Under Superfund

Superfund provides the federal government with the authority to respond directly, or to compel potentially responsible parties to respond to releases or threatened releases of hazardous substances or pollutants or contaminants.

RESPONSE AUTHORITY

Section 104 of Superfund authorizes federal government response to a release or threatened release of *hazardous substances* or *pollutants* or *contaminants*.

It is important to note that the definitions of hazardous substances [CERCLA Section 101(14)] and pollutants or contaminants [CERCLA Section 104(a)(2)] specifically exclude "petroleum, including crude oil or any fraction thereof," unless specifically listed. There is no definition of *petroleum* in Superfund. However, EPA interprets the *petroleum exclusion* provision to include crude oil and fractions of crude oil, including the hazardous substances, such as benzene, that are indigenous in those petroleum substances. Because these hazardous substances are found naturally in all crude oil and its fractions, they are included in the term *petroleum*. The term also includes hazardous substances that are normally mixed with or added to crude oil or crude oil fractions during the refining process, including hazardous substances whose levels are increased during refining. These substances are also part of *petroleum* because their addition is part of the normal oil separation and processing operations at refineries that produce the product commonly understood

282

to be petroleum. However, hazardous substances that are added to petroleum or that increase in concentration solely as a result of contamination of the petroleum during use are not part of the petroleum and thus are not excluded from Superfund (U.S. EPA Memorandum from the Office of General Counsel concerning the CERCLA Petroleum Exclusion, July 31, 1987).

In addition, the federal government is not authorized to respond to the following releases unless there is a public or an environmental health emergency, or no other person can respond to that release:

- A release of a naturally occurring substance in its unaltered form, or altered through natural conditions at a location where it is naturally found (e.g., radon gas).
- A release from building products contained in residential, community, or commercial structures where the exposure resulting from the products is within these structures (e.g., urea formaldehyde foam insulation, asbestos).
- A release into a public or private water supply due to the deterioration of the water supply system through ordinary use (e.g., asbestos pipes).

National Contingency Plan

Superfund requires that all actions taken in response to releases of hazardous substances shall, to the greatest extent possible, be in accordance with the provisions of the National Contingency Plan (NCP), which was revised on March 8, 1990 (55 *FR* 8666), and codified in 40 CFR Part 300. The NCP outlines the steps that the federal government must follow in responding to situations in which hazardous substances are released or are likely to be released into the environment. Response actions that are developed and implemented by private parties under Superfund also must be consistent with the NCP. The NCP implements the response authorities and responsibilities created by Superfund and the Clean Water Act. Actually a predecessor of Superfund, the NCP was originally written to implement provisions of Section 311 of the Clean Water Act, which addresses spills of oil and hazardous substances into waters of the United States. Pursuant to Section 105 of Superfund and Executive Order 12316, EPA is responsible for promulgating revisions to the NCP. This chapter discusses only the hazardous substance response provisions of the NCP.

The NCP has the following basic components:

- Methods for discovering sites at which hazardous substances have been disposed.

- Methods for evaluating and remedying releases that pose substantial danger to public health and the environment.
- Methods and criteria for determining the appropriate extent of cleanup.
- Means of assuring that remedial action measures are cost-effective.

The process established by the NCP for handling hazardous substances is triggered by the identification of potential hazardous waste sites under Superfund's Section 103 notification program, as discussed in Chapter 12. The process begins with a preliminary determination of whether there is an emergency requiring immediate action at a particular site. If there is, the next step is to act as quickly as possible to remove or stabilize the threat. Even after the necessary action has been taken to control the immediate threat, contamination may remain at the site. A more detailed analysis of the contamination may be needed to determine if further decontamination is required. If long-term action is deemed necessary, a decision is made regarding the relative national priority of responding to the threat at that site. If it is warranted, the site will enter the remedial action process, as explained in Chapter 14.

RESPONSE ACTIONS

Whether an action is managed by the government or by potentially responsible parties, two categories of response actions are identified by the NCP: removal and remedial actions.

Under Section 104(e), a Fund-financed initial response (removal) cannot take more than 12 months or cost more than $2 million. Beyond these limits, the action is considered a continued response (remedial). A continued response cannot receive federal funding unless the site has been finalized on the National Priorities List (NPL). However, there is a waiver available to allow a continued response if it is appropriate and consistent with future remedial actions.

Removal Response Action

A removal action involves cleanup or other actions that are taken in response to emergency conditions (e.g., spills) or on a short-term or temporary basis.

Under Superfund there are three categories of removal actions, which are:

- *Emergency,* which generally refers to a release that requires that removal activities begin on site within hours of the lead agency's determination that a removal action is appropriate.
- *Time-critical* is whre the lead agency determines that a removal action is appropriate and that there is a period of less than six months available before removal activities must begin on site.
- *Nontime-critical* where the lead agency determines that a removal action is appropriate and that there is a planning period of more than six months before on-site removal activities must begin. (It is important to note that an engineering evaluation/cost analysis is required to be prepared for all nontime-critical removal actions.)

Examples of removal response actions include: installation of security fences or other measures to limit access, installation of alternative water supplies, evacuation and housing of threatened individuals, segregation of incompatible wastes, and construction of temporary containment systems. A removal action generally requires far less preliminary planning than a remedial action because the emphasis is on finding a rapid and short-term solution to a serious problem.

According to OSWER Directive 9345.0-01, the following factors are to be considered in determining the appropriateness of a removal action at a site:

- Actual or potential exposure of nearby populations, animals, or the food chain to hazardous substances or pollutants or contaminants.
- Actual or potential contamination of drinking-water supplies or sensitive ecosystems.
- Hazardous substances or pollutants or contaminants, in drums, barrels, tanks, or other bulk storage containers, that may pose a threat of release.
- High levels of hazardous substances or pollutants or contaminants in soils, largely at or near the surface, that may migrate.
- Weather conditions that may cause hazardous substances or pollutants or contaminants to migrate or be released.
- Threat of fire or explosion.
- The availability of other appropriate federal or state response mechanisms to respond to the release.
- Other situations or factors that may pose threats to public health or welfare or the environment.

Superfund requires all removal actions to be conducted so as to contribute to the efficient performance of long-term remedial measures that EPA deems practicable.

Remedial Response Action

A remedial action tends to be long-term in nature and involves response actions that are consistent with a permanent remedy that is taken in lieu of, or in addition to, a removal action. The remedial action process is explained in detail in Chapter 14.

LIABILITY

Section 107 of Superfund sets forth the liabilities involved with releases *or* threatened releases of hazardous substances. The following entities are outlined as potentially liable under Section 107(a):

- The current owner or operator of a site that contains hazardous substances.
- Any person who owned or operated the site at the time when hazardous substances were disposed.
- Any person who arranged for the treatment, storage, or disposal of the hazardous substances at the site.
- Any generator who disposed of hazardous substances at the site.
- Any transporter who transported hazardous substances to the site.

The persons listed above are liable for:

- All costs of removal or remedial action incurred by the government.
- Any other necessary costs of response incurred by any other person consistent with the National Contingency Plan.
- Damages for injury to, destruction of, or loss of natural resources, including the reasonable costs for assessing them.
- The costs of any health assessment or health effects study carried out under Section 104(i).

It is important to note that Section 107(e)(1) prohibits a potentially responsible party from transferring or contracting away its liability under Section 107 to another party by means of an indemnification, hold harmless, or similar contract agreement. However, the provisions of this section do not bar an agreement to insure, hold harmless, or indemnify a party to such an agreement for liability under Section 107.

Liability Limits

Under Superfund, liability for damages for each release of a hazardous substance is limited to $50 million for owners and operators of vessels or facilities plus all costs of the response. However, there is no limit to liability when:

- There was willful misconduct or willful negligence.
- The primary cause of the incident was a violation of applicable safety, construction, or operating standards or regulations.
- The responsible party failed to provide assistance when requested to by a public official in compliance with the NCP.

Defenses to Liability

Section 107(b) provides four affirmative defenses to the liability provisions that can be asserted by a person:

- An act of God
- An act of war
- An act or omission of a third party
- Any combination of the foregoing

The Third-Party Defense

To prove the third-party defense set forth in Section 107(b)(3), a person must establish by a preponderance of evidence that:

1. The release or threat of release and . . . damages resulting there from were caused solely by . . . an act or omission of a third party other than an employee or agent of the defendant, or that one whose act or omission occurs in connection with a contractual relationship, existing directly or indirectly with the defendant . . . ;
2. Due care was exercised with respect to the hazardous substance concerned, taking into consideration the characteristics of such hazardous substance, in light of all relevant facts and circumstances; and
3. Precautions were undertaken against foreseeable acts or omissions of any such third party and the consequences that could frequently result from such acts of omissions.

Innocent Landowner Liability

The CERCLA statute of 1980 imposed *innocent landowner liability;* that is, a person who acquired property that contained hazardous substances may be liable for all response costs for a release regardless of whether the owner had knowledge of the substances. To address concerns that the strict liability standard under Superfund could cause inequitable results with respect to landowners who had not been involved in hazardous substance disposal activities, SARA included a new provision that created limited circumstances under which landowners who acquire property without the knowledge of the existence of hazardous substances may avail themselves of the third-party defense to liability contained in Section 107(b)(3).

Persons otherwise liable under Superfund are not liable if the release in question was caused by the act or omission of a third party, unless the third party's act or omission occurred in connection with a contractual relationship with the defendant. The protection afforded the innocent landowner under SARA is clarified with the definition of the term *contractual relationship* under Section 101(35): a person acquiring property through a contract, deed, or other such instrument will not be deemed to have a contractual relationship with the previous landowner if the subsequent owner can demonstrate that the person did not know and had no reason to know that any hazardous substance was present at the site at the time when the property was acquired. To show that the landowner had no reason to know of the hazardous substances at the time of acquisition, a person must satisfy *due diligence* requirements (below) to establish the third party defense.

Due Diligence

Section 101(35) extends the third party defense to persons who acquired the property after the disposal or placement of the hazardous substance only if, at the time of acquisition, the defendant "did not know and had no reason to know that any hazardous substance which is the subject of the release . . . was disposed of . . . at the facility." Section 101(35) expressly provides that for a defendant to prove that he or she had "no reason to know" of the disposal of hazardous substances, the defendant must demonstrate by a preponderance of the evidence that, prior to acquisition, he or she conducted all appropriate inquiry into the previous ownership and uses of the property consistent with good commercial or customary practice. A landowner who demonstrates that "all appropriate inquiry" has been conducted will not be deemed to have constructive knowledge under Section 122(g)(1)(B).

Under Section 101(35)(B), the following factors must be considered when determining whether "all appropriate inquiry" has been made:

- Any specialized knowledge or experience on the part of the defendant.
- Commonly known or reasonably ascertainable information about the property.

- Relationship of the purchase price to the value of the property if uncontaminated.
- Obviousness of the presence or likely presence of contamination at the property.
- Ability to detect such contamination by appropriate inspection.

These factors clearly indicate that a determination of what constitutes "all appropriate inquiry" under all circumstances must be made on a case-by-case basis. Generally, when determining whether a landowner has conducted all appropriate inquiry, EPA will require a more comprehensive inquiry for those involved in commercial transactions than for those involved in residential transactions for personal use. For example, an investigation along the lines of a survey for contamination may be recommended in some commercial transactions, whereas this type of inquiry would not typically be recommended for the purchaser of personal residential property. Thus, the determination will be made on the basis of what is reasonable under all of the circumstances [memorandum dated June 6, 1989, from Edward E. Reich, Assistant Administrator for Enforcement and Compliance Monitoring to EPA Regional Administrators title, "Guidance on Landowner Liability under Section 107(a)(1) of CERCLA, *De Minimis* Settlements under Section 122(g)(1)(B) of CERCLA, and Settlement with Prospective Purchasers of Contaminated Property"].

Miscellaneous Liability Provisions

The following sections outline the various doctrines of liability contained or practiced under Superfund. The doctrines used depend on whether the material in question is a hazardous substance or a pollutant or contaminant, as depicted in Figure 13-1.

Hazardous Substance Liability

Under Superfund, statutory liability is imposed on hazardous substances. Therefore, EPA does not have to prove that the defendant's actions were the cause of the alleged environmental or health threat. Statutory liability is not imposed on pollutants or contaminants or any other substance that does not meet the definition of a hazardous substance [Section 101(14)]. However, if cleanup costs are incurred by the government from responding to a release involving pollutants or contaminants, cost recovery is possible, although the government would have to file a civil action

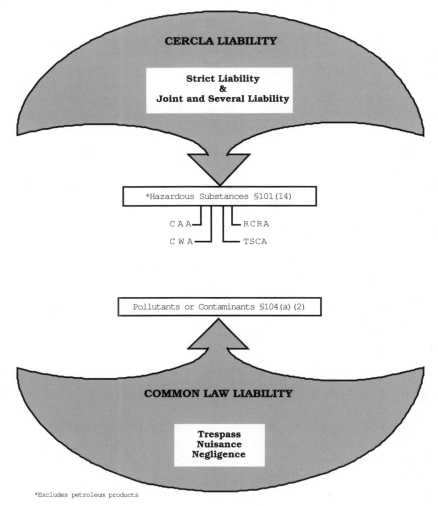

Figure 13-1. Liability under CERCLA

(lawsuit) and show *negligence, trespass,* or *nuisance* under common law doctrine on the part of the responsible party to obtain reimbursement for the response actions and potential punitive damages.

Strict Liability

Under Superfund, hazardous substances are governed under strict liability as established by the courts. Strict liability in tort law is liability without fault. Therefore, one who engages in an activity that has an inherent risk of injury is liable for all injuries proximately caused by his or her enterprise, even without showing negligence. Hence, one who handles hazardous substances is liable for all resulting injuries even if he or she uses the utmost care.

Joint and Several Liability

Superfund does not statutorily impose joint and several liability. This has been left to the courts to decide. However, the Department of Justice (DOJ) and EPA have applied a standard of joint and several liability in appropriate cases, and this position has been upheld by the courts. The term *joint and several* refers to the sharing of liabilities among a group of people collectively and also individually. Thus, if the government holds potentially responsible parties (PRPs) as jointly and severally liable for response costs, the government may sue some or all of the defendants together, or each one separately, and may collect equal or unequal amounts from each party. For example, at a site with ten PRPs, if one party disposed of 1000 tons of hazardous waste and nine parties disposed of one ton each, under joint and several liability, each party could be liable for the same amount or one party may be liable for the entire amount even though the parties did not dispose of equal amounts.

Response Action Liability

In general, no person is liable for costs or damages as a result of actions taken or omitted in the course of rendering care, assistance, or advice in accordance with the National Contingency Plan or at the direction of an appointed on-scene coordinator.

Response Action Contractor Liability

Under Section 119 of Superfund, any person who is a response action contractor with respect to any release or threatened release shall not be liable under any federal law to any person for injuries, costs, damages, expenses, or other liability that results from such a release. This will not apply in the case of negligence, gross negligence, or willful misconduct. This section does not apply to any PRP at the site or to a facility regulated under RCRA.

Section 104 allows qualified PRPs (as determined by EPA) to carry out the response action, conduct the remedial investigation, or conduct the feasibility study in accordance with the settlement provisions of Section 122. It is important to note that if a PRP is involved in a remedial action, that party's liability is not lessened by the response action contractor liability provisions under Section 119.

FEDERAL FACILITIES

Section 120(a) of SARA affirms that federal facilities are subject to the provisions of Superfund in the same manner as any nongovernmental entity. This section also outlines the process by which federal agencies are required to undertake remedial actions.

The selection of a remedy for a release is a joint determination by EPA and the affected federal agency. If the parties do not agree on the selection, EPA determines the remedy.

The same section establishes a schedule for response actions at appropriate federal facilities.

EPA is required to evaluate federal facilities for possible inclusion on the NPL and review the results of completed federal agency remedial investigations and feasibility studies.

Federal agencies must:

- Commence the RI/FS for a facility within 6 months of its listing on the NPL.
- Enter into an interagency agreement with EPA, within 6 months of EPA's review of the RI/FS concerning the review of alternatives, with joint selection of a remedy or EPA selection of a remedy if the parties are unable to agree, as well as a schedule for completion of the remedy and an arrangement for the operation and maintenance of the facility.
- Begin remedial action within 15 months of completing the RI/FS.
- Report annually to Congress regarding the progress achieved in implementing this section.

Chapter 14

Remedial Response

A Superfund-authorized action at a site involves either a short-term removal action or a long-term remedial response. Whereas a *removal action* is a relatively quick action taken over the short term to address a release, a *remedial action* is a long-term action that stops or substantially reduces a release or threatened release of hazardous substances that is serious but does not pose an immediate threat to public health or the environment.

REMEDIAL RESPONSE ACTION PROCESS

Generally, there is a basic ten-step process (which is not necessarily sequential) for a remedial response at a Superfund site, as outlined in Figure 14-1. The steps are:

1. Site discovery
2. Preliminary assessment
3. Site inspection
4. Hazard ranking analysis
5. National Priorities List determination
6. Remedial investigation and feasibility study
7. Remedy selection/record of decision
8. Remedial design
9. Remedial action
10. Project closeout

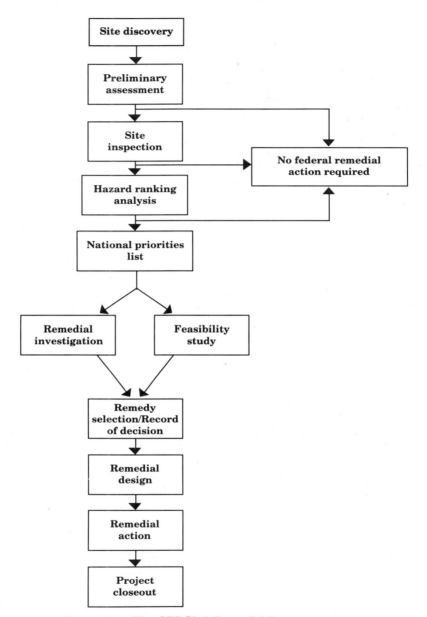

Figure 14-1. The CERCLA Remedial Response Process

Determination of the Lead Agency

The implementation of a remedial action at a particular site can be done by EPA, another federal agency, the state, and/or responsible parties. However, a lead agency must be selected that will have the primary responsibility for coordinating a response action. EPA, a state environmental agency, or another federal agency (such as the Department of Defense for military bases) may serve as the lead agency; however, EPA has final authority regarding remedy selection where it is not the lead agency. The selection of the lead agency is typically done after a site is placed on the National Priorities List. Selection is done through interagency negotiations involving EPA, states, and other federal agencies. The lead agency, which is represented by the remedial project manager (RPM), has the primary responsibility for coordinating a response action. The lead agency RPM is responsible for overseeing all technical, enforcement, and financial aspects of a remedial response.

State as Lead Agency

Where EPA and a state are involved in remedial activities, the lead agency is identified in a Superfund memorandum of agreement (SMOA), a cooperative agreement (CA), or a state Superfund contract (SSC). The SMOA is a general agreement that specifies the nature and the extent of interaction between EPA and the state for one or more sites. The CA is a site-specific agreement that establishes EPA and state responsibilities for a specific response action. The SSC is an agreement that documents any required cost shares and assurances necessary from a state but does not involve the disbursement of federal monies.

Other Federal Agency as Lead Agency

A federal agency other than EPA also may assume the roles and responsibilities of the lead agency. The division of authority and responsibility for the federal agency as the lead (and support agency) is specified in an interagency agreement (IAG). Because federal agencies conducting response activities are expected to comply with the NCP, CERCLA, and other EPA guidance as mandated by Section 120 of CERCLA, the IAG is essential in delineating the lead agency's responsibilities.

Responsible Party as Lead Agency

Pursuant to Section 104, a potentially responsible party (PRP) also may conduct response actions, provided that the PRP is qualified and otherwise capable. For a PRP-initiated response action, EPA or the state is the lead agency for overseeing the PRP's activities. PRPs may participate in the remedy selection process by recommending their own preferred alternative to the lead agency at the conclusion of the feasibility study and by submitting comments during the formal comment period held prior to the final remedy selection for the site.

SITE DISCOVERY

Specified releases of hazardous substances or pollutants or contaminants must be reported as described in Chapter 12. These releases are evaluated as to their potential threat to human health and the environment. In addition, sites also are discovered by citizen complaints, by employees, and through compliance inspections. Upon discovery, such potential sites are screened to identify release situations warranting further remedial response consideration.

These sites are entered into the Comprehensive Environmental Response, Compensation, and Liability Information System (CERCLIS), which is the national reporting, tracking, and management tool for Superfund. CERCLIS has incorporated into its system four other database systems, as follows:

- The Superfund Comprehensive Accomplishments Plan, which provides data on all response activities.
- The Removal Tracking System, which provides a comprehensive removal data base that includes start date, location, lead agency, and NPL status.
- The Case Management System, which contains general information on all enforcement activities including information on cost recovery and settlements.
- The Remedial/Removal Financial System Site File, which tracks the actual obligations for operable units for each facility (or site) and event for site activities conducted under IAGs, CAs, or contracts with states, political subdivisions, or other federal agencies.

PRELIMINARY ASSESSMENT

A *preliminary assessment* (PA) is an initial analysis of existing information to determine if a release of hazardous substances may be serious enough to require additional investigation or action. The PA is the first phase in the process of determining whether a site is releasing, or has the potential to release, hazardous substances or pollutants or contaminants into the environment, and whether it requires response action that is authorized by Superfund.

The preliminary assessment is a multistep process consisting of:

- Review of existing information
- Site reconnaissance
- Development of preliminary and projected HRS scores
- Application of qualitative criteria
- Prioritization for site inspection
- Report preparation
- Documentation
- CERCLIS tracking

During a PA, the investigator compiles and evaluates available information about a site and its surrounding environment, including information on potential waste sources, migration pathways, and receptors. The PA culminates in a brief report (EPA Form 2070-12) with formal recommendations. Although the PA does attempt to establish whether the site has the potential to adversely affect the environment, it is not intended to determine the exact magnitude of the release. This is accomplished when the site is scored under the hazard ranking system analysis (HRS) after completion of a site inspection and, more comprehensively, during the subsequent remedial investigation.

Preliminary Assessment Goals

According to OSWER Directive 9345.0-01, the preliminary assessment has four specific goals:

1. *Eliminate sites where remedial action is not required.* The first goal of the PA is to screen out those sites in the CERCLIS inventory that are statutorily ineligible for a Superfund remedial response, that pose no threat to public health or the environment, or at which no further action is warranted under the remedial program.
2. *Identify sites that require emergency response.* Superfund removal authority allows EPA to take immediate action at a site regardless of whether the site is on the National Priorities List (NPL). The PA can assist in determining if the site, or a portion of it, may qualify for a removal action, thereby warranting referral to the

removal program. This allows cleanup activities in advance of a determination about whether the site qualifies for the NPL.

3. *Compile information necessary to develop preliminary and projected HRS scores.* If the site may pose a threat that warrants remedial action, the PA collects data to develop preliminary and proposed HRS scores.

4. *Set priorities for site inspections.* The fourth goal of the PA is to set the priority of the site for a site inspection. Because more sites are typically referred for further action than resources can accommodate, EPA must establish priorities for further investigation.

Preliminary Assessment Petitions

Under Section 105(d) of Superfund, any person may formally petition EPA to conduct a preliminary assessment. The petition should concern a release or threatened release that affects or may affect the petitioner.

There is no specified format for the PA petition. However, a petition should contain basic information about the release and the petitioner. This information should include:

- The name, address, telephone number, and signature of the petitioner.
- The exact location of the actual or potential release. This may include marking on a street map or on a U.S. Geological Survey topographical map.
- A description of how the petitioner is, or may be, affected by the actual or potential release (e.g., contaminated groundwater, dead vegetation, or health affects).

The petition must be sent to the EPA Regional Administrator covering the site (see Appendix G). After receiving a PA petition, EPA determines if there is reason to believe that an actual or potential site exists, and if EPA has the legal authority to respond to the site. Within 12 months after a petition is received, EPA is required to review it and prepare a report. A copy of this report must be sent to the petitioner within the one-year time-frame. This report will state whether the petition was approved, and the reasons for the decision. If a petition is approved, EPA will conduct a preliminary assessment and provide a copy of the PA to the petitioner.

SITE INSPECTION

If the preliminary assessment indicates a suspected release of hazardous substances that may threaten human health or the environment, EPA can initiate a *site inspection,* which is conducted to ascertain the extent of the problem and to obtain information needed to determine whether a removal action is needed at the site, or whether it should be included on the NPL. In addition to sampling, inspections usually include a reconnaissance of the site's layout, surrounding topographical features, and the location of nearby populations, to document any risks the site may pose. Site inspections are divided into two tiers: screening site inspections (SSIs) and listing site inspections (LSIs).

The goals of the SSI are to:

- Collect additional data to calculate a better preliminary hazard ranking score.
- Establish priorities among sites most likely to qualify for the National Priorities List.
- Identify the most critical data requirements for a listing site inspection.

Those sites that are most likely to qualify for the National Priorities List are candidates for LSIs, which addresses the data requirements for a hazard ranking analysis. LSIs also are used to support the scoping phase of the remedial investigation and development of the remedial work plan.

HAZARD RANKING ANALYSIS

Because Superfund federal monies obviously cannot clean up all of the Nation's hazardous waste sites, a system of establishing priorities was developed. The criteria for establishing priorities for remedial action are based on the Hazard Ranking System (HRS), which was designed to help evaluate the relative risk to public health and the environment and to allow for the quick ranking of sites. The HRS score reflects the potential harm to human populations and the environment from the migration of hazardous substances involving groundwater, surface water, and air. A composite score, based on separate scores calculated for each of the possible contaminant migration routes, is determined. The score for each migration route is obtained by assigning a numerical value based on predetermined guidelines, contained in the HRS, to a set of factors that characterize the potential of the release to cause harm. An HRS numerical score for potential inclusion on the NPL is then determined. The HRS score is based on 100 points, and any site that receives a score of 28.5 is eligible for inclusion on the NPL. For EPA to compile a listing of 400 sites on the first NPL as mandated by CERCLA, it set the HRS score at 28.5 for NPL inclusion. Although the score was somewhat arbitrarily determined, it has remained the same.

States have the primary responsibility for identifying sites (although EPA may consider sites in addition to those submitted by states), computing HRS scores, and submitting candidate sites to their respective EPA regional office. The regional offices conduct a quality control review of the state's candidate sites and also may assist in investigating, monitoring, and scoring sites. EPA headquarters conducts further quality assurance audits to ensure accuracy and consistency among the various EPA and state offices involved in the scoring. EPA then proposes the new sites that meet the listing requirements in the *Federal Register* and solicits public comments on the proposal. After completion of the public comment period, a review of the comments which takes approximately eight months from the time of proposal, the final rulemaking is published in the *Federal Register*.

NATIONAL PRIORITIES LIST DETERMINATION

The primary purpose of the NPL is to identify, for EPA, the states, and the public, those facilities and sites that appear to present the most significant threat to human health or the environment. This list, which is periodically published in the *Federal Register*, is used to help direct priorities for action, including site cleanups, voluntary response, and enforcement measures.

The NPL was compiled as part of a cooperative effort involving the states and EPA. EPA developed the HRS scoring system to help evaluate the relative risk to public health and the environment posed by different sites. Each site submitted by the states and EPA is scored according to the HRS. The list is based primarily on HRS scores, in addition to those sites that are designated as the top-priority site in a particular state. Superfund requires these top-priority sites to be included among the 100 highest-priority sites on the NPL.

As discussed above, a site that receives an HRS score of 28.5 or greater is eligible for placement on the NPL. However, a site may be placed on the NPL regardless of its HRS score in the following situations [300.66(b)(4)]:

- If a state designates (only once) a site as its top-priority site.
- If the Agency for Toxic Substances and Disease Registry (ATSDR) issues a health advisory for a site.
- If EPA anticipates that it will be more cost-effective to use its remedial authority than to use its removal authority to respond to a release.

- If EPA determines that a release poses a significant threat to the public health.

The NPL does not determine priorities for removal actions. EPA may pursue removal actions at any site, whether listed or not, provided that the action is consistent with the NCP. Likewise, EPA may take enforcement actions, as well as conduct remedial investigations or feasibility studies, regardless of whether the site is on the NPL. However, a site's listing on the NPL must be finalized for it to receive fund monies for remedial construction. In addition, listing of a site on the NPL does not require any action by a private party, nor does it determine the liability of any party for the cost of cleanup at the site. It does not mean that the site necessarily represents an *immediate* threat to public health, although to get on the list by the HRS score, each site must represent some significant, long-term threat to public health.

Federal Facilities

Although Section 111(e)(3) of Superfund prohibits the use of fund monies for remedial actions at federal facilities, EPA lists federal facilities on the NPL. This action is consistent with the NPL's purpose of providing information to the public with respect to sites that present potential hazards.

RCRA Facilities

EPA published its policy for including sites on the NPL that are subject to Subtitle C of RCRA (51 *FR* 21057, June 10, 1986). Under this policy, sites not subject to RCRA Subtitle C corrective action requirements (discussed in Chapter 9) will remain eligible for NPL inclusion. Examples of RCRA Subtitle C, NPL-eligible sites include:

- Facilities that ceased treating, storing, or disposing of hazardous wastes prior to November 19, 1980.
- Sites at which only materials exempted from the statutory or regulatory definition of solid waste or hazardous waste are managed.
- Hazardous waste generators or transporters not required to have interim status or a RCRA permit.

Sites with releases that can be addressed under the RCRA Subtitle C corrective action provisions will not be placed on the NPL. However,

RCRA sites may be listed if they meet all of the other criteria for listing, and if they fall within one of the following categories:

- Facilities owned by persons who are bankrupt.
- Facilities that have lost authorization to operate, and for which there are additional indications that the owner or the operator will not be willing to undertake corrective action.
- Sites, analyzed on a case-by-case basis, whose owners or operators have shown an unwillingness to undertake corrective action.

REMEDIAL INVESTIGATION AND FEASIBILITY STUDY

Information obtained from the preliminary assessment, site inspection, and other sources is used to determine the general types of response actions applicable to the site for use in planning the remedial investigation. The National Contingency Plan (NCP) requires that a detailed remedial investigation (RI) and a feasibility study (FS) be conducted for sites listed on the NPL and targeted for remedial response under Section 104. The RI/FS process is the methodology that the Superfund program has established for characterizing the nature and extent of risks posed by uncontrolled hazardous waste sites and for evaluating potential remedial options.

Operable Units

Current practices in designing remedies for Superfund sites often divide sites into operable units that address discrete aspects of the site (such as source control, groundwater remediation) or different geographic portions of the site. An *operable unit* is defined in 40 CFR 300.6 as "a discernable part of the entire response action that decreases a release, threat of release, or pathway of exposure." RI/FSs may be conducted for the entire site and operable units broken out during or after the FS, or operable units may be treated individually from the start, with focused RI/FSs conducted for each operable unit.

The RI/FS Process

As shown in Figure 14-2, the RI and the FS are interdependent. Although the RI/FS process is presented in a fashion that makes the steps appear

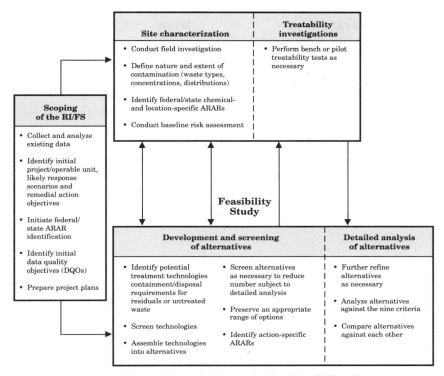

Figure 14-2. Phased Remedial Investigation/Feasibility Process

sequential and distinct, in practice the process is highly interactive. In fact, the RI and the FS are usually conducted concurrently. Whereas the RI emphasizes data collection and site characterization, the FS focuses on data analysis and evaluation of alternatives. Data collected in the RI influence the development of remedial alternatives in the FS, which in turn affects the data needs and scope of treatability studies and field investigations. In addition, because of the complex nature of many sites, new site characterization information may be compiled as the RI progresses, which may require reassessment of the types of response actions identified. In turn, this may require expanding the RI to obtain the data necessary to evaluate the new alternatives.

Management and coordination of RI/FS activities will affect the resources, timing, and completeness of the RI and the FS reports. Site-specific conditions will govern the extent of data collection and analysis for each level of both the RI and the FS processes.

Scoping of the RI/FS

Scoping is the initial phase of the RI/FS process. The scoping phase is the planning stage for the RI/FS process at a specific site, and many of the planning steps developed during scoping are continued and refined throughout the RI/FS process. Scoping activities typically begin with the collection of existing site data, including data from previous investigations such as the preliminary assessment and site investigation. On the basis of this information, site management planning is undertaken for preliminary identification of the boundaries of the study area, to determine likely remedial action objectives and whether interim actions may be necessary or appropriate, and to establish whether the site may best be remedied as one or several separate, operable units. Once an overall management strategy is selected, the RI/FS for a specific project, or the site as a whole, is planned.

When the involved parties agree on a general approach for managing the site, the next step is to scope the project(s) and develop specific project plans. Typical scoping activities include:

- Initiating the identification and discussion of potential ARARs.
- Determining the types of decisions to be made and identifying the data and other information needed to support those decisions.
- Assembling a technical advisory committee to assist in these activities, to serve as a review board for important deliverables, and to monitor progress, as appropriate, during the study.
- Establishing data quality objectives.
- Preparing the work plan, the sampling and analysis plan (which consists of the quality assurance project plan and the field sampling plan), the health and safety plan, and the community relations plan.

The scoping process is critical to the development of a sampling plan, which describes the sampling studies that will be conducted, including sample types, analyses, locations, and frequency. Planning needs, such as sampling operational plans, materials, record keeping, personnel needs, and sampling procedures, also are developed or identified for the investigation.

Risk Assessment

The primary purpose of Superfund is to protect human health and the environment from current and potential threats posed by uncontrolled hazardous substance releases. To assist in this mandate, EPA has developed a Superfund risk assessment program as part of its remedial response program. The Superfund risk assessment program is comprised of three separate parts:

- Human health and environmental evaluations
- Health assessments
- Endangerment assessments

Human Health and Environmental Evaluations

The goal of the Superfund human health and environmental evaluation is to provide a framework for obtaining the risk information needed for decision making at Superfund sites. Specifically, the process should provide:

- An analysis of baseline risks, thus helping to determine the need for action at sites.
- A basis for determining levels of chemicals that can remain onsite without threatening public health and the environment.
- A basis for comparing potential health impacts of various remedial alternatives.
- A consistent process for evaluating and documenting public health and environmental threats at sites.

The risk information generated by the human health and environmental evaluation process is designed to be used in the RI/FS. The baseline risk assessment contributes to site characterization and the subsequent development, evaluation, and selection of appropriate response alternatives. (*Baseline risks* are existing or potential risks to human health and the environment that might exist if no remedy or institutional control were applied at a site.) Such an assessment consists of data collection and analysis, exposure assessment, toxicity assessment, and risk characterization. The results of the baseline risk assessment are used to:

- Help determine whether response action is necessary at the site.
- Modify preliminary remediation goals.
- Help support selection of the no-action alternative.
- Document the magnitude of risk at a site, and the primary causes of that risk.

Health Assessment

A public health assessment must be conducted by the ATSDR for each site proposed or included on the NPL before the completion of the RI/

FS [Section 104(i)(6)]. The ATSDR health assessment, which is relatively qualitative in nature, should be distinguished from the human health evaluation, which is more quantitative than the ATSDR assessment.

EPA human health evaluations include quantitative, substance-specific estimates of the risk that a site poses to human health, estimates that depend on statistical and biological models using data from human epidemiological investigations and animal toxicity studies. The information generated from a human health evaluation is used in risk management decisions to establish cleanup levels and select a remedial alternative. ATSDR health assessments, although they also may employ quantitative data, are more qualitative in nature than the EPA evaluations, as the health assessments not only focus on the possible health threats posed by chemical contaminants attributable to a site, but consider all health threats, both chemical and physical, to which residents near a site may be subjected. These health assessments focus on the medical and public health concerns associated with exposures at a site and discuss especially sensitive populations, toxic mechanisms, and possible disease outcomes.

EPA considers the information in a health assessment along with the results of the baseline risk assessment to give a complete picture of health threats.

Endangerment Assessments

Prior to taking enforcement action against PRPs, EPA must make a determination that an imminent and substantial endangerment to public health or the environment exists because of a site. Such a legal determination is called an *endangerment assessment*. In the past, an endangerment assessment often was prepared as a study separate from the baseline risk assessment (human health and environmental evaluation). However, with the enactment of SARA and changes in EPA practices, the need to perform a detailed endangerment assessment as a separate effort from the baseline risk assessment has been eliminated. Elements included in the baseline risk assessment conducted at a Superfund site during the RI/FS process fully satisfy the requirements of the endangerment assessment.

Remedial Investigation

The remedial investigation (RI) is comprised of two phases: site characterization and treatability investigations. The data developed from these two phases support the evaluation of remedial alternatives.

It should be noted that:

- The RI must be conducted consistently with the National Contingency Plan.
- Data needs differ between an enforcement-led, a fund-led (federal financed), and a private-party-led remedial investigation (the data collection process must be tailored to meet specific investigative needs and objectives, including data quality and sufficiency).
- All supporting files and supporting documentation must be collected and retained.

Site Characterization

The site characterization process involves field sampling and laboratory analyses. Field sampling typically is phased so that results of the initial sampling efforts can be used to refine plans developed during scoping to better focus subsequent sampling efforts. Data quality objectives are revised as appropriate, based on an improved understanding of the site, to facilitate the efficient and accurate characterization of the site.

A preliminary site characterization summary is prepared to provide information on the site early in the process before preparation of the full RI report. This summary is useful in determining the feasibility of potential technologies and in assisting with the initial identification of ARARs.

Treatability Investigations

If existing site and/or treatment data are insufficient for adequate evaluation of alternatives, treatability tests may be necessary for the analysis of a particular technology for specific site wastes. Treatability investigations generally use bench-scale studies, but occasionally pilot-scale studies are necessary.

Bench- or pilot-scale studies may be needed in the RI for investigators to obtain enough data to select a remedial alternative. The bench and pilot studies of the RI specifically are concerned with waste treatability, scaleup of innovative technologies, technology application issues, and evaluation of specific alternatives. Bench and pilot studies also may be conducted during remedial alternative design or construction to more fully evaluate specific requirements of the selected alternative. However, these studies are outside the RI/FS process. In general, bench-scale studies are appropriate for the RI stage, whereas pilot-scale studies, if required, may be conducted during the final remedial design phase.

Feasibility Study

The feasibility study also is comprised of two phases: development and screening of alternatives and detailed analysis of alternatives.

Development and Screening of Alternatives

The development of alternatives generally begins soon after the RI/FS scoping process, when likely response scenarios are first identified. The development of alternatives requires:

- Identification of remedial action objectives.
- Identification of potential treatment, resource recovery, and containment technologies that will satisfy these objectives.
- Screening of the technologies based on their effectiveness, implementability, and cost.
- Assembling technologies and their associated containment or disposal requirements into alternatives for managing the contaminated media at the site or for the operable unit.

Alternatives can be developed to address a contaminated medium (e.g., soil), a specific area of the site (e.g., a surface impoundment), or the entire site. Alternatives for specific media and site areas can be studied separately in the FS process or combined into comprehensive alternatives for the entire site.

As practicable, a range of treatment alternatives is developed, varying primarily in the extent to which they rely on the long-term management of residuals and untreated wastes. The upper bound of the range would be an alternative that would eliminate, to the extent feasible, the need for any long-term management (including monitoring) at the site. The lower bound would consist of an alternative involving treatment as a principal element although some long-term management of portions of the site that did not constitute "principal threats" would be required. Between the upper and lower bounds of the treatment range, alternatives varying in the type and degrees of treatment and associated containment/disposal requirements should be included as appropriate, and a no-action alternative must be developed.

After development of the alternatives, the next step is to screen them. In this step, the universe of potentially applicable technology types and process options is reduced by evaluating the options with respect to their technical implementability. During screening, process options and entire technology types are eliminated from further consideration on the basis of technical implementability. This is accomplished by using readily available information (from the RI site characterization of contaminant types and concentrations and on-site characteristics) to screen out technologies and process options that cannot be effectively implemented at the site. As with all decision making during an RI/FS, the screening of technologies must be documented.

Detailed Analysis of Alternatives

The detailed analysis of alternatives consists of analyzing and presenting the relevant information needed to assist decision makers in selecting a site remedy, not the decision-making process itself. During this analysis, each alternative is assessed against the evaluation criteria described below. The results of the assessment are organized to compare the alternatives and identify the key tradeoffs among them. This approach is designed to provide decision makers with enough information to adequately compare alternatives, select an appropriate remedy for a site, and demonstrate satisfaction of the Superfund remedy selection requirements in the record of decision (ROD).

Superfund requires [Section 121(b)(1)(A)] an evaluation of long-term effectiveness and related considerations for each of the alternative remedial actions. Nine evaluation criteria have been developed to address the statutory requirements and to address the additional technical and policy considerations that EPA has determined to be important for selecting among remedial alternatives, as outlined in Figure 14-3. These evaluation criteria serve as a basis for conducting detailed analyses during the FS and for subsequently selecting an appropriate remedial action. The evaluation criteria are as follows:

- *Overall protection of human health and the environment,* which addresses whether or not a remedy provides adequate protection and describes how risks posed through each pathway are eliminated, reduced, or controlled through treatment, engineering controls, or institutional controls.
- *Compliance with ARARs,* which addresses whether or not a remedy will meet all of the applicable or relevant and appropriate requirements of other federal and state environmental statutes and/or provide grounds for invoking a waiver.
- *Long-term effectiveness and permanence,* which refers to the ability of a remedy to maintain reliable protection of human health and the environment over time, once cleanup goals have been met.

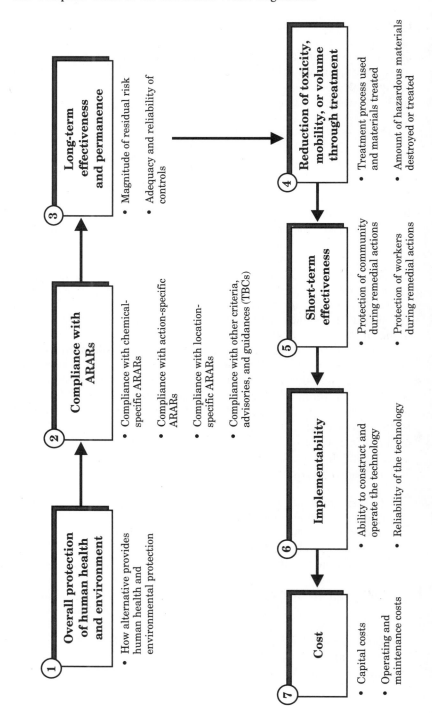

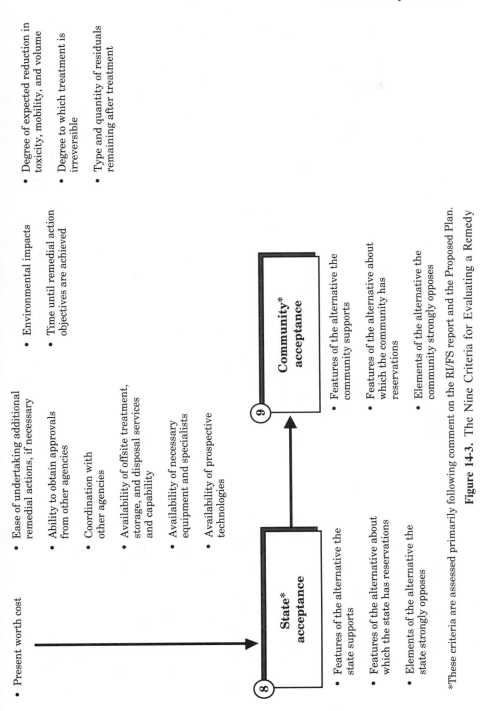

Figure 14-3. The Nine Criteria for Evaluating a Remedy

*These criteria are assessed primarily following comment on the RI/FS report and the Proposed Plan.

- Present worth cost

- Ease of undertaking additional remedial actions, if necessary
- Ability to obtain approvals from other agencies
- Coordination with other agencies
- Availability of offsite treatment, storage, and disposal services and capability
- Availability of necessary equipment and specialists
- Availability of prospective technologies

- Environmental impacts
- Time until remedial action objectives are achieved

- Degree of expected reduction in toxicity, mobility, and volume
- Degree to which treatment is irreversible
- Type and quantity of residuals remaining after treatment

State* acceptance ⑧

- Features of the alternative the state supports
- Features of the alternative about which the state has reservations
- Elements of the alternative the state strongly opposes

Community* acceptance ⑨

- Features of the alternative the community supports
- Features of the alternative about which the community has reservations
- Elements of the alternative the community strongly opposes

- *Reduction of toxicity, mobility, or volume through treatment,* which is the anticipated performance of the treatment technologies that a remedy may employ.
- *Short-term effectiveness,* which addresses the period of time needed to achieve protection and any adverse impacts on human health and the environment that may be posed during the construction and implementation period until cleanup goals are achieved.
- *Implementability,* which is the technical and administrative feasibility of a remedy, including the availability of materials and services needed to implement a particular option.
- *Cost,* which includes estimated capital and operation and maintenance costs, and net present worth costs.
- *State acceptance,* which addresses the technical or administrative issues and concerns that the support agency may have regarding each alternative.
- *Community acceptance,* which addresses the issues and concerns the public may raise regarding each of the alternatives.

Concerning cost considerations, the NCP states that "an alternative that far exceeds (for example, by an order of magnitude) the costs of other alternatives evaluated and does not provide substantially greater public health or environmental benefit should usually be excluded from further consideration." If the site is fund-financed, it also must be *fund-balanced.* This means that the cost required for site action must be weighed with other priority sites to determine if there is adequate money in the fund to respond to these sites.

Post-RI/FS Action

Following completion of the RI/FS, the results of the detailed analyses, when combined with the risk management judgments made by the decision maker, become the rationale for selecting a preferred alternative and preparing the proposed plan, as explained in the section on remedy selection. Therefore, the results of the detailed analysis, or more specifically the comparative analysis, should serve to highlight the relative advantages and disadvantages of each alternative so that the key tradeoffs can be identified. These tradeoffs, coupled with risk management decisions, will serve as the rationale for action, providing a transition between the RI/FS report and the development of the proposed plan and, ultimately, the record of decision.

Cleanup Requirements

Superfund does not specify cleanup standards *per se*. Section 121 of Superfund, however, requires that remedial actions be undertaken in compliance with *applicable* or *relevant* and *appropriate* environmental and public health requirements (ARARs). The requirements that must be complied with are those that are applicable or relevant to the hazardous substances or pollutants or contaminants at a site. Any such requirements may be waived under specified conditions, as outlined below, provided that protection of human health and the environment is still assured.

Applicable requirements are those cleanup standards, standards of control, and other environmental protection requirements, criteria, or limitations promulgated under federal or state law that specifically address a hazardous substance, pollutant or contaminant, remedial action, location, or other circumstance at a Superfund site. If a requirement is not applicable, it still may be relevant and appropriate.

Relevant and *appropriate requirements* are those cleanup standards, standards of control, and other environmental protection requirements, criteria, or limitations promulgated under federal or state law that, while not applicable to a hazardous substance, pollutant or contaminant, remedial action, location, or other circumstance at a Superfund site, address problems or situations similar to those encountered at the site, and whose use is well suited to the particular site. The relevance and appropriateness of a requirement can be judged by comparing a number of factors, including the characteristics of the remedial action, the substances in question, and the physical circumstances of the site.

Whereas the applicability determination is a legal one, the determination of relevancy and appropriateness relies on professional judgment, considering environmental and technical factors at the site. There is some flexibility in the relevance and appropriateness determination: a requirement may be relevant, in that it covers situations similar to that at the site, but it may not be appropriately applied for various reasons, and therefore may not be well suited to the site. In some situations, only portions of a requirement or regulation may be judged relevant and appropriate; but if a requirement is applicable, all substantive parts must be followed (OSWER Directive 9234.01).

For example, if closure requirements under Subtitle C of RCRA (e.g., the unit received hazardous waste after 1980) are applicable, the unit must be closed in compliance with one of the closure options available under Subtitle C. These closure options are closure by removal (clean closure) or closure with wastes or waste residues in place (landfill type closure). However, if Subtitle C is not applicable, then a hybrid closure, which could include other types of closure designs, also could be used. The hybrid closure option arises from a determination that only certain closure requirements in the two Subtitle C closure alternatives are relevant and appropriate.

On-site versus Off-site Actions

Section 121(e) of Superfund exempts any on-site action from having to obtain a federal, state, or local permit (e.g., RCRA, TSCA). On-site actions generally only need to comply with the technical aspects of the requirements, not with the administrative aspects; that is, neither permit applications nor other administrative reviews are considered ARARs for actions conducted on-site, and therefore they should not be pursued. However, the RI/FS, record of decision, and design documents should demonstrate full compliance with all technical requirements that are considered applicable or relevant and appropriate. Off-site actions do, however, require full compliance with all aspects of the applicable regulations. Thus, off-site actions only need to comply with applicable requirements, not with relevant and appropriate requirements.

The transfer of hazardous substances or pollutants or contaminants off-site is allowed only if the transfer is made to a facility operating in compliance with RCRA (or in compliance with TSCA or other federal laws where applicable) and applicable state requirements. As soon as a hazardous waste is removed off-site from a Superfund site, appropriate administrative requirements become applicable (e.g., permits, manifests).

In addition, any off-site transfer of hazardous substances or pollutants or contaminants to a land disposal facility is authorized only if:

- The unit to which the materials are being taken is not releasing hazardous waste into surface water or groundwater or soil.
- Releases from other units at the facility are controlled through RCRA Subtitle C corrective action.

Using ARARs

The ARARs should be identified on a site-specific basis and will depend on the specific chemicals at a site, the proposed remedy selection, and the site characteristics. The ARARs that may apply to a site remedial action should be identified and considered at various points in the remedial planning stages; specifically:

- During the scoping process of the RI/FS, chemical-specific and location-specific ARARs should be identified on a preliminary basis.
- During the site characterization phase of the remedial investigation, when the risk assessments are conducted to assess risks at a site, the chemical-specific and location-specific ARARs should be identified more comprehensively than they first were, and used to help determine the cleanup goals.
- During the development of remedial alternatives in the feasibility study, action-specific ARARs should be identified for each of the proposed alternatives and considered along with other ARARs.
- During the detailed analysis of alternatives, ARARs for each alternative should be examined as a group to determine what is needed to comply with other laws and to be protective of human health and the environment.
- When an alternative is selected, it must be able to attain the ARARs unless one of the six statutory waivers discussed below is invoked.
- During the remedial design phase, the technical specifications of construction must ensure attainment of the ARARs.

Exemptions

EPA is authorized to select a remedial action that protects human health and the environment but does not meet the ARARs for on-site actions if:

1. The remedial action is an interim measure, and the final remedy will attain the ARARs upon its completion.
2. Compliance with the ARARs will result in greater risk to human health and the environment than other options.
3. Compliance with the ARARs is technically impracticable.
4. An alternative remedial action will attain the equivalent of the ARARs.
5. In the case of state requirements, the state has not consistently applied state requirements in similar circumstances.
6. For Section 104 remedial actions, compliance with the ARARs will not provide a balance between protecting public health, welfare, and the environment at the facility and the availability of fund money for response at other facilities (*fund-balancing*).

If a remedial action results in any hazardous substances remaining on site, EPA is required to review the remedy at least every five years to assure that human health and the environment are being protected. If the review indicates that additional action is needed, EPA is required to take the action and report to Congress on the sites and the actions taken.

ARARs for Contaminated Water

In determining the applicable or relevant and appropriate actions involving contaminated surface water or groundwater, the most important factors to consider are the uses and potential uses of the water (52 *FR* 32499). The actual or potential use of water, and the manner in which it is used, will determine what requirements may be applicable or relevant and appropriate. For groundwater that is or may be used for drinking, the Maximum Contaminant Levels (MCLs) established under the Safe Drinking Water Act are generally the applicable or relevant and appropriate standard. If MCLs do not exist for contaminants identified at a site, health advisories established by EPA's Office of Drinking Water, reference doses, and carcinogenic potency factors are applicable or relevant and appropriate.

State ARARs

The requirement that ARARs must be attained also applies to any state requirement promulgated under a state environmental or facility-citing law that is more stringent than any federal requirement, and that has been identified to EPA in a timely manner.

The application of a state requirement that results in a statewide ban on land disposal is prohibited unless each of the following conditions is met:

- The state requirement is generally applicable and was adopted by formal means.
- The state requirement was adopted on the basis of hydrologic, geologic, or other relevant considerations and was not adopted to preclude on-site remedial actions or other land disposal for reasons unrelated to protection of human health and the environment.
- The state arranges for and pays the incremental costs of utilizing another treatment or disposal facility.

Prior to EPA's acceptance of a settlement with responsible parties, if the proposed remedial action does not attain an ARAR (federal or state), EPA must provide the state with an opportunity to concur with the remedy. If the state concurs, it may become a signatory to the consent decree. (A *consent decree* is an administrative order, having the force of law, that outlines the requirements for the responsible parties concerning a site's remedial action.) If the state does not concur and desires to have the ARAR met, it can intervene, as a matter of right, in the enforcement action before joining the consent decree for the purpose of conforming the remedial action to the ARAR. The remedial action must be made to conform to the ARAR if the state establishes, on the basis of the administrative record, that EPA's decision to waive the ARAR was not supported by substantial evidence. However, if the court determines that the remedial action does not need to conform to the ARAR, and the state desires to have the ARAR met, the consent decree must be modified to incorporate the ARAR if the state agrees to pay the additional costs associated with meeting it.

REMEDY SELECTION/RECORD OF DECISION

The remedy selection process, outlined in Figure 14-4, involves the selection of the preferred alternative, the issuance of a proposed plan, a public comment period for the preferred alternative, and, finally, the selection of the alternative documented in the record of decision (ROD).

It is important to note that at a site where waste will remain requires a review at least once every five years to ensure that the site remains safe.

Preferred Alternative Selection

After completion of the RI/FS, the lead agency (e.g., EPA, the state) identifies a *preferred alternative,* which is the protective, ARAR-compliant approach that is judged to provide the best balance of tradeoffs with respect to the nine evaluation criteria described above and depicted in Figure 14-3.

Proposed Plan

The preferred alternative for a site is presented to the public in a *proposed plan,* the purpose of which is to facilitate public participation in the remedy selection process by:

- Identifying the preferred alternative for a remedial action at a site or an operable unit and explaining the reasons for the preference.
- Describing other remedial options that were considered in detail in the RI/FS report.

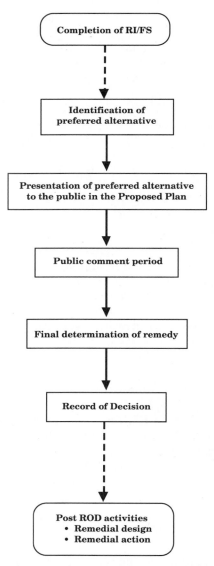

Figure 14-4. Remedy Selection Process

- Soliciting public review and comment on all the alternatives described.
- Providing information on how the public can be involved in the remedy selection process.

The proposed plan contains the "identified" preferred alternative, chosen on the basis of available information, but does not present a remedy "selected" for implementation. An important function of the proposed plan is to solicit public comment on all of the alternatives considered in the detailed analysis phase of the RI/FS because a remedy other than the preferred alternative may be selected.

Public Comment

Section 117(a)(2) of Superfund requires the lead agency to provide a reasonable opportunity for submission of written and oral comments and an opportunity for a public meeting, at or near the facility at issue, regarding the proposed plan and any proposed findings.

The lead agency must make the relevant documents (e.g., proposed plan, RI/FS) available to the public when the public comment period begins. This period must last a minimum of 30 days to allow time for the public to comment on the information contained in the RI/FS report [40 CFR 300.430(f)(3)(C)].

Record of Decision

The record of decision (ROD) serves as the final remedial action plan for a site or an operable unit. The ROD has the following purposes:

- It serves as a legal function, in that it certifies that the remedy selection process was carried out in accordance with the requirements of Superfund.
- It serves as a technical document that outlines the engineering components and remediation goals of the selected remedy.
- It is informational, providing the public with a consolidated source of information about the history, characteristics, and risks posed by the conditions at the site, as well as a summary of the cleanup alternatives considered, their evaluation, and the rationale behind the selected remedy.

The ROD consists of three basic components: a declaration, a decision summary, and a responsiveness summary.

Declaration

The declaration functions as an abstract for the key information contained in the ROD and is the section of the ROD signed by the EPA Regional Administrator. It provides a brief description of the selected remedy for the site and a formal statement explaining that the selected remedy complies with CERCLA and is consistent, to the extent practicable, with the NCP.

Decision Summary

The decision summary provides an overview of the site characteristics, the alternatives evaluated, and the analysis of those options. The decision summary also identifies the selected remedy and explains how the remedy fulfills statutory requirements.

Responsiveness Summary

The responsiveness summary addresses public comments received on the proposed plan, the RI/FS report, and other information in the administrative record.

REMEDIAL DESIGN

The *remedial design phase* is the engineering phase. The purpose of this phase is to develop a detailed set of plans and specifications for conducting the selected remedial action based on the ROD, cleanup levels to be attained, and site characteristics. At this point, for EPA-led sites, EPA may turn over the management of the cleanup action to the U.S. Army Corps of Engineers because of its experience in major construction projects. The Corps then hires its own contractors to perform the work, however, the EPA Regional Project Manager provides environmental oversight at the site. If a state or responsible party has the lead, it continues to manage the design and construction for the site under the oversight of the EPA RPM.

REMEDIAL ACTION

Following completion and approval of the remedial design, the remedial action phase is implemented. Otherwise known as the construction phase, the *remedial action phase* is the process in which remedial activities, including treatment, removal, and all other necessary tasks, are undertaken. The time required for this phase depends on the complexity of the site. When all phases of the remedial activities at a site have been completed and no further action is warranted, the site will enter the project closeout phase.

PROJECT CLOSEOUT

Project closeout is divided into three phases: NPL deletion, operation and maintenance, and final project closeout.

NPL Deletion

The NCP provides that sites may be deleted from, or recategorized on, the NPL when "no further response is appropriate" [40 CFR 300.66(c)(7)]. For a site to be eligible for deletion, at least one of the following criteria must be met:

- EPA, in consultation with the state, must have determined that responsible or other parties have implemented all appropriate response actions.
- All appropriate fund-financed responses must have been implemented, and EPA, in consultation with the state, must have determined that no further response is appropriate.
- Based on a remedial investigation, EPA, in consultation with the state, must have determined that no further response is appropriate.

EPA has established a new category for the NPL, the "construction completion" category. Sites may be categorized as "construction complete" only after remedies have been implemented and are operating properly. These may be sites awaiting deletion, sites awaiting five-year review or deletion, sites undergoing long-term remedial actions.

EPA must obtain state concurrence in order to delete a site from the NPL. In addition, EPA must provide the opportunity for public comment on a proposed deletion.

It is important to note that no site can be deleted from the NPL after completion of the cleanup until at least one five-year review has been conducted for those sites where waste remains. When a site is deleted from the NPL, it is technically closed out with respect to the federally funded remedial response. However, any site deleted from the NPL is eligible for further fund-financed remedial response actions if further conditions warrant such actions.

Operation and Maintenance

Following the completion of the remedial action, the state must assume responsibility for any operation and maintenance (O&M) requirements associated with the site remedy. EPA shares the costs of O&M for a period not to exceed one year, based on the date of project completion. The date is certified in the remedial action final inspection report and is formally approved by the Assistant Administrator of the Office of Solid Waste and Emergency Response (OSWER) or the EPA Regional Administrator.

Final Project Closeout

Upon the satisfactory completion of the fund-financed response, the site project is closed out.

Chapter 15

Miscellaneous Provisions Under Superfund

A number of provisions established under Superfund are indirectly part of the response action activities. This chapter discusses these provisions. The "miscellaneous" provisions that are addressed in this chapter are:

- Enforcement
- Natural resource damages
- Public participation
- Worker safety and health program

ENFORCEMENT

A major goal of Superfund is to encourage responsible parties to finance and conduct appropriate response actions and to recover the costs for response actions that were financed with fund money. Sections 106 and 107 of Superfund form the basis of this authority. The enforcement provisions of Section 106 authorize the use of administrative orders or the pursuit of civil actions to compel responsible parties to undertake cleanup action. Section 107 makes responsible parties liable for the costs incurred by federal or state governments or private parties that conduct response actions consistent with the NCP.

The Superfund enforcement process normally used by EPA to promote PRP involvement typically includes the following parts:

- EPA attempts to identify PRPs as early as possible. Once they have been identified, EPA notifies the parties of their potential liability.

- In the course of identifying the response work that must be done, EPA encourages PRPs to do work at the site.
- If EPA believes the PRPs to be willing and able to do the work, EPA attempts to negotiate an enforcement agreement with them. The enforcement agreement may be an agreement entered in court (e.g., judicial consent decree) or a mutual agreement outside of court (e.g., administrative order). Both types of agreement are enforceable in court.
- If a settlement is not reached, EPA can use its authority to issue a unilateral administrative order or to directly file suit against the PRPs. If the PRPs do not respond to an administrative order, EPA has the option of filing a lawsuit to compel performance.
- If the PRPs do not perform the response action and EPA undertakes the work, EPA may file suit against the PRPs and recover treble damages.

Settlements

EPA is authorized to enter into agreements with PRPs to conduct response actions and to decide if the specified settlement procedures should be used. EPA's decision is not subject to judicial review, but if the decision is negative, EPA is required to notify the PRPs of it.

Remedial action agreements must be entered into as consent decrees. (A *consent decree* is a legal document that specifies an entity's obligations when that entity enters into a settlement with the government); a consent decree is entered as an order by a federal district court or a state court. EPA is not required to make a finding of imminent and substantial endangerment, and entering into a consent decree is not an acknowledgment of an imminent and substantial endangerment or liability. Participation by a PRP in a settlement is not admissible in any judicial or administrative proceeding except as is consistent with federal rules of evidence. The use of administrative consent orders for unilateral orders is allowed for both removal and remedial actions.

PRP Searches

After site discovery, the first step is to search for and identify the potentially responsible parties (PRPs). Information from a local county clerk or registrar may identify a person or party paying property taxes, for example. In addition to an informational search, a field investigation may aid in the identification of responsible parties. An on-site visual investigation might include inspections of trash receptacles, drum labels, abandoned vehicles and license plates, and names of contract companies (e.g., for fences, trash removal, landscaping). If one PRP is located, that party is usually made aware that he or she could be liable for all response costs incurred and that identifying additional parties would redistribute the liability—an approach that often facilitates the search.

After they have been identified, EPA issues a notice to all PRPs. The *notice letter* states that the government has identified the party as a PRP liable for any cleanup costs incurred. This notice procedure allows the PRPs to organize and select representatives to meet with EPA in subsequent negotiations. PRPs who do not participate can be sued either by the government or by other PRPs for cost reimbursement after cleanup costs have been incurred.

Negotiations

Negotiation with potentially responsible parties is an integral part of the enforcement process. Negotiations are conducted either to secure responsible party action to fund or conduct cleanup or to recover federal funds already expended.

Negotiations for removal actions usually are of short duration, whereas negotiations for remedial actions generally last longer and may take place before, during, or after a response action, depending on site circumstances as well as the nature and immediacy of the threat.

Section 122 of Superfund sets forth procedures for negotiating settlements with PRPs for conducting response actions. This section essentially formalizes the settlement process that had been established under EPA's existing settlement policy, with some additions.

Special Notices and Enforcement Moratorium

Superfund authorizes EPA to issue a *special notice* calling for a temporary enforcement moratorium if negotiations would facilitate an agreement with PRPs to either undertake or finance the RI/FS. EPA is required to notify all parties as well as the state of such negotiation procedures, and to provide them with appropriate information when available. This information includes the names and addresses of other PRPs, the volume and nature of substances contributed by each PRP, and a ranking by volume of the substances. The PRPs who receive notice have 60 days to submit a proposal to undertake or finance the RI/FS. During this 60-day period, EPA may not initiate the RI/FS; however, additional studies or investigations authorized under Section 104(b) may be initiated. Nothing precludes EPA from undertaking response or enforcement actions if a site poses a significant threat to human health or the environment. If the PRPs do not submit a good-faith proposal within 60 days of notice, EPA may proceed with the RI/FS. If PRPs do submit a good faith effort within 60 days of notice, the enforcement moratorium continues until 90 days past the date of notice while EPA evaluates the proposal.

Nonbinding Preliminary Allocation of Responsibility

A nonbinding preliminary allocation of responsibility (NBAR) is a method used by EPA to allocate percentages of total response costs at a facility among PRPs, primarily based on the volume of waste contributed by a PRP. Its purpose is to expedite a settlement. NBARs are used to help promote a settlement if PRPs fail to determine allocations of responsibilities among themselves. An NBAR is not admissible as evidence in any proceeding including citizen suits, is not subject to court review, and does not constitute an apportionment or other statement of divisibility of harm or causation. Generally, an NBAR is prepared during the RI/FS. The costs incurred by EPA in preparing the NBAR must be reimbursed by the PRPs. The guidelines for preparing NBARs were promulgated on May 28, 1987 (52 *FR* 19919).

Covenants Not to Sue

Section 122(f) of SARA permits EPA to issue covenants not to sue for liability, including future liability, if certain conditions are met (e.g., the covenant is in the public interest and would expedite a response action approved by EPA). The criteria for such a covenant are the same as those provided in EPA's *settlement policy* (50 *FR* 5034, February 5, 1985). Such covenants are required to contain a reservation of rights, known as a reopener, for unknown conditions, except in extraordinary circumstances. (A *reopener* is a provision that reserves EPA's right to require settling parties to take further response action in addition to cleanup measures already provided for in a settlement agreement, notwithstanding the covenant not to sue.) EPA also will include in covenants not to sue a second reopener, covering situations in which additional information reveals that a remedy no longer protects public health or the environment. It is important to note that this reopener is triggered by a threshold of protection of public health or the environment rather than the imminent and substantial endangerment threshold.

It is mandatory for EPA to provide a covenant not to sue under Superfund for future releases under certain circumstances; for example, an on-site remedial action that meets the NCP is not selected, and the hazardous substances are transported off-site to a facility that meets the requirements of RCRA, or a remedial action involves treatment so the substances will no longer present any current or currently foreseeable future risks to public health, welfare, or the environment.

A covenant not to sue concerning future liability to the United States does not take effect until EPA certifies that the remedial action has been completed in accordance with Superfund at the facility subject to such covenant. The date of completion of the remedial action is the date at which remedial construction has been completed. The exact point when EPA can certify completion of a particular remedial action depends on the particular requirements of that remedial action; however, in general, the operation and maintenance activities are not included as the remedial action if they successfully attain the requirements set forth in the record of decision and the remedial design.

EPA considers a number of factors in determining whether to issue a covenant not to sue. These factors include:

- The effectiveness and reliability of the remedy.
- The nature of the risks remaining at the facility.
- The extent to which performance standards are included.
- The extent to which the response action provides a complete remedy.
- The extent to which the technology has been demonstrated to be effective.
- Whether the fund would be available for any additional remedial action.
- Whether the remedial action will be carried out, in whole or in part, by the responsible parties.

De Minimis *Settlements*

When practicable and in the public interest, Section 122(g) authorizes EPA to reach final settlements with PRPs if the settlement involves a minor portion of the response costs, and the waste sent to the site by the PRP is minimal in comparison to the other hazardous substances at the facility in terms of volume and toxicity (*de minimis*). Final settlements also may be negotiated with landowner PRPs if the landowner did not conduct or permit the disposal of hazardous waste at the site, did not contribute to the release of hazardous substances by an act or omission, and did not buy the property with the knowledge that waste had been disposed of at the site. Potentially responsible parties claiming a defense to liability, as opposed to being less culpable than other PRPs, must meet the new requirements of Section 101(f) to establish that defense.

Defining the *De Minimis* Waste Contributor

To qualify as a *de minimis* generator or transporter (contributor), the PRP must have contributed an amount of hazardous substances that is minimal in comparison to the total at the facility. The PRP also must have contributed hazardous substances that are not of significantly greater hazardous effect than others at the facility. For example, if all of the PRPs at a site disposed of the same solvent wastes, then those PRPs who had contributed a minimal amount in relation to the total could qualify for *de minimis* status. If, however, a PRP disposed of a minimal amount of waste that was more toxic or that exhibited other more serious hazardous effects than the other wastes at the site, then that PRP, despite the minimal volume of the contribution, would probably not qualify as a *de minimis* contributor. Even if a waste contributor meets the volume and toxicity requirements for *de minimis* contributor status, a possible settlement with a *de minimis* PRP must be determined by EPA to be "practicable and in the public interest."

Settlements

The goal of negotiations with *de minimis* parties is to achieve quick and standardized agreements through the expenditure of minimal enforcement resources and transaction costs. To attain this goal, the *de minimis* settlement does not require a commitment to perform work but rather a payment to be made to the fund. However, in appropriate cases, EPA can consider entering into *de minimis* settlements under which the settling parties agree to perform a discrete portion of the response action needed for the site, such as preparing an RI/FS or the cleanup of an operable unit. In exchange for this payment, the settling parties receive a statutory contribution protection under Section 122(g)(5) of SARA and may receive a covenant not to sue.

Releases from Liability

De minimis settlers may be granted a covenant not to sue for civil claims concerning the site that seek injunctive relief under Sections 106 and 107 of Superfund when EPA determines that such covenant is consistent with the public interest. Natural resource damage claims may not be released, however, and are expressly reserved unless the federal natural resource trustee has agreed in writing to such a covenant not to sue.

NATURAL RESOURCE DAMAGES

Before the enactment of SARA, Section 111 of Superfund authorized claims from the fund for the costs of the assessment of damages to natural resources and/or the costs of replacement, restoration, rehabilitation, or acquisition of equivalent natural resources as a result of injury due to a release. However, Section 517(a) of SARA prohibits fund expenditures to carry out Sections 111(a)(3), (b), (c)(1), and (c)(2), which are the authorizing provisions for natural resource damage claims.

Natural resource claims can only be asserted by trustees of the particular resource [Sections 111(a)(3) and (b) of Superfund]. Superfund authorizes trustees to obtain compensation through the claims process for two types of natural resource activities: damage assessment and restoration. *Restoration* includes restoring, rehabilitating, replacing, or acquiring the equivalent of an injured resource. *Damage assessment* is the process of determining the extent of injury to, destruction of, or loss of a natural resource. This may include the preliminary investigation of injury. Trustees also may include in such claims the reasonable and necessary costs associated with developing cost projections, developing an appropriate restoration plan, and obtaining public comments.

Other types of activities contemplated by Superfund to mitigate losses to natural resources include the replacement of the natural resource that has been injured, lost, or destroyed with an equivalent resource. An example of this would be creating an equivalent wetland or rehabilitating a functionally stressed wetland ecosystem, preferably in the same geographical area, for one injured by the release of a hazardous substance.

The Superfund amendments clarify the roles of federal and state trustees in performing natural resource damage assessments, limit the use of fund money for natural resource damage claims, and establish a three-year federal statute of limitations for filing such claims.

Natural Resources Trustees

Section 107(d) requires EPA and the governor of each state to designate officials to act on behalf of the public as trustees for natural resources under Superfund and Section 311 of the Clean Water Act. EPA is required to publish the identity of the designated federal trustees in the NCP. The governor of each state is required to notify EPA of the designated state trustees, who are required to assess damages for injury to, destruction of, or loss of natural resources under their trusteeship. Also, federal trustees are authorized to assess damages for natural resources under a state's trusteeship upon request and reimbursement from a state and at the federal officials' discretion.

Any funds recovered by a federal or a state trustee must be retained by the trustee for use only to restore, replace, or acquire the equivalent of such natural resources. However, liability for damages to natural resources under Section 107 is not limited to the cost of restoring, replacing, or acquiring such natural resources.

PUBLIC PARTICIPATION

EPA's public participation program has several components, as follows [40 CFR 300.430(f)(3)]:

- Before the adoption of any remedial action plan, the public must have access to a published notice and a brief analysis of the proposed action, as well as an opportunity for a public meeting.
- The final remedial action plan must be made available to the public before the commencement of any remedial action. If there are any significant changes to the proposed plan, a discussion of the reasons for these changes must be included.
- Responses to all significant public comments, criticisms, and new data submitted in written comments or during oral presentations must accompany the plan.
- After the adoption of a final remedial action plan, if there is remedial action, enforcement action, or settlements that differ in any significant aspects from the final plan, an explanation of the reasons for such changes must be published in a major local newspaper.

Citizen Suits

Superfund allows any person to take civil action against EPA for failure to undertake a nondiscretionary duty under Superfund or against any person (including personnel at federal facilities) for violation of any standard, regulation, condition, requirement, or order under Superfund.

No action can be commenced prior to 60 days after a plaintiff has given notices of violation to EPA, to the state where the alleged violation occurred, and to the alleged violator. An action cannot be commenced for a violation if EPA is "diligently" prosecuting the action under RCRA or Superfund.

Community Relations

EPA has established a community relations program to encourage public participation at Superfund sites. A community relations program for two-way communication is tailored to the needs of a community. For site-specific programs, EPA or state staff develop the program by interviewing residents, local officials, and community groups to ascertain the community's primary needs and the extent of the community's desire to participate in the decision-making process. This information is used to prepare a site-specific community relations plan. Community relations activities differ during removal actions and remedial actions.

Removal Actions

A removal action usually involves an immediate response designed for a quick cleanup. In this case, the community relations effort is limited to informing the public about the response action and its potential health and environmental effects.

Remedial Actions

A remedial action can take years to develop and implement. Because of its potential impact, a formal community relations plan is prepared. A plan is required for all remedial actions and for removal actions that last longer than 45 days. The plan outlines in detail the activities that will be conducted to ensure that members of the community can present their opinions and concerns about the site as well as be kept informed throughout the cleanup process. Typically, one of the first steps in the community relations program is to establish an information file at a local public building. This file is to contain site-related material such as news releases, technical reports, and fact sheets related to site activities. Each site also has a designated community relations contact, usually an EPA staff person located at a Regional Office, who is available to answer questions regarding the site.

Although EPA tries to include the community's preferences in selecting a remedy for a site, it may be forced to select a response action that is not the community's choice because the statute requires that the chosen remedy be cost-effective, fund-balanced, and selected as part of a permanent solution.

Enforcement Actions

EPA's general route of action is to pursue legal means to compel responsible parties to pay for or conduct the cleanup. Thus, in an enforcement-led site, EPA may be limited in the amount and nature of the information that it can make available to the public, as there might be sensitive or confidential information whose public disclosure could damage the government's legal case.

WORKER SAFETY AND HEALTH PROGRAM

Section 126 of SARA requires the Department of Labor (DOL) to promulgate regulations for the protection of the safety and health of any employee engaged in hazardous waste operations. These regulations were promulgated on March 6, 1989 (54 *FR* 9294), under 29 CFR 1910.120. In addition, Executive Order 12196 mandates that federal agencies are required to comply with these standards.

Program Components

The program requires each employer to develop and implement a written safety and health program that identifies, evaluates, and controls safety and health hazards and provides emergency response procedures for each hazardous waste site or treatment, storage, and/or disposal facility. This written program must include specific and detailed information on the following:

- An organizational workplan
- Site evaluation and control
- A site-specific program
- An information and training program
- A personal protective equipment program
- Monitoring
- A medical surveillance program
- Decontamination procedures
- Engineering controls and work practices
- Handling and labeling drums and containers
- Record keeping

The written safety and health program must be periodically updated and made available to all affected employees, contractors, and subcontractors. The employer also must inform contractors and subcontractors, or their representatives, of any identifiable safety and health hazards or potential fire or explosion hazards before they enter the work site.

Each of the components of the safety and health program is discussed in the following sections.

Workplan

The workplan must support the overall objectives of the control program and provide procedures for its implementation, and it must incorporate the employer's standard operating procedures for safety and health [29 CFR 1910.120(b)(1)]. A chain of command must be established to specify employer and employee responsibilities in carrying out the safety and health program.

The workplan should include the following:

- A list of supervisor and employee responsibilities and means of communication.
- The name of the person who supervises all of the hazardous waste operations.
- The name of the site supervisor with both the responsibility and the authority to develop and implement the site safety and health program and to verify compliance.

In addition to this organizational structure, the plan should define the tasks and objectives of site operation as well as the logistics and resources required to fulfill those tasks. The following topics should be addressed:

- The anticipated cleanup and/or operating procedures.
- A definition of work tasks and objectives and methods of accomplishment.
- The established personnel requirements for implementing the plan.
- The procedures needed to implement training, informational programs, and medical surveillance requirements.

Site Evaluation and Control

A trained person must conduct a preliminary evaluation of an uncontrolled hazardous waste site before entering the site [29 CFR 1910.120(c)(2)]. The evaluation must include all suspected conditions that are immediately dangerous to life or health, or that may cause serious harm to employees (e.g., confined space entry, potentially explosive or flammable situations, visible vapor clouds). As available, the evaluation must include information on the location and size of the site, site topography, site accessibility by air and roads, pathways for hazardous substances to disperse, a description of worker duties, and the time needed to perform given tasks.

The use of a buddy system also is required as a protective measure to assist in the rescue of any employee who becomes unconscious, trapped, or seriously disabled on site. In such a system, two employees must keep an eye on each other, and only one should be in a specific dangerous area at one time; then if one gets into trouble, the second can call for help.

Site-Specific Safety and Health Plan

The site-specific plan must include all of the basic requirements of the overall safety and health program, but must give attention to those characteristics unique to the particular site [29 CFR 1910.120(b)(4)]. For example, the site-specific plan may outline procedures for confined space entry, air and personal monitoring and environmental sampling, and a spill containment program to address the particular hazards present at the site.

The site safety and health plan must identify the hazards of each phase of the specific site operation and must be kept on the work site. Pre-entry briefings must be conducted prior to site entry and at other times as necessary to ensure that employees are aware of the site safety and health plan and its implementation. The employer also must ensure that periodic safety and health inspections are made of the site, and that all known deficiencies are corrected before any work is done at the site.

Information and Training Program

As part of the safety and health program, employers are required to develop and implement a program to inform workers (including contractors and subcontractors) who are performing hazardous waste operations of the level and degree of exposure that they are likely to encounter [29 CFR 1910.120(e) and (i)].

Employers also are required to develop and implement procedures for introducing effective new technologies that provide improved worker protection in hazardous waste operations. Examples include foams, absorbents, adsorbents, neutralizers, and the like.

The employer must develop a training program for all employees exposed to safety and health hazards during hazardous waste operations. Both supervisors and workers must be trained to:

- Recognize hazards and prevent them.
- Select, care for, and use respirators properly, as well as other types of personal protective equipment.
- Understand engineering controls and their use.
- Use proper decontamination procedures.
- Understand the emergency response plan, medical surveillance requirements, confined space entry procedures, spill containment program, and any appropriate work practices.

Employees at all sites must not perform any hazardous waste operations unless they have been trained to the level required by their job function and responsibility and have been certified by their instructor to have completed the necessary training. All applicable workers must receive refresher training that is sufficient for them to maintain or demonstrate their competency annually. These requirements may include recognizing and knowing the hazardous materials they will encounter and their risks, knowing how to select and use appropriate personal protective equipment, and knowing the appropriate control, containment, or confinement procedures and how to implement them. Training need not be repeated if the employee goes to work at a new site; however, the employee must receive any additional training required to work safely at the new site. An employee who worked at a hazardous waste site before 1987 and received equivalent training need not repeat the initial training specified in Table 15-1 if the employer can demonstrate satisfaction of the requirement in writing and certify that the employee has received such training.

Employees who receive the specified training must be given a written certificate upon successful completion of that training.

Personal Protective Equipment Program

The employer is required to develop a written *personal protective equipment program* for all employees involved in hazardous waste operations [29 CFR 1910.120(a)(5)]. This program must include an explanation of equipment selection and use, maintenance and storage, decontamination and disposal, training and proper fit, donning and doffing procedures,

Table 15-1. Personnel training requirements for hazardous waste site cleanup.

Staff		
Routine site employees	{	**40** hours initial **24** hours field **8** hours annual refresher
Routine site employees (minimal exposures)	{	**24** hours initial **8** hours field **8** hours annual refresher
Non-routine site employees	{	**24** hours initial **8** hours field **8** hours annual refresher
Supervisor/Managers of		
Routine site employees	{	**40** hours initial **24** hours field **8** hours hazardous waste management **8** hours annual refresher
Routine site employees (minimal exposure)	{	**24** hours initial **8** hours field **8** hours hazardous waste management **8** hours annual refresher
Nonroutine site employees	{	**24** hours initial **8** hours field **8** hours hazardous waste management **8** hours annual refresher

inspection, in-use monitoring, program evaluation, and equipment limitations.

The employer also must provide and require the use of personal protective equipment where engineering control methods are infeasible, to keep worker exposures at or below the permissible exposure limit. Personal protective equipment must be selected that is appropriate to the requirements and limitations of the site, the task-specific conditions and task duration, and the hazards and potential hazards identified at the site. As necessary, the employer must furnish the employee with positive-pressure self-contained breathing apparatus or positive-pressure air-line respirators equipped with an escape air supply, and with totally encapsulating chemical protective suits.

Monitoring

The employer must conduct monitoring before site entry at uncontrolled hazardous waste sites to identify conditions immediately dangerous to life and health, such as oxygen-deficient atmospheres and areas where toxic substance exposures are above permissible limits [29 CFR 1910.120(c)(6)]. Accurate information on the identification and quantification of airborne contaminants is essential for:

- Selecting personal protective equipment.
- Delineating areas where protection and controls are needed.
- Assessing the potential health effects of exposure.
- Determining the need for specific medical monitoring.

After hazardous waste cleanup operations begin, the employer must periodically monitor those employees who are likely to have relatively high exposures to determine if they have been exposed to hazardous substances in excess of permissible exposure limits. The employer must also monitor for any potential condition that is immediately dangerous to life and health or for higher exposures that may occur as a result of new work operations.

Medical Surveillance

The employer must [29 CFR 1910.120(f)] establish a medical surveillance program for the following:

- All employees exposed or potentially exposed to hazardous substances or health hazards above the permissible exposure limits for more than 30 days per year.
- Workers exposed above the published exposure levels (if there is no permissible exposure limit for the hazardous substances) for 30 days or more a year.
- Workers who wear approved respirators for 30 or more days per year on site.
- Workers who are exposed to unexpected or emergency releases of hazardous wastes above exposure limits (without wearing appropriate protective equipment), or who show signs, symptoms, or illness that may have resulted from exposure to hazardous substances.

All examinations must be performed under the supervision of a licensed physician, without cost to the employee, without loss of pay, and at a reasonable time and place. Examinations must include a medical and work history with special emphasis on symptoms related to the handling of hazardous substances and health hazards and to fitness for duty, including the ability to wear any required personal protective equipment under conditions that may be expected at the work site. These examinations must be given as follows:

- Prior to job assignments and annually thereafter (or every two years if a physician determines that is sufficient).
- At the termination of employment.*
- Before reassignment to an area where medical examinations are not required.*
- If the examining physician believes that a periodic follow-up is medically necessary.
- As soon as possible for employees injured or becoming ill from exposure to hazardous substances during an emergency, or who develop signs or symptoms of overexposure from hazardous substances.

The employer must give the examining physician a copy of the standard and its appendixes, a description of the employee's duties related to his or her exposure, the exposure level or anticipated exposure level, a description of any personal protective and respiratory equipment used or to be used, and any information from previous medical examinations. The employer must obtain a written opinion from the physician that contains the results of the medical examination and any detected medical conditions that would place the employee at an increased risk from exposure, any recommended limitations on the employee or upon his or her use of personal protective equipment, and a statement that the employee has been informed by the physician of the results of the medical examination. The physician is not to reveal in the written opinion given to the employer any specific findings or diagnoses unrelated to employment.

Decontamination Procedures

Decontamination procedures are a component of the site-specific safety and health plan and, consequently, must be developed, communicated

---

*If the employee has not had an examination within the last six months.

to employees, and implemented before workers enter a hazardous waste site [29 CFR 1910.120(k)]. As necessary, the site safety and health officer must require and monitor decontamination of the employee or decontamination and disposal of the employee's clothing and equipment, as well as the solvents used for decontamination, before the employee leaves the work area. If an employee's nonimpermeable clothing becomes grossly contaminated with hazardous substances, the employee must immediately remove that clothing and take a shower. Impermeable protective clothing must be decontaminated before the employee removes it.

Protective clothing and equipment must be decontaminated, cleaned, laundered, maintained, or replaced to retain its effectiveness. The employer must inform any person who launders or cleans such clothing or equipment of the potentially harmful effects of exposure to hazardous substances.

Engineering Controls and Work Practices

To the extent feasible, the employer must institute engineering controls and work practices to help reduce and maintain employee exposure at or below permissible exposure limits [29 CFR 1910.120(g)]. To the extent that they are not feasible, engineering and work practice controls may be supplemented with personal protective equipment. Examples of suitable and feasible engineering controls include the use or pressurized cabs or control booths on equipment and/or the use of remotely operated materials handling equipment. Examples of safe work practices include removing all nonessential employees from potential exposure when drums are opened, wetting down dusty operations, and placing employees upwind of potential hazards.

Handling and Labeling Drums and Containers

Before drums or containers are handled, the employer must make sure that they meet the required OSHA, EPA, and Department of Transportation (DOT) regulations, and are properly inspected and labeled [29 CFR 1910.120(j)]. Damaged drums or containers must be emptied of their contents by using a device classified for the material being transferred, and they must be properly discarded. In areas where spills, leaks, or ruptures occur, the employer must furnish employees with salvage drums or containers, a suitable quantity of absorbent material, and approved fire-extinguishing equipment in the event of small fires. The employer also must inform employees of the appropriate hazard warnings for labeled drums and the removal of soil or coverings, as well as the dangers of handling unlabeled drums or containers without prior identification of their contents. To the extent feasible, the moving of drums or containers must be kept to a minimum, and a program must be implemented to contain and isolate hazardous substances being transferred into drums or containers. In addition, an approved EPA ground-penetrating device must be used to determine the location and depth of any improperly discarded drums or containers.

Record Keeping

OSHA requires employers to provide employees with information to assist in the management of their own safety and health. The standard "Access to Employee Exposure and Medical Records" [29 CFR 1910.20] permits direct access to these records by employees exposed to hazardous materials, or by their designated representatives, and by OSHA. The rule applies to, but does not require, medical and exposure records maintained by the employer.

The employer must keep exposure records for 30 years and medical records for at least the duration of employment plus 30 years. Records of employees who have worked for less than one year need not be retained after employment, but the employer must provide these records to the employee upon termination of his or her employment. First-aid records of one-time treatment need not be retained for any specified period. The employer must inform each employee of the existence, location, and availability of these records. Under the hazardous waste standard, at a minimum, medical records must include the following information [29 CFR 1910.120(j)(8)]:

- Employee's name and social security number.
- Physician's written opinions.
- Employee's medical complaints related to exposure to hazardous substances.
- Information provided to the treating physician.

The Toxic Substances
Control Act

The Toxic Substances Control Act (TSCA) was enacted on October 11, 1976. TSCA's authority allows EPA to prohibit or control the manufacturing, importing, processing, use, and disposal of any *chemical substance that presents an unreasonable risk of injury to human health or the environment.* Certain substances are statutorily excluded from TSCA regulation, including pesticides (active ingredients only), foods, food additives, drugs, cosmetics, tobacco, firearms, and nuclear material.

TSCA regulations apply to any person who manufactures, imports, processes, uses, or disposes of *chemical substances.* However, because this book focuses on hazardous waste regulation, this part addresses only the use, management, disposal, and cleanup of PCBs.

The major sections of TSCA include:

- *Section 4,* which requires a chemical manufacturer, importer, or processor to test certain existing chemical substances for specified toxicity information, provided that EPA can justify the need for such data.
- *Section 4(e),* which authorizes the formation of the Interagency Testing Committee (ITC), composed of representatives of selected federal agencies, who must establish and continuously update a priority list of at least 50 chemical substances that the ITC recommends for testing.
- *Section 5,* which requires manufacturers or importers to submit to EPA a premanufacture notification (PMN) at least 90 days before manufacturing or importing a *new* chemical substance. In addition, this section outlines regulatory control options for new chemical substances. However, Section 5 also provides EPA with the au-

thority to limit or control the manufacture, processing, and use of existing chemicals by requiring the submission of a premanufacture notice prior to any "significant new use" of certain chemical substances, as determined by EPA.

- *Section 6,* which outlines the regulatory controls for *existing* chemical substances. These control options range from labeling to bans on manufacturing.
- *Section 6(e),* which requires EPA to control the manufacture, processing, distribution, use, and disposal of polychlorinated biphenyls (PCBs).
- *Section 7,* which authorizes EPA to take any action on any chemical substance if there is an "imminent hazard."
- *Section 8(a),* which requires manufacturers, importers, and processors to report information on manufacturing, importing, processing, use, disposal, worker exposure, and production volumes for specified chemical substances.
- *Section 8(b),* which establishes the TSCA inventory, a listing of all chemical substances (as defined) in commerce in the United States. If a substance is on the inventory, it is considered to be *existing;* if not, it is a *new* chemical substance.
- *Section 8(c),* which requires manufacturers, importers, processors, and distributors to retain records of the allegations of workers and citizens regarding adverse reactions to the chemical substances they manufacture, process, or distribute.
- *Section 8(d),* which requires manufacturers, importers, and processors to report any unpublished health and safety study data on specified chemicals.
- *Section 8(e),* which requires manufacturers, importers, and processors to report any "substantial risks to human health or the environment" for any chemical substance.
- *Section 9,* which requires EPA to refer regulation of a chemical substance to another agency if that agency's authority is more appropriate than that of EPA.
- *Section 12,* which requires industrial organizations to notify EPA when exporting specified chemicals. EPA in turn notifies the appropriate foreign governments.
- *Section 13,* which sets forth importing requirements for chemical substances.
- *Section 21,* which allows citizens to petition EPA for the regulation of any chemical substance.
- *Section 22,* which provides a national defense waiver for any TSCA regulation.
- *Section 23,* which allows for the protection of employee rights.

TSCA does not contain any provisions for state authorization; therefore, EPA has sole TSCA enforcement authority (although a state may assist EPA upon mutual agreement). However, a number of states regulate PCBs as a hazardous waste or regulate materials containing less than 50 parts per million (ppm) PCBs.

TSCA's authority is very broad, but primarily focuses on controlling the chemical manufacturing and processing industry. As noted, because this book focuses on waste management, only PCBs will be discussed in the following chapters.

TSCA's Relationship to Other Statutes

The Resource Conservation and Recovery Act

The authority concerning disposal under TSCA is significantly different from that of RCRA. TSCA regulates individual chemical substances, whereas RCRA regulates waste streams that may contain multiple chemical substances. EPA may regulate a chemical substance under TSCA only if it is found that the substance "presents an unreasonable risk of injury to human health or the environment." To determine an unreasonable risk under TSCA, EPA must conduct an economic cost/benefit analysis. RCRA does not require the use of economic considerations in its rulemaking.

PCBs are not listed as hazardous waste under RCRA, although they are an Appendix VIII hazardous constituent and an Appendix IX groundwater constituent. There have been numerous unsuccessful attempts to transfer the regulation of PCBs from TSCA to the RCRA program. However, the recent promulgation of manifesting, notification, and tracking requirements for PCBs in 1989 will probably ensure that the PCB program will remain under TSCA.

RCRA Mixed Wastes

A *mixed waste* contains a RCRA hazardous waste and PCBs of 500 ppm or greater (e.g., when a PCB item is decontaminated with a specified solvent that also is a RCRA hazardous waste, in accordance with 40 CFR 761.79 of TSCA). The policy for managing mixed wastes is to administer the most stringent regulation of each appropriate statute to the mixed waste stream [50 *FR* 49261 and 40 CFR 761.1(e)]. In real terms, this means that storage for the mixed waste would be only 90 days (RCRA), rather than 275 (TSCA), and that disposal of the waste would require incineration at 99.9999 percent destruction and removal efficiency (TSCA). A TSCA incinerator does not meet all of the RCRA incinerator requirements, nor does a RCRA incinerator meet all of the TSCA requirements; therefore, the only way to properly dispose of mixed waste is to send it to a dually permitted (RCRA and TSCA) incinerator.

Importing Hazardous Wastes

When importing hazardous wastes into the United States, the importer, who must be a U.S. citizen, must comply with Section 13 of TSCA. This section requires all importers of chemical substances to certify that such shipments either are in compliance with all applicable rules and regulations of TSCA or are not subject to TSCA. Chemicals that are not subject to TSCA under Section 13 (i.e., materials that are not included in the definition of "chemical substance") include active pesticide ingredients, drugs, cosmetics, and nuclear materials. In determining whether a material is in compliance with TSCA, two items of primary concern are: (1) every chemical component in the waste stream must be an *existing* chemical (i.e., included in EPA's TSCA Chemical Substances Inventory); and (2) none of the chemical components of the waste stream can be prohibited from importation. It should be noted that a material must be a hazardous waste to be subject to RCRA, whereas a material must be defined as a chemical substance to be subject to TSCA. Hazardous waste is a subset of chemical substances. Regulatory information pertaining to the import status of chemical substances under TSCA can be obtained from EPA's TSCA Industry Assistance Hotline at 202-554-1404.

Superfund

PCBs are designated as a hazardous substance under Superfund [Section 101(14)] because of the Clean Water Act. Therefore, any person involved in a release or threatened release of PCBs is liable for any and all costs incurred for a cleanup of released or threatened release of PCBs.

Reportable Quantities

Pursuant to Section 103 of Superfund, a spill of one pound of PCBs is a reportable quantity subject to immediate notification of the National Response Center (800-424-8802). (Previously, the RQ for PCBs was ten pounds; however, on August 14, 1989 (54 *FR* 33418), EPA changed the RQ to one pound.) As discussed in Chapter 12, the spill must be one pound of "pure" PCBs. For example, if a transformer containing dielectric fluid that has 100,000 ppm (10 percent) PCBs spills, ten pounds of fluid must be released to constitute one pound of released PCBs. However, if the exact concentration of PCBs is unknown (assuming it is greater than 500 ppm), a spill of one pound or greater of fluid must be reported.

The National Environmental Policy Act

EPA has concluded that many of its actions do not require an environmental impact statement because EPA's actions constitute functional equivalency, as discussed previously. The functional equivalence exclusion that relates to TSCA actions has been tested in court only for cleanup actions involving PCBs; but it appears that, as far as EPA is concerned, when conducting or overseeing an action concerning TSCA, EPA can use the functional equivalence exclusion if the specified criteria are met as established by case law. [See *Environmental Defense Fund, Inc. v. EPA*, 489 F.2d 1247, 1257 (D.C. Cir. 1973), *Twitty v. State of N.C.*, 527 F.Supp. 778 (1981), *Maryland v. Train*, 415 F.Supp. 116, 121–22 (1976), and *Warren County v. State of N.C.*, 528 F.Supp. 276 (1981).]

Chapter 16

Key PCB Definitions

This chapter contains key regulatory definitions of PCB-related TSCA terms used throughout Part III. These definitions are listed in 40 CFR 761.3 and 761.123.

Annual report means the written document submitted each year by each disposer and commercial storer of PCB waste to the appropriate EPA Regional Administrator. The annual report is a brief summary of the information included in the annual document log.

Annual document log means the detailed information maintained at the facility on the PCB waste handling at the facility.

Capacitor means a device for accumulating and holding a charge of electricity and consisting of conducting surfaces separated by a dielectric. Types of capacitors are as follows:

(1) *Small capacitor* means a capacitor which contains less than 1.36 kg (3 lbs.) of dielectric fluid. The following assumptions may be used if the actual weight of the dielectric fluid is unknown. A capacitor whose total volume is less than 1,639 cubic centimeters (100 cubic inches) may be considered to contain less than 1.36 kg (3 lbs.) of dielectric fluid and a capacitor whose total volume is more than 3,278 cubic centimeters (200 cubic inches) must be considered to contain more than 1.36 kg (3 lbs.) of dielectric fluid. A capacitor whose volume is between 1,639 and 3,278 cubic centimeters may be considered to contain less than 1.36 kg (3 lbs.) of dielectric fluid if the total weight of the capacitor is less than 4.08 kg (9 lbs.).

(2) *Large high-voltage capacitor* means a capacitor which contains 1.36 kg (3 lbs.) or more of dielectric fluid and operates at 2,000 volts (a.c. or d.c.) or above.

(3) *Large low voltage capacitor* means a capacitor which contains 1.36 kg (3 lbs.) or more of dielectric fluid and which operates below 2,000 volts (a.c. or d.c.).

Certification means a written statement regarding a specific fact or representation that contains the following language:

> Under civil and criminal penalties of law for the making or submission of false or fraudulent statements or representations (18 U.S.C. 1001 and 15 U.S.C. 2615). I certify that the information contained in or accompanying this document is true, accurate, and complete. As to the identified section(s) of this document for which I cannot personally verify truth and accuracy, I certify as the company official having supervisory responsibility for the persons who, acting under my direct instructions, made the verification that this information is true, accurate, and complete.

Chemical substance (1) except as provided in paragraph (2) of this definition, means any organic or inorganic substance of a particular molecular identity, including: any combination of such substances occurring in whole or part as a result of a chemical reaction or occurring in nature, and any element or uncombined radical.

(2) Such term does not include: any mixture; any pesticide (as defined in the Federal Insecticide, Fungicide, and Rodenticide Act) when manufactured, processed, or distributed in commerce for use as a pesticide; tobacco or any tobacco product; any source material, special nuclear material, or by-product material (as such terms are defined in the Atomic Energy Act of 1954 and regulations issued under such Act); any article the sale of which is subject to the tax imposed by section 4181 of the Internal Revenue Code of 1954 (determined without regard to any exemptions from such tax provided by section 4182 or section 4221 or any provisions of such Code); and any food, food additive, drug, cosmetic, or device (as such terms are defined in section 201 of the Federal Food, Drug, and Cosmetic Act) when manufactured, processed, or distributed in commerce for use as a food, food additive, drug, cosmetic, or device.

Chemical waste landfill means a landfill at which protection against risk of injury to health or the environment from migration of PCBs to land, water, or the atmosphere is provided from PCBs and PCB Items deposited therein by locating, engineering, and operating the landfill as specified in section 761.75.

Commercial storer of PCB waste means the owner or operator of each facility which is subject to the PCB storage facility standards of §761.65, and who engages in storage activities involving PCB waste generated by others, or PCB waste that was removed while servicing the equipment owned by others and brokered for disposal. The receipt of a fee or any other form of compensation for storage services is not necessary to qualify as a commercial storer of PCB waste. It is sufficient under this definition that the facility stores PCB waste generated by others or the facility removed the PCB waste while servicing equipment owned by others. A generator who stores only the generator's waste is subject to the storage requirements of §761.65, but is not required to seek approval as a commercial storer of PCB waste.

Designated facility means the off-site disposer or commercial storer of PCB waste designated on the manifest as the facility that will receive a manifested shipment of PCB waste.

Disposal means to intentionally or accidentally discard, throw away, or otherwise complete or terminate the useful life of PCBs and PCB Items. Disposal includes spills, leaks, and other uncontrolled discharges of PCBs as well as actions related to containing, transporting, destroying, degrading, decontaminating, or confining PCBs and PCB Items.

Disposer of PCB waste as the term is used in subparts J and K of this part [761], means any person who owns or operates a facility approved by EPA for the disposal of PCB waste which is regulated for disposal under the requirements of subpart D of this part [761].

Double wash/rinse means a minimum requirement to cleanse solid surfaces (both impervious and nonimpervious) two times with an appropriate solvent or other material in which PCBs are at least 5 percent soluble (by weight). A volume of PCB-free fluid sufficient to cover the contaminated surface completely must be used in each wash/rinse. The wash/rinse requirement does not mean the mere spreading of solvent or other fluid over the surface, nor does the requirement mean a once-over wipe with a soaked cloth. Precautions must be taken to contain any runoff resulting from the cleansing and to dispose properly of wastes generated during the cleansing.

EPA identification number means the 12-digit number assigned to a facility by EPA upon notification of PCB waste activity under §761.205.

Fluorescent light ballast means a device that electrically controls fluorescent light fixtures and that includes a capacitor containing 0.1 kg or less of dielectric.

Generator of PCB waste means any person whose act or process produces PCBs that are regulated for disposal under subpart D of this part [761], or whose act first causes PCBs or PCB Items to become subject to the disposal requirements of subpart D of this part [761], or who has physical control over the PCBs when a decision is made that the use of the PCBs has been terminated and therefore is subject to the disposal requirements of subpart D of this part [761]. Unless another provision of this part specifically requires a site-specific meaning, "generator of PCB waste" includes all of the sites of PCB waste generation owned or operated by the person who generates PCB waste.

High-concentration PCBs means PCBs that contain 500 ppm or greater PCBs, or those materials which EPA requires to be assumed to contain 500 ppm or greater PCBs in the absence of testing.

High-contact industrial surface means a surface in an industrial setting which is repeatedly touched, often for long periods of time. Manned machinery and control panels are examples of high-contact industrial surfaces. High-contact industrial surfaces are generally of impervious solid material. Examples of low-contact industrial surfaces include ceilings, walls, floors, roofs, roadways and sidewalks in the industrial area, utility poles, unmanned machinery, concrete pads beneath electrical equipment, curbing, exterior structural building components, indoor vaults, and pipes.

High-contact residential/commercial surface means a surface in a residential/commercial area which is repeatedly touched, often for relatively long periods of time. Doors, wall areas below 6 feet in height, uncovered flooring, windowsills, fencing, banisters, stairs, automobiles, and children's play areas such as outdoor patios and sidewalks are examples of high-contact residential/commercial surfaces. Examples of low-contact residential/commercial surfaces include interior ceilings, interior wall areas above 6 feet in height, roofs, asphalt roadways, concrete roadways, wooden utility poles, unmanned machinery, concrete pads beneath electrical equipment, curbing, exterior structural building components (e.g., aluminum/vinyl siding, cinder block, asphalt tiles), and pipes.

High-efficiency boiler means a boiler that operates at a minimum of 50 million BTU-hours. If the boiler uses natural gas or oil as primary fuel, the carbon monoxide concentration in the stack would be 50 ppm or less and the excess oxygen would be at least 3 percent when PCBs are burned. If the boiler uses coal as the primary fuel, the carbon monoxide concentration in the stack would be 100 ppm or less and the excess oxygen would be at least 3 percent when PCBs are being burned.

Impervious solid surfaces means solid surfaces which are nonporous and thus unlikely to absorb spilled PCBs within the short period of time required for cleanup of spills under this policy [the PCB Spill Cleanup Policy]. Impervious solid surfaces include, but are not limited to, metals, glass, aluminum siding, and enameled or laminated surfaces.

Incinerator means an engineered device using controlled flame combustion to thermally degrade PCBs and PCB Items. Examples of devices used for incineration include rotary kilns, liquid injection incinerators, cement kilns, and high-temperature boilers.

Industrial buildings means a building directly used in manufacturing or techniclaly productive enterprises. Industrial buildings are not generally or typically accessible to other than workers. Industrial buildings include buildings used directly in the production of power, the manufacture of products, the mining of raw materials, and the storage of textiles, petroleum products, wood and paper products, chemicals, plastics, and metals.

In or near commercial buildings means within the interior of, on the roof of, attached to the exterior wall of, in the parking area serving, or within 30 meters of a non-industrial non-substation building. Commercial buildings are typically accessible to both members of the general public and employees, and include: (1) Public assembly properties, (2) educational properties, (3) institutional properties, (4) residential properties, (5) stores, (6) office buildings, and (7) transportation centers (e.g., airport terminals, subway stations, bus stations or train stations).

Laboratory means a facility that analyzes samples for PCBs and is unaffiliated with any entity whose activities involve PCBs.

Leak or *leaking* means any instance in which a PCB Article, PCB Container, or PCB Equipment has any PCBs on any portion of its external surface.

Low-concentration PCBs means PCBs that are tested and found to contain less than 500 ppm PCBs or those PCB-containing materials which EPA requires to be assumed to be at concentrations below 500 ppm (i.e., untested mineral oil dielectric fluid).

Manifest means the shipping document EPA form 8700-22 and any continuation sheet attached to EPA form 8700-22, originated and signed by the generator of PCB waste in accordance with the instructions included with the form and subpart K of this part [761].

Manufacture means to produce, manufacture, or import into the customs territory of the United States.

Mark means the descriptive name, instructions, cautions, or other information applied to PCBs and PCB Items, or other objects subject to these regulations.

Marked means the marking of PCB Items and PCB storage areas and transport vehicles by means of applying a legible mark by painting, fixation of an adhesive label, or by any other method that meets the requirements of these regulations.

Nonimpervious solid surfaces means solid surfaces which are porous and are more likely to absorb spilled PCBs prior to completion of the cleanup requirements prescribed in this policy [the PCB Spill Cleanup Policy]. Nonimpervious solid surfaces include, but are not limited to, wood, concrete, asphalt, and plasterboard.

Nonrestricted access areas means any area other than restricted access, outdoor electrical substations, and other restricted access locations, as defined in this section. In addition to residential/commercial areas, these areas include unrestricted access rural areas (areas of low density development and population where access is uncontrolled by either manmade barriers or naturally occurring barriers, such as rough terrain, mountains, or cliffs).

On-site means within the boundaries of a contiguous property unit.

Other restricted access (nonsubstation) locations means areas other than electrical substations that are at least 0.1 kilometer (km) from a residential/commercial area and limited by man-made barriers (e.g., fences and walls) that are substantially limited by naturally occurring barriers such as mountains, cliffs, or rough terrain. These facilities are in remote rural locations. Areas where access is restricted but that are less than 0.1 km from a residential/commercial area are considered to be residential/commercial areas.

Outdoor electrical substations means outdoor, fenced-off, and restricted access areas used in the transmission and/or distribution of electrical power. Outdoor electrical substations restrict public access by being fenced or walled off as defined under section 761.30(1)(1)(ii). For purposes of this TSCA policy [the PCB Spill Cleanup Policy], outdoor electrical substations are defined as being located at least 0.1 km from a residential/commercial area. Outdoor fenced-off restricted access areas used in the transmission and/or distribution of electrical power which are located less than 0.1 km from a residential/commercial area are considered to be residential/commercial areas.

PCB wastes means those PCBs and PCB Items that are subject to the disposal requirements of subpart D of this part [761].

PCB transformer means any transformer that contains 500 ppm PCB or greater.

PCB Equipment means any manufactured item, other than a PCB Container or a PCB Article Container, which contains a PCB Article or other PCB Equipment, and includes microwave ovens, electronic equipment, and fluorescent light ballasts and fixtures.

PCB Item is defined as any PCB Article, PCB Article Container, PCB Container, or PCB Equipment, that deliberately or unintentionally contains or has as a part of it any PCB or PCBs.

PCB-Contaminated Electrical Equipment means any electrical equipment, including but not limited to transformers (including those used in railway locomotives and self-propelled cars), capacitors, circuit breakers, reclosers, voltage regulators, switches (including sectionalizers and motor starters), electromagnets, and cable, that contain 50 ppm or greater PCB, but less than 500 ppm PCB. Oil-filled electrical equipment other than circuit breakers, reclosers, and cable whose PCB concentration is unknown must be assumed to be PCB-Contaminated Electrical Equipment. (See Section 761.30(a) and (h) for provisions permitting reclassification of electrical equipment containing 500 ppm or greater PCBs to PCB-Contaminated Electrical Equipment.)

PCB Container means any package, can, bottle, bag, barrel, drum, tank, or other device that contains PCBs or PCB Articles and whose surface(s) has been in direct contact with PCBs.

PCB Article means any manufactured article, other than a PCB Container, that contains PCBs and whose surface(s) has been in direct contact with PCBs. "PCB Article" includes capacitors, transformers, electric motors, pumps, pipes, and any other manufactured item (1) which is formed to a specific shape or design during manufacture, (2) which has end use function(s) dependent in whole or in part upon its shape or design during end use, and (3) which has either no change of chemical composition during its end use or those changes of composition which have no commercial purpose separate from that of the PCB Article.

PCB and *PCBs* means any chemical substance that is limited to the biphenyl molecule that has been chlorinated to varying degrees or any combination of substances which contain such substance. (Refer to section 761.1(b) for applicable concentrations of PCBs.) PCB and PCBs as contained in PCB Items are defined in Section 761.3. For any purposes under this part [761], inadvertently generated non-Aroclor PCBs are defined as the total PCBs calculated following division of the quantity of monochlorinated biphenyls by 50 and dichlorinated biphenyls by 5.

PCB Article Container means any package, can, bottle, bag, barrel, drum, tank, or other device used to contain PCB Articles or PCB Equipment, and whose surface(s) has not been in direct contact with PCBs.

Posing an exposure risk to food or feed means being in any location where human food or animal feed products could be exposed to PCBs released from a PCB Item. A PCB Item poses an exposure risk to food or feed if PCBs released in any way from the PCB Item have a potential pathway to human food or animal feed. EPA considers human food or animal feed to include items regulated by the U.S. Department of Agriculture or the Food and Drug Administration as human food or animal feed; this includes direct additives. Food or feed is excluded from this definition if it is used or stored in private homes.

Qualified incinerator means one of the following:

(1) An incinerator approved under the provisions of section 761.70. Any concentration of PCBs can be destroyed in an incinerator approved under section 761.70.

(2) A high-efficiency boiler approved under the provisions of Section 761.60(a)(3). Only PCBs in concentrations below 500 ppm can be destroyed in a high-efficiency boiler approved under Section 761.60(a)(3).

(3) An incinerator approved under section 3005(c) of the Resource Conservation and Recovery Act (42 U.S.C. 6925(c)) (RCRA). Only PCBs in concentrations below 50 ppm can be destroyed in a RCRA-approved incinerator. The manufacturer seeking to qualify a process as a controlled waste process by disposing of wastes in a RCRA-approved incinerator must make a determination that the incinerator is capable of destroying less readily burned compounds than the PCB homologs to be destroyed. The manufacturer may use the same guidance used by EPA in making such a determination when issuing an approval under section 3005(c) of RCRA. The manufacturer is also responsible for obtaining a reasonable assurance that the incinerator, when burning PCB wastes, will be operated under conditions which have been shown to enable the incinerator to destroy the less readily burned compounds.

Requirements and standards means:

(1) "Requirements" as used in this policy [the PCB Spik Cleanup Policy] refers to both the procedural responses and numerical decontamination levels set forth in this policy as constituting adequate cleanup of PCBs.

(2) "Standards" refers to the numerical decontamination levels set forth in this policy.

Residential/commercial areas means those areas where people live or reside or where people work in other than manufacturing or farming industries. Residential areas include housing and the property on which housing is located as well as playgrounds, roadways, sidewalks, parks, and other similar areas within a residential community. Commercial areas are typically accessible to both members of the general public and employees and include public assembly properties, institutional properties, stores, office buildings, and transportation centers.

Responsible party means the owner of the PCB equipment, facility, or other source of PCBs or his/her designated agent (e.g., a facility manager or foreman).

Rupture of a PCB Transformer means a violent or non-violent break in the integrity of a PCB Transformer caused by an overtemperature and/or overpressure condition that results in the release of PCBs.

Sale for purposes other than resale means sale of PCBs for purposes of disposal and for purposes of use, except where use involves sale for distribution in commerce. PCB Equipment which is first leased for purposes of use any time before July 1, 1979, is considered sold for purposes other than resale.

Significant exposure means any exposure of human beings or the environment to PCBs as measured or detected by any scientifically acceptable analytical method.

Small quantities for research and development means any quantity of PCBs:

(1) that is originally packaged in one or more hermetically sealed containers of a volume of no more than five (5.0) milliliters, and

(2) that is used only for purposes of scientific experimentation or analysis, or chemical research on, or analysis of, PCBs, but not for research or analysis for the development of a PCB product.

Soil means all vegetation, soils, and other ground media, including but not limited to, sand, grass, gravel, and oyster shells. It does not include concrete and asphalt.

Spill area means the area of soil on which visible traces of the spill can be observed plus a buffer zone of 1 foot beyond the visible traces. Any surface or object (e.g., concrete sidewalk or automobile) within the visible traces area or on which visible traces of the spilled material observed is included in the spill area. This area represents the minimum area assumed to be contaminated by PCBs in the absence of precleanup sampling data and is thus the minimum area that must be cleaned.

Spill boundaries means the actual area of contamination as determined by postcleanup verification sampling or by precleanup sampling to determine actual spill boundaries. EPA can require additional cleanup when necessary to decontaminate all areas within the spill boundaries to the levels required in this policy [the PCB Spill Cleanup Policy] (e.g., additional cleanup will be required if postcleanup sampling indicates that the area decontaminated by the responsible party, such as the spill area as defined in this section, did not encompass the actual boundaries of PCB concentration).

Spill means both intentional and unintentional spills, leaks, and other uncontrolled discharges where the release results in any quantity of PCBs running off or about to run off the external surface of the equipment or other PCB source, as well as the contamination resulting from those releases. This policy [the PCB Spill Cleanup Policy] applies to spills of 50 ppm or greater PCBs. The concentration of PCBs spilled is determined by the PCB concentration in the material spilled as opposed to the concentration of PCBs in the material onto which the PCBs were spilled. Where a spill of untested mineral oil occurs, the oil is presumed to contain greater than 50 ppm but less than 500 ppm PCBs and is not subject to the relevant requirements of this policy.

Standard wipe test means, for spills of high-concentration PCBs on solid surfaces, a cleanup to numerical surface standards and sampling by a standard wipe test to verify that the numerical standards have been met. This definition constitutes the minimum requirements for an appropriate wipe testing protocol. A standard-size template (10 centimeters (cm) × 10 cm) will be used to delineate the area of cleanup; the wiping medium will be a gauze pad or glass wool of known size which has been saturated with hexane. It is important that the wipe be performed very quickly after the hexane is exposed to air. EPA strongly recommends that the gauze (or glass wool) be prepared with hexane in the laboratory and that the wiping medium be stored in sealed glass vials until it is used for the wipe test. Further, EPA requires the collection and testing of field blanks and replicates.

Storage for disposal means temporary storage of PCBs that have been designated for disposal.

Totally enclosed manner means any manner that will ensure no exposure of human beings or the environment to any concentration of PCBs.

Transfer facility means any transportation-related facility including loading docks, parking areas, and other similar areas where shipments of PCB waste are held during the normal course of transportation. Transport vehicles are not transfer facilities under this definition, unless they are used for the storage of PCB, rather than for actual transport activities. Storage areas for PCB waste at transfer facilities are subject to the storage facility standards of §761.65, but such storage areas are exempt from the approval requirements of §761.65(d) and the recordkeeping requirements of §761.180, unless the same PCB waste is stored there for a period of more than 10 consecutive days between destinations.

Transport vehicle means a motor vehicle or rail car used for the transportation of cargo by any mode. Each cargo-carrying body (e.g., trailer, railroad freight car) is a separate transport vehicle.

Transporter of PCB waste means, for the purposes of subpart K of this part [761], any person engaged in the transportation of regulated PCB waste by air, rail, highway, or water for purposes other than consolidation by a generator.

Waste oil means used products primarily derived from petroleum, which include, but are not limited to, fuel oils, motor oils, gear oils, cutting oils, transmission fluids, hydraulic fluids, and dielectric fluids.

Chapter 17

Use, Storage, and Disposal of PCBs

Section 6(e) of the Toxic Substances Control Act (TSCA) specifically compels EPA to regulate the manufacture, importation, use, and disposal of polychlorinated biphenyls (PCBs). Other provisions of TSCA direct EPA to regulate chemicals that present an "unreasonable risk of injury to health and the environment," but Section 6(e) is the only provision of TSCA that directly controls the manufacture, processing, distribution in commerce, use, and disposal of a specific chemical substance—PCBs.

INTRODUCTION

Section 6(e) of TSCA directly bans the manufacture of new PCBs; prohibits the processing, distribution in commerce, and use of all PCBs in any way other than a *totally enclosed manner;* and regulates the disposal of PCBs. Although PCBs are banned, Congress gave EPA the authority to grant the following limited exceptions to that ban:

- EPA can authorize particular uses of PCBs provided that such use does not present an unreasonable risk to public health and the environment.
- EPA can exempt certain activities from the ban on the manufacture, processing, and distribution in commerce of PCBs, provided that such activity does not present an unreasonable risk and that good faith efforts have been made to find a substitute for the PCBs for the required activity.

Exemptions to the ban on the manufacture, processing, and distribution in commerce of PCBs can be granted only upon petition on a case-by-case basis through rulemaking. Exemptions cannot be granted for more than a one-year period.

In general, EPA will hold the owners of equipment containing PCBs responsible for compliance with the TSCA regulations. However, in cases involving PCB use by a person who does not own the equipment or PCB equipment located on property owned by a third party, EPA will consider the facts of each case to determine whether the user or the landowner should be held responsible for compliance either in addition to or instead of the owner of the PCBs (TSCA Compliance Program Policy No. 6-PCB-1, March 4, 1981).

What PCBs Are

Polychlorinated biphenyls are produced by substituting chlorine atoms for the hydrogen atoms on a biphenyl (double benzene ring) molecule. The number and the location of the chlorine attachments determine the physical properties and characteristics of a PCB molecule. There are 10 positions on a biphenyl ring that through various combinations can yield 209 possible PCB compounds. Commercial PCB products are most often mixtures of many types of PCB molecules. For regulatory purposes, a biphenyl ring chlorinated to *any* degree is considered a PCB [40 CFR 761.3]. This includes monochlorinated biphenyls. Generally, PCBs used in electrical equipment tend to be viscous and heavy (11 to 13 pounds per gallon), similar to a light honey, but they may also be solid and waxy. They are extremely stable, nonflammable, lipid-soluble, and resistant to degradation. These properties are ideal in an industrial application, but also are thought to be a cause of negative environmental effects. Because of their lipid solubility, PCB molecules can move up the food chain, bioaccumulating in higher trophic-level organisms. The toxicological properties of PCBs depend on the amount and location of the chlorination. With the exception of chloracne (skin lesions), toxic effects in humans are not well documented. Documented toxic effects in animals include adverse reproductive effects, liver lesions, cancer, and developmental toxicity. Low concentrations of PCBs have been shown to be highly toxic to fish (47 *FR* 37344-5, August 25, 1982). PCBs also are known by their generic name, Aroclor.

Between 1929 and 1977, PCBs were primarily manufactured for use in electrical equipment; and the majority of PCB equipment marketed in the United States is still in service. PCBs that were intentionally manufactured for use as a dielectric fluid, they were often mixed with certain organic solvents, such as chlorinated benzenes; thus, the dielectric fluid present in electrical equipment containing PCBs generally is not 100 percent PCB.

Polychlorinated terphenyls (PCTs) also were manufactured as a commercial product and are similar in properties to PCBs. Although PCTs are not specifically covered by the TSCA PCB regulations, most were contaminated with up to 10,000 ppm PCB, and so would be regulated.

PCBs IN ELECTRICAL EQUIPMENT

The two major categories of PCBs are those intentionally manufactured for use in electrical and other types of equipment and the PCBs produced inadvertently as by-products and impurities. The intentional manufacture of PCBs other than for research purposes is now prohibited; however, PCBs are still contained in electrical equipment and other types of equipment that were manufactured before the ban.

EPA's strategy for regulating PCBs has focused on the regulation of PCBs in electrical equipment and of by-product PCBs. This chapter addresses only PCBs in electrical equipment.

On May 31, 1979, EPA promulgated a final rule (44 *FR* 31512) covering the manufacture, processing, distribution in commerce, use, and disposal of PCBs. The rule did the following:

1. Classified the use of PCBs in transformers, capacitors, and electromagnets as totally enclosed.
2. Established requirements for the marking and disposal of PCBs in concentrations over 50 ppm.
3. Established a regulatory cutoff of 50 ppm for the manufacture, processing, distribution in commerce, and use of PCBs.
4. Authorized the use of PCBs for 11 specific activities.

The Environmental Defense Fund (EDF) sought judicial review of provisions 1, 3, and 4 in the U.S. Circuit Court of Appeals for the District of Columbia. The court ruled that the EPA lacked substantial evidence to support the classification of transformers, capacitors, and electromagnets as totally enclosed and the regulatory cutoff of 50 ppm for the manufacture, processing, distribution in commerce, and use of PCBs.

If the court's decision had gone into effect, the use of all transformers, capacitors, and electromagnets containing PCBs would have been immediately banned. Because most electrical transformers and capacitors at the time contained PCBs, this ban would have had a disastrous economic impact on industry and consumers alike. Thus, EPA and EDF filed a joint motion with the court requesting a stay of the court's mandate until additional rulemaking could be completed. The court granted the request and compelled EPA to begin additional rulemaking.

Major rules subsequent to the May 1979 rule include the following additions:

- On August 25, 1982 (42 *FR* 37357), EPA promulgated the Electrical Equipment Use Rule in response to the EDF suit. It further defined the concept of a totally enclosed manner of PCB use and regulated exposure risks to food and feed.
- On July 17, 1985 (50 *FR* 29199), EPA promulgated the Fire Rule. This rule regulates transformers *in or near commercial buildings* and is designed to prevent threats to human health or the environment from PCB transformers involved in fires.
- On December 21, 1989 (54 *FR* 52716), EPA promulgated the Notification and Manifesting Rule. This rule requires notification of PCB activity, manifesting, commercial storer permitting, and additional record-keeping requirements.

Overview of the PCB Regulatory Program

The regulations governing PCBs are contained in 40 CFR, Part 761. (Also consult Appendix B of this book, which contains a regulatory checklist for PCBs.) These regulations are designed to ensure the proper disposal of PCBs and PCB items while minimizing risk to health and the environment during use, handling, and storage. The regulations, with some exceptions, apply to any substance, mixture, or item with a concentration of 50 ppm PCBs or greater, or contaminated by a source of PCBs 50 ppm or greater. Specific requirements include:

- *Record keeping:* Certain records (e.g., manifests, certificates of disposal, inspection logs) must be kept by facilities using, storing, and disposing of PCBs.
- *Marking:* Items must be clearly identified if they contain PCBs [40 CFR 761.40].
- *Storage:* PCBs and PCB items must be stored in accordance with requirements designed to ensure safe storage prior to disposal [40 CFR 761.65].
- *Disposal:* Except as provided, PCBs and PCB items must be disposed of by high-temperature incineration [40 CFR 761.60 and 761.20(e)].

- *Tracking:* Generators of waste PCBs and PCB items must notify EPA of their activities and must ship all PCB waste with a uniform hazardous waste manifest, and must receive certificates of disposal [54 *FR* 52716, December 21, 1989].

The regulations also address prohibited uses, authorized uses, inspections, distribution in commerce, and spill cleanup (discussed in Chapter 18).

PCB Classifications

Intentionally generated polychlorinated biphenyls (e.g., commercial products) are classified as follows, based on their PCB concentration:

Non-PCB: <50 ppm PCB
PCB-contaminated: between 50 and 500 ppm PCB
PCB: 500 ppm or greater PCB

In addition to the PCB content, classification also is based on the type of equipment. The equipment includes:

- Transformers
- Capacitors
- Hydraulic systems
- Miscellaneous equipment

Reclassification

PCB electrical equipment may be reclassified to PCB-contaminated or non-PCB status [40 CFR 761.30(a)(2)(v)]. Reclassifying involves the draining of all of the existing dielectric fluid, then filling the equipment with non-PCB dielectric fluid. Provided that the dielectric fluid is retested following a minimum of three months' *in-service* use after the date of filling, and it has a PCB concentration of less than 500 ppm or less than 50 ppm (47 *FR* 37354, August 25, 1982), the item may then be reclassified and handled appropriately. The dielectric fluid must attain a minimum temperature of 50 degrees Centigrade at least once during the in-service period.

Transformers

Electrical transformers are often filled with a dielectric liquid that increases the resistance of the unit to arcing and acts as a heat transfer medium, helping to cool the coils. Most transformers are filled with transformer oil, but about 2 to 3 percent of liquid-filled transformers are filled with a chlorinated fire-resistant fluid that meets the definition established in the National Electrical Code for *askarel,** the generic name for nonflammable insulating liquids used in transformers. Prior to 1979, transformer askarel contained 60 to 100 percent PCBs. Askarel transformers were made in a variety of sizes containing from 3 to 3000 gallons of PCB liquid, and they are generally used in hazardous locations where flammability is a concern.

Transformers are presumed to contain 500 ppm or greater PCB unless it is demonstrated otherwise (44 *FR* 31517, May 31, 1979). This demonstration can be accomplished by analysis, identification labels, or manufacturer's documentation. When one is testing for PCBs, there is no required test method. However, the owner is responsible for the integrity of the test.

EPA identified the following four major economic sectors that control most of the PCB transformers in service:

- The industrial sector
- Electric utilities
- Commercial buildings
- Railroads and subways

Industrial Sector

This sector includes metals, chemicals, paper and lumber, mining, automobiles, food, textiles, and glass. PCB transformers are likely to be located in several areas:

- Inside buildings in hazardous locations.
- Near high-voltage electrical equipment generating high temperatures (e.g., metal processing equipment, kilns, and the like).
- In powerhouses that distribute electrical power throughout the facility.

---

*Many transformer manufacturers identified PCB askarel liquid by a trade name. These trade names include Chlorextol, Asbestol, Pyranol, Saf-T-Kuhl, EEC-18, No-Flamol, Inerteen, Nepolin, and Dykanol.

Electrical Utilities

PCB transformers can be found in:

- Distribution substations
- Generating facilities (usually only in hazardous locations)
  - Nuclear facilities
  - Areas near coal conveyors
  - Electrostatic precipitators

Commercial Buildings

PCB transformers are often used inside commercial buildings to meet fire-code restrictions. Most commercial building owners contract the servicing of their transformers to transformer maintenance and repair companies.

Railroads and Subways

PCBs are used in onboard transformers in electric railroad locomotives and self-propelled cars. These transformers reduce the high-voltage current from overhead lines. Subways use PCB transformers, which are typically located underground, to distribute power to subway cars.

Mineral Oil-Filled Transformers

Transformers that have mineral oil as a dielectric are presumed to be PCB-contaminated (between 50 and 500 ppm) unless it is demonstrated otherwise. If testing the mineral oil demonstrates that the fluid has a PCB concentration of 500 ppm or greater, the item is classified as a PCB item (44 *FR* 31517, May 31, 1979). EPA has established a time frame for bringing "newly discovered" mineral-oil transformers into compliance with PCB transformer requirements [40 CFR 761.30(a)(1)(xv)(B) and (C)]. A transformer owner has 7 days from testing to label and, if the transformer is located in or near a commercial building, 30 days to notify the appropriate fire response personnel and building owners of the discovery.

Capacitors

PCBs were used as the dielectric fluid in most capacitors manufactured between 1920 and 1978. All non-PCB capacitors (except large, high-voltage capacitors) manufactured since July 1, 1978, are required to be labeled "NO PCBs" [40 CFR 761.40(g)]. Capacitors are presumed to have a concentration of 500 ppm or greater unless demonstrated otherwise (47 *FR* 37347, August 25, 1982).

Hydraulic Systems

PCBs were widely used by steel manufacturing and die casting plants in hydraulic systems on machines that handled hot metals to reduce fire hazards. Hydraulic systems normally leak several times their capacity each year because the fluid is pressurized to several thousand pounds per square inch and may leak at connections. PCBs may be used in hydraulic systems only at concentrations less than 50 ppm because they are not considered to be totally enclosed [40 CFR 761.30(e)].

Miscellaneous Electrical Equipment

All oil-filled switches, electromagnets, and voltage regulators are presumed to be PCB-contaminated unless demonstrated otherwise. All oil-filled cable, reclosers, and circuit breakers can be assumed to be non-PCB (<50) unless verification shows otherwise (47 *FR* 37353, August 25, 1982).

Batch Testing

Dielectric fluid removed from mineral-oil-filled electrical equipment may be collected in a common container, provided that no other chemical substances are added to the container. This common container option does not allow dilution of the collected oil. Dielectric fluid that is presumed or known to contain at least 50 ppm PCB must not be mixed with mineral oil known or assumed to contain less than 50 ppm PCB. For the purposes of complying with the marking and disposal requirements, representative samples may be taken from either the common containers or the individual electrical equipment to determine the PCB concentration. However, if any PCBs at a concentration of 500 ppm or greater have been added to the container or equipment, the total contents must be considered to have a PCB concentration of 500 ppm or greater [40 CFR 761.60(g)(i)].

PROHIBITIONS

The regulatory programs addressing PCBs in electrical equipment are divided into two major categories: items, processes, and uses that are prohibited and items, processes, and uses that are specifically authorized.

Totally Enclosed Manner

Pursuant to 40 CFR 761.20(a), no person may use any PCB or PCB item regardless of concentration in any manner other than a *totally enclosed manner* within the United States unless specifically authorized to do so by 40 CFR 761.30.

The following activities are considered *totally enclosed:* the distribution in commerce of intact nonleaking electrical equipment, such as transformers, capacitors, electromagnets, voltage regulators, switches, sectionalizers, motor starters, circuit breakers, reclosers, and cable that contain PCBs at any concentration, and the processing and distribution in commerce of PCB equipment containing an intact nonleaking PCB capacitor.

Manufacturing and Importing

No person may manufacture or import PCBs for any use within the United States or manufacture PCBs for export from the United States without an exemption. A petition for an exemption can be granted through the formal rulemaking process. An exemption is not needed to manufacture PCBs made in an "excluded manufacturing process," nor is one needed to import PCBs in concentrations of less than 50 ppm for purposes of disposal [40 CFR 761.20(b)(1) to (b)(2)]. Not included in this ban are PCBs imported from U.S. Territories or U.S. military installations [40 CFR 761.20(b)(1)].

PCBs in concentrations of 50 ppm or greater may not be imported or exported for the purpose of disposal [40 CFR 761.20(b)(2) and 761.20(c)(3)].

Dilution

Dilution to circumvent disposal requirements is prohibited. For example, if *any* amount of PCB fluid (500 ppm or greater) is introduced to PCB-contaminated or non-PCB fluid or equipment, the entire mixture or equipment must be classified, and handled as PCB (i.e., 500 ppm or greater) regardless of the actual level [40 CFR 761.1(b)].

Waste Oil

Waste oil with any detectable levels of PCBs cannot be used as a sealant, coating, pesticide carrier, road oil, rust preventive, or dust control agent [40 CFR 761.20(d)]. All untested waste oil to be burned for energy recovery must be assumed to contain quantifiable (2–49 ppm) levels of PCBs, and may be burned only in "qualified incinerators" as defined in 40 CFR 761.3 [40 CFR 761.20(e)].

AUTHORIZATIONS

The PCB items, processes, and uses described in this section are authorized under the Toxic Substances Control Act.

Transformers

PCB and PCB-contaminated transformers may be used for the remainder of their useful service life, provided that they are intact and nonleaking, except as noted below [40 CFR 761.30(a)]. A PCB transformer that is not in use, but is intended for reuse, is considered an in-service transformer for the purposes of the rule and is authorized for the remainder of its useful service life.

Since October 1, 1985, the use and storage for reuse of PCB transformers that pose an exposure risk to food or feed and the installation of PCB transformers in or near commercial buildings has been prohibited [40 CFR 761.30(a)(1)].

In or Near Commercial Buildings

On July 17, 1985 (50 *FR* 29201), EPA promulgated additional requirements for PCB transformers *in or near commercial buildings,* which means within the interior of, on the roof of, attached to the exterior wall of, in the parking area serving, or within 30 meters of a nonindustrial nonsubstation building [40 CFR 761.3]. Commercial buildings are typically accessible to both members of the general public and employees.

This rule was promulgated in response to the severe potential health and environmental effects caused by PCB transformers involved in fires. These severe effects include the generation of dioxins and furans as a result of the incomplete combustion of PCBs during a fire.

As of October 1, 1990, all network PCB transformers with higher secondary voltages (secondary voltages equal to or greater than 480 volts, including 480/227-volt systems) in or near commercial buildings must have been removed or reclassified to PCB-contaminated or non-PCB. In addition, all radial PCB transformers and lower secondary network PCB transformers (network transformers with secondary voltages below 480 volts) in use in or near commercial buildings must be removed, reclassified, or equipped with electrical protection to avoid PCB transformer failures from sustained high current faults by October 1, 1993 (except for those located in sidewalk vaults), provided that the building owner notified EPA prior to the October 1, 1990, deadline. Current-limiting fuses or other equivalent technology must be used to detect sustained high current faults and provide for complete deenergization immediately upon detection before transformer failure occurs. The installation, setting, and maintenance of current-limiting fuses or other equivalent technology to avoid PCB transformer failures from sustained high current faults must be completed in accordance with good engineering practices [40 CFR 761.30(a)(1)(iv)].

As of October 1, 1990, all radial transformers with higher secondary voltage in use in or near commercial buildings must have been removed, reclassified, or equipped with protection to avoid transformer failures caused by sustained low current faults. Pressure- and temperature-sensitive (or equally effective) devices must be used in these transformers to detect sustained low current faults. Equipment must be disconnected to ensure complete deenergization in the event of a sensed abnormal condition (e.g., an overpressure or overtemperature condition in the transformer) caused by a sustained low current fault. The disconnect equipment must be configured to operate automatically within 30 to 60 seconds of the receipt of a signal indicating an abnormal condition from a sustained low current fault or to allow for manual deenergization from a *manned on-site control center* upon the receipt of an audio or visual signal indicating an abnormal condition caused by a sustained low current fault. If automatic operation is selected, and a circuit breaker is utilized for disconnection, it must also have the capacity to be manually opened if necessary. The detection and deenergization equipment must be properly installed and maintained and set sensitive enough to detect abnormal operations rapidly [40 CFR 761.30(a)(1)(v)(B)].

In addition, as of December 1, 1985, all PCB transformers located in or near commercial buildings must have been registered with building owners and with the fire response personnel with primary jurisdiction [40 CFR 761.30(a)(1)(vi)]. For a PCB transformer(s) located *in* a commercial building, the owner of the transformer must register it with the building owner of record if different. For a PCB transformer(s) located *near* a commercial building, the transformer owner must register it with all owners of buildings located within 30 meters of the PCB transformer(s). In defining *commercial building,* EPA includes residential buildings (e.g., apartments, hotels, dormitories, condominiums) but does not include single family homes (51 *FR* 47243, December 31, 1986). Information that must be provided to building owners and fire response personnel includes, but is not limited to:

- The specific location of the PCB transformer(s).
- The principal constituent of the dielectric fluid in the transformer(s) (e.g., PCBs, mineral oil, chlorobenzenes).
- The type of transformer installation (e.g., 208/120-volt network, 208/ 120-volt radial, 208-volt network, 480-volt network, 480/277-volt network, 480-volt radial, 480/277-volt radial).
- The name and telephone number of the person to contact in the event of a fire involving a PCB transformer.

Combustible materials including, but not limited to, paints, solvents, plastics, paper, and sawdust must not be stored within a PCB transformer enclosure, within 5 meters of a PCB enclosure, or within 5 meters of a PCB transformer [40 CFR 761.30(a)(1)(viii)].

If a PCB transformer is involved in a fire-related incident, the owner or the operator of the transformer must immediately report the incident to the National Response Center (800-424-8802). A *fire-related incident* is defined as any incident involving a PCB transformer that involves the generation of sufficient heat and/or pressure (by any source) to result in the violent or nonviolent rupture of a PCB transformer and the release of PCBs. The owner or the operator also must take measures as soon as it is practically and safely possible to contain and control any potential releases of PCBs and incomplete combustion product into water [40 CFR 761.30(a)(1)(xi)]. These measures should include:

- The blocking of all floor drains in the vicinity of the transformer.
- The containment of water run-off.
- The control and treatment (prior to release) of any water used in subsequent cleanup operations.

Resale

Transformers may be sold, provided that they were originally purchased or sold for purposes other than resale before July 1, 1979. In addition, the transformer must be intact, nonleaking, marked as a PCB transformer, and in working condition [40 CFR 761.20(c)(1)].

Servicing

PCB transformers are serviced periodically and repaired when malfunctioning. Servicing includes:

- Sampling of the fluid to test its dielectric strength.
- "Topping off" with additional dielectric fluid.
- Replacement of gaskets, bushings, and insulators that may involve partial draining of the transformer.
- Removal and filtering of the PCB liquid and refilling of the unit.
- Removal of the PCB liquid and its replacement with non-PCB fluid.

Any PCB transformer being serviced or rebuilt cannot have its core removed at any time; however, it may be "topped off" with dielectric fluid of any concentration. PCB-contaminated transformers can have their core removed but can have only dielectric fluid with less than 500 ppm PCB added. If dielectric fluid containing PCBs above 500 ppm is introduced to a PCB-contaminated or non-PCB transformer, the transformer must be classified as a PCB transformer regardless of the actual PCB concentration. PCBs removed from any servicing activity must be captured and either reused as dielectric fluid or disposed of in accordance with 40 CFR 761.60. Any dielectric fluid containing PCBs at concentrations of 50 ppm or greater and used for servicing transformers must be stored in accordance with the storage for disposal requirements of 40 CFR 761.65, addressed in the storage section of this chapter [40 CFR 761.30(a)(2)].

Leaks

If a PCB transformer is found to have a leak that results in *any* quantity of PCBs running off or about to run off its external surface, the transformer must be repaired or replaced to eliminate the source of the leak.

PCB waste resulting from the cleanup of spills or leaks must be stored and disposed of in accordance with 40 CFR 761.60(a) [47 *FR* 37347, August 25, 1982 and 40 CFR 761.60(d)].

Capacitors

PCBs at any concentrations may be used in capacitors for the remainder of their useful lives if the capacitors are intact and nonleaking, except for the following instances that involve special restrictions [40 CFR 761.30(l)].

Food and Feed

Large capacitors that are used or stored for reuse and pose an exposure risk to food or feed were prohibited after October 1, 1988 [40 CFR 761.30(l)(1)(i)].

In evaluating the *exposure risk* from a capacitor, it is best to consider a hypothetical situation in which PCBs are discharged in any way from the capacitor, such as through a leak or a rupture. Assuming that such a discharge occurs, thereby releasing all or a portion of the contained PCBs, and considering the capacitor's location and any relevant factors, it must be determined whether contact between PCBs and food or feed is possible. PCB items that are located directly adjacent to, or above, food or feed products are presumed to pose an exposure risk to food or feed unless there is some type of secondary containment, or other physical structure, that prevents discharges of PCBs from contaminating food or feed.

Restricted Access

Large capacitors can be used after October 1, 1988, only if they are located at a restricted access electrical substation or in a restricted access indoor location that has adequate roof, walls, and floor to contain any release of PCBs within the indoor location [40 CFR 761.30(l)(1)(ii)]. A *restricted access* electrical substation is an outdoor fenced or walled-in facility that restricts public access and is used in the transmission or distribution of electrical power (47 *FR* 37349, August 25, 1982).

Courtesy of Lab Safety Supply, Inc., Janesville, WI.

Figure 17-1. PCB Label

MARKING

The following items *must* be marked with an appropriate PCB label, as depicted in Figure 17-1. The label must be placed on the exterior of the PCB item or vehicle in a place that can be easily seen and read by anyone inspecting or servicing it [40 CFR 761.40]. It is necessary to mark:

- All PCB transformers (PCB-contaminated transformers are not required to be marked).
- All large PCB capacitors.
- Equipment containing a PCB transformer or a PCB large high-voltage capacitor.
- All containers used to store PCB items.

- All access modes to PCB transformer locations in or near commercial buildings.
- PCB storage areas.
- Any transport vehicle, carrying one or more PCB transformers *or* 99.4 pounds of PCB liquid greater than 50 ppm, which must be marked on all four sides.
- Electrical motors using PCB coolants.
- Hydraulic systems using PCB hydraulic fluid.
- Heat transfer systems using PCBs.

Note: Although small PCB capacitors themselves were not required to be labeled with a PCB label as of January 1, 1979, all equipment containing small capacitors must be marked at the time of manufacture with the statement "This equipment contains PCB capacitors" [40 CFR 761.40(d)].

INSPECTION

A visual inspection of certain PCB transformers in use, or stored for reuse, must be conducted at least once every three months, except as noted below. These inspections may take place at any time during the three-month time periods January–March, April–June, July–September, and October–December, provided that there is a minimum of 30 days between inspections. The visual inspection must include observations for any leaks on or around the transformer. In-service PCB-contaminated transformers require no inspection. Transformers and their required inspections are as follows:

- In-service transformers with a PCB content of more than 60,000 ppm require a quarterly inspection.
- In-service transformers with a PCB content of between 500 and 60,000 ppm require only an annual inspection.
- In-service transformers with a PCB content of more than 60,000 ppm but with 100 percent secondary containment require only an annual inspection.

Records of a transformer's inspection and maintenance history must be prepared, and must be kept for at least three years after disposal of the transformer. These records must contain the following information:

- The name of the person conducting the inspection.
- The date of each visual inspection and the date when any leak was discovered.

- The transformer's location.
- The location of any leaks.
- An estimate of the amount of any dielectric fluid released from the leak.
- The date and description of any cleanup, containment, replacement, or repair performed on the transformer.
- The results of any containment and daily inspection required for uncorrected active leaks.

STORAGE

Storage Area Requirements

PCB items destined for disposal must be stored in an area that complies with 40 CFR 761.65(b). The requirements for the storage area are as follows:

- The roof and walls must be adequate for protection from precipitation.
- An adequate floor is required, with continuous curbing at a minimum height of 6 inches. The floor and curbing must provide containment for at least 25 percent of the total internal volume of all stored PCB items or two times the internal volume of the largest PCB item, whichever is greater.
- The storage area cannot have drain valves, floor drains, expansion joints, sewer lines, or other openings that could permit liquids to flow from the curbed area.
- The floor must be made of a smooth and impervious material (e.g., Portland cement, steel).
- The storage area cannot be located within a 100-year floodplain.

Any container used for the storage of PCBs must comply with the Shipping Container Specification System under the Department of Transportation (DOT). Liquid PCBs must be stored in Specification 5, 5B, 6D with 2S, 6D with 2SL, or 17E containers. Nonliquid PCBs must be stored in Specification 5, 5B, or 17C containers [40 CFR 761.65(c)(6)].

Inspections during Storage

All PCB items in storage must be checked for leaks at least once every 30 days [40 CFR 761.65(c)(5)]. Any leaking PCB items and their contents must be immediately transferred to properly marked nonleaking containers. Any spilled or leaked materials must be immediately cleaned up in accordance with the PCB Spill Cleanup Policy (see Chapter 18) and must be disposed of in accordance with 40 CFR 761.60(a)(4).

Temporary Storage

Certain PCB items may be stored temporarily in an area that does not comply with the storage requirements of 40 CFR 761.65(b), for up to 30 days from the date of their removal from service, provided that a notation is attached to the PCB item indicating the date when the item was removed from service, and the storage area is marked with a PCB mark [40 CFR 761.65(c)(1)]. The PCB items are:

- Nonleaking PCB articles and equipment.
- Leaking PCB articles and PCB equipment if the items are placed in a nonleaking PCB container that contains sufficient sorbent materials to absorb any liquid PCBs remaining in the PCB items.
- PCB containers holding nonliquid PCBs such as contaminated soil, rags, and debris.
- PCB containers containing liquid PCBs at a concentration between 50 and 500 ppm, provided that a Spill Prevention, Control, and Countermeasure Plan (SPCC) has been prepared for the temporary storage area in accordance with 40 CFR Part 112. In addition, each container must bear a notation that the PCBs in the drum do not exceed a concentration of 500 ppm.

Nonleaking and structurally undamaged PCB large high-voltage capacitors and PCB-contaminated electrical equipment that have not been drained of free-flowing dielectric fluid may be stored beyond 30 days on pallets next to a PCB storage area that complies with the requirements of 40 CFR 761.65(b), if the storage area has immediately available unfilled storage space equal to 10 percent of the volume of capacitors and equipment stored outside of the storage area. The capacitors and equipment temporarily stored outside of the storage area must be checked for leaks at least weekly [40 CFR 761.65(c)(2)]. PCB-contaminated electrical equipment that has all free-flowing dielectric fluid removed is no longer regulated under TSCA.

Bulk Storage

Large containers, such as storage tanks, can be used to store bulk PCB liquids for up to one year. These storage tanks must meet the design and construction standards adopted by the Occupational Safety and Health Administration (OSHA) contained in 29 CFR 1910.106 for flammable and combustible liquids. In addition, bulk storage facilities must have an SPCC plan similar to the plans required for oil spill prevention [40 CFR 761.65(c)(7)].

For each batch of PCBs stored in bulk, records must be maintained that indicate the exact quantity of the batch and the date when the batch was added to the container. The record also must include the date, quantity, and disposition of any PCBs removed from the container [40 CFR 761.65(c)(8)].

Storage Time Limits

In accordance with 40 CFR 761.65(a), all PCB items, articles, or containers must be *disposed* of within one year of the date when they were placed into storage. Because the one-year storage deadline is applicable to the generator and disposal facility, EPA has established policy (48 *FR* 52304, November 17, 1983) concerning the appropriate storage time-limits for the generator and disposal facility. This policy states that a generator has 275 days (from the date it went into storage) to remove the PCB item and deliver it to the disposal facility. The disposal facility has 90 days (from the date it received the PCB item) to dispose of the PCB item. If the one-year storage limit is violated, the party that exceeds his or her time limit (i.e., 275 days for the generator or 90 days for the disposer) is in violation. For example, a PCB transformer was put into storage on July 1, 1991, but was not disposed of until September 1, 1992. The generator, however, sent the transformer in a timely fashion, and it was received by the disposer on January 1, 1992. In this case, the disposer was in violation for having exceeded the 90-day limit, whereas the generator was in compliance with the 275-day limit.

Every PCB item that is destined for disposal must have the date when the item was taken out of service marked on it. The storage area must be arranged and managed so that PCB items can be located by the date when they entered storage [40 CFR 761.65(c)(8)].

An item being stored for reuse can be stored indefinitely if it is intact, nonleaking, and in working order. Any PCB item being stored for reuse is subject to all in-use requirements, such as quarterly inspections and marking.

Laboratories

Laboratories storing samples are conditionally exempt from the notification and approval requirements for commercial storers provided that they comply with 40 CFR 761.65(b)(1)(i) through (b)(1)(iv). A *laboratory* is defined in 40 CFR 761.3 as a facility that analyzes PCBs and is unaffiliated with any entity whose activities involve PCBs.

DISPOSAL OF PCBs

Disposal Facilities

All disposal facilities, except for high-efficiency boilers, must possess a permit issued under the Toxic Substances Control Act if they dispose of PCBs in concentrations at or above 50 ppm. The EPA Regional Administrator issues permits to facilities operating within regional boundaries. Mobile units that will be operating in more than one EPA region must obtain an operating permit from the Assistant Administrator for the Office of Pesticides and Toxic Substances located in Washington, DC.

The technical requirements for the disposal units are not addressed in this book because of their complexity and because they affect only a very small part of the regulated community. The requirements, however, can be found in 40 CFR 761.70 for incinerators, 40 CFR 761.60(a)(2)(iii) for high-efficiency boilers, and 40 CFR 761.75 for landfills.

Disposal Requirements for PCB Items

Transformers

There are two options for the disposal of PCB transformers. The first option permits the transformer and the PCB dielectric fluid to be burned together in an approved high-temperature incinerator. With the second option, all of the free-flowing dielectric fluid is removed from the transformer. The drained transformer carcass must then be filled with a specified solvent (e.g., xylene, toluene, kerosene) for 18 hours, then drained again. The original PCB dielectric fluid and the solvent used to decontaminate the carcass must be incinerated (if the solvent also is a hazardous waste, the incinerator also must be authorized under RCRA), and the carcass must be disposed of in a TSCA-permitted landfill [40 CFR 761.60(b)(l)].

PCB-Contaminated Transformers

All free-flowing PCB-contaminated dielectric fluid must be removed. This fluid must either be incinerated, burned in a high-efficiency boiler, disposed of in a landfill (provided that the dielectric is nonignitable), or disposed of in an alternatively approved manner by EPA. The carcass, provided that all free-flowing liquid is removed, is no longer regulated [40 CFR 761.60(b)(4)].

Capacitors

Large capacitors must be incinerated or disposed of by any other method that EPA has specifically permitted under TSCA [40 CFR 761.60(b)(2)].

Intact and nonleaking small capacitors can be disposed of in a municipal landfill (subject to state rules), except for those of PCB capacitor manufacturers or manufacturers of equipment containing capacitors (such as telephone booths, light fixtures) [40 CFR 761.60(b)(2)(ii)]. Manufacturers must dispose of small capacitors in TSCA-permitted incinerators [40 CFR 761.60(b)(2)]. Other persons with leaking small capacitors have the option of either land disposal in a TSCA landfill or incineration (March 4, 1985, memorandum from John Moore, Assistant Administrator, Office of Pesticide and Toxic Substances to Gary O'Neal, Director of Air and Toxics, Region X).

Note: Consult Sections 104, 106, and 107 of Superfund (Chapter 13 in this book) for potential liabilities regarding incurred cleanup costs. If *any* PCB article releases PCB (a CERCLA hazardous substance) into the environment, it may warrant a Superfund response that the generator will be responsible for the cleanup. Therefore, major consequences can arise from disposing of small capacitors in a nonsecured manner.

Containers

All PCB containers must be incinerated or decontaminated, after which the containers can be disposed of or reused [40 CFR 761.60(c)]. Any solvent may be used for decontamination if the solubility of the PCBs in the solvent is 5 percent or more by weight. Each rinse must use a volume of the solvent equal to approximately 10 percent of the container capacity. The solvent may be reused until it contains 50 ppm PCB. The solvent must be disposed of as a PCB liquid [40 CFR 761.79(a)]. The solvents recommended for decontamination of PCB containers are xylene, toluene, and kerosene (44 *FR* 31546, May 31, 1979).

Containers used to contain only PCBs at a concentration less than 500 ppm can be disposed of as municipal solid waste, provided that the PCBs were in a liquid state, the container is first drained of all liquid, and the liquid is disposed of accordingly.

Liquids

Liquids containing PCBs at a concentration of 500 ppm or greater must be incinerated [40 CFR 761.60(a)]. Liquids containing PCBs at concentrations less than 500 ppm may be incinerated, burned in a high-efficiency boiler, or disposed of in a TSCA-approved landfill, provided that the waste is nonignitable, and such waste is pretreated and/or stabilized to eliminate the presence of free liquids prior to final disposal [40 CFR 761.60(a)(2) for mineral oil and 40 CFR 761.60(a)(3) for non-mineral oil].

Containerized liquids with PCB concentrations of less than 500 ppm may be incinerated or disposed of in an approved landfill. Containers that are landfilled must be surrounded by an amount of inert sorbent material capable of absorbing all of the liquid contents of the container (such as an overpack) [40 CFR 761.75(b)(8)].

Land Disposal Restrictions

The Hazardous and Solid Waste Amendments established the land disposal restrictions for certain RCRA hazardous wastes. Phase II of those restrictions includes the ban on disposing of liquid PCBs at concentrations greater than or equal to 50 ppm in or on the land. However, for a waste containing PCBs in concentrations at or above 50 ppm to be subject to the RCRA land disposal ban, the PCBs must either be mixed with a RCRA-listed hazardous waste (decontamination solvent) or exhibit a characteristic of hazardous waste, as only those wastes that are identified as hazardous are subject to RCRA. Also, the waste must be a liquid waste as determined by the paint filter test.

Soil and Debris

Soil, rags, absorbents, dredge materials, municipal sewage treatment sludges, and debris that contain PCBs at concentrations of 50 ppm or greater may be disposed of in either a TSCA landfill or an incinerator. However, processing liquid PCBs into nonliquid forms to circumvent the incineration requirements is prohibited [40 CFR 761.60(a)(4) and (a)(5)].

Alternative Disposal Methods

Any alternative method of disposal may be approved by EPA, provided that the method has a destruction efficiency that is similar to the other methods, and it is protective of human health and the environment. Current examples of alternative disposal methods include solvent extraction, dechlorination, and biodegradation [40 CFR 761.60(e)].

Note: This is a major difference between RCRA and TSCA. Whereas RCRA stipulates the disposal methods with little or no flexibility, TSCA sets performance standards to foster the development of alternative disposal methods.

TRACKING

EPA established comprehensive tracking requirements for shipments of PCB wastes on December 21, 1989 (54 *FR* 52716). These regulations were established to track shipments of PCB waste, similarly to the RCRA hazardous waste program, from the cradle to the grave. The requirements for tracking include:

- Notification of PCB waste activity
- EPA identification number
- Manifest system
- One-year exception reporting
- Certificate of disposal
- Record keeping

Notification of PCB Waste Activity

As of February 5, 1990, certain generators and all transporters, commercial storers, and disposers of PCB waste must notify EPA of their activities [40 CFR 761.205(a)]. *PCB waste* means those PCBs and PCB items that are subject to the disposal requirements of 40 CFR 761.60. That is, PCBs and PCB items become subject to the disposal requirements when it has been determined that they no longer serve their intended purpose and are to be disposed of. Items unregulated for disposal, such as intact, nonleaking small capacitors and drained PCB-contaminated equipment, are not subject to the disposal requirements of 40 CFR 761.60 and, therefore, are not included in the definition of PCB waste.

It is important to note that non-exempt generators, commercial storers, transporters, and disposers of PCB waste who begins PCB waste activities after February 5, 1990, must, prior to handling any PCB waste, notify EPA and obtain an EPA identification number. In the case of disposers and commercial storers of PCB waste, new entrants into the regulated community are required to obtain an EPA identification number and approval before they commence disposal or storage operations [54 *FR* 52723, December 21, 1989].

Generators

Only generators who maintain PCB storage areas subject to the 40 CFR 761.65(b) and (c)(7) storage facility standards are required to notify EPA of PCB waste activities. Generators who do not maintain 761.65(b) or (c)(7) storage areas are exempt from the requirements to notify EPA and obtain EPA identification numbers. Thus persons who store PCB waste temporarily per 40 CFR 761.65(c)(1) are exempt from notification. Because they are not, however, excluded from manifest requirements, these generators must use the generic identification number "40 CFR PART 761" on their manifests [40 CFR 761.205(c)(l)].

Facilities That Have Previously Notified under RCRA

In situations where facilities have previously been issued an EPA identification number for hazardous waste activities under RCRA, the owner or the operator can indicate on Item II of EPA form 7710-53 the facility's RCRA identification number. After verification, EPA will use the existing RCRA number for TSCA purposes. It is important to note that even though a facility may already have an EPA identification number, a person engaged in PCB waste activities must still give notification of these activities [40 CFR 761.205(b)]. Generators exempt from TSCA notification, however, may elect to use their previously issued RCRA identification number without having to notify [40 CFR 761.205(c)(1)].

EPA Identification Number

As of June 4, 1990, generators of PCB waste must not process, store, offer for transport, transport, or dispose of PCBs without having an EPA identification number. In addition, transporters, commercial storers, and disposers must not accept PCB waste without an EPA identification number. An EPA identification number is obtained by submitting EPA form 7710-53, Notification of PCB Waste Activity, as described above [40 CFR 761.202]. After notification and verification of the information, persons will be issued a unique 12-digit EPA identification number. The notification form must be sent to:

Chief, Chemical Regulations Branch, Room NE-117
Office of Toxic Substances (TS-798)
U.S. Environmental Protection Agency
401 M St., SW
Washington, DC 20460

Manifest System

A generator who transports or offers for transportation PCB waste for off-site commercial storage or disposal must use a uniform hazardous waste manifest, EPA Form 8700-22 [40 CFR 761.207(a)].

Any person shipping PCB waste to a state (the consignment state) that supplies and requires use of its manifest must use that state's manifest. If the consignment state does not require use of its own manifest, and the state in which the PCB waste was generated (the generator state) supplies and requires the use of its manifest, the person shipping the PCB waste must use the generator state's manifest. If both states require use of their manifests, the manifest of the consignment state must be used. If neither the consignment state nor the generator state requires use of its own manifest, the shipper can use a manifest from any source [40 CFR 761.207(b)–(f)].

The generator must:

- Sign the manifest certification by hand.
- Obtain the handwritten signature of the initial transporter and the date of acceptance on the manifest.
- Retain one copy in its records.
- Give to the transporter the remaining copies of the manifest, which will accompany the shipment of PCB waste.

40 CFR 761.208(a)(4) requires generators who use independent transporters to ship waste to a storage or disposal facility to confirm, by telephone or by other means of confirmation agreed to by both parties, that the commercial storer or disposer actually received the manifested waste.

Samples

A sample is exempt [40 CFR 761.65(i)] from the manifesting requirements when:

- It is being transported to the laboratory for the purposes of testing or from the laboratory after being tested.
- It is being stored by the sample collector before being transported to a laboratory, stored in a laboratory before testing, stored by a laboratory after testing but before being returned to the sample collector, or stored because of a court case or enforcement action.

In addition, for a sample to qualify for such an exemption, while being transported to or from the laboratory, it is necessary for sample handlers to:

- Comply with applicable DOT regulations [49 CFR 173.345] or U.S. Postal Regulations [49 CFR 652.2 and 652.3].
- See that the sample collector's name, mailing address, and telephone number accompany the sample.
- See that the laboratory's name, address, and telephone number accompanied the manifest.
- See that the quantity, date or shipment, and description of the sample are contained in the shipment.
- Package the sample so that it does not leak, spill, or vaporize from its packaging.

When the concentration of the PCB sample has been determined, and its use terminated, the sample must be properly disposed of [40 CFR 761.65(i)(4)].

Manifest Exception Reporting

If the generator has not received the hand-signed manifest within 35 days after the initial transporter accepted the PCB waste, the generator must contact the disposer or commercial storer to determine whether the PCB waste has actually been received [40 CFR 761.215(a)]. If the PCB waste has not been received, the generator must contact the transporter(s) to determine the whereabouts of the PCB waste. If the generator has not received a hand-signed manifest from an EPA-approved facility within ten days from the date of contacting the transporter(s), the generator must submit an exception report to the EPA Regional Administrator for the region in which the generator is located.

The exception report must contain both of the following [40 CFR 761.215(b)]:

- A legible copy of the manifest of concern.
- A cover letter signed by the generator describing the efforts taken to locate the missing shipment.

One-Year Exception Reporting

Pursuant to 40 CFR 761.65(a) of the TSCA storage rules for PCB waste, the storage of PCB waste prior to disposal is limited to one year from removal of service. Under EPA policy, as discussed earlier, the one-year storage limit is allocated between the initial generator (three months) and the approved disposal facility (nine months). When either party exceeds its respective time limit, a *one-year exception report* must be filed with the appropriate EPA Regional Administrator.

The one-year exception report must include a legible copy of a manifest or other written communication relevant to the transfer and disposal of the affected PCBs or PCB item. In addition, a cover letter signed by the submitter also must be included, describing:

- The date(s) when the PCBs or the PCB item was removed from service for disposal.
- The date(s) when the affected PCBs or PCB item was received by the submitter of the report, if applicable.
- The date(s) when the affected PCBs or PCB item was transferred to a designated disposal facility.
- The identity of the transporter, commercial storer, or disposers known to be involved in the transaction.
- The reason, if known, for the delay in bringing about the disposal of the affected PCBs or PCB item within the one-year time limit.

Certificate of Disposal

The owner or the operator of a disposal facility that accepts a PCB waste shipment must prepare a certificate of disposal for that shipment [40 CFR 761.218(a)]. The certificate must include:

- The identity of the disposal facility, by name, address, and EPA identification number.
- The identity of the PCB waste, including reference to the manifest number.
- A statement certifying that disposal has occurred, including the date of disposal and the process employed.
- The following certification statement:

> Under civil and criminal penalties of law for the making or submission of false or fraudulent statements or representations (18 U.S.C. 1001 and 15 U.S.C. 2615), I certify that the information contained in or accompanying this document is true, accurate, and complete. As to the identified

section(s) of this document for which I cannot personally verify truth and accuracy, I certify as the company official having supervisory responsibility for the persons who, acting under my direct instructions, made the verification that this information is true, accurate, and complete.

The certificate of disposal must be sent to the generator within 30 days of the date of disposal [40 CFR 761.218(b)]. The disposer, the commercial storer, and the generator must keep a copy of each certificate as part of their facility records [40 CFR 761.218(c) and (d)].

Record Keeping

Each owner or operator of a facility only using or storing [i.e., commercial storers and disposal facilities must comply with the record-keeping requirements contained in 40 CFR 761.180(b) and (c)] at one time at least 45 kg (99.4 lb) of PCBs contained in PCB containers, one or more PCB transformers, or 50 or more PCB large high- or low-voltage capacitors must develop and maintain records at the facility on the disposition of the PCBs and PCB items [40 CFR 761.180(a)]. An owner or an operator must prepare and maintain *annual records*. An owner or an operator also must prepare a written *annual document log* prepared for each facility by July 1 covering the previous calendar year (January through December). Annual documents are a yearly summary denoting the handling and disposition of PCBs dealt with during the previous year. The annual document log does not have to be submitted unless requested by EPA. An owner or an operator of multiple facilities may maintain the records and annual documents at one designated facility that is normally occupied for at least eight hours a day, provided that the identity of the designated facility is available at each facility using or storing PCBs and PCB items.

The following information must be included in the *annual records:*

- All signed manifests produced during the previous year.
- All certificates of disposal received during the previous year.

The following information must be included in the *annual document log:*

- The name, address, and EPA identification number of the facility and the calendar year being reported.
- The unique manifest number of every manifest generated by the facility during the calendar year. The following information from each manifest also must be included (and also must be kept on

unmanifested waste that may be stored at the facility, and on waste received from or shipped to a facility owned or operated by the same operator [40 CFR 761.180(a)(2)(ii) and (vii)]):

- For *bulk PCB waste* (e.g., tanker or truck), its weight in kilograms, the first date when it was removed from service for disposal, the date when it was placed into transport for off-site storage or disposal, and the date of disposal.
- The serial number or other means of identifying each *PCB article,* the weight in kilograms of the PCB waste in each transformer or capacitor, the date when it was removed from service for disposal, the date when it was placed in transport for off-site storage or disposal, and the date of disposal.
- A unique number identifying each *PCB container,* a description of the contents of each PCB container (e.g., liquid, soil, and cleanup debris) including the total weight of the material in kilograms in each PCB container, the first date when material was placed in each PCB container for disposal, the date when each container was placed in transport for off-site storage or disposal, and the date of disposal.
- A unique number identifying each *PCB article container,* a description of the contents of each PCB article container (e.g., capacitors, electric motors, pumps) including the total weight in kilograms of the contents of each PCB article container, the first date when a PCB article was placed in each PCB article container for disposal, the total weight of the PCB articles in kilograms in each PCB article container, the date when the PCB article container was placed in transport for off-site storage or disposal, and the date of disposal.

• A record of each telephone call, or other means of verification agreed upon by both parties, made to each designated commercial storer or designated disposer to confirm receipt of PCB waste transported by an independent transporter, as required by 40 CFR 761.208(a)(4).

• The total quantities (in kilograms) and number of PCB items (e.g., transformers, capacitors) and PCBs remaining in service at the end of each calendar year.

Weight Calculations

The most accurate way to calculate the weight of the PCBs in PCB items is to have the dielectric analyzed by a laboratory. However, if the exact weight of the dielectric fluid is unknown, assumptions about its weight may be used. As a general rule, Aroclor fluids weigh approximately 12 pounds per gallon, mineral oil weighs approximately 8 pounds per gallon, and dielectric fluid from capacitors weighs approximately 14 pounds per gallon [EPA regulatory interpretation letter from Glen Kuntz, Office of Toxic Substances, Washington, DC to Moorehead Electrical Machinery Company, 1981 (date unspecified)]. In addition, regardless of the PCB concentration, the weight of the PCBs in a liquid may be reported as the weight of the fluid itself.

Record Retention

The annual document must be maintained for at least three years after the facility ceases using or storing PCBs and PCB items in the prescribed quantities. Annual records, manifests, and certificates of disposal also must be maintained for three years [40 CFR 761.180(a)].

In addition to the above-mentioned record-keeping requirements, records of inspections and maintenance history must be prepared and maintained for PCB transformers for at least three years after the disposal of the transformer [40 CFR 761.30(a)(xii)].

TSCA ENFORCEMENT PROVISIONS

Enforcement Overview

Under the authority of TSCA, EPA can inspect any establishment where *chemical substances* are manufactured, processed, imported to, stored, or held before or after their distribution in commerce. The term chemical substance, under TSCA, includes PCBs. No inspection can include financial, sales, pricing, personnel, or research data, unless specified in an inspection notice. EPA can, however, subpoena witnesses, documents, and other information as necessary to carry out TSCA.

Civil actions concerning violations of or lack of compliance with TSCA may be brought to a U.S. district court to restrain or compel the taking of an action. Any chemical substance or mixture, including PCBs that were manufactured, processed, or distributed in commerce in violation of TSCA, may be subject to seizure.

Specific enforcement strategies for implementing TSCA regulations have been developed by EPA. These strategies identify and rank possible violations of a particular regulation, identify the tools available for compliance monitoring and how they will be used, provide a formula for determining the application of inspection resources, and establish policy for determining civil penalties under the regulation. This policy is known as the *TSCA Civil Penalty Policy* (March 10, 1980). In addition, on April 9, 1990, EPA issued the *PCB Penalty Policy,* which is used to determine penalties for violations of the PCB rules in conjunction with the *TSCA Civil Penalty Policy.*

Citizen Suits

Under Section 21 of TSCA, any person may bring a civil suit to restrain a violation of TSCA by any party or to compel EPA to perform any nondiscretionary duty required by this law. In addition, any person may petition EPA to issue, amend, or repeal a rule under the testing, reporting, or restriction sections of TSCA. EPA has 90 days to respond to a petition. If no action is taken or a petition is denied, the party has the opportunity for judicial review in a U.S. district court. In both civil suits and citizens' petitions, the court may award reasonable legal costs and attorneys' fees, if appropriate.

Enforcement Provisions

Civil and Criminal Penalties

Any person who fails or refuses to comply with any requirement under TSCA may be subject to a civil penalty of up to $25,000 per day per violation. Persons who knowingly or willfully violate the law, in addition to any civil penalties, may be fined up to $25,000 for each day of violation, imprisoned for up to one year, or both.

Imminent Hazard

Although it has not been used to date, EPA may issue an Imminent Hazard Order under Section 7 of TSCA. An imminent hazard exists when a chemical substance or mixture *presents an imminent and unreasonable risk of serious or widespread injury to health or the environment.* When such a condition exists, EPA is authorized to initiate an action in a U.S. district court. Remedies to an imminent hazard may include seizure, recall, replacement, and notification of the affected population.

Chapter 18

PCB Spill Cleanup Requirements

EPA has established a national PCB spill cleanup policy applicable to spills of PCBs at concentrations of 50 ppm or greater. This chapter describes that policy, as well as spill reporting requirements for PCBs in addition to those addressed in Chapter 12.

INTRODUCTION

On April 2, 1987, EPA promulgated (52 *FR* 10688) its new National PCB Spill Cleanup Policy. This policy established criteria that EPA uses in determining the adequacy of spill cleanup involving materials containing PCBs at concentrations of 50 ppm or greater.

EPA considers intentional as well as unintentional spills, leaks, and other uncontrolled discharges of PCBs at concentrations of 50 ppm or greater to be improper disposal of PCBs [40 CFR 761.60(d)(1)]. The term *spill* means spills, leaks, or other uncontrolled discharges of PCBs for which the release results in any quantity of PCBs running off or about to run off the surface of the equipment or other PCB source, as well as the contamination resulting from those releases [40 CFR 761.123]. When PCBs are improperly disposed of as a result of a spill of material containing 50 ppm or greater, EPA has the authority under Section 17 of TSCA, as well as under Sections 104, 106, and 107 of Superfund (because PCBs are a hazardous substance), to compel persons to take actions to rectify damages or clean up contamination resulting from the spill.

Previously, EPA stated (47 *FR* 37354, August 25, 1982) that it would not charge a party with a disposal violation if the responsible party could show that the spill, leak, or uncontrolled discharge occurred during the authorized use of electrical equipment, and that adequate cleanup measures were initiated within 48 hours. The new TSCA PCB Spill Cleanup Policy has not changed the first part of this policy in regard to citing a facility for a disposal violation. However, EPA has changed the action-initiation time frames used for purposes of complying with the policy, as discussed later in this chapter.

Before the promulgation of the new TSCA cleanup policy, persons responsible for a spill were required to contact the appropriate EPA Regional PCB Coordinator for a determination of adequate cleanup levels and procedures. The result was inconsistent cleanup policies, depending on the region; so EPA issued the policy to form a nationally consistent PCB Spill Cleanup Policy. However, it is strongly recommended that if a spill containing PCBs in concentrations greater than 50 ppm occurs, the appropriate EPA Regional PCB Coordinator should be consulted (see Appendix G of this book). The reason for this recommendation is that the new policy is extremely complex and allows for little flexibility in cleanup procedures, but the EPA regional office has the authority to deviate from the policy in specific instances [40 CFR 761.120(c)]. Thus, by contacting the EPA Regional PCB Coordinator, one can mitigate the complexity of the policy, obtain specific information as it applies to a particular spill situation, and reduce one's potential liabilities by following EPA's recommendation.

Compliance with the Policy

Although a spill containing PCBs of 50 ppm or greater concentration is considered improper disposal, this policy establishes requirements that EPA considers to ensure adequate cleanup of spilled PCBs. Cleanup in accordance with this policy means compliance with its procedural as well as numerical requirements [40 CFR 761.135]. Compliance with the policy creates a presumption against both enforcement action for penalties and the need for further cleanup under TSCA. EPA does reserve the right, however, to initiate appropriate action to compel cleanup if, upon review of the records of cleanup or sampling following cleanup, EPA finds that the decontamination levels in the policy have not been achieved. EPA also reserves the right to seek penalties if it is believed that the responsible party has not made a good-faith effort to comply with all provisions of the policy, such as prompt notification of a spill when required [40 CFR 761.120(b)].

Applicability

This policy is applicable to any spill of material containing PCBs of 50 ppm or greater concentration occurring after the effective date of the policy, May 4, 1987. Spills that occurred before the effective date of this policy are not covered. Spills that occurred before the effective date but were discovered after it are to be cleaned up to requirements established at the discretion of the EPA regional office [40 CFR 761.120(a)]. Other spills that are not subject to this policy, and that should be addressed by EPA regional offices, include spills directly into surface water, drinking water, sewers, grazing lands, and vegetable gardens. EPA retains the authority [40 CFR 761.135] to require additional, more stringent, less stringent, or alternative decontamination procedures for any spill that warrants such action, based on a finding by the EPA Regional Administrator that further cleanup is necessary to prevent unreasonable risk, or if there is a finding that the cleanup standards are unwarranted because of risk-mitigating factors, impracticable compliance, or cost-prohibitive factors. The EPA Regional Administrator must notify the Director of the Office of Toxic Substances in Washington, DC to allow for disapproval of the Regional Administrator's finding.

PCB SPILL REPORTING REQUIREMENTS

Any spill of material containing PCBs of 50 ppm or greater concentration that directly discharges into surface water, sewers, drinking-water supplies, grazing land, or vegetable gardens must be reported as soon as possible after discovery, but in no case later than 24 hours after discovery. This notification is to be directed to the appropriate EPA Regional PCB Coordinator [40 CFR 761.125(a)(1)(i)–(ii)].

All spills involving 10 pounds or more of pure PCBs by weight from materials containing PCBs of 50 ppm or greater concentration, and not covered in the above paragraph, must be reported to the appropriate EPA Regional PCB Coordinator [40 CFR 761.125(a)(1)(iii)]. The National Response Center also must be notified as required by Section 103 of Superfund whenever a spill of one pound or more occurs (see Chapter 12).

Any other spill of material containing PCBs of 50 ppm or greater concentration, although not reportable, must still be cleaned up in accordance with EPA's PCB Spill Cleanup Policy [40 CFR 761.125(a)(1) (iv)]). Note that regardless of the quantity of PCB material spilled, the spill is covered under Section 107 of Superfund regarding the liabilities of releases of hazardous substances (see Chapter 13).

PCB SPILL CLEANUP REQUIREMENTS

Two types of spills are addressed by this policy: low-concentration spills of less than one pound; and low-concentration spills of one pound or more and/or high-concentration spills of any amount.

Under this policy, all contaminated soils, solvents, rags, and other materials resulting from the cleanup of PCBs must be stored, labeled, and disposed of in accordance with the applicable provisions of 40 CFR Part 761 (see Chapter 17) [40 CFR 761.125(a)(2)].

If the visible traces of a spill are insufficient, yet there is evidence of a leak or a spill, the spill boundary is to be determined by using a statistically based sampling scheme [40 CFR 761.125(a)(3)].

Small-Quantity Low-Concentration Spills

These requirements apply to low-concentration spills (PCB concentrations between 50 and 500 ppm) that involve less than one pound of PCBs by weight (less than 270 gallons of untested mineral oil). *By weight* means the actual amount of PCB molecules in a material and does not refer to other substances contained in the mixture. For spills involving untested mineral oil, it is presumed that the mineral oil is PCB-contaminated (between 50 and 500 ppm) unless demonstrated to be otherwise (44 *FR* 31517, May 31, 1979). Any spill in this category must be cleaned up in accordance with the appropriate requirements within 48 hours of its discovery [40 CFR 761.125(b)].

Solid Surfaces

Solid surfaces, except for indoor residential areas, must be double washed/rinsed. *Double wash/rinse* means a minimum requirement to cleanse solid surfaces (both impervious and nonimpervious) two times with an appropriate solvent or other material in which PCBs are at least 5 percent soluble (by weight). A volume of PCB-free fluid sufficient to cover the contaminated surface completely must be used in each wash/rinse. The wash/rinse requirement does not mean the mere spreading of solvent or other fluid over the surface, nor does the requirement mean a once-over wipe with a soaked cloth. Precautions must be taken to contain any resultant run-off and to dispose properly of wastes generated during the cleansing [40 CFR 761.125(b)].

Indoor, residential solid surfaces must be cleaned to 10 micrograms per 100 square centimeters by using a standard wipe test, which means, for spills on solid surfaces, a cleanup to numerical surface standards and sampling by a standard wipe test to verify that the numerical standards have been met. This definition constitutes the minimum requirements for an appropriate wipe testing protocol [40 CFR 761.125(b)(i)]. A standard-size template (10 cm × 10 cm) should be used to delineate the area of cleanup; the wiping medium should be a gauze pad or glass wool of known size that has been saturated with hexane. It is important that the wipe be performed very quickly after the hexane is exposed to air. The gauze (or glass wool) should be prepared with hexane in the laboratory, and the wiping medium should be stored in sealed glass vials until it is used for the wipe test.

Soils

All soil within a spill area (including a minimum buffer of one lateral foot beyond and 10 inches below the visible spill boundary) must be excavated. The ground must be restored to its original configuration by backfilling with clean, less than 1 ppm PCB, soil [40 CFR 761.125(b)(ii)].

High-Concentration and Large Low-Concentration Spills

The following criteria are applicable to any high-concentration spill (500 ppm or greater), and all low-concentration spills involving one pound or more of PCBs by weight (including 270 pounds or more of untested mineral oil) [40 CFR 761.125(c)].

Immediate Steps

The following four actions must be taken within 24 hours (or 48 hours for PCB transformers) of spill discovery [40 CFR 761.125(c)(1)]:

1. Notify, if applicable, the appropriate EPA regional office and, if required by Section 103 of Superfund, the National Response Center (800-424-8802).
2. Cordon off the immediate spill area plus a three-foot buffer zone. Clearly visible warning signs, denoting avoidance of the area, are to be placed adjacent to the cordoned area.
3. Record and document the area of visible contamination to establish the spill boundaries. If visible observations are not adequate to

delineate the boundaries, appropriate statistical sampling must be used.

4. The cleanup of all visible traces of fluid on hard surfaces and all visible traces of fluid on soil, gravel, sand, oyster shells, and other similar media must be initiated.

It is important to note that there is no time limit for the completion of the cleanup of spills in this category. However, EPA will consider the promptness of the completion of cleanup in determining whether a responsible party made good-faith efforts to clean up in accordance with this policy (52 *FR* 10693, April 2, 1987).

Decontamination Requirements for Electrical Substations

Electrical substations, considered restricted-access areas, must be cleaned up to the following requirements [40 CFR 761.125(c)(2)]:

- Solid surfaces must be cleaned up to a PCB level of 100 micrograms per 100 square centimeters as determined by a standard wipe test.
- Contaminated soils must be cleaned up to 25 ppm *or* 50 ppm.

The 50-ppm soil cleanup option requires the prominent display of a sign that, at a minimum, includes information concerning the date of the spill, the quantity of spilled material, the concentration of PCBs remaining at the spill site, and the recommendation for using protective clothing [40 CFR 761.125(c)(2)(ii)].

Decontamination Requirements for Other Restricted-Access Areas

Spills that occur in restricted-access locations other than electrical substations must be cleaned up as follows [40 CFR 761.125(c)(3)]:

- High-contact solid surfaces and low-contact, indoor, impervious solid surfaces must be cleaned to 10 micrograms per 100 square centimeters.
- Low-contact indoor, nonimpervious surfaces can be cleaned up either to 10 micrograms per 100 square centimeters, or to 100 micrograms per 100 square centimeters if the spill is also encapsulated.
- Low-contact outdoor surfaces must be cleaned to 100 micrograms per 100 square centimeters.
- Contaminated soil is to be cleaned to 25 ppm PCBs by weight.

Decontamination Requirements for Nonrestricted Access Areas

Spills that occur in nonrestricted-access areas must be cleaned in accordance with the following criteria [40 CFR 761.125(c)(4)]:

- Furnishings, toys, and other easily replaceable household items must be disposed of in accordance with 40 CFR 761.60 and replaced by the responsible party.
- Indoor solid surfaces, indoor vault areas, high-contact outdoor solid surfaces, and low-contact outdoor impervious solid areas must be cleaned to 10 micrograms per 100 square centimeters.
- Low-contact outdoor, nonimpervious soil surfaces are to be cleaned either to 10 micrograms per 100 square centimeters, or to 100 micrograms per 100 square centimeters if the spill also is encapsulated.
- Contaminated soil must be cleaned up to a minimum depth of 10 inches and to a minimum PCB concentration of 10 ppm. However, if less than 1 ppm of PCBs is found in the soil before the 10-inch minimum is reached, no further excavation is required. The resultant hole then must be filled in with a cap of clean soil, that is, less than 1 ppm of PCBs (53 *FR* 40883, October 19, 1988).

Post-Cleanup Sampling Requirements

Post-cleanup sampling is required to verify that the required cleanup levels, under this policy, were attained [40 CFR 761.130]. The responsible party may use any statistically valid, reproducible sampling scheme (either random or grid samples), provided that the following two requirements are met:

1. The sampling area is equal to the greater of: an area equal to the area cleaned plus an additional one-foot boundary or an area 20 percent larger than the original area of contamination.
2. The sampling scheme must ensure a 95 percent confidence level against false-positives.

The number of samples must be sufficient to ensure that areas of contamination of a radius of two feet or more within the sampling area will be detected, except that the minimum number of samples is 3 and the maximum number of samples is 40. The sampling scheme must include calculation for expected variability due to analytical error [40 CFR 761.130(c)].

EPA recommends the use of the EPA guidance manuals *Verification of PCB Spill Cleanup by Sampling and Analysis* and *Field Manual for Grid Sampling of PCB Spill Sites to Verify Cleanup* for the purposes of sampling for PCBs under this policy (contact EPA's TSCA Assistance hotline at 202-554-1404 for copies). The major advantage of using the recommended sampling schemes is that they are designed to characterize the degree of contamination within the entire sampling area with a high degree of confidence while requiring fewer samples than other grid or random sampling schemes. These recommended schemes allow some sites to be characterized on the basis of using composite samples instead of grab samples [40 CFR 761.130(e)].

Record-Keeping Requirements

The responsible party must document the cleanup with written records [40 CFR 761.125(c)(5)]. These records must be maintained for at least five years, and must contain the following information:

- The source of the spill.
- The date and the time of the spill.
- The date and the time when cleanup was completed or terminated.
- The cost of the cleanup.
- A brief description of the spill location and the materials contaminated, including the location and type (e.g., outdoor electrical substation).
- Precleanup sampling data used to establish the spill boundaries, if required.
- A description of the decontamination procedures for solid surfaces and a listing of those solid surfaces.
- The depth and amount of soil excavated.
- Postcleanup verification sampling data, sampling methodology, and analytical techniques used.

Certification of Decontamination

As part of the record-keeping requirements, a certification statement signed by the responsible party stating that the cleanup requirements have been met, and that the information contained in the record is true to the best of his or her knowledge, is required [40 CFR 761.125(c)(5)].

Appendix A

RCRA Compliance Inspection Checklist

Section I—Generator Checklist for RCRA

Note: Because state laws in many cases are more stringent than federal law, these checklists should be used as guides only.

Section A—EPA ID Number

Does generator have EPA Identification Number?   Yes___ No___

Section B—Hazardous Waste Determination

1. Has it been determined what hazardous waste(s) is generated at this facility?   Yes___ No___

2. Are records of the determinations kept (262.40)?   Yes___ No___

3. a. Are solid wastes that exhibit hazardous characteristics generated?   Yes___ No___

   b. How are waste characteristics determined (testing, knowledge of process)?

4. Identify total quantities of hazardous waste generated per month, for the last 12 months, for both acutely hazardous waste and other hazardous waste.

Jan	Feb	Mar	Apr	May	Jun	Jul	Aug	Sep	Oct	Nov	Dec

5. Does facility qualify as a small-quantity generator (SQG) for the entire last 12-month period (261.5)?   Yes___ No___

6. Is generator exempted or conditionally exempted from regulation because it:

   a. Is a small-quantity generator (261.5)?　　　　　　　　Yes___ No___

   b. Produces nonhazardous waste at this time (261.4)?　　Yes___ No___

Section C—Uniform Hazardous Waste Manifest System

1. Has hazardous waste been shipped off-site since November 19, 1980 (262 Subpart B)?　　　　　　　　　　　Yes___ No___

   (If no, skip to Section D, question 4.)

2. If not exempt, is the waste manifested on Uniform Hazardous Waste Manifests?　　　　　　　　　　　　　　Yes___ No___

   If so, do the manifests contain:

   a. Name and mailing address of generator?　　　　　　Yes___ No___

   b. Name and EPA ID Number of each transporter?　　　Yes___ No___

   c. DOT waste description, including proper shipping name, hazardous class, and UN/NA identification number?　　　　　　　　　　　　　　　　　　　Yes___ No___

   d. Number and type of containers (if applicable)?　　　Yes___ No___

   e. Quantity of each waste transported?　　　　　　　　Yes___ No___

   f. Name, EPA ID Number, and site address of facility designated to receive the waste?　　　　　　　　　Yes___ No___

   g. The following certification?　　　　　　　　　　　　Yes___ No___

    I hereby declare that the contents of this consignment are fully and accurately described above by proper shipping name and are classified, packed, marked, and labeled, and are in all respects in proper condition for transport by highway according to applicable international and national government regulations.

    Unless I am a small-quantity generator who has been exempted by statute of regulation from the duty to make a waste minimization certification under Section 3002(b) of RCRA, I also certify that I have a program in place to reduce the volume and toxicity of waste generated to the degree I have determined to be economically practicable, and I have selected the method of treatment, storage or disposal currently available to me which minimizes the present and future threat to human health and the environment.

3. Does the facility designated to receive the waste have:

   a. A RCRA permit?　　　　　　　　　　　　　　　　Yes___ No___

   b. Interim status?　　　　　　　　　　　　　　　　　Yes___ No___

   c. A permit, license, or registration from a state to manage municipal or industrial solid waste (for SQGs)?　　Yes___ No___

4. a. Are copies of the manifests retained?   Yes___ No___

   b. Were all manifests signed and dated?   Yes___ No___

   c. Were the handwritten signature and date of accep-
      tance from the initial transporter obtained?   Yes___ No___

   d. Is one copy of the manifest signed by the generator
      and transporter retained?   Yes___ No___

   e. Do return copies of the manifest include a facility
      owner/operator signature and date of acceptance?   Yes___ No___

   f. If the copy of the manifest from the facility was not
      returned within 45 days, was an Exception Report
      filed?   Yes___ No___

      If yes, did it contain:

      (1) A legible copy of the manifest?   Yes___ No___

      (2) A cover letter explaining efforts to locate waste
          and the results of those efforts?   Yes___ No___

   g. Have copies been retained for 3 years?   Yes___ No___

Section D—Pretransport Requirements

1. Does the generator package waste?   Yes___ No___

2. Is the waste packaged in accordance with DOT requirements 40 CFR 173, 178, and 179?   Yes___ No___

3. Inspect containers to be shipped.

   a. Are containers leaking, corroding, or bulging?   Yes___ No___

   b. Is there evidence of heat generation from incompati-
      ble wastes in containers?   Yes___ No___

   c. Are containers labeled according to DOT (49 CFR
      172 Subpart E)?   Yes___ No___

   d. Are containers marked according to DOT require-
      ments (49 CFR 172 Subpart D)?   Yes___ No___

   e. Is each container of 110 gallons or less marked with
      the following words?   Yes___ No___

HAZARDOUS WASTE—Federal Law Prohibits Improper Disposal. If found,
contact the nearest police or public safety authority or the U.S. Environmental
Protection Agency.

Generator's Name and Address _____.

Manifest Document Number _____.

4. Accumulation time (262.34):

   a. Is facility a permitted storage facility?   Yes___ No___

   b. Has all hazardous waste, generated in excess of the SQG limits, been shipped off-site or sent to on-site treatment, storage, or disposal within 90 days?   Yes___ No___

      (1) Is the waste placed in containers and managed in accordance with the container management requirements for facility owners or operators?   Yes___ No___

      (2) Is the date upon which each period of accumulation began clearly marked on each container?   Yes___ No___

      (3) Are the words "Hazardous Waste" clearly marked on each container of 110 gallons or less and visible for inspection?   Yes___ No___

      (4) For quantities in excess of the respective SQG rates, are the facility standards for Preparedness and Prevention (Part 265 Subpart C) and Contingency Plan/Emergency Procedures (Part 265 Subpart D) complied with?   Yes___ No___

      (5) For hazardous waste generated below the respective SQG rates, is the facility complying with the requirements for SQGs?   Yes___ No___

      (6) Do the facility hazardous waste management personnel have the requisite training documented in their personal file (265.16)?   Yes___ No___

   c. Have hazardous wastes, generated at a rate between 100 kg/mo and 1,000 kg/mo, been accumulated less than 180 days (or 270 days if the facility of choice is over 200 miles away)?   Yes___ No___

   d. Is the total amount of all hazardous waste accumulated on-site and generated below 100 kg/mo, less than 1,000 kg?   Yes___ No___

   e. Is the total amount of hazardous waste, accumulated on-site, generated at a rate between 100 kg/mo and 1,000 kg/mo, less than 6,000 kg?   Yes___ No___

   f. Are the containers being inspected for leakage or corrosion (265.174)?   Yes___ No___

   g. Is ignitable or reactive hazardous waste handled?   Yes___ No___

      (1) If yes, does the generator locate ignitable or reactive wastes at least 15 meters (50 feet) inside the facility's property line (265.176)?   Yes___ No___

      (2) Are the ignitable or reactive wastes separate from sources of ignition (265.17)?   Yes___ No___

Section E—Record Keeping and Records

1. Are the following records kept (262.40)?

   (*Note:* The following must be kept for a minimum of 3 years.)

   a. Manifests or signed copies from designated facilities?   Yes___ No___

   b. Biennial reports (does not apply to SQGs)?   Yes___ No___

   c. Exception reports (does not apply to SQGs)?   Yes___ No___

   d. Test results or other means of determination, as required?   Yes___ No___

2. Where are facility records kept (at the facility, off-site, etc.)? _____

   _____

3. Who is responsible for keeping the records? _____

   _____ Title: _____

   _____

Section II—Transporter Checklist for RCRA

Section A—General Transporter Information

1. Does the transporter have an EPA Identification Number?   Yes___ No___

2. Does more than one transporter or address use this identification number?   Yes___ No___

3. Identify the mode(s) of transportation used:

   ___Air ___Rail ___Highway ___Water ___Other

4. Is hazardous waste exported out of the United States?   Yes___ No___

5. Is hazardous waste imported into the United States?   Yes___ No___

   (If yes, complete "Generator Checklist" for these hazardous wastes.)

6. Are hazardous wastes of different DOT shipping descriptions mixed by placing them in a single container?   Yes___ No___

   (If yes, complete "Generator Checklist" for these mixtures.)

Section B—Transfer Facilities

1. Are manifested shipments of hazardous waste stored in containers meeting requirements of 40 CFR 262.30 at a transfer facility?   Yes___ No___

2. Is all manifested hazardous waste, temporarily stored by the transporter, shipped off-site within 10 days?   Yes___ No___

Section C—Manifest and Record Keeping Requirements

1. Are all shipments of hazardous wastes accomplished by manifest?   Yes___ No___

2. Does all required information appear on the manifest (40 CFR 172.205)?   Yes___ No___

3. If hazardous waste(s) is exported out of the United States, are the date of exit and the name and address of the receiving facility indicated on the manifest?   Yes___ No___

4. Are copies of manifests and shipping papers retained for the required 3-year period?   Yes___ No___

Section D—Manifest Compliance

1. Is all waste shipped to either the designated facility listed on the manifest or the alternate facility (when applicable) or the next designated transporter?   Yes___ No___

Section E—Pretransport Review

1. Has the generator complied with the following requirements?

    a. Has the generator packaged wastes in accordance with DOT requirements (49 CFR 173)?   Yes___ No___

    b. Has the generator packaged wastes in repacks?   Yes___ No___

    c. Has the generator labeled wastes in accordance with DOT requirements (49 CFR 172, Subpart E)?   Yes___ No___

    d. Has the generator marked wastes in accordance with DOT requirements (49 CFR 172, Subpart D)?   Yes___ No___

    e. Has the generator marked each container of 110 gallons or less used in such transportation with the following words and information displayed in accordance with the requirements of 49 CFR 172.304?   Yes___ No___

HAZARDOUS WASTE—Federal Law Prohibits Improper Disposal. If found, contact the nearest police or public safety authority or the U.S. Environmental Protection Agency.

Generator's Name and Address: _____.

Manifest Document Number: _____.

f. Did generator placard or offer the initial transporter the appropriate placards according to DOT (49 CFR 172, Subpart F)?   Yes__ No__

Section F—Emergency Action

1. Has the transporter ever been involved in a discharge of hazardous wastes?   Yes__ No__

   a. If yes, was the National Response Center (800-424-8802 or 202-426-2675), U.S. Coast Guard, the state, and the principal office of the transporter notified?   Yes__ No__

   b. Was a written report submitted to DOT within 10 days following the discharge?   Yes__ No__

2. Has the transporter obtained an Emergency Identification Number from EPA for the cleanup operation?   Yes__ No__

Section G—Transport Vehicle Inspection

1. Company/name/designation of vehicle: _____

   _____

2. Truck driver's name: _____

3. What hazardous wastes are listed on the manifest?

4. Form of containerization of hazardous wastes:

   _____ drums, size: _____ gallons (ea), _____ amount (i.e., 30 drums)

   _____ portable tanks—number _____ volume (ea) _____

   _____ gondola

   _____ tanker—type _____ volume (ea) _____

5. What is the condition of containerization (intact, leaking, corroded, fuming, damaged, improperly sealed, poor condition, improper lining, and so forth)?

   _____

   _____

6. Is truck properly placarded and marked (49 CFR, Subpart F)?   Yes__ No__

7. Did generator have to repackage wastes by truck driver's request?   Yes___ No___

Section III—TSDFs: Checklist for the General Standards

Section A—General Facility Standards

1. Does the facility have an EPA Identification Number?   Yes___ No___

2. Has the facility received hazardous waste from a foreign source?   Yes___ No___

   (If yes, was a notice filed with the Regional Administrator 4 weeks in advance of the initial shipment?)   Yes___ No___

Waste Analysis

3. Does the facility have a written waste analysis plan?   Yes___ No___

4. Does the plan include:

   a. Parameters for which each waste will be analyzed?   Yes___ No___

   b. Rationale for the selection of these parameters?   Yes___ No___

   c. Test methods used to test for these parameters?   Yes___ No___

   d. Sampling method used to obtain sample?   Yes___ No___

   e. Frequency with which the initial analysis will be reviewed or repeated?   Yes___ No___

      (If yes, does it include requirements to retest when the process or operation generating the waste has changed?) Yes___ No___

   f. (For off-site facilities) Waste analyses that generators have agreed to supply?   Yes___ No___

   g. (For off-site facilities) Procedures that are used to inspect and analyze each movement of hazardous waste, including:

      (1) Procedures to be used to determine the identity of each movement of waste?   Yes___ No___

      (2) Sampling method to be used to minimize the possibility for the unauthorized entry of persons or livestock onto the active portions of the facility?   Yes___ No___

Security

5. Is there adequate security to minimize the possibility of the unauthorized entry of persons or livestock onto the active portions of the facility?   Yes___ No___

   If yes, is security provided through:

   a. 24-hour surveillance system (e.g., television monitoring or guards)?   Yes___ No___

   or

   b. (1) Artificial or natural barrier around facility (e.g., fence or fence and cliff)?   Yes___ No___

   and

      (2) Means to control entry through entrances (e.g., attendant, television monitors, locked entrance, controlled roadway access)?   Yes___ No___

6. Is a sign with the legend "Danger—Unauthorized Personnel Keep Out" posted at the entrance to the active portion of the facility?   Yes___ No___

General Inspection Requirements

7. a. Is a written schedule for inspection maintained with respect to the following?   Yes___ No___

      (1) Monitoring equipment, if applicable?   Yes___ No___

      (2) Safety and emergency equipment?   Yes___ No___

      (3) Security devices?   Yes___ No___

      (4) Operating and structural equipment, if applicable?   Yes___ No___

      (5) Identifying the types of problems to be looked for during inspection?   Yes___ No___

         (a) Malfunction or deterioration (e.g., inoperative sump pump, leaking fitting, eroding dike, corroded pipes or tanks, etc.)?   Yes___ No___

         (b) Operator error?   Yes___ No___

         (c) Discharges (e.g., leaks from valves or pipes, joint breaks, etc.)?   Yes___ No___

   b. Is a written schedule for these inspections maintained at the facility?   Yes___ No___

      (1) Are records of these inspections maintained in an inspection log?   Yes___ No___

(2) If yes, does it include:

    (a) Date and time of inspection?   Yes___ No___

    (b) Name of inspector?   Yes___ No___

    (c) Notation of observations?   Yes___ No___

    (d) Date and nature of repairs or remedial action?   Yes___ No___

(3) Are there any malfunctions or other deficiencies noted in the inspection log that remain uncorrected?   Yes___ No___

(4) Are records of the inspection log maintained at the facility for at least 3 years?   Yes___ No___

Personnel Training

8. Is a personnel training program in place?   Yes___ No___

  a. If yes:

    (1) Is the program directed by a person trained in hazardous waste management procedures?   Yes___ No___

    (2) Is the program designed to prepare employees to respond effectively to hazardous waste emergencies?   Yes___ No___

    (3) Is a training review given annually?   Yes___ No___

  b. Are the following records kept:

    (1) Job title and written job description of each position?   Yes___ No___

    (2) Description of the type and amount of introductory and continuing training?   Yes___ No___

    (3) Documentation that training has been given to employees?   Yes___ No___

  c. Are these records maintained at the facility? Yes___ No___

Requirements for Ignitable, Reactive, or Incompatible Waste

9. Is ignitable or reactive waste handled?   Yes___ No___

  a. If yes, is waste separated and confined from sources of ignition or reaction?   Yes___ No___

  b. Are "No Smoking" signs posted in hazardous areas where ignitable or reactive wastes are handled? Yes___ No___

10. Is waste stored in containers?   Yes___ No___

    a. Are containers leaking, corroding, or bulging?   Yes___ No___

    b. Has the facility ever placed incompatible wastes together?   Yes___ No___

Section B—Preparedness and Prevention

1. Is there evidence of fire, explosion, or contamination of the environment?   Yes___ No___

2. Is the facility equipped with:

    a. Easily accessible internal communications or alarm system?   Yes___ No___

    b. Telephone or two-way radio to call emergency response personnel?   Yes___ No___

    c. Portable fire extinguishers, fire control equipment, spill control equipment, and decontamination equipment?   Yes___ No___

        (1) Is this equipment tested and maintained as necessary to assure its proper operation?   Yes___ No___

    d. Water of adequate volume for hoses, sprinklers, or water spray system?   Yes___ No___

        (1) Describe source of water: _____

        (2) Indicate flow rate and/or pressure and storage capacity, if applicable:

_____

3. Is there sufficient aisle space to allow unobstructed movement of personnel and equipment?   Yes___ No___

4. Have arrangements been made with the local authorities to familiarize them with characteristics of the facility?   Yes___ No___

5. In the case that more than one police or fire department might respond, is there a designated primary authority?   Yes___ No___

    If yes, indicate primary authority: _____

6. Have agreements with state emergency response teams, emergency response contractors, and equipment suppliers been made?   Yes___ No___

    Are they readily available to the emergency coordinator?   Yes___ No___

7. Have arrangements been made to familiarize local hospitals with the properties of hazardous waste handled and type of injuries that could result from fires, explosions, or releases at the facility?   Yes___ No___

8. If the state or local authorities declined to enter into the above-referenced agreements, is there documentation of this?   Yes___ No___

Section C—Contingency Plan and Emergency Procedures

1. Does the facility have a contingency plan?   Yes___ No___

   a. If yes, does it contain:

      (1) Actions to be taken in response to emergencies?   Yes___ No___

      (2) Description of arrangements with police, fire, and hospital officials?   Yes___ No___

      (3) List of names, addresses, phone numbers, or personnel qualified to act as emergency coordinator?   Yes___ No___

      (4) List of all emergency equipment at the facility?   Yes___ No___

      (5) Evacuation plan for facility personnel?   Yes___ No___

2. Is a copy of the contingency plan maintained at the facility?   Yes___ No___

3. Has a copy been supplied to local police and fire departments?   Yes___ No___

4. Is the plan a revised SPCC plan?   Yes___ No___

5. Is there an emergency coordinator on-site or within short driving distance of the plant at all times?   Yes___ No___

   If yes, list primary emergency coordinator: _____

Section D—Manifest System, Record Keeping and Reporting

1. Has the facility received hazardous waste from off-site?   Yes___ No___

   If no, proceed to question 5.

   If yes, are copies of all manifests retained?   Yes___ No___

2. Have any shipments of hazardous waste been received from a rail or water (bulk shipment) transporter?   Yes___ No___

   a. If yes, is it accompanied by shipping papers?

      (1) Have the shipping papers been signed and a copy returned to the generator?   Yes___ No___

      (2) Has a signed copy been given to the transporter?   Yes___ No___

3. Has the facility received any shipments of hazardous
   waste that were inconsistent with the manifest?   Yes___ No___

   a. If yes, has the discrepancy been resolved with the
      generator and the transporter?   Yes___ No___

   b. If no, has the Regional Administrator been notified?   Yes___ No___

4. Has any waste been received (that does not come under
   the small-generator exclusion) not accompanied by a
   manifest?   Yes___ No___

   If yes, has an unmanifested waste report been submitted?   Yes___ No___

5. Does the facility have a written operating record?   Yes___ No___

   a. Is a copy maintained at the facility?   Yes___ No___

   b. Does the record include:

      (1) Description and quantity of each hazardous waste
          and the methods and dates of its treatment, stor-
          age, or disposal at the facility?   Yes___ No___

      (2) Location and quantity of each hazardous waste?   Yes___ No___

          (a) Is this information cross-referenced with spe-
              cific manifest document numbers, if applica-
              ble?   Yes___ No___

      (3) Location and quantity of each hazardous waste
          recorded on a map or diagram of each cell or dis-
          posal area (for disposal facilities only)?   Yes___ No___

      (4) Results of waste analyses?   Yes___ No___

      (5) Reports of incidents involving implementation of
          the contingency plan (if applicable)?   Yes___ No___

      (6) Results of required inspections?   Yes___ No___

      (7) Monitoring, testing, or analytical data where re-
          quired?   Yes___ No___

      (8) Closure cost estimates and, for land disposal fa-
          cilities, post-closure cost estimates?   Yes___ No___

Appendix B

TSCA Compliance Checklist (PCB Compliance)

A. Inventory

1. Does facility contain in-service, stored for future use, or for disposal:

   a. Large high- or low-voltage PCB capacitors? Yes___ No___

   b. PCB transformers? Yes___ No___

   c. PCB-contaminated transformers? Yes___ No___

2. If company has PCB-contaminated transformers, how was it determined that the transformers contained 50 to 500 ppm PCB?

   _____

   _____

3. Are there any other PCB Items (electromagnets, hydraulic systems, etc.)? Yes___ No___ N/A___

   If yes, list number and type of item; whether it is in-service, in storage or sent to disposal; and if it is properly marked:

   _____

   _____

   _____

B. Storage and Handling

1. Does the facility have its own storage site for PCBs? Yes___ No___

   (If no, go to Section D)

2. Does storage site meet physical requirements
   [761.42(a)]?   Yes___ No___

   a. Does it provide protection from rainfall?   Yes___ No___

   b. Does it meet floor requirements with 6-inch continu-
      ous curbing?   Yes___ No___

   c. Does it meet containment volume requirements?   Yes___ No___

      (1) What is the containment volume of the storage site?

      _____

                     (Length × Width × Height)

      (2) What is the internal volume of the largest PCB article or container
          stored within the storage site?

      _____

      (3) What is the total internal volume of all PCB articles and containers
          within the storage site?

      _____

          Is item (1) greater than two times item (2)?   Yes___ No___

          or

          25% of item (3)?   Yes___ No___

   d. (1) Is the area within the curbed area void of drains,
          valves, expansion joints, or other openings?   Yes___ No___

      (2) If no, document location of opening, drainage patch, and ultimate
          disposal location in logbook, and describe below:

      _____

      _____

      _____

   e. Is storage site located above the 100-year floodplain? Yes___ No___

   f. Are storage areas adequately marked?   Yes___ No___

3. Containers:

   a. Are all PCB items that are located within storage
      areas dated [761.65(c)(8)]?   Yes___ No___

   b. Do PCB containers comply with DOT specifications
      except as noted in 3c and 3d below [761.65(c)(6)?   Yes___ No___

   c. Are any nonliquid PCBs being stored in containers
      larger than those specified in DOT regulations
      [761.65(c)(6)]?   Yes___ No___

    (1) Do these containers provide as much protection
and have the same strength as DOT containers?   Yes___ No___

  d. Are any liquid PCBs being stored in containers
larger than those specified in DOT regulations
[761.42(c)(7)]?   Yes___ No___

    (1) Do the containers comply with OSHA specifica-
tions?   Yes___ No___

    (2) Has SPCC plan been prepared and implemented?   Yes___ No___

4. Storage Site Operations:

  a. Are all PCB items arranged so they can be located
by date? [761.65(c)(8)]   Yes___ No___

  b. Are good housekeeping procedures being implemented?   Yes___ No___

  c. Is movable equipment decontaminated by approved
procedures?   Yes___ No___

  d. Are PCB items stored and handled in a manner
that protects them from accidental breakage or
damage?   Yes___ No___

5. Other Storage Areas:

  a. Are any of the following temporarily being stored
outside the prescribed area [761.65(c)(1)]:

    (1) Nonleaking PCB articles and PCB equipment?   Yes___ No___

    Is the date removed from service noted on the ar-
ticle or equipment?   Yes___ No___

    (2) Leaking PCB articles and PCB equipment placed
in a nonleaking PCB container?   Yes___ No___

    Is the date removed from service noted on the
container?   Yes___ No___

    Have they been there less than 30 days?   Yes___ No___

    (3) Containers of liquid PCBs at concentrations of 50
to 500 ppm?   Yes___ No___

    Is SPCC plan available pertaining to temporary
storage area?   Yes___ No___

    Are containers marked to indicate that the liquid
does not exceed 500 ppm?   Yes___ No___

    Is the date removed from service noted on the
containers?   Yes___ No___

Have containers been there less than 30 days?   Yes___ No___

b. Are there any large high-voltage capacitors or PCB-contaminated transformers next to the storage site [761.65(c)(2)]?   Yes___ No___

Are they on pallets?   Yes___ No___

Is there adequate space within the storage site to contain 10% of the volume of these capacitors and transformers?   Yes___ No___

C. Decontamination

1. Are PCB transformers or other equipment containing PCB substances or mixtures drained or decontaminated prior to disposal, and is all movable equipment decontaminated?   Yes___ No___

(If no, go to Section E)

2. Is the drainage and solvent-filling site adequate to protect against spills and leaks and consequent contamination of surrounding areas and waterways?   Yes___ No___

3. Do solvents to be used for PCB removal contain less than 50 ppm PCB [761.79]?   Yes___ No___

4. Was a sample of the solvent that was used for PCB removal obtained?   Yes___ No___

5. Was the rinse volume of the solvent approximately equal to 10% of the container's total volume [761.79(a)]?   Yes___ No___

6. Are PCB transformers completely filled with solvent and allowed to stand for at least 18 hours before being drained [761.60(b)(1)]?   Yes___ No___

7. Are the drained PCB chemical substances or PCB solvent mixtures properly disposed of or stored in the same manner as PCB mixtures?   Yes___ No___

8. Are solvents or materials that have been used for decontamination of PCB equipment disposed of or stored in the same manner as PCB mixtures?   Yes___ No___

9. Does the facility have written decontamination procedures?   Yes___ No___

D. Record Keeping

1. Do records indicate the date when PCBs were:

a. Removed from service?   Yes___ No___

    b. Placed in storage for disposal?   Yes___ No___

    c. Placed in transport for disposal?   Yes___ No___

2. Do records indicate the quantity of the above items as follows:

    a. The weights of PCBs and PCB items in PCB containers?   Yes___ No___

    b. The identification of contents of PCB containers?   Yes___ No___

    c. The number of PCB transformers?   Yes___ No___

    d. The weight of PCBs in PCB transformers?   Yes___ No___

    e. The number of PCB large, high- and low-voltage capacitors?   Yes___ No___

3. Do records indicate the quantities of PCBs remaining in service, broken down as follows:

    a. The weight of PCBs and PCB items in PCB containers?   Yes___ No___

    b. The identification of contents of PCB containers?   Yes___ No___

    c. The number of PCB transformers?   Yes___ No___

    d. The weight of PCBs in PCB transformers?   Yes___ No___

    e. The number of PCB large, high- and low-voltage capacitors?   Yes___ No___

4. Is the information requested in questions 1, 2, and 3 above compiled in an annual document? (This document must be prepared by July 1 and cover the previous calendar year.)   Yes___ No___

5. Are copies of manifests maintained?   Yes___ No___

E. Disposal

1. Are PCB articles or containers, which were stored for disposal after January 1, 1983, disposed of within 1 year?   Yes___ No___

2. What items are disposed of, stating the disposal methods?

_____

_____

3. Are certificates of disposal available for each item as required?   Yes___ No___

Appendix C

The RCRA-Listed Hazardous Wastes

EPA Waste Number	Hazardous Waste	Hazard Code[1]

HAZARDOUS WASTES FROM NONSPECIFIC SOURCES

F001   The following spent halogenated solvents used in degreasing: tetrachloroethylene, trichloroethylene, methylene chloride, 1,1,1-trichloroethane, carbon tetrachloride, and chlorinated fluorocarbons, all spent solvent mixture/blends used in degreasing containing, before use, a total of ten percent or more (by volume) of one or more of the above halogenated solvents or those solvents listed in F002, F004, and F005; and still bottoms from the recovery of these spent solvents and spent solvent mixtures.   (T)

F002   The following spent halogenated solvents: tetrachloroethylene, methylene chloride, trichloroethylene, 1,1,1-trichloroethane, chlorobenzene, 1,1,2-trichloro-1,2,2-trifluoroethane, o-dichlorobenzene, trichlorofluoromethane and, 1,1,2-trichloroethane; all spent solvent mixtures/blends containing, before use, a total of ten percent or more of the above halogenated solvents or those listed in F001, F004, or F005; and still bottoms from the recovery of these spent solvents and spent solvent mixtures.   (T)

[1]Hazard codes are: (C) = corrosive, (T) = toxic, (R) = reactive, (H) = acutely hazardous, and (I) = ignitable.

EPA Waste Number	Hazardous Waste	Hazard Code[1]
F003	The following spent nonhalogenated solvents: xylene, acetone, ethyl acetate, ethyl benzene, ethyl ether, methyl isobutyl ketone, n-butyl alcohol, cyclohexanone, methanol; all spent solvent mixtures/blends containing, before use, one or more of the above nonhalogenated solvents, and, a total of ten percent or more (by volume) of one or more of those solvents listed in F001, F002, F004, and F005; and still bottoms from the recovery of these spent solvents and spent solvent mixtures.	(I)
F004	The following spent nonhalogenated solvents: cresols and cresylic acid, nitrobenzene; all spent solvent mixtures/blends containing, before use, a total of ten percent or more (by volume) of one or more of the above nonhalogenated solvents or those solvents listed in F001, F002, and F005; and the still bottoms from the recovery of these spent solvents and spent solvent mixtures.	(T)
F005	The following spent nonhalogenated solvents: toluene, methyl ethyl ketone, carbon disulfide, isobutanol, pyridine benzene, 2-ethoxyethanol, and 2-nitropropane; all spent solvent mixtures/blends containing, before use, a total of ten percent (or more) by volume of one or more of the above nonhalogenated solvents or those listed in F001, F002, and F004; and the still bottoms from the recovery of these spent solvents and spent solvent mixtures.	(I,T)
F006	Wastewater treatment sludges from electroplating operations except from the following processes: (1) sulfuric acid anodizing of aluminum; (2) tin plating on carbon steel; (3) zinc plating (segregated basis) on carbon steel; (4) aluminum or zinc-aluminum plating on carbon steel; (5) cleaning/stripping associated with tin, zinc, and aluminum plating on carbon steel; and (6) chemical etching and milling of aluminum.	(T)
F019	Wastewater treatment sludges from the chemical conversion coating of aluminum.	(T)
F007	Spent cyanide plating bath solutions from electroplating operations (except for precious metals electroplating spent cyanide plating bath solutions).	(R,T)

EPA Waste Number	Hazardous Waste	Hazard Code[1]
F008	Plating bath residues from the bottom of plating baths from electroplating operations for which cyanides are used in the process (except for precious metals electroplating bath sludges).	(R,T)
F009	Spent stripping and cleaning bath solutions from electroplating operations for which cyanides are used in the process (except for precious metals electroplating spent stripping and cleaning bath solutions).	(R,T)
F010	Quenching bath sludges from oil baths from metal heat treating operations for which cyanides are used in the process (except for precious metals heat treating quenching bath sludges).	(R,T)
F011	Spent cyanide solutions from salt bath pot cleaning from metal heat treating operations (except for precious metals heat treating spent cyanide solutions from salt bath pot cleaning).	(R,T)
F012	Quenching wastewater treatment sludges from metal heat treating operations for which cyanides are used in the process (except for precious metals heat treating quenching wastewater treatment sludges).	(T)
F024	Wastes including but not limited to distillation residues, heavy ends, tars, and reactor clean-out wastes from the production of chlorinated aliphatic hydrocarbons, having carbon content from one to five, utilizing free radical catalyzed processes (does not include light ends, spent filters and filter aids, spent dessicants, wastewater, wastewater treatment sludges, spent catalysts and wastes listed in 261.32).	(T)
F020	Wastes (except wastewater and spent carbon from hydrogen chloride purification) from the production or manufacturing use (as a reactant, chemical intermediate, or component in a formulating process) of tri- or tetrachlorophenol or of intermediates used to produce their pesticide derivatives (does not include wastes from the production of hexachlorophene from highly purified 2,4,5-trichlorophenol).	(H)
F021	Wastes (except wastewater and spent carbon from hydrogen chloride purification) from the production or manufacturing use (as a reactant, chemical intermediate, or component in a formulating process) of pentachlo-	(H)

EPA Waste Number	Hazardous Waste	Hazard Code[1]
	rophenol or of intermediates used to produce its derivatives.	
F022	Wastes (except wastewater and spent carbon from hydrogen chloride purification) from the manufacturing use (as a reactant, chemical intermediate, or component in a formulating process) of tetra-, penta-, or hexachlorobenzenes under alkaline conditions.	(H)
F023	Wastes (except wastewater and spent carbon from hydrogen chloride purification) from the production of materials on equipment previously used for the production or manufacturing use (as a reactant, chemical intermediate, or component in a formulating process) of tri- and tetrachlorophenols (does not include wastes from equipment used only for the production or use of hexachlorophene from highly purified 2,4,5-trichlorophenol).	(H)
F026	Wastes (except wastewater and spent carbon from hydrogen chloride purification) from the production of materials on equipment previously used for the manufacturing use (as a reactant, chemical intermediate, or component in a formulating process) of tetra-, penta-, or hexachlorobenzene under alkaline conditions.	(H)
F027	Discarded unused formulations containing tri-, tetra-, or pentachlorophenol or discarded unused formulations containing compounds derived from these chlorophenols (does not include formulations containing hexachlorophene synthesized from prepurified 2,4,5-trichlorophenol as the sole component).	(H)
F028	Residues resulting from the incineration or thermal treatment of soil contaminated with EPA hazardous wastes numbered F020, F021, F022, F023, F026, and F027.	(T)
F039	Leachate resulting from the treatment, storage, or disposal of wastes classified by more than one waste code under Subpart D, or from a mixture of wastes classified under Subparts C and D of this part [261]. (Leachate resulting from the management of one or more of the following EPA Hazardous Wastes and no other hazardous wastes retains its hazardous waste code(s): F020, F021, F022, F023, F026, F027, and/or F028.)	(T)

EPA Waste Number	Hazardous Waste	Hazard Code[1]

HAZARDOUS WASTES FROM SPECIFIC SOURCES

Wood Preservatives

K001   Bottom sediment sludge from the treatment of waste-   (T)
        waters from wood preserving processes that use creo-
        sote and/or pentachlorophenol.

Inorganic Pigments

K002   Wastewater treatment sludge from the production of   (T)
        chrome yellow and orange pigments.

K003   Wastewater treatment sludge from the production of   (T)
        molybdate orange pigments.

K004   Wastewater treatment sludge from the production of   (T)
        zinc yellow pigments.

K005   Wastewater treatment sludge from the production of   (T)
        chrome green pigments.

K006   Wastewater treatment sludge from the production of   (T)
        chrome oxide green pigments (anhydrous and hy-
        drated).

K007   Wastewater treatment sludge from the production of   (T)
        iron blue pigments.

K008   Oven residue from the production of chrome oxide   (T)
        green pigments.

Organic Chemicals

K009   Distillation bottoms from the production of acetalde-   (T)
        hyde from ethylene.

K010   Distillation side cuts from the production of acetalde-   (T)
        hyde from ethylene.

K011   Bottom stream from the wastewater stripper in the   (R,T)
        production of acrylonitrile.

K013   Bottom stream from the acetonitrile column in the pro-   (R,T)
        duction of acrylonitrile.

K014   Bottoms from the acetonitrile purification column in   (T)
        the production of acrylonitrile.

K015   Still bottoms from the distillation of benzyl chloride.   (T)

EPA Waste Number	Hazardous Waste	Hazard Code[1]
K016	Heavy ends or distillation residues from the production of carbon tetrachloride.	(T)
K017	Heavy ends (still bottoms) from the purification column in the production of epichlorohydrin.	(T)
K018	Heavy ends from the fractionation column in ethyl chloride production.	(T)
K019	Heavy ends from the distillation of ethylene dichloride in ethylene dichloride production.	(T)
K020	Heavy ends from the distillation of vinyl chloride in vinyl chloride monomer production.	(T)
K021	Aqueous spent antimony catalyst waste from fluoromethanes production.	(T)
K022	Distillation bottom tars from the production of phenol/acetone from cumene.	(T)
K023	Distillation light ends from the production of phthalic anhydride from naphthalene.	(T)
K024	Distillation bottoms from the production of phthalic anhydride from naphthalene.	(T)
K093	Distillation light ends from the production of phthalic anhydride from o-xylene.	(T)
K094	Distillation bottoms from the production of phthalic anhydride from o-xylene.	(T)
K025	Distillation bottoms from the production of nitrobenzene by the nitration of benzene.	(T)
K026	Stripping still tails from the production of methyl ethyl pyridines.	(T)
K027	Centrifuge and distillation residues from toluene diisocyanate production.	(R,T)
K028	Spent catalyst from the hydrochlorinator reactor in the production of 1,1,1-trichloroethane.	(T)
K029	Waste from the product steam stripper in the production of 1,1,1-trichloroethane.	(T)
K095	Distillation bottoms from the production of 1,1,1-trichloroethane.	(T)
K096	Heavy ends from the heavy ends column from the production of 1,1,1-trichloroethane.	(T)

EPA Waste Number	Hazardous Waste	Hazard Code[1]
K030	Column bottoms or heavy ends from the combined production of trichloroethylene and perchloroethylene.	(T)
K083	Distillation bottoms from aniline production.	(T)
K103	Process residues from aniline extraction from the production of aniline.	(T)
K104	Combined wastewater streams generated from nitrobenzene/aniline production.	(T)
K085	Distillation or fractionation column bottoms from the production of chlorobenzenes.	(T)
K105	Separated aqueous stream from the reactor product washing step in the production of chlorobenzenes.	(T)
K111	Product washwaters from the production of dinitrotoluene via nitration of toluene.	(C,T)
K112	Reaction by-product water from the drying column in the production of toluenediamine via hydrogenation of dinitrotoluene.	(T)
K113	Condensed liquid light ends from the purification of toluenediamine in the production of toluenediamine via hydrogenation of dinitrotoluene.	(T)
K114	Vicinals from the purification of toluenediamine in the production of toluenediamine via hydrogenation of dinitrotoluene.	(T)
K115	Heavy ends from the purification of toluenediamine in the production of toluenediamine via hydrogenation of dinitrotoluene.	(T)
K116	Organic condensate from the solvent recovery column in the production of toluene diisocyanate via phosgenation of toluenediamine.	(T)
K117	Wastewater from the reactor vent gas scrubber in the production of ethylene dibromide via bromination of ethene.	(T)
K118	Spent adsorbent solids from purification of ethylene dibromide via bromination of ethene.	(T)
K136	Still bottoms from the purification of ethylene dibromide in the production of ethylene dibromide via bromination of ethene.	(T)

EPA Waste Number	Hazardous Waste	Hazard Code[1]

Inorganic Chemicals

K071	Brine purification muds from the mercury cell process in chlorine production for which separately prepurified brine is not used.	(T)
K073	Chlorinated hydrocarbon waste from the purification step of the diaphragm cell process using graphite anodes in chlorine production.	(T)
K106	Wastewater treatment sludge from the mercury cell process in chlorine production.	(T)

Pesticides

K031	By-product salts generated in the production of MSMA and cacodylic acid.	(T)
K032	Wastewater treatment sludge from the production of chlordane.	(T)
K033	Wastewater and scrub water from the chlorination of cyclopentadiene in the production of chlordane.	(T)
K034	Filter solids from the filtration of hexachlorocyclopentadiene in the production of chlordane.	(T)
K097	Vacuum stripper discharge from the chlordane chlorinator in the production of chlordane.	(T)
K035	Wastewater treatment sludges generated in the production of creosote.	(T)
K036	Still bottoms from toluene reclamation distillation in the production of disulfoton.	(T)
K037	Wastewater treatment sludges from the production of disulfoton.	(T)
K038	Wastewater from the washing and stripping of phorate production.	(T)
K039	Filter cake from the distillation of diethylphosphorodithioic acid in the production of phorate.	(T)
K040	Wastewater treatment sludge from the production of phorate.	(T)
K041	Wastewater treatment sludge from the production of toxaphene.	(T)

EPA Waste Number	Hazardous Waste	Hazard Code[1]
K098	Untreated process wastewater from the production of toxaphene.	(T)
K042	Heavy ends or distillation residues from the distillation of tetrachlorobenzene in the production of 2,4,5-T.	(T)
K043	2,6-Dichlorophenol waste from the production of 2,4-D.	(T)
K099	Untreated wastewater from the production of 2,4-D.	(T)

Explosives

K044	Wastewater treatment sludges from the manufacturing and processing of explosives.	(R)
K045	Spent carbon from the treatment of wastewater containing explosives.	(R)
K046	Wastewater treatment sludges from the manufacturing, formulation, and loading of lead-based initiating compounds.	(R)
K047	Pink/red water from TNT operations.	(R)

Petroleum Refining

K048	Dissolved air floatation (DAF) float from the petroleum refining industry.	(T)
K049	Slop oil emulsion solids from the petroleum refining industry.	(T)
K050	Heat exchanger bundle cleaning sludge from the petroleum refining industry.	(T)
K051	API separator sludge from the petroleum refining industry.	(T)
K052	Tank bottoms (leaded) from the petroleum refining industry.	(T)

Iron and Steel

K061	Emission control dust/sludge from the primary production of steel in electric furnaces.	(T)
K062	Spent pickle liquor generated by steel finishing operations of facilities within iron and steel industry SIC codes 331 and 332.	(C,T)

EPA Waste Number	Hazardous Waste	Hazard Code[1]
K064	Acid plant blowdown slurry/sludge resulting from the thickening of blowdown slurry from primary copper production.	(T)
K065	Surface impoundment solids contained in and dredged from surface impoundments at primary lead smelting facilities.	(T)
K066	Sludge from treatment of process wastewater and/or acid plant blowdown from primary zinc production.	(T)
K088	Spent potliners from primary aluminum reduction.	(T)
K090	Emission control dust or sludge from ferrochromium silicon production.	(T)
K091	Emission control dust or sludge from ferrochromium production.	(T)

Secondary Lead

K069	Emission control dust/sludge from secondary lead smelting.	(T)
K100	Waste leaching solution from acid leaching of emission control dust/sludge from secondary lead smelting.	(T)

Veterinary Pharmaceuticals

K084	Wastewater treatment sludges generated during the production of veterinary pharmaceuticals from arsenic or organo-arsenic compounds.	(T)
K101	Distillation tar residues from the distillation of aniline-based compounds in the production of veterinary pharmaceuticals from arsenic or organo-arsenic compounds.	(T)
K102	Residue from the use of activated carbon for decolorization in the production of veterinary pharmaceuticals from arsenic or organo-arsenic compounds.	(T)

Ink Formulation

K086	Solvent washes and sludges, caustic washes and sludges, or water washes and sludges from cleaning tubs and equipment used in the formulation of ink from pigments, driers, soaps, and stabilizers containing chromium and lead.	(T)

EPA Waste Number	Hazardous Waste	Hazard Code[1]

Coking

K060	Ammonia still lime sludge from coking operations.	(T)
K087	Decanter tank tar sludge from coking operations.	(T)

COMMERCIAL CHEMICAL PRODUCTS

The following P code wastes are considered acutely hazardous (H):

P023	Acetaldehyde, chloro-		P046	Benzeneethanamine, al-pha,alpha-dimethyl
P002	Acetamide, N-(aminothiox-omethyl)-		P014	Benzenethiol
P057	Acetamide, 2-fluoro-		P001	2H-1-Benzopyran-2-one, 4-hydroxy-3-(3-oxo-1-phenyl-butyl)-, and salts
P058	Acetic acid, fluoro-, so-dium salt			
P066	Acetimidic acid, N-[(meth-ylcarbamoyl)oxy]thio-, methyl ester		P028	Benzyl chloride
			P015	Beryllium dust
P002	1-Acetyl-2-thiourea		P016	Bis(chloromethyl) ether
P003	Acrolein		P017	Bromoacetone
P070	Aldicarb		P018	Brucine
P004	Aldrin			
P005	Allyl alcohol		P021	Calcium cyanide
P006	Aluminum phosphide		P022	Carbon bisulfide
P007	5-(Aminomethyl)-3-isoxazolol		P022	Carbon disulfide
			P095	Carbonic dichloride
P008	4-alpha-Aminopyridine		P023	Chloroacetaldehyde
P009	Ammonium picrate (R)		P024	*p*-Chloroaniline
P119	Ammonium vanadate		P029	Copper cyanide
P010	Arsenic acid		P030	Cyanides (soluble cyanide salts), not elsewhere speci-fied
P012	Arsenic (III) oxide As_2O_3			
P011	Arsenic (V) oxide As_2O_5			
P011	Arsenic pentoxide		P031	Cyanogen
P012	Arsenic trioxide		P033	Cyanogen chloride
P038	Arsine, diethyl		P034	2-Cyclohexyl-4,6-dinitro-phenol
P054	Aziridine			
P013	Barium cyanide		P036	Dichlorophenylarsine
P024	Benzenamine, 4-chloro-		P037	Dieldrin
P077	Benzenamine, 4-nitro-		P038	Diethylarsine
P028	Benzene, (chloromethyl)-		P041	Diethyl-*p*-nitrophenyl phosphate
P042	1,2-Benzenediol, 4-[(1-hy-droxy-2-(methyl-amino) ethyl)]-		P040	O,O-Diethyl O-pyrazinyl phosphorothioate

P043	Diisopropyl fluorophosphate (DEP)
P044	Dimethoate
P045	3,3-Dimethyl-1-(methylthio)-2-butanone, O-[(methylamino)carbonyl] oxime
P071	O,O-Dimethyl O-*p*-nitrophenyl phosphorothioate
P082	Dimethylnitrosamine
P046	alpha,alpha-Dimethylphenethylamine
P047	4,6-Dinitro-*o*-cresol and salts
P048	2,4-Dinitrophenol
P020	Dinoseb
P085	Diphosphoramide, octamethyl
P039	Disulfoton
P049	2,4-Dithiobiuret
P050	Endosulfan
P088	Endothal
P051	Endrin
P042	Epinephrine
P101	Ethyl cyanide
P054	Ethylenimine
P097	Famphur
P056	Fluorine
P057	Fluoroacetamide
P058	Fluoroacetic acid, sodium salt
P065	Fulminic acid, mercury (II) salt (R,T)
P059	Heptachlor
P051	1,2,3,4,10,10-Hexachloro-6,7-epoxy-1,4,4a,5,6,7,8,8a-octahydro-endo, endo-1,4:5,8-dimethanonaphthalene
P037	1,2,3,4,10,10,-Hexachloro-6,7-epoxy-1,4,4a,5,6,7,8,8a-octahydro-endo, exo-1,4:5,8-dimethanonaphthalene

P060	1,2,3,4,10,10-Hexachloro-1,4,4a,5,8,8a-hexahydro-1,4:5,8-endo, endo-dimethanonaphthalene
P004	1,2,3,4,10,10-Hexachloro-1,4,4a,5,8,8a-hexahydro-1,4:5,8-endo, exo-dimethanonaphthalene
P062	Hexaethyltetraphosphate
P116	Hydrazinecarbothioamide
P068	Hydrazine, methyl-
P063	Hydrocyanic acid
P063	Hydrogen cyanide
P096	Hydrogen phosphide
P064	Isocyanic acid, methyl ester
P007	3(2H)-isoxazolone, 5-(aminomethyl)-
P092	Mercury, (acetato-O) phenyl-
P065	Mercury fulminate (R,T)
P016	Methane, oxybis(chloro)-
P112	Methane, tetranitro- (R)
P118	Methanethiol, trichloro-
P050	6,9-Methano-2,4,3-benzodioxathiepin, 6,7,8,9,10,10-hexachloro- 1,5,5a,6,9,9a-hexahydro-, 3-oxide
P059	4,7-Methano-1H-indene, 1,4,5,6,7,8,8-heptachloro-3a,4,7,7a-tetrahydro-
P066	Methomyl
P067	2-Methylaziridine
P068	Methyl hydrazine
P064	Methyl isocyanate
P069	2-Methyllactonitrile
P071	Methyl parathion
P072	alpha-Naphthylthiourea
P073	Nickel carbonyl
P074	Nickel cyanide
P075	Nicotine and salts
P076	Nitric oxide
P077	*p*-Nitroaniline

P078	Nitrogen dioxide
P076	Nitrogen (II) oxide
P078	Nitrogen (IV) oxide
P081	Nitroglycerine (R)
P082	N-Nitrosodimethylamine
P084	N-Nitrosomethylvinyl-amine
P085	Octamethylpyrophosphor-amide
P087	Osmium oxide
P087	Osmium tetroxide
P088	7-Oxabicyclo-[2.2.1] hep-tane-2,3-dicarboxylic acid
P089	Parathion
P034	Phenol, 2-cyclohexyl-4,6-dinitro-
P048	Phenol, 2,4-dinitro-
P047	Phenol, 2-methyl-4,6-dini-tro- and salts
P020	Phenol, 2,4-dinitro-6-(1-methylpropyl)-
P009	Phenol, 2,4,6-trinitro-, am-monium salt (R)
P092	Phenylmercury acetate
P093	Phenylthiourea
P094	Phorate
P095	Phosgene
P096	Phosphine
P041	Phosphoric acid, diethyl 4-nitrophenyl ester
P044	Phosphorodithioic acid, O,O-dimethyl S-[2-(methyl-amino)-2-oxyethyl] ester
P043	Phosphorofluoric acid, bis(1-methylethyl)ester
P094	Phosphorothioic acid, O,O-diethyl S-(ethylthio) methyl ester
P089	Phosphorothioic acid, O,O-diethyl O(p-nitrophenyl) ester
P040	Phosphorothioic acid, O,O-diethyl O-pyrazinyl ester

P097	Phosphorothioic acid, O,O-dimethyl O-[p(dimethyl-amino)-sulfonyl) phenyl] ester
P110	Plumbane, tetraethyl-
P098	Potassium cyanide
P099	Potassium silver cyanide
P070	Propanal, 2-methyl-2-(methylthio)-O-[(methylam-ino) carbonyl]oxime
P101	Propanenitrile
P027	Propanenitrile, 3-chloro
P069	Propanenitrile, 2-hydroxy-2-methyl-
P081	1,2,3-Propanetriol, trini-trate- (R)
P017	2-Propanone, 1-bromo-
P102	Propargyl alcohol
P003	2-Propenal
P005	2-Propen-1-ol
P067	1,2-Propylenimine
P102	2-Propyn-1-ol
P008	Pyridinamine
P075	Pyridine, (S)-3-(1-methyl-2-pyrrolidinyl)-, and salts
P111	Pyrophosphoric acid, tetra-ethyl ester
P103	Selenourea
P104	Silver cyanide
P105	Sodium azide
P106	Sodium cyanide
P107	Strontium sulfide
P108	Strychnidin-10-one, and salts
P018	Strychnidin-10-one, 2,3-di-methoxy-
P108	Strychnine and salts
P115	Sulfuric acid, thallium (I) salts
P109	Tetraethyldithiopyrophos-phate
P110	Tetraethyl lead
P111	Tetraethylpyrophosphate

P112	Tetranitromethane (R)	P123	Toxaphene
P062	Tetraphosphoric acid, hexaethyl ester	P118	Trichloromethanethiol
P113	Thallic oxide	P119	Vanadic acid, ammonium salt
P113	Thallium (III) oxide		
P114	Thallium (I) selenite	P120	Vanadium pentoxide
P115	Thallium (I) sulfate	P120	Vanadium (V) oxide
P109	Thiodiphosphoric acid, tetraethyl ester	P084	Vinylamine, N-methyl-N-nitroso-
P045	Thiofanax	P001	Warfarin, when present at concentrations greater than 0.3%
P049	Thiomidodicarbonic diamide		
P014	Thiophenol		
P116	Thiosemicarbazide	P121	Zinc cyanide
P026	Thiourea, (2-chlorophenyl)-	P122	Zinc phosphide, when present at concentrations greater than 10%
P072	Thiourea, 1-naphthalenyl-		
P093	Thiourea, phenyl		

The following U code wastes are nonacutely hazardous:

U001	Acetaldehyde (I)		1,1a,2,8,8a,8b-hexahydro-8a-methoxy-5-methyl-
U034	Acetaldehyde, trichloro-		
U187	Acetamide, N-(4-ethoxyphenyl)-	U157	Benz(j)aceanthrylene, 1,2-dihydro-3-methyl-
U005	Acetamide, N-9H-fluoren-2-yl-	U016	3,4-Benzacridine
U112	Acetic acid, ethyl ester (I)	U017	Benzal chloride
U144	Acetic acid, lead salt	U192	Benzamide, 3-5-dichloro-N-(1,1-diethyl-2-propynyl)-
U214	Acetic acid, thallium (1+) salt		
U002	Acetone (I)	U018	Benz(a)anthracene
U003	Acetonitrile (I,T)	U094	Benzanthracene, 7,12-dimethyl-
U004	Acetophenone		
U005	2-Acetylaminofluorene	U012	Benzenamine (I,T)
U006	Acetyl chloride (C,R,T)	U014	Benzenamine, 4,4'-carbonimidoylbis(N,N-dimethyl)-
U007	Acrylamide		
U008	Acrylic acid (I)	U049	Benzenamine, 4-chloro-2-methyl-
U009	Acrylonitrile		
U011	Amitrole	U093	Benzenamine, N,N'-dimethyl-4-phenylazo-
U012	Aniline (I,T)		
U014	Auramine	U158	Benzenamine, 4,4'-methylenebis(2-chloro)-
U015	Azaserine		
U010	Azirino (2',3',3',4)pyrrolo (1,2-a)indole-4,7-dione, 6-amino-8-[((aminocarbonyl)oxy)methyl]-	U222	Benzenamine, 2-methyl-, hydrochloride
		U181	Benzenamine, 2-methyl-,5-nitro
		U019	Benzene

U038	Benzeneacetic acid, 4-chloro-alpha-(4-chlorophenyl)-alpha-hydroxy, ethyl ester	U020	Benzenesulfonyl chloride (C,R)
U030	Benzene, 1-bromo-4-phenoxy-	U207	Benzene, 1,2,4,5-tetrachloro-
U037	Benzene, chloro	U061	Benzene, 1,1'-(2,2,2-trichloroethylidene)bis[1-chloro-
U221	Benzenediamine, ar-methyl-	U247	Benzene, 1,1'-(2,2,2-trichloroethylidene)[4-methoxy-
U190	1,2-Benzenedicarboxylic acid anhydride		
U028	1,2-Benzenedicarboxylic acid [bis(2-ethyl-hexyl)] ester	U023	Benzene, (trichloromethyl)- (C,R,T)
U069	1,2-Benzenedicarboxylic acid, dibutyl ester	U234	Benzene, 1,3,5-trinitro (R,T)
U088	1,2-Benzenedicarboxylic acid, diethyl ester	U021	Benzidine
U102	1,2-Benzenedicarboxylic acid, dimethyl ester	U202	1,2-Benzisothiazolin-3-one, 1,1-dioxide
U107	1,2-Benzenedicarboxylic acid, di-*n*-octyl ester	U203	1,3-Benzodioxole, 5-(2-propenyl)-
U070	Benzene, 1,2-dichloro-	U141	1,3-Benzodioxole, 5-(1-propenyl)-
U071	Benzene, 1,3-dichloro-	U090	1,3-Benzodioxole, 5-propyl-
U072	Benzene, 1,4-dichloro-		
U060	Benzene, 1,1-(2,2-dichloroethylidene)bis[4-chloro-	U064	Benzo[rst]pentaphene
U017	Benzene, (dichloromethyl)-	U197	*p*-Benzoquinone
U223	Benzene, 1,3-diisocyanato-methyl- (R,T)	U023	Benzotrichloride (C,R,T)
U239	Benzene, dimethyl- (I,T)	U085	2,2'-Bioxirane (I,T)
U201	1,3-Benzenediol	U021	[1,1'-Biphenyl]-4,4'-diamine
U127	Benzene, hexachloro-	U073	[1,1'-Biphenyl]-4,4'-diamine, 3,3'-dichloro-
U056	Benzene, hexahydro- (I)		
U220	Benzene, methyl-	U091	[1,1'-Biphenyl]-4,4'-diamine, 3,3'-dimethoxy-
U105	Benzene, 1-methyl-2,4-dinitro-	U095	[1,1'-Biphenyl]-4,4'-diamine, 3,3'-dimethyl-
U106	Benzene, 2-methyl-1,3-dinitro-	U027	Bis(2-chloroisopropyl) ether
U055	Benzene, (1-methylethyl) (I)	U024	Bis(2-chloromethoxy) ethane
U169	Benzene, nitro- (I,T)	U028	Bis(2-ethyhexyl)phthalate (DEHP)
U183	Benzene, pentachloro-	U225	Bromoform
U185	Benzene, pentachloronitro-	U030	4-Bromophenyl phenyl ether
U020	Benzenesulfonic acid chloride (C,R)	U128	1,3-Butadiene, 1,1,2,3,4,4-hexachloro

U172	1-Butanamine, N-butyl-N-nitroso-
U031	1-Butanol (I)
U159	2-Butanone (I,T)
U160	2-Butanone peroxide (R,T)
U053	2-Butenal
U074	2-Butene, 1,4-dichloro-(I,T)
U143	2-Butenoic acid, 2-methyl-, 7-[(2,3-dihydroxy)-3-methyl-1-oxobutoxy) methyl]-2,3,5,7a-tetra-hydro-1-pyrrolizin-1-yl ester, [1S[alpha(Z),7(2S,3R), 7aalpha]]-
U031	n-Butyl alcohol (I)

U136	Cacodylic acid
U032	Calcium chromate
U238	Carbamic acid, ethyl ester
U178	Carbamic acid, methylni-troso-, ethyl ester
U114	Carbamodithioic acid, 1-2-ethanediylbis-, salts and esters
U062	Carbamothioic acid, bis(1-methylethyl)-S-(2,3,-di-chloro-2-propenyl) ester
U215	Carbonic acid, dithallium (I) salt
U033	Carbonic difluoride
U156	Carbonochloridic acid, methyl ester (I,T)
U033	Carbon oxyfluoride (R,T)
U211	Carbon tetrachloride
U034	Chloral
U035	Chlorambucil
U036	Chlordane
U026	Chlornaphazine
U037	Chlorobenzene
U039	4-Chloro-m-cresol
U041	1-Chloro-2,3-epoxypropane
U042	2-Chloroethyl vinyl ether
U044	Chloroform
U046	Chloromethyl methyl ether
U047	beta-Chloronaphthalene
U048	o-Chlorophenol

U049	4-Chloro-o-toluidine, hy-drochloride
U032	Chromic acid, calcium salt
U050	Chrysene
U051	Creosote
U052	Cresols (Cresylic acid)
U053	Crotonaldehyde
U055	Cumene (I)
U246	Cyanogen bromide
U197	2,5-Cyclohexadiene-1, 4-dione
U056	Cyclohexane (I)
U057	Cyclohexanone (I)
U130	1,3-Cyclopentadiene, 1,2,3,4,5,5-hexachloro-
U058	Cyclophosphamide

U240	2,4-D, salts and esters
U059	Daunomycin
U060	DDD
U061	DDT
U062	Diallate
U133	Diamine (R,T)
U063	Dibenz(a,h)anthracene
U064	Dibenz(a,i)pyrene
U066	1,2-Dibromo-3-chloropro-pane
U069	Dibutyl phthalate
U070	o-Dichlorobenzene
U071	m-Dichlorobenzene
U072	p-Dichlorobenzene
U073	3,3'-Dichlorobenzidine
U074	1,4-Dichloro-2-butene (I,T)
U075	Dichlorodifluoromethane
U078	1,1-Dichloroethylene
U079	1,2-Dichloroethylene
U025	Dichloroethyl ether
U081	2,4-Dichlorophenol
U082	2,6-Dichlorophenol
U240	2,4-Dichlorophenoxyacetic acid, salts and esters
U083	1,2-Dichloropropane
U084	1,3-Dichloropropene
U085	1,2:3,4-Diepoxybutane (I,T)
U108	1,4-Diethylene dioxide
U086	N,N-Diethylhydrazine

U087	O,O-Diethyl-S-methyl-dithiophosphate	U209	Ethane, 1,1,2,2-tetrachloro-
U088	Diethyl phthalate	U218	Ethanethioamide
U089	Diethylstilbestrol	U359	Ethanol, 2-ethoxy-
U148	1,2-Dihydro-3,6-pyradizinedione	U227	Ethane, 1,1,2-trichloro-
U090	Dihydrosafrole	U004	Ethanone, 1-phenyl-
U091	3,3'-Dimethoxybenzidine	U043	Ethene, chloro-
U092	Dimethylamine (I)	U042	Ethene, (2-chloroethoxy)-
U093	Dimethylaminoazobenzene	, U079	Ethene, 1,1-dichloro-
U094	7,12-Dimethylbenz(a)anthracene	U079	Ethene, 1,2-dicloro-(E)-
		U210	Ethene, tetrachloro-
U095	3,3'-Dimethylbenzidine	U228	Ethene, trichloro
U096	alpha,alpha-Dimethylbenzylhydroperoxide (R)	U112	Ethyl acetate (I)
		U113	Ethyl acrylate (I)
U097	Dimethylcarbamoyl chloride	U238	Ethyl carbamate (urethane)
		U038	Ethyl 4,4'-dichlorobenzilate
U098	1,1-Dimethylhydrazine	U359	Ethylene glycol monoethyl ether
U099	1,2-Dimethylhydrazine		
U101	2,4-Dimethylphenol	U114	Ethylenebisdithiocarbamic acid, salts, and esters
U102	Dimethyl phthalate		
U103	Dimethyl sulfate	U067	Ethylene dibromide
U105	2,4-Dinitrotoluene	U077	Ethylene dichloride
U106	2,6-Dinitrotoluene	U115	Ethylene oxide (I,T)
U107	Di-n-octyl phthalate	U116	Ethylene thiourea
U108	1,4-Dioxane	U117	Ethyl ether
U109	1,2-Diphenylhydrazine	U076	Ethylidene dichloride
U110	Dipropylamine (I)	U118	Ethylmethacrylate
U111	Di-N-propylnitrosamine	U119	Ethylmethanesulfonate
U001	Ethanal (I)	U120	Fluoranthene
U174	Ethanamine, N-ethyl-N-nitroso-	U122	Formaldehyde
		U123	Formic acid (C,T)
U155	1,2-Ethanediamine, N,N-dimethyl-N'-2-pyridinyl-N'-(2-thienylmethyl)-	U124	Furan (I)
		U125	2-Furancarboxaldehyde (I)
		U147	2,5-Furandione
U067	Ethane, 1,2-dibromo-	U213	Furan, tetrahydro- (I)
U076	Ethane, 1,1-dichloro-	U125	Furfural (I)
U077	Ethane, 1,2-dichloro-	U124	Furfuran (I)
U131	Ethane, hexachloro-		
U024	Ethane, 1,1'-[methylenebis(oxy)]bis(2-chloro)-	U206	D-Glucopyranose, 2-deoxy-2(3-methyl-3-nitrosoureido)-
U117	Ethane, 1,1'-oxybis- (I)		
U025	Ethane, 1,1'-oxybis(2-chloro)-	U126	Glycidylaldehyde
		U163	Guanidine, N-nitroso-N-methyl-N'nitro-
U184	Ethane pentachloro-		
U208	Ethane, 1,1,1,2-tetrachloro-		

U127	Hexachlorobenzene	U046	Methane, chloromethoxy-
U128	Hexachlorobutadiene	U068	Methane, dibromo-
U129	Hexachlorocyclohexane	U080	Methane, dichloro-
	(gamma isomer)	U075	Methane, dichlorodifluoro-
U130	Hexachlorocyclopentadiene	U138	Methane, iodo-
U131	Hexachloroethane	U119	Methanesulfonic acid,
U132	Hexachlorophene		ethyl ester
U243	Hexachloropropene	U211	Methane, tetrachloro-
U133	Hydrazine (R,T)	U153	Methanethiol (I,T)
U086	Hydrazine, 1,2-diethyl-	U225	Methane, tribromo-
U098	Hydrazine, 1,1-dimethyl-	U044	Methane, trichloro-
U099	Hydrazine, 1,2-dimethyl-	U121	Methane, trichlorofluoro-
U109	Hydrazine, 1,2-diphenyl-	U123	Methanoic acid (C,T)
U134	Hydrofluoric acid (C,T)	U154	Methanol (I)
U134	Hydrogen fluoride (C,T)	U155	Methapyrilene
U135	Hydrogen sulfide	U142	1,3,4-Metheno-2H-cyclo-
U096	Hydroperoxide, 1-methyl-		buta[cd]pentalen-2-one,
	1-phenylethyl- (R)		1,1a,3,3a,4,5,5,5a,5b,6-
U136	Hydroxydimethylarsine		decachlorooctahydro-
	oxide	U247	Methoxychlor
		U154	Methyl alcohol (I)
U116	2-Imidazolidinethione	U029	Methyl bromide
U137	Indeno(1,2,3-cd)pyrene	U186	1-Methylbutadiene (I)
U190	1,3-Isobenzofurandione	U045	Methyl chloride (I,T)
U140	Isobutyl alcohol (I,T)	U156	Methyl chlorocarbonate
U141	Isosafrole		(I,T)
		U226	Methyl chloroform
U142	Kepone	U157	3-Methylcholanthrene
		U158	4,4'-Methylenebis(2-chlo-
U143	Lasiocarpine		roaniline)
U144	Lead acetate	U068	Methylene bromide
U146	Lead, bis(acetato-	U080	Methylene chloride
	O)tetrahydroxytri-	U159	Methyl ethyl ketone (I,T)
U145	Lead phosphate	U160	Methyl ethyl ketone per-
U146	Lead subacetate		oxide (R,T)
U129	Lindane	U138	Methyl iodide
		U161	Methyl isobutyl ketone (I)
U147	Maleic anhydride	U162	Methyl methacrylate (I,T)
U148	Maleic hydrazide	U163	N-Methyl-N'-nitro-N-nitro-
U149	Malononitrile		soguanidine
U150	Melphalan	U161	4-Methyl-2-pentanone (I)
U151	Mercury	U164	Methylthiouracil
U152	Methacrylonitrile (I,T)	U010	Mitomycin C
U092	Methanamine, N-methyl-		
	(I)		
U029	Methane, bromo-	U059	5,12-Naphthacenedione,
U045	Methane, chloro- (I,T)		(8S-*cis*)-8-acetyl-10-[(3-

	amino-2,3,6-trideoxy-alpha- L-lyxo-hexopyranosyl)- oxyl]-7,8,9,10-tetrahydro- 6,8,11- trihydroxy-1-methy- oxy-	U184 U185	Pentachloroethane Pentachloronitrobenzene (PCNB)
U165	Naphthalene	U186	1,3-Pentadiene (I)
U047	Naphthalene, 2-chloro-	U187	Phenacetin
U166	1,4-Naphthalenedione	U188	Phenol
U236	2,7-Naphthalenedisulfonic	U048	Phenol, 2-chloro-
	acid, 3,3'-[(3,3'-dimethyl-	U039	Phenol, 4-chloro-3-methyl-
	(1,1'biphenyl)-4,4'diyl)]-	U081	Phenol, 2,4-dichloro-
	bis(azo)bis(5-amino-4-hy-	U082	Phenol, 2,6-dichloro-
	droxy)-, tetrasodium salt	U089	Phenol, 4,4'-(1,2-diethyl-
U167	1-Naphthylamine		1,2-ethenediyl)bis-
U168	2-Naphthylamine	U101	Phenol, 2,4-dimethyl-
U167	alpha-Naphthylamine	U170	Phenol, 4-nitro-
U168	beta-Naphthylamine	U242	Phenol, pentachloro-
U026	2-Naphthylamine, N,N'-	U212	Phenol, 2,3,4,6-tetrachloro-
	bis(2-chloromethyl)-	U230	Phenol, 2,4,5-trichloro-
U217	Nitric acid, thallium (1 +)	U231	Phenol, 2,4,6-trichloro-
	salt	U150	L-Phenylalanine, 4-[bis(2-
U169	Nitrobenzene (I,T)		chloroethyl)amino]-
U170	p-Nitrophenol	U145	Phosphoric acid, lead salt
U171	2-Nitropropane (I)	U087	Phosphorodithioic acid
U172	N-Nitrosodi-n-butylamine		O,O-diethyl-, S-methyles-
U173	N-Nitrosodiethanolamine		ter
U174	N-Nitrosodiethylamine	U189	Phosphorous sulfide (R)
U176	N-Nitroso-N-ethylurea	U190	Phthalic anhydride
U177	N-Nitroso-N-methylurea	U191	2-Picoline
U178	N-Nitroso-N-methylure-	U192	Pronamide
	thane	U194	1-Propanamine (I,T)
U179	N-Nitrosopiperidine	U111	1-Propanamine, N-nitroso-
U180	N-Nitrosopyrrolidine		N-propyl-
U181	5-Nitro-o-toluidine	U110	1-Propanamine, N-propyl-
			(I)
U193	1,2-Oxathiolane, 2,2-	U066	Propane, 1,2-dibromo-3-
	dioxide		chloro-
U058	2H-1,3,2-Oxazaphospho-	U149	Propanedinitrile
	rine, 2-[bis(2-chloroethyl)	U171	Propane, 2-nitro- (I)
	amino] tetrahydro-, oxide	U027	Propane, 2,2'-oxybis (2-
	2-		chloro)-
U115	Oxirane (I,T)	U193	1,3-Propane sultone
U041	Oxirane, 2-(chloromethyl)-	U235	1-Propanol, 2,3-dibromo-,
			phosphate(3:1)
U182	Paraldehyde	U140	1-Propanol, 2-methyl- (I,T)
U183	Pentachlorobenzene	U007	2-Propenamide
		U243	1-Propene, hexachloro-
		U009	2-Propenenitrile
		U008	2-Propenoic acid (I)

U113	2-Propenoic acid, ethyl ester (I)	U218	Thioacetamide
U118	2-Propenoic acid, 2-methyl-, ethyl ester	U153	Thiomethanol (I,T)
		U244	Thioperoxydicarbonic diamide, tetramethyl
U162	2-Propenoic acid, 2-methyl-, methyl ester (I,T)	U219	Thiourea
U233	Propionic acid, 2-(2,4,5-trichlorophenoxy)-	U244	Thiuram
		U220	Toluene
U194	n-Propylamine (I,T)	U221	Toluenediamine
U083	Propylene dichloride	U223	Toluene diisocyanate (R,T)
U148	3,6-Pyridazinedione, 1-2-dihydro-	U328	o-Toluidine
		U222	o-Toluidine hydrochloride
U196	Pyridine	U353	p-Toluidine
U191	Pyridine, 2-methyl-	U011	1H-1,2,4-Triazol-3-amine
U237	2,4(1H,3H)-Pyrimidine-dione, 5-[bis(2-chloro-ethyl)amino]-	U226	1,1,1-Trichloroethane
		U227	1,1,2-Trichloroethane
		U228	Trichloroethylene
U164	4(1H)-Pyrimidinone, 2,3-dihydro-6-methyl-2-thioxo-	U121	Trichloromonofluoromethane
U180	Pyrrolidine, 1-nitroso-	U234	sym-Trinitrobenzene (R,T)
		U182	1,3,5-Trioxane, 2,4,5-tri-methyl-
U200	Reserpine	U235	Tris(2,3-dibromopropyl) phosphate
U201	Resorcinol		
		U236	Trypan blue
U202	Saccharin and salts		
U203	Safrole	U237	Uracil mustard
U204	Selenious acid	U176	Urea, N-ethyl-N-nitroso-
U204	Selenium dioxide	U177	Urea, N-methyl-N-nitroso-
U205	Selenium sulfide (R,T)		
U015	L-Serine, diazoacetate (ester)	U043	Vinyl chloride
U206	Streptozotocin	U248	Warfarin, when present at concentrations of 0.3% or less
U103	Sulfuric acid, dimethyl ester		
U189	Sulfur phosphide (R)	U239	Xylene (I)
U207	1,2,4,5-Tetrachlorobenzene	U200	Yohimban-16-carboxylic acid, 11,17-dimethoxy-18-[(3,4,5-trimethoxy-ben-zoyl)oxy]-methyl ester
U208	1,1,1,2-Tetrachloroethane		
U209	1,1,2,2-Tetrachloroethane		
U210	Tetrachloroethylene		
U213	Tetrahydrofuran (I)	U249	Zinc phosphide, when present at concentrations of 10% or less
U214	Thallium (I) acetate		
U215	Thallium (I) carbonate		
U216	Thallium chloride		
U217	Thallium (I) nitrate		

Appendix D

The Hazardous Constituents (The Appendix VIII Constituents)

Common Name	Common Name	Common Name
Acetonitrile	Arsenic and com-	Beryllium and com-
Acetophenone	pounds, N.O.S.	pounds, N.O.S.
2-Acetylaminefluorene	Arsenic acid	Bis(2-chloromethoxy)
Acetyl chloride	Arsenic pentoxide	ethane
1-Acetyl-2-thiourea	Arsenic trioxide	Bis(2-chloroethyl) ether
Acrolein	Auramine	Bis(chloromethyl) ether
Acrylamide	Azaserine	Bis(2-ethylhexyl)
Acrylonitrile		phthalate
Aflatoxins	Barium and compounds,	Bromoacetone
Aldicarb	N.O.S.	Bromoform
Aldrin	Barium cyanide	4-Bromophenyl phenyl
Allyl alcohol	Benz(c)acridine	ether
Aluminum phosphide	Benz(a)anthracene	Brucine
4-Aminobiphenyl	Benzal chloride	Butyl benzyl phthalate
5-(Aminomethyl)-3-isox-	Benzene	
azolol	Benzenearsonic acid	Cacodylic acid
4-Aminopyridine	Benzidine	Cadmium and com-
Amitrole	Benzo(b)fluoranthene	pounds, N.O.S.
Ammonium vanadate	Benzo(j)fluoranthene	Calcium chromate
Aniline	Benzo(a)pyrene	Calcium cyanide
Antimony and com-	p-Benzoquinone	Carbon disulfide
pounds, N.O.S.	Benzotrichloride	Carbon oxyfluoride
Aramite	Benzyl chloride	Carbon tetrachloride

435

Common Name	Common Name	Common Name
Chloral	Cyanogen	Dichloropropanol,
Chlorambucil	Cyanogen bromide	N.O.S.
Chlordane (alpha and	Cyanogen chloride	Dichloropropene,
gamma isomers)	Cycasin	N.O.S.
Chlorinated benzenes,	2-Cyclohexyl-4,6-dini-	1,3-Dichloropropene
N.O.S.	trophenol	Dieldrin
Chlorinated ethane,	Cyclophosphamide	1,2:3,4-Diepoxybutane
N.O.S.		Diethylarsine
Chlorinated fluorocar-	2,4-D, salts and esters	1,4-Diethyleneoxide
bons, N.O.S.	Daunomycin	Diethyl phthalate
Chlorinated naphtha-	DDD	N,N'-Diethylhydrazine
lene, N.O.S.	DDE	O,O-Diethyl S-methyl
Chlorinated phenol,	DDT	dithiophosphate
N.O.S.	Diallate	Diethyl-*p*-nitrophenyl
Chlornaphazin	Dibenz(a,h)acridine	phosphate
Chloroacetaldehyde	Dibenz(a,j)acridine	O,O-Diethyl O-pyra-
Chloroalkyl ethers,	Dibenz(a,h)anthracene	zinyl phosphorothio-
N.O.S.	7H-Dibenzo(c,g)	ate
p-Chloroaniline	carbazole	Diethylstilbesterol
Chlorobenzene	Dibenzo(a,e)pyrene	Dihydrosafrole
Chlorobenzilate	Dibenzo(a,h)pyrene	Diisopropylfluoro-
p-Chloro-*m*-cresol	Dibenzo(a,i)pyrene	phosphate (DFP)
1-Chloro-2,3-epoxypro-	1,2-Dibromo-3-chloro-	Dimethoate
pane	propane	3,3'-Dimethoxybenzi-
Chloroform	Dibutyl phthalate	dine
Chloromethyl methyl	*o*-Dichlorobenzene	*p*-Dimethylaminoazo-
ether	*m*-Dichlorobenzene	benzene
beta-Chloronaphthalene	*p*-Dichlorobenzene	7,12-Dimethylbenz[a]
o-Chlorophenol	Dichlorobenzene,	anthracene
1-(*o*-Chlorophenyl)	N.O.S.	3,3'-Dimethylbenzidine
thiourea	3,3'-Dichlorobenzidine	Dimethylcarbamoyl
Chloroprene	1,4-Dichloro-2-butene	chloride
3-Chloropropionitrile	Dichlorodifluoromethane	1,1-Dimethylhydrazine
Chromium and com-	Dichloroethylene,	1,2-Dimethylhydrazine
pounds, N.O.S.	N.O.S.	alpha,alpha-Dimethyl-
Chrysene	1,1-Dichloroethylene	phenethylamine
Citrus red No. 2	1,2-Dichloroethylene	2,4-Dimethylphenol
Coal tar	Dichloroethyl ether	Dimethyl phthalate
Copper cyanide	Dichloroisopropyl	Dimethyl sulfate
Creosote	Dichloromethyl ether	Dinitrobenzene, N.O.S.
Cresol (Cresylic acid)	2,4-Dichlorophenol	4,6-Dinitro-*o*-cresol and
Crotonaldehyde	2,6-Dichlorophenol	salts
Cyanides (soluble salts	Dichlorophenylarsine	2,4-Dinitrophenol
and complexes)	Dichloropropane,	2,4-Dinitrotoluene
N.O.S.	N.O.S.	2,6-Dinitrotoluene

Common Name	Common Name	Common Name
Dinoseb	Hexachlorobenzene	Methyl bromide
Di-*n*-octyl phthalate	Hexachlorobutadiene	Methyl chloride
Diphenylamine	Hexachlorocyclopen-	Methyl chlorocarbonate
1,2-Diphenylhydrazine	tadiene	Methyl chloroform
Di-*n*-propylnitrosamine	Hexachlorodibenzo-*p*-	3-Methylcholanthrene
Disulfoton	dioxins	4,4'-Methylenebis(2-
Dithiobiuret	Hexachlorodibenzo-	chloroaniline)
	furans	Methylene bromide
Endosulfan	Hexachloroethane	Methylene chloride
Endothal	Hexachlorophene	Methyl ethyl ketone
Endrin and metabolites	Hexachloropropene	(MEK)
Epichlorhydrin	Hexaethyl tetraphos-	Methyl ethyl ketone
Epinephrine	phate	peroxide
Ethyl carbamate (Ure-	Hydrazine	Methyl hydrazine
thane)	Hydrogen cyanide	Methyl iodide
Ethyl cyanide	Hydrogen fluoride	Methyl isocyanate
Ethylenebisdithiocar-	Hydrogen sulfide	2-Methyllactonitrile
bamic acid, salts and		Methyl methacrylate
esters	Indeno(1,2,3-cd)pyrene	Methyl methanesulfo-
Ethylene dibromide	Iron dextran	nate
Ethylene dichloride	Isobutyl alcohol	Methyl parathion
Ethylene glycol mono-	Isodrin	Methylthiouracil
ethyl ether	Isosafrole	Mitomycin C
Ethyleneimine		MNNG
Ethylene oxide	Kepone	Mustard gas
Ethylenethiourea		
Ethylidene dichloride	Lasiocarpine	Naphthalene
Ethyl methacrylate	Lead and compounds,	1,4-Naphthoquinone
Ethyl methanesulfonate	N.O.S.	alpha-Naphthylamine
	Lead acetate	beta-Naphthylamine
Famphur	Lead phosphate	alpha-Naphthylthiourea
Fluoranthene	Lead subacetate	Nickel and compounds,
Fluorine	Lindane	N.O.S.
Fluoroacetamide		Nickel carbonyl
Fluoroacetic acid, so-	Maleic anhydride	Nickel cyanide
dium salt	Maleic hydrazide	Nicotine and salts
Formaldehyde	Malononitrile	Nitric oxide
	Melphalan	*p*-Nitroaniline
Glycidylaldehyde	Mercury and com-	Nitrobenzene
	pounds, N.O.S.	Nitrogen dioxide
Halomethanes, N.O.S.	Mercury fulminate	Nitrogen mustard and
Heptachlor	Methacrylonitrile	hydrochloride salt
Heptachlor epoxide (al-	Methapyrilene	Nitrogen mustard N-ox-
pha, beta, and gamma	Methomyl	ide and hydrochloride
isomers)	Methoxychlor	salt

Common Name	Common Name	Common Name
Nitroglycerin	Phorate	Tetrachlorodibenzo-*p*-
p-Nitrophenol	Phosgene	dioxins
2-Nitropropane	Phosphine	Tetrachlorodibenzo-
Nitrosamines, N.O.S.	Phthalic acid esters,	furans
N-Nitrosodi-*n*-butyl-	N.O.S.	Tetrachloroethane,
amine	Phthalic anhydride	N.O.S.
N-Nitrosodiethanol-	2-Picoline	1,1,1,2-Tetrachloro-
amine	Polychlorinated biphe-	ethane
N-Nitrosodiethylamine	nyls, N.O.S.	1,1,2,2-Tetrachloro-
N-Nitroso-N-ethylurea	Potassium cyanide	ethane
N-Nitrosomethylethyl-	Potassium silver cya-	Tetrachloroethylene
amine	nide	2,3,4,6-Tetrachloro-
N-Nitroso-N-methylurea	Pronamide	phenol
N-Nitroso-N-methyl-	1,3-Propane sultone	Tetraethyldithiopyro-
urethane	Propargyl alcohol	phosphate
N-Nitrosomethylvinyl-	*n*-Propylamine	Tetraethyl lead
amine	Propylene dichloride	Tetraethyl pyrophos-
N-Nitrosomorpholine	1,2-Propylenimine	phate
N-Nitrosonornicotine	Propylthiouracil	Tetranitromethane
N-Nitrosopiperidine	Pyridine	Thallium and com-
N-Nitrosopyrrolidine		pounds, N.O.S.
N-Nitrososarcosine	Reserpine	Thallic oxide
5-Nitro-*o*-toluidine	Resorcinol	Thallium (I) acetate
		Thallium (I) carbonate
Octamethylpyrophos-		Thallium (I) chloride
phoramide	Saccharin and salts	Thallium (I) nitrate
Osmium tetroxide	Safrole	Thallium selenite
	Selenium and com-	Thallium (I) sulfate
Paraldehyde	pounds, N.O.S.	Thioacetamide
Parathion	Selenium dioxide	Thiofanox
Pentachlorobenzene	Selenium sulfide	Thiomethanol
Pentachlorodibenzo-*p*-	Selenourea	Thiophenol
dioxins	Silver and compounds,	Thiosemicarbazide
Pentachlorodibenzo-	N.O.S.	Thiourea
furans	Silver cyanide	Thiram
Pentachloroethane	Silvex (2,4,5-TP)	Toluene
Pentachloronitrobenzene	Sodium cyanide	Toluenediamine
(PCNB)	Streptozotocin	Toluene-2,4-diamine
Pentachlorophenol	Strontium sulfide	Toluene-2,6-diamine
Phenacetin	Strychnine and salts	Toluene-3,4-diamine
Phenol		Toluene diisocyanate
Phenylenediamine	TCDD	*o*-Toluidine
Phenylmercury acetate	1,2,4,5-Tetrachloroben-	*o*-Toluidine hydrochlo-
Phenylthiourea	zene	ride

Common Name	Common Name	Common Name
p-Toluidine	Trichloropropane,	Uracil mustard
Toxaphene	N.O.S.	
1,2,4-Trichlorobenzene	1,2,3-Trichloropropane	Vanadium pentoxide
1,1,2-Trichloroethane	O,O,O-Triethyl phos-	Vinyl chloride
Trichloroethylene	phorothioate	
Trichloromethanethiol	1,3,5-Trinitrobenzene	
Trichloromonofluoro-	Tris(1-aziridinyl)phos-	Warfarin and salts
methane	phine sulfide	
2,4,5-Trichlorophenol	Tris(2,3-dibromopropyl)	
2,4,6-Trichlorophenol	phosphate	Zinc cyanide
2,4,5-T	Trypan blue	Zinc phosphide

Appendix E

Groundwater Monitoring Constituents (The Appendix IX Constituents)

Common Name	Common Name	Common Name
Acenaphthene	*Barium	Bis(2-chloro-1-methyl-
Acenaphthylene	*Benzene	ethyl) ether; 2,2'-
Acetone	Benzo(a)anthracene	Dichlorodiisopropyl
Acetonitrile (Methyl	(Benzanthracene)	ether
cyanide)	*Benzo(b)fluoranthene	Bis(2-ethylhexyl)
*Acetophenone	Benzo(k)fluoranthene	phthalate
2-Acetylaminofluorene	Benzo(ghi)perylene	Bromodichloromethane
(2-AAF)	*Benzo(a)pyrene	*Bromoform (Tribromo-
*Acrolein	Benzyl alcohol	methane)
*Acrylonitrile	*Beryllium	*4-Bromophenyl phenyl
*Aldrin	alpha-BHC	ether
Allyl chloride	beta-BHC	*Butyl benzyl phthalate
*4-Aminobiphenyl	delta-BHC	(Benzyl butyl
*Aniline	gamma-BHC; Lindane	phthalate)
Anthracene	Bis(2-chloroethoxy)	
*Antimony	methane	*Cadmium
*Aramite	Bis(2-chloroethyl)	*Carbon disulfide
*Arsenic	ether	*Carbon tetrachloride

*These constituents also are Appendix VIII hazardous constituents.

440

Common Name	Common Name	Common Name
*Chlordane	*Dichlorodifluoro-	Endosulfan sulfate
*p-Chloroaniline	methane	*Endrin
*Chlorobenzene	1,1-Dichloroethane	Endrin aldehyde
*Chlorobenzilate	1,2-Dichloroethane	Ethylbenzene
*p-Chloro-m-cresol	(Ethylene dichloride)	Ethyl methacrylate
Chloroethane (Ethyl	*1,1-Dichloroethylene	Ethyl methanesulfo-
chloride)	(Vinylidene chloride)	nate
*Chloroform	trans-1,2-Dichloroeth-	
2-Chloronaphthalene	ylene	*Famphur
2-Chlorophenol	*2,4-Dichlorophenol	*Fluoranthene
4-Chlorophenyl phenyl	*2,6-Dichlorophenol	*Fluorene
ether	1,2-Dichloropropane	
*Chloroprene	cis-1,3-Dichloropro-	*Heptachlor
*Chromium	pene	*Heptachlor epoxide
*Chrysene	trans-1,3-Dichloropro-	*Hexachlorobenzene
Cobalt	pene	*Hexachlorobutadiene
Copper	*Dieldrin	*Hexachlorocyclo-
*m-Cresol	*Diethyl phthalate	pentadiene
*o-Cresol	O,O-Diethyl O-2-pyra-	*Hexachloroethane
*p-Cresol	zinyl phosphoro-	*Hexachlorophene
*Cyanide	thioate (Thionazin)	*Hexachloropropene
	*Dimethoate	2-Hexanone
	*p-(Dimethylamino)	
*2,4-D (2,4-Dichloro-	azobenzene	*Indeno(1,2,3-cd)pyrene
phenoxyacetic acid)	*7,12-Dimethylbenz(a)	*Isobutyl alcohol
4,4'-DDD	anthracene	*Isodrin
4,4'-DDE	*3,3'-Dimethylbenzidine	Isophorone
4,4'-DDT	*alpha,alpha-Dimethyl-	*Isosafrole
*Diallate	phenethylamine	
*Dibenz(a,h)anthracene	*2,4-Dimethylphenol	*Kepone
Dibenzofuran	*Dimethyl phthalate	
Dibromochloromethane	m-Dinitrobenzene	*Lead
(Chlorodibromometh-	*4,6-Dinitro-o-cresol	
ane)	*2,4-Dinitrophenol	
*1,2-Dibromo-3-chloro-	*2,4-Dinitrotoluene	*Mercury
propane (DBCP)	*2,6-Dinitrotoluene	*Methacrylonitrile
1,2-Dibromoethane	*Dinoseb (DNBP or 2-	*Methapyrilene
(Ethylene dibromide)	sec-Butyl-4,6-dinitro-	*Methoxychlor
Di-n-butyl phthalate	phenol)	*Methyl bromide (Bro-
*o-Dichlorobenzene	*Di-n-octyl phthalate	momethane)
*m-Dichlorobenzene	1,4-Dioxane	*Methyl chloride (Chlo-
*p-Dichlorobenzene	*Diphenylamine	romethane)
*3,3'-Dichlorobenzidine	*Disulfoton	*3-Methylcholanthrene
trans-1,4-Dichloro-2-		*Methylene bromide
butene	Endosulfan I and II	(Dibromomethane)

Common Name	Common Name	Common Name
*Methylene chloride (Dichloromethane)	*N-Nitrosopiperidine	*1,2,4,5-Tetrachloroben- zene
*Methyl ethyl ketone (MEK)	*N-Nitrosopyrrolidine	*1,1,1,2-Tetrachloroeth-
*Methyl iodide (Iodo- methane)	*5-Nitro-o-toluidine	ane
*Methyl methacrylate	*Parathion	*1,1,2,2-Tetrachloroeth- ane
*Methyl methanesulfo- nate	*Polychlorinated bi- phenyls (PCBs)	*Tetrachloroethylene (Perchloroethylene
2-Methylnaphthalene	Polychlorinated di- benzo-p-dioxins	or Tetrachloroeth- ene)
*Methyl parathion (Par- athion methyl)	(PCDDs)	*2,3,4,6-Tetrachloro- phenol
4-Methyl-2-pentanone (Methyl isobutyl ke- tone)	Polychlorinated diben- zofurans (PCDFs)	*Tetraethyl dithiopyro- phosphate (Sulfo- tepp)
	*Pentachlorobenzene *Pentachlorethane *Pentachloronitro-	
*Naphthalene	benzene	*Thallium
*1,4-Naphthoquinone	*Pentachlorophenol	Tin
1-Naphthylamine	*Phenacetin	*Toluene
2-Naphthylamine	Phenanthrene	*o-Toluidine
*Nickel	*Phenol	*Toxaphene
o-Nitroaniline	p-Phenylenediamine	*1,2,4-Trichlorobenzene
m-Nitroaniline	*Phorate	1,1,1-Trichloroethane
*p-Nitroaniline	*2-Picoline	(Methylchloroform)
*Nitrobenzene	*Pronamide	*1,1,2-Trichloroethane
o-Nitrophenol	Propionitrile (Ethyl cy-	*Trichloroethylene
*p-Nitrophenol	anide)	(Trichloroethene)
4-Nitroquinoline 1-ox- ide	Pyrene	Trichlorofluoromethane
*N-Nitrosodi-n-butyl-	*Pyridine	*2,4,5-Trichlorophenol *2,4,6-Trichlorophenol
amine	*Safrole	*1,2,3-Trichloropropane
*N-Nitrosodiethylamine	*Selenium	*O,O,O-Triethyl phos-
N-Nitrosodimethyl- amine	*Silver	phorothioate
N-Nitrosodiphenyl- amine	*Silvex (2,4,5-TP) Styrene	sym-Trinitrobenzene
N-Nitrosodipropyl- amine (Di-n-propyl-	Sulfide	Vanadium Vinyl acetate
nitrosamine)	2,4,5-T (2,4,5-Trichlo-	*Vinyl chloride
N-Nitrosomethylethyl- amine	rophenoxyacetic acid)	Xylene (total)
*N-Nitrosomorpholine	*2,3,7,8-TCDD (2,3,7,8- Tetrachlorodibenzo- p-dioxin)	Zinc

Appendix F

Classification of Permit Modifications

Modifications	Class
A. General Permit Provisions	
1: Administrative and informational changes.	1
2: Correction of typographical errors.	1
3: Equipment replacement or upgrading with functionally equivalent components (e.g., pipes, valves, pumps, conveyors, controls).	1
4: Changes in the frequency of or procedures for monitoring, reporting, sampling, or maintenance activities by the permittee:	
(a) To provide for more frequent monitoring, reporting, sampling or maintenance.	1
(b) Other changes.	2
5: Schedule of compliance:	
(a) Changes in interim compliance dates, with prior approval of the Director.	*1
(b) Extension of final compliance date.	3
6: Changes in expiration date of permit to allow earlier permit termination, with prior approval of the Director.	*1
7: Changes in ownership or operational control of a facility, provided the procedures of §270.40(b) are followed.	*1
B. General Facility Standards	
1: Changes to waste sampling or analysis methods:	
(a) To conform with agency guidance or regulations.	1
(b) Other changes.	2

*Class 1 modifications requiring prior EPA approval.

443

Modifications	Class
2: Changes to analytical quality assurance/control plan:	
(a) To conform with agency guidance or regulations.	1
(b) Other changes.	2
3: Changes in procedures for maintaining the operating record.	1
4: Changes in frequency or content of inspection schedules.	2
5: Changes in the training plan:	
(a) That affect the type or decrease the amount of training given to employees.	2
(b) Other changes.	1
6: Contingency plan:	
(a) Changes in emergency procedures (i.e., spill or release response procedures).	2
(b) Replacement with functionally equivalent equipment, equipment upgrade, or relocation of emergency equipment listed.	1
(c) Removal of equipment from emergency equipment list.	2
(d) Changes in name, address, or phone number of coordinators or other persons or agencies identified in the plan.	1

Note: When a permit modification (such as introduction of a new unit) requires a change in facility plans or other general facility standards, that change shall be reviewed under the same procedures as the permit modification.

C. Groundwater Protection

1: Changes to wells:	
(a) Changes in the number, location, depth, or design of upgradient or downgradient wells of permitted groundwater monitoring system.	2
(b) Replacement of an existing well that has been damaged or rendered inoperable, without change of location, design, or depth of the well.	1
2: Changes in groundwater sampling or analysis procedures or monitoring schedule, with prior approval of the Director.	*1
3: Changes in statistical procedure for determining whether a statistically significant change in groundwater quality between upgradient and downgradient wells has occurred, with prior approval of the Director.	*1
4: Changes in point of compliance.	2
5: Changes in indicator parameters, hazardous constituents, or concentration limits (including ACLs):	
(a) As specified in the groundwater protection standard.	3
(b) As specified in the detection monitoring program.	2
6: Changes to a detection monitoring program as required by §264.98(j), unless otherwise specified in this Appendix.	2

Modifications	Class
7: Compliance monitoring program:	
(a) Addition of compliance monitoring program as required by §264.98(h)(4) and §264.99.	3
(b) Changes to a compliance monitoring program as required by §264.99(k), unless otherwise specified in this Appendix.	2
8: Corrective action program:	
(a) Addition of a corrective action program as required by §264.99(i)(2) and §264.100.	3
(b) Changes to a corrective action program as required by §264.100(h), unless otherwise specified in this Appendix.	2

D. Closure

1: Changes to the closure plan:	
(a) Changes in estimate of maximum extent of operations or maximum inventory of waste on-site at any time during the active life of the facility, with prior approval of the Director.	*1
(b) Changes in the closure schedule for any unit, changes in the final closure schedule for the facility, or extension of the closure period, with prior approval of the Director.	*1
(c) Changes in the expected year of final closure, where other permit conditions are not changed, with prior approval of the Director.	*1
(d) Changes in procedures for decontamination of facility equipment or structures, with prior approval of the Director.	*1
(e) Changes in approved closure plan resulting from unexpected events occurring during partial or final closure, unless otherwise specified in this Appendix.	2
2: Creation of a new landfill unit as part of closure.	3
3: Addition of the following new units to be used temporarily for closure activities:	
(a) Surface impoundments.	3
(b) Incinerators.	3
(c) Waste piles that do not comply with §264.250(c).	3
(d) Waste piles that comply with §264.250(c).	2
(e) Tanks or containers (other than specified below).	2
(f) Tanks used for neutralization, dewatering, phase separation, or component separation, with prior approval of the Director.	*1

E. Post-Closure

1: Changes in name, address, or phone number of contact in post-closure plan.	1
2: Extension of post-closure care period.	2
3: Reduction in the post-closure care period.	3

Modifications	Class
4: Changes to the expected year of final closure, where other permit conditions are not changed.	1
5: Changes in post-closure plan necessitated by events occurring during the active life of the facility, including partial and final closure.	2

F. Containers

1: Modification or addition of container units:
  (a) Resulting in greater than 25% increase in the facility's container storage capacity. — 3
  (b) Resulting in up to 25% increase in the facility's container storage capacity. — 2
2: (a) Modification of a container unit without increasing the capacity of the unit. — 2
  (b) Addition of a roof to a container unit without alteration of the containment system. — 1
3: Storage of different wastes in containers:
  (a) That require additional or different management practices from those authorized in the permit. — 3
  (b) That do not require additional or different management practices from those authorized in the permit. — 2

Note: See §270.42(g) for modification procedures to be used for the management of newly listed or identified wastes.

4: Other changes in container management practices (e.g., aisle space, types of containers, segregation). — 2

G. Tanks

1: (a) Modification or addition of tank units resulting in greater than 25% increase in the facility's tank capacity, except as provided in G(1)(d) of this Appendix. — 3
  (b) Modification or addition of tank units resulting in up to 25% increase in the facility's tank capacity, except as provided in G(1)(d) of this Appendix. — 2
  (c) Addition of a new tank that will operate for more than 90 days using any of the following physical or chemical treatment technologies: neutralization, dewatering, phase separation, or component separation. — *1
  (d) After prior approval of the Director, addition of a new tank that will operate for up to 90 days using any of the following physical or chemical treatment technologies: neutralization, dewatering, phase separation, or component separation. — 1

Modifications	Class
2: Modification of a tank unit or secondary containment system without increasing the capacity of the unit.	2
3: Replacement of a tank with a tank that meets the same design standards, and whose capacity differs by no more than 1% to 10% from that of the replaced tank, provided that:	1
(1) The capacity difference is no more than 1500 gallons.	
(2) The facility's permitted tank capacity is not increased.	
(3) The replacement tank meets the same conditions in the permit.	
4: Modification of a tank management practice.	2
5: Management of different wastes in tanks:	
(a) That require additional or different management practices, a different tank design, different fire protection specifications, or a significantly different tank treatment process from that authorized in the permit.	3
(b) That do not require additional or different management practices, a different tank design, different fire protection specifications, or a significantly different tank treatment process from that authorized in the permit.	2

Note: See §270.42(g) for modification procedures to be used for the management of newly listed or identified wastes.

H. Surface Impoundments

1: Modification or addition of surface impoundment units that results in increasing the facility's surface impoundment storage or treatment capacity.	3
2: Replacement of a surface impoundment unit.	3
3: Modification of a surface impoundment unit without increasing the facility's surface impoundment storage or treatment capacity.	3
4: Modification of a surface impoundment management practice.	2
5: Treatment, storage, or disposal of different wastes in surface impoundments:	
(a) That require additional or different management practices or different designs of the liner or leak detection system than authorized in the permit.	3
(b) That do not require additional or different management practices or different designs of the liner or leak detection system than authorized in the permit.	2

Note: See §270.42(g) for modification procedures to be used for the management of newly listed or identified wastes.

Modifications	Class

I. Enclosed Waste Piles

For all waste piles except those complying with §264.250(c), modifications are treated the same as for a landfill. The following modifications are applicable only to waste piles complying with §264.250(c).

1: Modification or addition of waste pile units:
    (a) Resulting in greater than 25% increase in the facility's waste pile storage or treatment capacity.   3
    (b) Resulting in up to 25% increase in the facility's waste pile storage or treatment capacity.   2
2: Modification of waste pile unit without increasing the capacity of the unit.   2
3: Replacement of a waste pile unit with another waste pile unit of the same design and capacity and meeting all waste pile conditions in the permit.   1
4: Modification of a waste pile management practice.   2
5: Storage or treatment of different wastes in waste piles:
    (a) That require additional or different management practices or different design of the unit.   3
    (b) That do not require additional or different management practices or different design of the unit.   2

Note: See §270.42(g) for modification procedures to be used for the management of newly listed or identified wastes.

J. Landfills and Unenclosed Waste Piles

1: Modification or addition of landfill units that result in increasing the facility's disposal capacity.   3
2: Replacement of a landfill.   3
3: Addition or modification of a liner, leachate collection system, leachate detection system, run-off control, or final cover system.   2
4: Modification of a landfill unit without changing a liner, leachate collection system, leachate detection system, run-off control, or final cover system.   2
5: Modification of a landfill management practice.   2
6: Landfill different wastes:
    (a) That require additional or different management practices, or different design of the liner, leachate collection system, or leachate detection system.   3
    (b) That do not require additional or different management practices, or different design of the liner, leachate collection system, or leachate detection system.   2

Note: See §270.42(g) for modification procedures to be used for the management of newly listed or identified wastes.

Modifications	Class

K. Land Treatment

1: Lateral expansion of or other modification of a land treatment unit to increase areal extent. ... 3

2: Modification of run-on control system. ... 2

3: Modification of run-off control system. ... 3

4: Other modifications of land treatment unit component specifications or standards required in permit. ... 2

5: Management of different wastes in land treatment units:
(a) That require a change in permit operating conditions or unit design specifications. ... 2
(b) That do not require a change in permit operating conditions or unit design specifications. ... 2

Note: See §270.42(g) for modification procedures to be used for the management of newly listed or identified wastes.

6: Modification of a land treatment unit management practice to:
(a) Increase rate or change method of waste application. ... 3
(b) Decrease rate of waste application. ... 1

7: Modification of a land treatment unit management practice to change measures of pH or moisture content, or to enhance microbial or chemical reactions. ... 2

8: Modification of a land treatment unit management practice to grow food-chain crops, to add to or replace existing permitted crops with different food-chain crops, or to modify operating plans for distribution of animal feeds resulting from such crops. ... 3

9: Modification of operating practice due to detection of releases from the land treatment unit pursuant to §264.278(g)(2). ... 3

10: Changes in the unsaturated zone monitoring system, resulting in a change to the location, depth, or number of sampling points, or that replace unsaturated zone monitoring devices or components of devices with devices or components that have specifications different from permit requirements. ... 3

11: Changes in the unsaturated zone monitoring system that do not result in a change to the location, depth, or number of sampling points, or that replace unsaturated zone monitoring devices or components of devices with devices or components having specifications different from permit requirements. ... 2

12: Changes in background values for hazardous constituents in soil and soil-pore liquid. ... 2

13: Changes in sampling, analysis, or statistical procedure. ... 2

14: Changes in land treatment demonstration program prior to or during the demonstration. ... 2

15: Changes in any condition specified in the permit for a land treatment unit to reflect results of the land treatment demonstration,

Modifications	Class
provided that performance standards are met, and the Director's prior approval has been received.	*1
16: Changes to allow a second land treatment demonstration to be conducted when the results of the first demonstration have not shown the conditions under which the wastes can be treated completely, provided that the conditions for the second demonstration are substantially the same as the conditions for the first demonstration.	*1
17: Changes to allow a second land treatment demonstration to be conducted when the results of the first demonstration have not shown the conditions under which the wastes can be treated completely, where the conditions for the second demonstration are not substantially the same as the conditions for the first demonstration.	3
18: Changes in vegetative cover requirements for closure.	2

L. Incinerators

1: Changes to increase by more than 25% any of the following limits authorized in the permit: a thermal feed rate limit, or an organic chlorine feed rate limit. The Director will require a new trial burn to substantiate compliance with the regulatory performance standards unless this demonstration can be made through other means.   3

2: Changes to increase by up to 25% any of the following limits authorized in the permit: a thermal feed rate limit, a waste feed limit, or an organic chlorine feed rate limit. The Director will require a new trial burn to substantiate compliance with the regulatory performance standards unless this demonstration can be made through other means.   2

3: Modification of an incinerator unit by changing the internal size or geometry of the primary or secondary combustion units, by adding a primary or secondary combustion unit, by substantially changing the design of any component used to remove HCl or particulate from the combustion gases, or by changing other features of the incinerator that could affect its capability to meet the regulatory performance standards. The Director may require a new trial burn to demonstrate compliance with the regulatory performance standards.   2

4: Modification of an incinerator unit in a manner that would not likely affect the capability of the unit to meet the regulatory performance standards but which would change the operating conditions or monitoring requirements specified in the permit. The Director may require a new trial burn to demonstrate compliance with the regulatory performance standards.   2

Modifications	Class

5: Operating requirements:
  (a) Modification of the limits specified in the permit for minimum combustion gas temperature, minimum combustion gas residence time, or oxygen concentration in the secondary combustion chamber. The Director will require a new trial burn to substantiate compliance with the regulatory performance standards unless this demonstration can be made through other means.   3
  (b) Modification of any stack gas emission limits specified in the permit, or modification of any conditions in the permit concerning emergency shutdown or automatic waste feed cutoff procedures or controls.   3
  (c) Modification of any other operating condition or any inspection or record-keeping requirement specified in the permit.   3

6: Incineration of different wastes:
  (a) If the waste contains a POHC that is more difficult to incinerate than authorized by the permit, or if incineration of the waste requires compliance with regulatory performance standards unless this demonstration can be made through other means.   3
  (b) If the waste does not contain a POHC that is more difficult to incinerate than authorized by the permit, and if incineration of the waste does not require compliance with different regulatory performance standards than specified in the permit.

Note: See §270.42(g) for modification procedures to be used for the management of newly listed or identified wastes.

7: Shakedown and trial burn:
  (a) Modification of the trial burn plan or any of the permit conditions applicable during the shakedown period for determining operational readiness after construction, the trial burn period, or the period immediately following the trial burn.   2
  (b) Authorization of up to an additional 720 hours of waste incineration during the shakedown period for determining operational readiness after construction, with the prior approval of the Director.   *1
  (c) Changes in the operating requirements set in the permit for conducting a trial burn, provided that such change is minor and has received the prior approval of the Director.   *1
  (d) Changes in the operating requirements set in the permit to reflect the results of the trial burn, provided that such change is minor and has received the prior approval of the Director.   *1

8: Substitution of an alternate type of fuel that is not specified in the permit.   1

Appendix G

Information Sources

This appendix contains various sources of further information concerning hazardous waste. The information is divided into four sections:

- Regulatory information sources
- Publication sources
- Federal regulatory agencies
- State regulatory agencies

REGULATORY INFORMATION SOURCES

The Federal Register

The *Federal Register* is the most complete and helpful source of regulatory information. Proposed and final regulations, as well as selected notices, publications, interpretations, and other related federal government information, are published in the *Federal Register*. Each regulation (final and proposed) that is published contains a preamble, which is essentially a discussion of EPA's rationale for the regulation and background information and interpretive guidance.

Published daily, the *Federal Register* is available for $340 per year from:

Superintendent of Document
U.S. Government Printing Office
Washington, DC 20402
202-783-3238

Code of Federal Regulations

Each year the *Federal Register* is codified into *The Code of Federal Regulations* (CFR). The CFR contains promulgated final regulations only, not preambles or proposed regulations. This annual document, issued by the Government Printing Office, is updated in July of each year, but is not available until January or

February of the following year. Title 40 of the CFR contains EPA's regulations, and Title 49 contains DOT's regulations.

Dockets

Official files of rulemaking documents, including public hearing transcripts, litigation records, and public comments, can be obtained as follows:

RCRA	202-475-9377
Superfund	202-382-3587
TSCA	202-382-3587
Underground tanks	202-475-9720
Clean air	202-382-7548
Drinking water	202-475-9598
Pesticides	703-557-4434

Written Regulatory Interpretation

A person can obtain an interpretation of a regulation or policy by writing to EPA and requesting it. However, at least six weeks is needed for one to obtain a response. To expedite a response, a letter could be routed through a congressional representative. There is a set time for a response to a letter from a member of Congress requesting a regulatory interpretation, usually 15 working days.

Freedom of Information

The Freedom of Information Act (FOIA), enacted in 1966, established an effective statutory right of access to federal government records. Under the provisions of FOIA, all records under the custody and control of federal executive branch agencies (with specific exceptions) are covered. FOIA requests are required to be responded to within 10 working days. Additionally, the requester can be charged for reasonable research and copying fees.

For further information concerning the limitations and procedures of the Freedom of Information Act, one should contact the Government Printing Office for the publication *Your Right to Federal Records, Questions and Answers on the Freedom of Information Act and the Privacy Act* (order no. 052-071-00752-1, $1.75).

Hotlines and Clearinghouses

The following hotlines may be consulted:

RCRA/Superfund Hotline
(8:30 to 7:30 EST)   800-424-9346
                     202-382-3000
TSCA Hotline
(8:30 to 5:00 EST)   202-554-1404

Small Business/Asbestos Hotline
 (8:00 to 4:30 EST)   800-368-5888
                        703-557-1938
DOT Hazardous Materials
Information Hotline   202-366-4488

Miscellaneous Information Sources

The following information sources are available to provide information on other
federal regulatory programs.

Safe Drinking Water Act	800-426-4791
	202-382-5533
SARA Title III	800-535-0202
Pesticides (regulatory)	703-557-7760
Pesticides (nonregulatory)	317-494-6614
Air (regulatory)	919-629-5651
Air (nonregulatory)	919-541-0850
Water	202-382-5400
OSHA	202-523-7031
Acid Rain	202-382-7407
Marine Protection	202-382-7166
Radiation Program	703-557-9710
NOAA	202-377-4190
NIOSH	202-472-7134
EPA Personnel Locator	202-382-2090
EPA, Freedom of Information	202-382-4048
EPA Library (main)	202-382-5922
EPA Library (pesticides and toxic substances)	202-382-3568

PUBLICATION SOURCES

EPA Office of Research and Development

EPA's Office of Research and Development (ORD), located in Cincinnati, Ohio,
conducts an Agency-wide integrated program of research and development relevant to pollution sources and control, fate and transport processes, health and
ecological effects, measurement and monitoring, and risk assessment. It may be
contacted at the following number:

   ORD Publications   513-569-7562

Government Printing Office

The Government Printing Office (GPO) has many publications available concerning pollution control, including both EPA and other federal agency publications. Because GPO has thousands of documents, it does not send a list of

publications. However, one can call or write to GPO and order up to six selected "subject bibliographies" free of charge (e.g., Air Pollution, SB# 46; Environmental Protection, SB# 88; Waste Management, SB# 95; Water Pollution, SB# 50). The following telephone number is used:

U.S. GPO   202-783-3238

The National Technical Information Service

NTIS is a depository for federal government publications, and in recent years, EPA has sent a majority of its publications to NTIS for distribution. A complete listing of all NTIS documents is contained in *U.S. Government Reports and Announcement Documents*, which is available at any U.S. Government Depository Library. NTIS may be contacted at:

National Technical Information Service
U.S. Department of Commerce
5285 Port Royal Road
Springfield, VA 22161
703-487-4650

The General Accounting Office

The General Accounting Office is an independent government agency that provides oversight functions on behalf of Congress. Periodically, Congress requests that GAO conduct an investigation of a particular federal program, and upon completion of the investigation GAO prepares and distributes its report. These reports provide in-depth information on the program of interest. You can telephone GAO at the following number to obtain a list of publications issued for the previous year:

The General Accounting Office   202-275-6241

The Office of Technology Assessment

The Office of Technology Assessment (OTA) supplies Congress with analyses and recommendations on particular government programs as requested. Many reports on selected EPA programs offer excellent summaries and insights. OTA provides a list of publications, and it may be called at the following number:

The Office of Technology Assessment   202-224-8996

Miscellaneous Publication Sources

Additional information is available from the following sources:

Air	919-541-2777
Pesticides	703-557-4460
EPA's National Enforcement	
Investigations Center	303-236-5122

Drinking Water	202-382-5533
Water Planning and Standards	202-382-7115
Radiation	703-557-9351

FEDERAL REGULATORY AGENCIES

Pertinent addresses and/or phone numbers of several agencies are listed below.

Environmental Protection Agency

Headquarters

401 M Street, SW
Washington, DC 20590

Personnel Locater

202-382-2090

EPA Regional Offices

Region I	JFK Federal Building Room 2203 Boston, MA 02203 617-565-3698
Region II	26 Federal Plaza New York, NY 10278 212-264-9628
Region III	841 Chestnut Street Philadelphia, PA 19107 215-597-9492
Region IV	345 Courtland Street, NE Atlanta, GA 30365 404-347-2234
Region V	230 South Dearborn Street Chicago, IL 60604 312-353-7579
Region VI	1445 Ross Avenue Suite 1200 Dallas, TX 75270 214-655-6700
Region VII	726 Minnesota Avenue Kansas City, KS 66101 913-236-2930

Region VIII	One Denver Place 999 18th Street Suite 500 Denver, CO 80202 303-293-7540
Region IX	75 Hawthorne Place San Francisco, CA 94105 415-556-6608
Region X	1200 Sixth Avenue Seattle, WA 98101 206-442-2782

States in EPA's Regions

Region I	Connecticut, Maine, Massachusetts, New Hampshire, Rhode Island, Vermont
Region II	New Jersey, New York, Puerto Rico
Region III	Delaware, District of Columbia, Maryland, Pennsylvania, Virginia, West Virginia
Region IV	Alabama, Florida, Georgia, Kentucky, Mississippi, North Carolina, South Carolina, Tennessee
Region V	Illinois, Indiana, Michigan, Minnesota, Ohio, Wisconsin
Region VI	Arkansas, Louisiana, New Mexico, Oklahoma, Texas
Region VII	Iowa, Kansas, Missouri, Nebraska
Region VIII	Colorado, Montana, North Dakota, South Dakota, Utah, Wyoming
Region IX	Arizona, California, Guam, Hawaii, Nevada
Region X	Alaska, Idaho, Oregon, Washington

EPA Regional Contacts

Region I
RCRA	617-565-3698
CERCLA	617-565-3279
TSCA	617-565-3715

Region II
RCRA	212-264-8672
CERCLA	212-264-6136
TSCA	212-264-2525

Region III
RCRA   215-597-8132
CERCLA   215-597-7668
TSCA   215-597-9800

Region IV
RCRA   404-347-4097
CERCLA   404-347-3864
TSCA   404-347-4727

Region V
RCRA   312-353-7570
CERCLA   312-353-1428
TSCA   312-353-2000

Region VI
RCRA   214-655-6705
CERCLA   214-655-9899
TSCA   214-655-6444

Region VII
RCRA   913-236-2855
CERCLA   913-236-2835
TSCA   913-236-2800

Region VIII
RCRA   303-293-1519
CERCLA   303-293-1742
TSCA   303-293-1603

Region IX
RCRA   415-556-8910
CERCLA   415-556-8389
TSCA   415-556-8071

Region X
RCRA   206-442-1987
CERCLA   206-442-4153
TSCA   206-442-5810

U.S. Department of Justice

Land and Natural Resources Division

This division is responsible for civil and criminal enforcement of environmental regulations, primarily on behalf of the Environmental Protection Agency. The telephone number is 202-633-2701.

U.S. Department of Labor (OSHA)

Office of Public Information
(Provides general information about OSHA.)
202-523-8145

Publications Office
(Distributes OSHA publications.)
202-523-6098

OSHA Regional Offices

Region I
Boston, MA
617-565-7164

Region II
New York, NY
212-944-3426

Region III
Philadelphia, PA
215-596-1201

Region IV
Atlanta, GA
404-347-3573

Region V
Chicago, IL
312-353-2220

Region VI
Dallas, TX
214-767-4764

Region VII
Kansas City, MO
816-347-5861

Region VIII
Denver, CO
303-837-3883

Region IX
San Francisco, CA
415-995-5680

Region X
Seattle, WA
206-442-5930

U.S. Coast Guard

Office of Environmental Protection
202-267-2200

Hazardous Materials Branch
202-267-1217

National Response Center
800-424-8802
202-426-2675

STATE REGULATORY AGENCIES

ALABAMA

Air
205-271-7700

SARA Title III
205-271-7700
Emergency Response
800-843-0699

Hazardous Waste
205-271-7737

Transportation
205-271-7735

Underground Storage Tanks
205-271-7700

Water
205-271-7700

ALASKA

Air
907-465-2666

SARA Title III
907-465-2600
Emergency Response
800-478-9300

Hazardous Waste
907-465-2671

Transportation
907-465-2671

Underground Storage Tanks
907-561-2020

Water
907-465-2653

ARIZONA

Air
602-257-2300

SARA Title III
602-231-6326

Hazardous Waste
602-257-2270

Transportation
602-257-2211

Underground Storage Tanks
602-542-1024

Water
602-257-2300

ARKANSAS

Air
501-562-7444

SARA Title III
501-562-7444

Hazardous Waste
501-562-7444

Transportation
501-562-7444

Underground Storage Tanks
501-562-7444

Water
501-562-7444

CALIFORNIA

Air
916-322-5840

SARA Title III
916-427-4287
Emergency Response
800-852-7550

Hazardous Waste
916-445-4171

Transportation
916-324-2430

Underground Storage Tanks
916-739-4400

Water
916-445-9552

COLORADO

Air
303-331-8500

SARA Title III
303-377-6326

Hazardous Waste
303-320-8333

Transportation
303-331-4830

Underground Storage Tanks
303-331-4830

Water
303-331-4525

CONNECTICUT

Air
203-566-5524

SARA Title III
203-566-4856

Hazardous Waste
203-566-5712

Transportation
203-566-8843

Underground Storage Tanks
203-566-4630

Water
203-566-3245

DELAWARE

Air
302-739-4403

SARA Title III
302-739-4321

Hazardous Waste
302-739-3689

Transportation
302-739-4781

Underground Storage Tanks
302-323-4588

Water
302-739-4860

DISTRICT OF COLUMBIA

Air
202-727-7395

SARA Title III
202-727-6161

Hazardous Waste
202-727-7395

Transportation
202-783-3194

Underground Storage Tanks
202-783-3186

Water
202-727-7395

FLORIDA

Air
904-488-1344

SARA Title III
904-488-1472

Hazardous Waste
904-488-0300

Transportation
904-488-0300

Underground Storage Tanks
904-488-3935

Water
904-488-3601

GEORGIA

Air
404-656-6900

SARA Title III
404-656-4713
Emergency Response
800-241-4113

Hazardous Waste
404-656-2833

Transportation
404-656-2833

Underground Storage Tanks
404-669-3927

Water
404-656-4708

HAWAII

Air
808-548-8548

SARA Title III
808-543-8249

Hazardous Waste
808-548-8548

Transportation
808-548-2270

Underground Storage Tanks
808-543-8228

Water
808-548-8548

IDAHO

Air
208-334-5898

SARA Title III
208-334-5888

Hazardous Waste
208-334-5879

Transportation
208-334-5879

Underground Storage Tanks
208-334-5845

Water
208-334-5855

ILLINOIS

Air
217-782-7326

SARA Title III
Emergency Response
800-782-7860

Hazardous Waste
217-333-8941

Transportation
217-524-6175

Underground Storage Tanks
217-785-1020

INDIANA

Air
317-232-8218

SARA Title III
Emergency Response
317-241-4336

Hazardous Waste
317-232-3292

Transportation
317-232-4535

Underground Storage Tanks
317-243-5022

Water
317-243-5012

IOWA

Air
515-281-5145

SARA Title III
515-281-6175
Emergency Response
515-281-8694

Hazardous Waste
515-281-8693

Transportation
913-236-2887

Underground Storage Tanks
515-281-5145

Water
515-281-5385

KANSAS

Air
913-206-1593

SARA Title III
913-296-1690

Hazardous Waste
913-296-1590

Transportation
913-296-1607

Underground Storage Tanks
913-206-1660

Water
913-296-1535

KENTUCKY

Air
502-564-3382

SARA Title III
502-564-8682
Emergency Response
502-564-7815

Hazardous Waste
502-564-3350

Transportation
502-564-6716

Underground Storage Tanks
502-564-3410

Water
502-564-3410

LOUISIANA

Air
504-342-9047

SARA Title III
504-925-6113
Emergency Response
504-925-6595

Hazardous Waste
504-342-1354

Transportation
504-342-1354

Underground Storage Tanks
504-342-7808

Water
504-342-6363

MAINE

Air
207-289-7688

SARA Title III
207-289-4080
Emergency Response
800-452-8735

MAINE (*continued*)

Hazardous Waste
207-289-2651

Transportation
207-289-2651

Underground Storage Tanks
207-289-2651

Water
207-289-2811

MARYLAND

Air
301-631-3255

SARA Title III
301-631-3774

Hazardous Waste
301-631-3304

Transportation
301-631-3343

Underground Storage Tanks
301-631-3442

Water
301-396-4411

MASSACHUSETTS

Air
617-292-5856

SARA Title III
617-292-5993

Hazardous Waste
617-292-5961

Transportation
617-292-5580

Underground Storage Tanks
617-566-4500

Water
617-292-5636

MICHIGAN

Air
517-335-9218

SARA Title III
517-373-8481

Hazardous Waste
517-373-2730

Transportation
517-373-2730

Underground Storage Tanks
517-373-9837

Water
517-373-7917

MINNESOTA

Air
612-296-2233

SARA Title III
612-296-2233

Hazardous Waste
612-631-3774

Transportation
612-297-2760

Underground Storage Tanks
612-296-7282

Water
612-296-7202

MISSISSIPPI

Air
601-961-5100

SARA Title III
601-960-9000

Hazardous Waste
601-961-4733

Transportation
601-961-5171

Underground Storage Tanks
601-961-5171

Water
601-961-5100

MISSOURI

Air
314-751-3443

SARA Title III
314-751-7929
Emergency Response
314-634-2436

Hazardous Waste
314-751-3176

Transportation
314-751-9428

Underground Storage Tanks
314-751-3031

Water
314-751-1300

MONTANA

Air
406-444-2544

SARA Title III
406-444-3948
Emergency Response
406-444-6911

Hazardous Waste
406-444-2821

Transportation
406-444-2821

Underground Storage Tanks
406-444-5970

Water
406-444-2406

NEBRASKA

Air
402-471-2186

SARA Title III
402-471-4230

Hazardous Waste
402-471-2186

Transportation
402-471-4217

Underground Storage Tanks
402-471-2186

Water
402-471-2674

NEVADA

Air
702-885-4670

SARA Title III
702-885-4240
Emergency Response
702-885-5300

Hazardous Waste
702-885-4670

Transportation
702-885-5872

Underground Storage Tanks
800-992-0900

Water
702-885-4360

NEW HAMPSHIRE

Air
603-271-1370

SARA Title III
603-271-2231
Emergency Response
800-346-4009

Hazardous Waste
603-271-2900

Transportation
603-271-2900

NEW HAMPSHIRE (*continued*)

Underground Storage Tanks
603-271-3503

Water
603-271-3503

NEW JERSEY

Air
609-292-5383

SARA Title III
609-633-2163
Emergency Response
609-292-7172

Hazardous Waste
609-633-1408

Transportation
609-292-5196

Underground Storage Tanks
609-984-3156

Water
609-984-3156

NEW MEXICO

Air
505-827-0070

SARA Title III
505-827-9224
Emergency Response
505-827-9126

Hazardous Waste
505-827-0020

Transportation
505-827-2929

Underground Storage Tanks
505-827-2894

Water
505-827-2793

NEW YORK

Air
518-457-3446

SARA Title III
518-457-4107
Emergency Response
518-457-7362

Hazardous Waste
518-457-3446

Transportation
518-457-3245

Underground Storage Tanks
518-457-4351

Water
518-457-3446

NORTH CAROLINA

Air
919-733-7015

SARA Title III
919-733-7015
Emergency Response
919-733-3867

Hazardous Waste
919-733-2178

Transportation
919-733-2178

Underground Storage Tanks
919-733-3221

Water
919-733-7015

NORTH DAKOTA

Air
701-224-2348

SARA Title III
701-224-2434
Emergency Response
701-224-2121

Hazardous Waste
701-224-2366

Transportation
701-224-2366

Underground Storage Tanks
701-224-2366

Water
701-224-2354

OHIO

Air
614-644-2270

SARA Title III
614-644-2260
Emergency Response
800-282-9378

Hazardous Waste
614-466-7220

Transportation
614-644-2934

Underground Storage Tanks
614-466-2416

Water
614-644-3020

OKLAHOMA

Air
405-271-5220

SARA Title III
405-521-2481
Emergency Response
405-521-2481

Hazardous Waste
405-271-5338

Transportation
405-271-7054

Underground Storage Tanks
405-521-3107

Water
405-271-2540

OREGON

Air
503-229-5696

SARA Title III
503-378-2885
Emergency Response
800-452-0311

Hazardous Waste
503-229-5696

Transportation
503-229-5913

Underground Storage Tanks
503-229-6631

Water
503-229-5696

PENNSYLVANIA

SARA Title III
717-657-4585
Emergency Response
717-783-8150

Hazardous Waste
717-787-9870

Transportation
717-787-7381

Underground Storage Tanks
717-657-4080

Water
717-787-2666

PUERTO RICO

Air
809-725-5140

PUERTO RICO (*continued*)

SARA Title III
809-722-1175
Emergency Response
809-723-1657

Hazardous Waste
809-722-1175

Transportation
809-725-5140

Underground Storage Tanks
809-725-0717

Water
809-725-5140

RHODE ISLAND

Air
401-277-2808

SARA Title III
401-421-7333
Emergency Response
401-274-7754

Hazardous Waste
401-277-2797

Transportation
401-277-2797

Underground Storage Tanks
401-277-2234

Water
401-277-3961

SOUTH CAROLINA

Air
803-734-4750

SARA Title III
803-734-0424
Emergency Response
803-253-6488

Hazardous Waste
803-734-5200

Transportation
803-734-5200

Underground Storage Tanks
803-758-5213

Water
803-734-5300

SOUTH DAKOTA

Air
605-773-3153

SARA Title III
605-773-3153
Emergency Response
605-773-3231

Hazardous Waste
605-773-3153

Transportation
605-773-3153

Underground Storage Tanks
605-773-3296

Water
605-773-3751

TENNESSEE

Air
615-741-3031

SARA Title III
615-252-3300
Emergency Response
800-258-3300

Hazardous Waste
615-741-3424

Transportation
615-741-3424

Underground Storage Tanks
615-741-4094

Water
615-741-6610

TEXAS

Air
512-451-5711

SARA Title III
512-465-2138
Emergency Response
512-463-7727

Hazardous Waste
512-458-7111

Transportation
512-463-8175

Underground Storage Tanks
512-463-6804

Water
512-463-8177

UTAH

Air
801-538-6108

SARA Title III
801-538-6121
Emergency Response
801-538-6333

Hazardous Waste
801-538-6101

Transportation
801-538-6170

Underground Storage Tanks
801-538-6170

Water
801-538-6146

VERMONT

Air
802-244-7831

SARA Title III
802-828-2286
Emergency Response
800-641-5005

Hazardous Waste
802-244-8755

Transportation
802-828-2070

Underground Storage Tanks
802-244-8755

Water
802-244-6951

VIRGINIA

Air
804-786-6035

SARA Title III
804-225-2513
Emergency Response
800-552-2075

Hazardous Waste
804-225-2667

Transportation
804-225-2667

Underground Storage Tanks
804-367-6685

Water
804-367-0056

WASHINGTON

Air
206-459-6256

SARA Title III
206-459-9191
Emergency Response
800-262-5990

Hazardous Waste
206-459-6316

Transportation
206-459-6322

Underground Storage Tanks
206-459-6316

Water
206-438-7085

WEST VIRGINIA

Air
304-348-2275

SARA Title III
304-348-5380

Hazardous Waste
304-348-2107

Transportation
304-348-3338

Underground Storage Tanks
304-348-5935

Water
304-348-2981

WISCONSIN

Air
608-266-7718

SARA Title III
608-266-3232
Emergency Response
608-266-3232

Hazardous Waste
608-266-1327

Transportation
608-266-2111

Underground Storage Tanks
608-266-7605

Water
608-266-8631

WYOMING

Air
307-777-7391

SARA Title III
307-777-7566

Hazardous Waste
307-777-7752

Transportation
307-777-7752

Underground Storage Tanks
307-777-7781

Water
307-777-7781

Appendix H

Acronyms

AA	— Assistant Administrator
ACL	— Alternate Concentration Level
ADI	— Acceptable Daily Intake
AEA	— Atomic Energy Act
ALJ	— Administrative Law Judge
ANPR	— Advanced Notice of Proposed Rulemaking
AO	— Administrative Order
APA	— Administrative Procedures Act
AQCRs	— Air Quality Control Regions
ARARs	— Applicable or Relevant and Appropriate Requirements
ASHAA	— Asbestos School Hazard Abatement Act
ATA	— American Trucking Association
ATSDR	— Agency for Toxic Substances and Disease Registry
ATS	— Action Tracking System
AX	— Administrator's Office
BAT	— Best Available Technology Economically Achievable
BDAT	— Best Demonstrated Available Technology
BOD	— Biological Oxygen Demand
BRC	— Below Regulatory Concern
BPT	— Best Practicable Control Technology
BTU	— British Thermal Unit
CA	— Cooperative Agreement
CAA	— Clean Air Act
CAAA	— Clean Air Act Amendments
CAG	— Carcinogen Assessment Group
CAP	— Criteria Air Pollutants
CAS	— Chemical Abstract Service
CASRN	— Chemical Abstract Service Registry Number

CBA   — Cost Benefit Analysis
CDC   — Center for Disease Control
CERCLA — Comprehensive Environmental Response, Compensation, and Liability Act
CERCLIS — Comprehensive Environmental Response, Compensation, and Liability Information System
CERI   — Center for Environmental Research Information
CFR   — Code of Federal Regulations
CGL   — Comprehensive General Liability
CHIP   — Chemical Hazard Information Profile
CLP   — Contract Laboratory Program
CM   — Corrective Measures
CMI   — Corrective Measures Implementation
CMS   — Corrective Measures Study
CPF   — Carcinogenic Potency Factor
CSF   — Carcinogenic Slope Factor
CWA   — Clean Water Act

DOC   — Department of Commerce
DOD   — Department of Defense
DOE   — Department of Energy
DOJ   — Department of Justice
DOL   — Department of Labor
DOT   — Department of Transportation
DQOs   — Data Quality Objectives
DRE   — Destruction and Removal Efficiency

EA   — Environmental Assessment
EDD   — Enforcement Decision Document
EDF   — Environmental Defense Fund
EIL   — Environmental Impairment Liability
EIR   — Exposure Information Report
EIS   — Environmental Impact Statement
EPA   — Environmental Protection Agency
EPCRA   — Emergency Planning and Community Right-to-Know Act
EPOW   — Extraction Procedure for Oily Wastes
EP TOX   — Extraction Procedure Toxicity Test
ERCS   — Emergency Response Cleanup Services
ERL   — Environmental Research Laboratory
ERRIS   — Emergency and Remedial Response Information System
ESA   — Endangered Species Act

FDA   — Food and Drug Administration
FFDCA   — Federal Food, Drug, and Cosmetic Act
FHSA   — Federal Hazardous Substances Act
FIFRA   — Federal Insecticide, Fungicide, and Rodenticide Act
FIT   — Field Investigation Team

FML	— Flexible Membrane Liner
FOIA	— Freedom of Information Act
FONSI	— Finding of No Significant Impact
FR	— *Federal Register*
FS	— Feasibility Study
FWPCA	— Federal Water Pollution Control Act
FY	— Fiscal Year
GA	— Grant Agreement
GLP	— Good Laboratory Practices
GPO	— Government Printing Office
GWPS	— Groundwater Protection Standard
HA	— Health Advisory
HAP	— Hazardous Air Pollutant
HCA	— Hazardous Communications Act
HEEP	— Health and Environmental Effects Profile
HMT	— Hazardous Materials Table
HMTA	— Hazardous Materials Transportation Act
HMTR	— Hazardous Materials Transportation Regulations
HOC	— Halogenated Organic Compound
HRS	— Hazard Ranking System
HSL	— Hazardous Substance List
HSWA	— Hazardous and Solid Waste Amendments of 1984
HW	— Hazardous Waste
IAG	— Interagency Agreement
IM	— Interim Measure
ISCL	— Interim Status Compliance Letter
ITC	— Interagency Testing Committee
LAER	— Lowest Achievable Emissions Rate
LCRS	— Leachate Control and Removal System
LD_{50}	— Lethal Dose fifty percent
LLW	— Low-Level Radioactive Waste
LOIS	— Loss of Interim Status
LQG	— Large-Quantity Generator
MCL	— Maximum Contaminant Level
MCLG	— Maximum Contaminant Level Goal
MOA	— Memorandum of Agreement
MOD	— Memorandum of Decision
MOU	— Memorandum of Understanding
MPRSA	— Marine Protection, Research, and Sanctuaries Act
MQG	— Medium-Quantity Generator
MSCA	— Multi-Site Cooperative Agreement
MSDS	— Material Safety Data Sheet

MTB   — Materials Transportation Board
MTU   — Mobile Treatment Unit

NAA   — Non-attainment Areas
NAAQS   — National Ambient Air Quality Standards
NACE   — National Association of Corrosion Engineers
NBAR   — Nonbinding Preliminary Allocation of Responsibility
NCP   — National Contingency Plan
NDD   — Negotiation Decision Document
NEC   — National Electric Code
NEIC   — National Enforcement Investigations Center
NEPA   — National Environmental Policy Act
NESHAP   — National Emission Standards for Hazardous Air Pollutants
NIEHS   — National Institute of Environmental Health Sciences
NIMBY   — Not In My Backyard
NIOSH   — National Institute of Occupational Safety and Health
NLAP   — National Lab Audit Program
NOD   — Notice of Decision
NOD   — Notice of Deficiency
NOEL   — No Observed Effect Level
NOID   — Notice of Intent to Deny Permit
NON   — Notice of Noncompliance
NOS   — Not Otherwise Specified
NOV   — Notice of Violation
NPDES   — National Pollutant Discharge Elimination System
NPDWR   — National Primary Drinking Water Regulations
NPL   — National Priorities List
NRC   — National Response Center
NRC   — Nuclear Regulatory Commission
NRDC   — Natural Resources Defense Council
NRT   — National Response Team
NSPS   — New Source Performance Standards
NTIS   — National Technical Information Service
NTP   — National Toxicological Program

OECM   — Office of Enforcement and Compliance Monitoring
OERR   — Office of Emergency and Remedial Response
O&M   — Operation and Maintenance
OMB   — Office of Management and Budget
O/O   — Owner or Operator
OPP   — Office of Pesticide Programs
ORC   — Office of Regional Counsel
ORM   — Other Regulated Material
ORNL   — Oak Ridge National Laboratory
OSC   — On-Scene Coordinator
OSHA   — Occupational Safety and Health Administration

OSW	— Office of Solid Waste
OSWER	— Office of Solid Waste and Emergency Response
OTA	— Office of Technology Assessment
OTS	— Office of Toxic Substances
OUST	— Office of Underground Storage Tanks
OWPE	— Office of Waste Programs Enforcement
PA	— Preliminary Assessment
PAT	— Permit Assistance Team
PCB	— Polychlorinated Biphenyl
PCP	— Pentachlorophenol
PFLT	— Paint Filter Liquids Test
PL	— Public Law
PMN	— Premanufacture Notification
POHC	— Principal Organic Hazardous Constituent
POTW	— Publicly Owned Treatment Works
ppb	— Parts Per Billion
ppm	— Parts Per Million
ppt	— Parts Per Trillion
PRP	— Potentially Responsible Party
PSD	— Prevention of Significant Deterioration
QA	— Quality Assurance
QC	— Quality Control
RA	— Regional Administrator
RA	— Remedial Action
RAMP	— Remedial Action Master Plan
RCRA	— Resource Conservation and Recovery Act
RD	— Remedial Design
RD&D	— Research, Demonstration, and Development
REM	— Remedial Planning Contractor
RFA	— RCRA Facility Assessment
RfD	— Reference Dose
RFI	— RCRA Facility Inspection
RI	— Remedial Investigation
RIA	— Regulatory Impact Analysis
RIM	— Regulatory Information Memorandum
RIP	— RCRA Implementation Plan
RMCL	— Recommended Maximum Contaminant Level
ROD	— Record of Decision
RPAR	— Rebuttable Presumption Against Registration
RPM	— Remedial Project Manager
RQ	— Reportable Quantity
RS	— Remedial Selection
RTECS	— Registry of Toxic Effects of Chemical Substances

SAB	— Science Advisory Board
SARA	— Superfund Amendments and Reauthorization Act
SBA	— Small Business Administration
SCAP	— Superfund Comprehensive Accomplishments Plan
SCRP	— Superfund Community Relations Plan
SDWA	— Safe Drinking Water Act
SI	— Site Identification
SIC	— Standard Industrial Classification
SIP	— State Implementation Plan
SITE	— Superfund Innovative Technology Evaluation
SMOA	— Superfund Memorandum of Agreement
SNARL	— Significant No Adverse Reaction Level
SPCC	— Spill Prevention, Control, and Countermeasure Plan
SQG	— Small-Quantity Generator
SSC	— State Superfund Contract
SWDA	— Solid Waste Disposal Act
SWMU	— Solid Waste Management Unit
TAT	— Technical Assistance Team
TC	— Toxicity Characteristic
TCLP	— Toxicity Characteristic Leaching Procedure
TOC	— Total Organic Carbon
TOX	— Total Organic Halogen
TSCA	— Toxic Substances Control Act
TSD	— Treatment, Storage, and/or Disposal
TSDF	— Treatment, Storage, and/or Disposal Facility
TSS	— Total Suspended Solids
UCR	— Unit Cancer Risk
UIC	— Underground Injection Control
UN/NA	— United Nations/North America
USCG	— United States Coast Guard
USDW	— Underground Source of Drinking Water
USGS	— United States Geological Survey
USPS	— United States Postal Service
UST	— Underground Storage Tank
VOC	— Volatile Organic Compound

Index

Index

Abandoned, 25
Aboveground tank, 7
Absorbent material, 106, 187
Acceptability of a shipment, 83
Accidental occurrence, 160
Accumulation of hazardous waste, 48, 56, 64, 66, 72–74, 75–77, 97, 106, 165, 187
Accumulation units, 76
Acronyms, 471–476
Act of God, 261
Action in authorized states, 249–250
Activated carbon, 51–52, 221–222
Active fault zone, 115
Active life, 7, 120, 131, 137, 139, 208
Active portion, 7
Acutely hazardous waste, 65
Acutely hazardous waste containers, 45
Administrative actions, 242–245
Administrative orders, 243–245, 249, 324
Administrative record, 198
Administrative review, 192
Agricultural waste, 27
Aisle space, 78, 116, 117
Alternate concentration limits, 135, 136–137
Alternate groundwater monitoring program, 124
Alternative disposal method, 378, 379–380
Alternative water supply, 261, 284
Amendments to the closure plan, 141–143
Amendments to the post-closure plan, 155
Analytical procedures, 122, 132
Ancillary equipment, 7, 163–164

Annual cost update, 155
Annual document log, 347, 385–386
Annual records, 385
Anodizing, 30
Appeals, 145
Appendix VII constituents, 33, 46
Appendix VIII constituents, 33, 46, 151, 176, 179, 228, 343
Appendix IX constituents, 33, 46, 134, 137, 151, 343
Application, 7
Approval of the closure plan, 141, 143–145
Approval of the post-closure plan, 143, 155–156
Approved program, 7
Aqueous, 34, 35
Aquifer, 7
ARARs, 303, 304, 307, 309, 310, 313–317
Aroclor, 359, 386–387
Askarel, 363
Assessment monitoring, 128–129
Atomic Energy Act, 40
Attorney General's statement, 253
Authorized representative, 7

Background quality, 123, 124, 132, 134, 135, 137, 146
Baghouse dust, 52
Barrel, 261
Baseline risk, 305
Batch testing PCBs, 365
Batteries, 49, 54–55, 65

BDAT, 216–217
Bench-scale test, 307
Beneficiation, 27
Benzene, 31
Beyond facility boundary, 227, 331
Biennial report, 62, 70, 71, 110
Blasting agent, 92
Boiler, 8–9, 55, 56, 60, 183
Broader in scope, 253–254
Bulk storage, 375–376, 386
Burners of waste fuel, 56, 57, 60
Burning for energy recovery, 25, 48, 49,
  55–60
By-products, 3, 50, 52
Byproduct material, 26

Cable, 365, 366
California waste, 217, 223–225
Capacitor, 347–348, 362, 364–365, 371,
  372, 375, 378, 381
Carrier, 80, 81, 83, 83
Case-by-case extensions, 220
Cement kiln, 13, 56, 363
Cement kiln dust, 27
CERCLIS, 281, 296, 297
Certification, 9, 56, 170, 212, 348, 361,
  384–385
Certification of closure, 145, 146, 148,
  152, 157
Certification of decontamination, 396
Certification of disposal, 362, 380, 384–
  385
Certification of post-closure, 156
Chain-of-custody, 122, 132
Change of ownership, 190
Changes during interim status, 189
Changing generator categories, 65
Characteristic hazardous waste, 24, 33–37,
  40, 45, 46, 48, 55, 147, 148, 379
Chemical conversion coating, 30
Chemical milling, 30
Chemical, physical, and biological treat-
  ment, 161, 183, 229
Chemical substances, 109, 341, 348, 387
Chemical waste landfill, 348
CHEMTREC, 104
Chromium wastes, 27
Circuit boards, 30
Circuit breakers, 365, 366, 368
Citizen suits, 250, 251, 330–331, 342, 388
Civil actions, 242, 245–246, 289, 381
Civil penalty policy, 249

Claimant, 261
Claims, 257, 261, 329
Class A explosive, 91
Class B explosive, 92
Class C explosive, 92
Class 1 permit modification, 202, 203–204
Class 2 permit modification, 147–148, 155,
  202, 204–206, 207, 208
Class 3 permit modification, 138, 148, 202,
  205, 206–207, 208
Class I violation, 248, 249
Class II violation, 248, 249
Classification of hazardous waste, 84, 85–
  95
Clean Air Act, 150, 260
Clean Water Act, 25, 46, 192, 260, 273,
  275, 277, 279–280, 283, 329, 344
Clean closure, 139, 143, 148–151, 155,
  172, 175, 230, 313
Clean closure of a regulated unit, 150–151
Cleanup levels, 149–150, 151, 237, 259,
  320
Cleanup requirements, 141, 147–153, 313–
  317, 389–396
Closed portion, 9
Closure, 9, 73, 76, 105, 109, 120, 139–154,
  163, 165, 170, 172–173, 175–175, 177,
  178, 180, 182, 188, 194, 195, 208, 209,
  248
Closure certification, 140, 145, 146, 148,
  152, 157
Closure cost estimate, 109, 110, 156–158,
  195
Closure notices, 143, 144, 153–154
Closure performance standard, 139, 152
Closure period, 142, 146–147
Closure plan, 139–145, 153, 165, 175
Closure plan approval, 143–145
Coastal waters, 261
Coking wastes, 32, 49
Combustible liquid, 91, 92
Commercial chemical products, 29, 35, 50,
  52, 65
Commercial storer of PCB waste, 349,
  376, 380
Community relations, 331–332
Compliance action, 245, 246
Compliance assessment, 197, 198
Compliance history, 205
Compliance inspection, 240–242, 296
Compliance monitoring, 134–138
Compliance order, 143, 243, 244

Compliance period, 135–138
Compliance point, 135
Compliance schedule, 246
Compliance with RCRA, 397–409
Compliance with TSCA, 359, 410–414
Component, 9
Compressed gas, 45
Compressed gas containers, 45
Confidentiality, 194
Confined aquifer, 9
Congress, 1, 24, 25, 40, 107, 186, 211,
    214, 245, 258, 260, 292, 316
Consent decree, 316–317, 324
Constituents of hazardous waste, 33, 46,
    120, 122, 133
Constituting disposal, 52, 53–54
Construction, 320–321
Contained-in rule, 39–40
Container storage, 73, 143, 153, 161, 162–
    163, 229, 251
Containers, 9, 61, 72, 73, 75, 148, 162,
    183, 208, 220, 229, 375, 378, 379, 385
Containment system, 131, 154, 155, 162,
    164, 172
Contaminated debris, 147
Contaminated groundwater, 39–40, 147
Contaminated soils, 147, 162, 163
Contingency plan, 9, 62, 78–79, 107, 109,
    117–118, 119, 195
Contingent closure plan, 141, 165
Continued response, 284
Continuous release, 277–278
Contractual relationship, 262–263, 287–288
Cooperative agreement, 295, 296
Corporate guarantee, 160
Corrective action, 3, 9, 27, 46, 129, 135,
    138, 190, 202, 208, 227–239, 245, 246,
    259, 314
Corrective action orders, 227
Corrective action under 3008(h), 128, 227,
    230–231, 243, 244
Corrective action under 3004(u), 150, 154,
    173, 209, 227–230
Corrective action under 3004(v), 227, 231
Corrective measures, 138, 232, 236–237
Corrective measures implementation, 232,
    233, 234, 238–239
Corrective measures study, 232, 233, 234
Corrosive wastes, 28, 35, 90, 91, 92, 121
Counting hazardous waste, 64–65
Covenants not to sue, 326–327
Cracking batteries, 55

Criminal actions, 242, 247, 388
Criteria for listing wastes, 28–29
Critical time response, 285
Crude oil, 57
Cutting oil, 57
Cyanide, 31, 35

Damages, 263
Data quality objectives, 307
De minimis mixtures, 37
De minimis settlements, 289, 327–329
De minimis waste contributor, 328
Decision summary, 320
Declaration, 320
Decontamination, 112, 140, 141, 147, 148,
    149, 151, 162, 172, 338–339, 378, 390,
    394–395
Deed notation, 153–154, 195, 209
Defenses to CERCLA liability, 286–289
Delisting, 25, 32–33, 255
Delivery of waste, 82
Derived-from rule, 39, 108, 214
Designated facility, 9–10, 44, 54, 69, 70,
    82, 119, 349
Detailed analysis of alternatives, 303, 309–
    312
Detection monitoring, 123–128, 137
Determination of secondary materials, 50–
    52
Determining generator categories, 64–65
Development and screening of alterna-
    tives, 303, 308–309
Dielectric, 344–345, 347, 362, 370, 374,
    375, 377, 386
Dike, 172
Dilution, 217, 366–367
Dioxin wastes, 25, 31, 163, 178, 222–223
Director, 10
Dirty closure, 148, 151–153
Discarded material, 25, 39
Discharge, 10, 389
Disposal, 10, 105–106, 186, 220, 349, 361,
    365, 376, 377–380, 384, 386
Disposal facility, 10, 377
Disposer of PCB waste, 349
Distillation, 48, 54, 214
Domestic sewage, 25
DOT, 34, 45, 36, 43, 46, 57, 68, 80, 81,
    85, 86, 87, 89, 90, 93, 95, 97, 98, 100,
    101, 102, 103, 104, 374, 383
Double liners, 171
Double-walled tanks, 167, 168

Double wash/rinse, 349, 392
Downgradient monitoring wells, 123, 126, 127
Draft permit, 10, 192, 198–200, 202, 207, 239
DRE, 180
Drilling fluids, 27
Drinking water suitability, 123, 124–125, 316
Drinking water supply, 263, 275
Driver qualifications, 83
Drum, 3
Drum reconditioning, 45–46
Due care, 287
Due diligence, 288–289
Dust suppressor, 32, 53

Electrical equipment, 360–361, 362, 366, 390
Electroless plating, 30
Electromagnets, 365, 366
Electroplating wastes, 30–31
Elementary neutralization unit, 10, 65, 106, 187, 228
Emergency coordinator, 74, 79, 118
Emergency equipment, 116, 118
Emergency permit, 11, 210
Emergency Planning and Community Right-to-Know Act, 278, 279
Emergency procedures, 72, 74–75, 78–79, 107, 118–119
Emergency Response Guidebook, 104
Emergency response information, 102–104
Emergency response training, 112–113
Empty containers, 29, 44–46, 65
Empty paper bags, 45
Empty tank, 45
Endangerment assessment, 305, 306
Energy recovery, 25, 48, 49, 55–60
Enforcement, 240–252, 252, 255, 323–329, 332, 343, 387–388
Enforcement actions, 242–247
Engineering controls, 339
Engineering evaluation/cost analysis, 285
Environment, 263, 276
Environmental evaluations, 305
Environmental impact statement, 187, 260, 345
EPA action in authorized States, 249–250
EPA hazardous waste number, 11, 67, 218
EPA identification number, 44, 54, 56, 59,
60, 67, 71, 81, 82, 108, 109, 110, 349, 380, 381–382, 385
EPA-recommended limits, 149–150, 151, 237
Equivalency demonstration, 151, 152
Equivalent number, 11
Ethyl alcohol, 34, 49
Etiologic agent, 91
Exception reporting, 62, 69, 380, 383, 384
Excluded wastes, 25–27
Exclusions from general facility standards, 106
Exclusions from permitting, 186–187
Exclusions from recycling, 49
Existing facility, 129, 187–188
Existing portion, 11
Existing tank system, 11
Expected date of closure, 143
Explosives, 32, 36, 91
Exposure information report, 193, 196–197, 209
Exposure risk, 371
Extension to closure period, 147
Extraction procedure, 36
Extremely hazardous substance, 278

Facility, 12, 228, 263
Facility inspections, 240–242, 296
Facility mailing list, 203, 204
Facility personnel, 110, 111
Fact sheet, 193, 198, 199–200
Farmers, 106, 187, 281
Feasibility study, 234, 236, 263–264, 270, 292, 293, 294, 302–304, 308–312, 313, 314, 319, 325, 326, 328
Federal agency as lead agency, 295
Federal facilities, 291–292, 301
Federal Insecticide Fungicide and Rodenticide Act, 31
Federally permitted release, 264–265, 277
Fertilizer, 22, 53
Final closure, 12, 139, 140, 147
Final permit, 200
Final project closeout, 327
Financial assurance, 153, 156–160, 190, 209
Financial responsibility, 105, 156–160, 165, 189, 190
Financial test and guarantee 158, 160
Fines, 243, 244, 245, 246, 247, 248, 249, 278, 387–388
Fire, 84, 117, 118, 285

Fire-fighting equipment, 74, 78, 116
Fire-related incident, 369
First third wastes, 215
Flammable compressed gas, 45
Flammable gas, 90, 91
Flammable liquid, 90, 91
Flammable solids, 90, 91
Flash point, 34, 90, 92
Floodplain, 2, 115–116, 195
Fluorescent light ballast, 349
Fly ash, 32
Food and feed, 371
Food-chain crops, 12, 176
Free liquids, 12, 167, 177, 217
Freeboard, 12, 73, 164, 171
Freedom of Information Act, 194
Fund, 265
Fund balancing, 312, 315

General facility standards, 105, 107–120, 172, 188
Generator, 12, 56, 59, 61–79, 148, 164–165, 137, 214, 216–219, 247, 250, 281, 286, 380, 381, 382
Generator categories, 64
Generator of PCB wastes, 350
Geotextiles, 42
Grant agreement, 250
Groundwater, 2, 12, 39–40, 105, 106, 109, 115, 120–138, 191, 197, 209, 233, 237–248, 265, 299, 314, 316
Groundwater assessment monitoring, 121, 128–129, 133, 154
Groundwater assessment outline, 121–122
Groundwater compliance monitoring, 134–138, 196
Groundwater detection monitoring, 123–128, 133–134, 196
Groundwater monitoring at interim status units, 120–129, 140, 151
Groundwater monitoring at permitted units, 129–138, 140, 151
Groundwater monitoring constituents, 47, 134, 151, 440–442
Groundwater monitoring parameters, 123–126, 133–137
Groundwater monitoring point of compliance, 135
Groundwater monitoring statistical comparisons, 127–128, 132–133
Groundwater monitoring system, 122–123, 196

Groundwater monitoring variances and waivers, 120–121, 123, 124, 131
Groundwater monitoring wells, 123
Groundwater protection standard, 134, 135–136, 137, 138
Groundwater quality, 120, 123, 126, 132
Groundwater sampling, 121–122, 132
Guarantor, 265

Halogens, 57, 58, 225
Hammer provision, 214, 216
Hazard class, 86, 89–92
Hazard communication, 112
Hazardous constituents, 46, 122, 129, 134, 135, 141, 148, 151, 228, 230, 233, 234, 285
Hazardous Materials Table, 81, 86–87, 90, 93, 95–96, 97
Hazardous Materials Transportation Act, 61, 80, 81, 83, 84, 90, 273, 279
Hazardous substance, 89, 257, 258, 265–266, 274, 281, 282, 283, 286, 287, 289, 290, 305, 313, 329, 373, 391
Hazardous substance liability, 289
Hazardous Substance Response Trust Fund, 258
Hazardous waste constituents, 12, 28, 46–47, 176, 228, 230, 233, 244
Hazardous waste fuel, 55
Hazardous waste management unit, 12–13
Health assessment, 305–306
High-concentration PCBs, 350
High-contact industrial surface, 350
High-efficiency boiler, 350, 377, 379
High-priority violator, 248, 249
Hotels, 27, 369
Household wastes, 27
Human health evaluation, 305
Hydraulic system, 362, 365, 373

Identification of shipping name, 86, 87, 89
Identification process, 23–24, 27–28, 63
Ignitable compressed gas, 34–35
Ignitable hazardous waste, 28, 34–35, 37, 73, 90, 114, 148, 149, 162, 164, 169, 172, 174
Imminent endangerment order, 244, 245
Imminent hazard, 191, 245, 247, 388
Impervious solid surface, 351
Importing hazardous waste, 108–109, 344
Importing PCBs, 366
Imposition of fines, 249

Imprisonment, 247, 388
In operation, 13
In or near commercial buildings, 351, 361, 367–370, 373
In service, 362, 373
In situ mining waste, 16, 27
Inactive portion, 13
Incident reports, 84
Incinerator, 13, 143, 148, 153, 161, 178–183, 229, 252, 344, 351, 367, 377, 378
Incompatible wastes, 13, 162, 164, 169, 177
Indian tribe, 266
Indicator parameters, 124, 126–128
Individual generation site, 13
Industrial buildings, 351
Industrial furnace, 13–14, 55, 60
Inflation factor, 157
Informal action, 243
Information and training program, 334–335
Information sources, 452
Inground tank, 14
Inherently wastelike, 25
Initial response, 284
Injection well, 14, 162, 184–185, 192, 211, 229
Inner liner, 14, 45
Innocent landowner liability, 287–289
Inorganic pigments, 32
Inspections, 109, 114–115, 162, 165, 169, 171–172, 175, 182, 195, 208, 240–243, 361, 373–375, 376
Insurance, 158, 159, 160, 195
Interagency agreement, 395, 296
Interim authorization, 251–252
Interim status, 48, 56, 66, 107, 130, 141, 143, 146, 148, 150, 154, 165–170, 186, 187–190, 208, 230, 241, 244, 248
Interim status corrective action orders, 128, 207, 230–231
Interim status termination, 143, 246
Invoice, 59–60
Iron and steel, 32
Irrigation return flows, 26
Irritating material, 91, 92

Judicial action, 244, 245–247, 248, 251, 253
Joint and several liability, 290–291

Kiln dust, 2, 27
Knowledge of waste, 63
Kraft paper mills, 26

Labelling, 67, 84, 86, 97–100, 247
Labels, 61, 247, 372
Laboratory, 351, 376–377, 392
Laboratory errors, 127
Laboratory samples, 41–42
Land disposal, 14, 316
Land disposal restrictions, 63, 69–70, 171, 177, 211–226, 379
Land disposal restrictions schedule, 214–216
Land disposal restrictions variance, 218–220
Land treatment, 123, 131, 143, 161, 175–177, 183, 229
Land treatment facility, 15, 211
Landfill, 14–15, 72, 75, 123, 139, 141, 143, 147, 148, 149, 161, 173, 175, 277–178. 183, 211, 217, 229, 314, 378, 379
Landfill cell, 15
Large high-voltage capacitor, 348, 385
Large low-voltage capacitor, 348, 385
Large-quantity generator, 61, 62, 64, 66–71, 75–79
Leachate, 15, 39, 129
Leachate collection/control system, 43, 141, 152, 213
Lead-acid batteries, 50, 54–55, 65
Lead agency, 266, 295–296, 319
Leak, 72, 83, 105, 169, 351, 370–371, 373, 375, 389
Leak-detection system, 15, 76
Legitimate energy recovery, 55
Legitimate recycling, 60
Letter of credit, 158, 159
Liability, 194, 242, 262, 263, 266, 275, 285–291, 323, 330, 343, 359, 373, 391
Liability coverage, 160
Liability defenses, 286
Liability limits, 286
Liability of contractors, 291
Liability of landowners, 287–289
Liability transfer, 286
Liner, 15, 141, 147, 167, 168, 177
Listed hazardous wastes, 24, 28–32, 147, 379, 415–434
Listing Background Document, 28, 31
Listing site inspection, 299
Location standards, 2, 115–116
Low-concentration PCBs, 351
Low-level Radioactive mixed waste, 37, 40–41, 255
Low-priority violator, 248, 249

Major facility, 15, 199
Major permit modifications, 202
Management, 15
Management of migration, 266
Manifest, 15, 56, 61, 62, 67–69, 81–82, 100, 104, 107, 247, 252, 343, 351, 361, 380, 382–384, 385
Manifest acquisition protocol, 69, 382
Manifest discrepancy, 119
Manifest document number, 15, 218, 385
Manned on-site control center, 368
Manufacture, 351
Manufacturing PCBs, 366
Manure, 27
Marketers, 55–56. 59, 61
Mark, 352
Marking, 67, 76–77, 84, 85, 86, 96–97, 361, 365, 372–373, 375, 376
Maximum contaminant levels, 135, 149, 237, 316
Medical surveillance, 112, 337–338
Medical waste, 37, 40
Medical Waste Tracking Act, 40
Medium-priority violator, 248, 249
Medium-quantity generator, 61, 66–75, 164–165
Memorandum of agreement, 250, 252, 253, 255
Metal heat treating waste, 31
Mineral oil, 364, 365, 387, 392
Mining overburden, 16, 27
Minor permit modifications, 202, 203
Minimum technological requirements, 171, 174, 177, 213
Miscellaneous liability, 289
Miscellaneous units, 16, 162, 183–184
Mixed waste, 343–344
Mixture, 37–38
Mixture rule, 37–39, 277
Mixtures of hazardous waste, 25
Mobile incinerator, 39, 181
Mobile treatment unit, 39, 43–44, 377
Modification to closure plan, 144
Monitoring, 337
Monitoring and analysis action, 243, 244–245, 246
More stringent, 253–254
Motels, 27
Motor starters, 366
Movement, 16
Multiple hazards, 90
Multiple labelling, 98–100

National contingency plan, 260, 266, 273, 283–284, 286, 295, 301, 302, 307, 312, 323, 327
National Priorities List, 2, 284, 293, 294, 298, 297, 299, 300–302, 321–322
Nationwide variance, 219
Natural resources, 257, 267, 323, 328, 329–330
Navigable waters, 267
Negligence, 286, 289, 290
Negotiation, 325
NEPA, 87, 259–260, 345
New chemical substance, 341
New hazardous waste management facility, 16, 133
New tank system, 16, 148, 170–171
No-migration petition, 218, 219–220
Nonacutely hazardous waste containers, 45
Nonbinding preliminary allocation of responsibility, 326
Noncompliance, 242, 246, 247
Nonimpervious solid surface, 352
Nonrestricted access, 352
Nonspecific source waste, 29, 30–31
Nonsudden accidental occurrence, 160
Nontime critical response, 285
Notice letter, 325
Notice of deficiency, 187, 192, 193, 197
Notification, 60, 107–109, 127–128, 138, 212, 275, 343
Notification of closure, 143, 144, 153–154
Notification of hazardous waste activity, 67, 107, 187, 281
Notification of hazardous waste management facilities, 280–281
Notification of PCB waste activity, 380–382
NPDES, 25, 39, 192, 277
Nuclear materials, 108
Nuisance, 289, 290

Off-shore facility, 267
Off-site, 314, 327
Off specification fuels, 58, 59
Off specification oil, 58, 59
Oil, 1, 49, 367
Oil and gas waste, 26, 27
Omnibus permit authority, 191
On-scene coordinator, 267
Onshore facility, 267
On-site, 16, 314, 327, 352

On-site treatment, 76
Onground tank, 16
Open burning, 16–17, 42, 212
Open dumping, 2
Operable unit, 267, 302, 328
Operating log, 109–110
Operating record, 109–110
Operation and maintenance, 321–322
Operation during interim status, 188, 189–190
Operator, 17
Ore processing waste, 26, 27
Organic peroxide, 91
ORM, 92
ORM-A, 92, 97
ORM-B, 92, 97
ORM-C, 92, 97
ORM-D, 92, 97
ORM-E, 92, 93, 97
Outside assistance, 117
Owner, 267–268
Ownership transfer, 190
Oxidizer, 34, 35, 90, 91

Packaging, 67, 84, 86, 95–96
Paint filter test, 163, 379
Paper bags, 45
Part A permit application, 54, 57, 107, 148, 187, 188, 189, 192, 195, 230, 246, 281
Part B permit application, 54, 192, 193, 194–198, 208, 220, 229, 246
Part 264 versus Part 265, 107
Partial closure, 17, 139, 140, 147
Pay-in period, 151
PCB article, 353, 386
PCB article container, 353, 372, 386
PCB classifications, 362
PCB container, 353, 386
PCB-contaminated electrical equipment, 353, 375, 380
PCB-contaminated transformer, 364, 367, 368, 370, 372, 377–378
PCB definition, 359–360
PCB equipment, 353
PCB item, 353, 372, 375, 376, 377–378
PCB transformer, 344, 353, 362, 363, 364, 366, 367, 371, 372, 376, 377, 385
PCB waste, 353, 380, 381, 382, 383, 384
PCBs, 225–226, 341, 342, 343, 344, 358–396
PCTs, 360

Penalties, 243, 244, 245, 246, 247, 248, 249, 278. 387–388
Pentachlorophenol, 31
Permit, 17, 48, 56, 66, 82, 107, 129, 134, 135, 136, 144, 146, 150, 158, 180, 186, 190–210, 228, 239, 241, 248, 251, 253, 259, 314, 377
Permit appeal, 201
Permit application process, 192, 197
Permit compliance schedules, 198, 237
Permit-by-rule, 192
Permit conditions, 186, 190–191, 247, 248
Permit denial, 192, 193, 200–201
Permit duration, 200
Permit exclusions, 186–187
Permit issuance, 200, 255
Permit modifications, 138, 147–148, 155, 194, 201–208, 443–451
Permit review, 192, 193, 197–198
Permit shield, 191
Person, 17, 268
Personnel, 17
Personnel protective equipment, 42, 113, 335–337
Personnel training, 62, 67, 72, 74, 77, 110–113, 195, 334–335, 336
Pesticide wastes, 32, 106, 187
Petitions, 4–5, 32, 151, 201, 219–220, 298
Petroleum, 32, 49, 175, 280, 282–283
Petroleum contaminated media, 27
pH, 35, 37, 126, 127, 176
Phosphate kilns
Physical construction, 189
Pickle liquor, 50
Pile, 17
Pilot-scale test, 307
Placarding, 67, 83, 84, 86, 100–103
Placarding table, 102, 103
Placement, 211
Plan, 268
Point of compliance, 155
Point source, 17–18, 25
Poison A, 90, 91
Poison B, 90, 91
Poisons, 95
Pollutant or contaminant, 268–269, 282, 285, 286, 290, 313
Posing an exposure risk to food or feed, 354
Post-cleanup sampling, 395–396
Post closure, 137, 139, 148, 149, 150, 151,

152, 154–156, 173, 177, 178, 189, 194, 248
Post-closure care period, 108
Post-closure certification, 156
Post-closure cost estimate, 109, 110, 157–158, 195, 209
Post-closure period, 120, 154
Post-closure permit, 129, 150, 151, 154, 172, 208–209
Post-closure plan, 154–156, 165, 195, 208
Post-closure plan amendments, 155
Post-closure plan approval, 143, 155–156
Potentially responsible party, 258, 282, 291, 306, 324–326, 327, 390, 396
POTW, 18, 25, 65, 187
Pre-transport requirements, 67
Precious metal recovery, 54
Preferred alternative, 317
Preliminary assessment, 233
Preliminary assessment petition, 298
Preliminary review, 197, 198, 235
Preparedness and prevention, 72, 74, 77–78, 107, 116–117, 195
Prevention of ignition or reaction of wastes
Printed circuit boards, 30
Priority classification scheme, 247–249
Prior releases, 150, 154, 173, 209, 227–230
Product storage waste, 41, 64, 140, 229
Program description, 252
Prohibited wastes, 213–214
Project closeout, 293, 294, 321–322
Proper shipping name, 86, 87, 94
Proposed plan, 317–318
Public hearings, 144, 155, 193, 198, 205, 239
Public notice, 198, 204
Public participation, 199–200, 207, 239, 317–319, 323, 330–332
Publicly owned treatment works, 18, 25, 65, 187
Pulping liquor, 13, 26

Qualified incinerator, 354

Radial transformer, 368
Radioactive material, 90, 91
Radioactive mixed waste, 255
Railroad boxcars, 49
Raw materials, 41
RCRA facility assessment, 193, 232, 233–235, 246

RCRA facility investigation, 232, 233, 235–236, 239
RD&D permits, 209–210
Reactive hazardous waste, 28, 35, 73, 114, 162, 164, 172, 174
Recalcitrant violator, 248
Reclamation, 54, 66
Reclassification, 362
Reclosers, 365, 366
Reconstruction, 189
Record keeping, 107, 109, 241, 247, 340, 361, 373–374, 376, 380, 385–387, 390
Record of decision, 234, 293, 294, 309, 314, 317–320
Recovery of waste, 220
Recycling, 24, 25, 32, 47–60, 218, 229
Recycling activity, 49, 52–55
Recycling process, 48
Redefinition of solid waste, 47
Regional project manager, 295, 320
Regulated unit, 130, 132, 134, 135, 137, 150–151, 154, 229
Relationship between RCRA and AEA, 37, 40–41, 255
Relationship between RCRA and CWA, 25, 192
Relationship between RCRA and HMTA, 80–104
Relationship between RCRA and MPRSA, 192
Relationship between RCRA and NEPA, 187
Relationship between RCRA and OSHA, 110–113
Relationship between RCRA and SDWA, 184–185, 192
Relationship between RCRA and Superfund, 2, 3, 234, 246, 250
Relationship between RCRA and TSCA, 108–109, 225–226, 343
Relationship between Superfund and CWA, 273, 279–280
Relationship between Superfund and HMTA, 273, 279
Relationship between Superfund and NEPA, 259–260
Relationship between Superfund and OSHA, 332–340
Relationship between Superfund and SARA Title III, 273, 278–279
Relationship between TSCA and AEA, 348

Relationship between TSCA and FFDCA, 348
Relationship between TSCA and FIFRA, 348
Relationship between TSCA and NEPA, 345
Relationship between TSCA and OSHA, 376
Relationship between TSCA and Superfund, 344, 343, 373, 389, 392, 393
Release, 228, 230, 258, 269, 275, 282–283
Remedial action, 209, 230, 234, 270–271, 275, 285, 293, 294, 314, 317, 320–321, 327, 330, 331–332
Remedial action objectives, 368
Remedial design, 234, 293, 294, 320
Remedial investigation, 234, 269–270, 292, 293, 294, 302–305, 306–307, 314, 319, 325–326, 328
Remedy evaluation criteria, 309–312
Remedy selection, 232, 233, 234, 237, 292, 293, 294, 317–320
Removal action, 250, 271, 284–285, 293, 331
Reopener, 326
Reportable quantity, 74–75, 79, 83, 89–90, 118, 170, 274–280, 344–345, 391, 393
Representative sample, 18
Required notices, 108–109
Resale of PCB items, 370
Residential/commercial area, 355
Response, 271, 284–285
Response action contractor liability, 291
Response action liability, 291
Responsible party, 355
Responsible party as lead agency, 296
Restoration, 329
Restricted access, 371
Restricted waste, 208, 213–214, 216
Retrofitting, 165
Reversion of State programs, 255
Revision of State programs, 254–255
Risk assessment, 304–306
RQ, 74–75, 79, 83, 89–90, 118, 176, 274–280, 344–345
Run-off, 18, 17
Run-on, 18, 163, 174, 177

Safety and health, 112, 323, 332–340
Sale for purposes other than resale, 355
Sample collection, 122, 132

Sample exclusion, 41–44, 376–377
Sample preservation, 122, 132
Sample quantity limits, 43
Sample shipment, 122, 132, 383–384
Sampling and analysis plan, 121–122, 132, 141
Sampling under 3013(a), 243, 244–245, 246
SARA Title III, 273, 278–279
Satellite accumulation areas, 72–73, 77
Saturated zone, 18, 121
Schedule of compliance, 18
Scoping of the RI/FS, 303, 304
Scrap metal, 49, 52
Screening site inspection, 299
Second third wastes, 215–216
Secondary containment, 76, 141, 164, 165, 166–168, 371, 373
Secondary lead, 32
Secondary materials, 27, 49, 53
Sectionalizers, 366
Security, 110, 113, 195
Seismic, 115–116
Servicing of PCB transformers, 370
Settlements, 324
Settlement policy, 326
Sewage exclusion, 25, 26
Shipper, 80, 81, 84
Shipping name, 86, 87, 94
Shipping papers, 44, 83, 100, 104
Signatory requirements, 194, 201
Significant discrepancy, 119
Site, 18
Site characterization, 303, 307
Site discovery, 293, 294, 296
Site evaluation, 333–334
Site inspection, 293, 294, 298–299, 304
Site investigation, 233
Site visit, 197, 198
Sludge, 18, 50, 52
Small capacitor, 347–348, 373, 378, 380
Small quantities for research and development, 355
Small-quantity generators, 2, 61, 65–66, 71
Soil, 355–356, 285, 379, 392, 394
Solid waste, 1, 18, 24–25, 39, 47, 48
Solid Waste Disposal Act, 1
Solid waste management unit, 18, 150, 154, 196, 228–229, 233, 235, 237
Solvent mixtures, 30

Solvent wastes, 30, 48, 50, 221–222, 377, 378
Source control action, 271
Source control maintenance measures, 271
Source material, 26
Space heaters, 60
SPCC plan, 78, 117, 375, 376
Special notices, 325–326
Special nuclear material, 26
Special-study waste, 26
Specific source waste, 29, 31–32
Specific recycling activities, 52–54
Specification oil, 58, 59
Speculative accumulation, 52, 53
Spent, 30
Spent materials, 50–51
Spill, 82–83, 140, 275, 285, 345, 356, 371
Spill area, 356
Spill boundaries, 356, 392, 393–394
Spill cleanup, 362, 289–396
Spill residues, 52, 140
Standard wipe test, 356–357
State as lead agency, 295
State authorization, 4, 240, 251–255, 345
State program description, 252
State program elements, 252–254
State Superfund contract, 295
Statement of basis, 193, 198, 199–200
Statistical comparisons, 127–128, 132–133
Storage, 3, 19, 53, 54, 105, 186, 220–221, 247, 361,372, 374–377, 384, 387
Storage for disposal, 357
Storage time, 62, 72, 75, 376, 384
Strict liability, 289–290
Student's t-test, 127, 132
Substantially equivalent, 251
Subtitle D, 1–2
Subtitle I, 1
Sudden accidental occurrence, 160
Suitability of drinking water, 123, 124–125, 316
Sulfide, 35
Sulfuric acid, 27
Surety bond, 158, 159
Surface impoundment, 3, 19, 72, 75, 121, 123, 139, 141, 143, 147, 148, 149, 150, 161, 171–173, 183, 208, 211, 213, 229, 230, 308
Survey plat, 140, 153, 157
Superfund, 61, 74, 79, 83, 118, 170, 228, 230, 236, 246, 250, 257–340

Superfund memorandum of agreement, 295
SW-846, 28, 36, 122
Switches, 365, 366

Tank, 19, 45, 72, 73–74, 75, 76, 84, 143, 148, 150, 153, 163, 183, 208, 220, 229, 251, 285, 375–376
Tank assessments,
Tank cleanup waste, 27
Tank closure, 170
Tank systems, 3, 7, 20, 161, 163–174
Tanning wastes, 27
TCLP, 36, 217, 221
Technical name, 94–95
Temporary authorization, 206, 207–208
Temporary storage, 375
Termination of interim status, 143
Territorial sea, 271
Test methods, 28, 36, 122, 363
Testing hazardous wastes, 28, 36, 63, 122
Thermal treatment, 20, 161, 182–183
Third third wastes, 215
Total organic carbon, 33, 133, 221
Total organic halogen, 33
Totally enclosed manner, 357, 358, 360, 366
Totally enclosed treatment facility, 20, 65, 106, 187 , 281
Toxic Substances Control Act, 108–109, 149, 226, 314, 341–396
Toxicity characteristic, 27, 28, 36–37
Tracking PCBs, 362, 380–387
Training, 62, 67, 72, 74, 77, 110–113, 195, 334–335, 336
Transfer facility, 80, 82, 106, 187, 357
Transfer of liability, 286
Transfer of ownership, 190
Transformer, 344, 353, 362, 363–364, 366, 367–371, 374, 377
Transport vehicle, 20, 357, 373
Transport vehicle waste, 41
Transporter, 20, 57, 80–104, 216, 247, 250, 271–272, 279, 286, 280, 386
Transporter of PCB waste, 357, 380
Treatability investigations, 303, 307
Treatability samples, 42–44
Treatability study, 42
Treatment, 20, 70, 105, 106, 186, 208, 247
Treatment standards, 211, 213, 216–226
Treatment zone, 20, 177

Trespass, 289, 290
Trial burns, 181
Trust fund, 158–159
Trustees, 329–330

UN/NA number, 85, 86, 93, 104
Underground injection, 21, 162, 183, 184–185, 192, 211, 229
Underground storage tank cleanup waste, 27
Underground tank, 21
Unfit-for-use tank system, 21
Unit marking, 76–77
Unmanifested waste, 120, 385–386
Unstable waste handling, 114
Upgradient monitoring wells, 123, 128, 134
Uppermost aquifer, 21
Use constituting disposal, 52, 53–54
Used oil, 49, 55, 57–60, 65
Utility wastes, 27

Variances, 120–121, 123, 168, 179, 213, 218–220
Vault system, 167, 168, 212
Verification of data accuracy, 197, 198
Vessel, 21, 272
Veterinary pharmaceuticals, 32
Violators, 248–249
Virgin sulfuric acid, 27
Visual site inspection, 235, 373
Voltage regulator, 365, 366

Waivers, 120–121, 123, 168, 179, 213, 284
Warning letter, 197, 243
Waste accumulation, 48, 56, 64, 66, 72–74, 75–77, 97, 106, 165, 187
Waste analysis, 109, 110, 113–114, 165, 169, 172, 174, 176, 179–180, 195, 218
Waste analysis plan, 114
Waste identification samples
Waste handling, 107, 339–340
Waste management area, 122, 132, 196
Waste minimization, 70–71, 109
Waste mixtures, 37–39
Waste oil, 1, 357, 367
Waste pile, 72, 75, 131, 139, 141, 143, 148, 150, 161, 174–175, 183
Wastes contained in nonwastes, 39–40
Wastes from specific sources, 29, 30–31
Wastes from nonspecific sources, 29, 30–31
Wastes derived from other wastes, 39
Wastewater, 39, 52, 221
Wastewater treatment unit, 21, 65, 106, 187, 228, 281
Waters of the United States, 279–280
Weight calculation, 386–387
Well, 22
Wetlands, 116, 184, 278–279, 329
Worker health and safety, 112, 323, 332–340
Work plan, 332, 333

Zero headspace extraction vessel, 37
Zone of engineering control, 22